A HISTORY OF TWENTIETH-CENTURY BRITISH WOMEN'S POETRY

A History of Twentieth-Century British Women's Poetry offers a uniquely detailed record and analysis of a vast array of publications, activities and achievements by major figures as well as lesser-known poets. This comprehensive survey is organised into three historical periods (1900–45, 1945–80 and 1980–2000), each part introduced by an evaluative overview in which emerging poets are mapped against cultural and literary events and trends. Four chapters in each section consider the major figures, including Charlotte Mew, Sylvia Townsend Warner, Stevie Smith, Elizabeth Jennings, Sylvia Plath, Anne Stevenson, Eavan Boland, Carol Rumens, Denise Riley, Grace Nichols and Carol Ann Duffy. The individual essays reflect and stimulate continuing debates about the nature of women's poetry. They offer new critical approaches to reading poems that engage with, for example, war, domesticity, Modernism, linguistic innovation, place, the dramatic monologue, Postmodernism and the lyric. A chronology and detailed bibliography of primary and secondary sources, covering more than 200 writers, make this an invaluable reference source for scholars and students of British poetry and women's writing.

JANE DOWSON is Senior Lecturer in English at De Montfort University, Leicester.

ALICE ENTWISTLE is Senior Lecturer in English at the University of the West of England, Bristol.

A HISTORY OF TWENTIETH-CENTURY BRITISH WOMEN'S POETRY

JANE DOWSON AND ALICE ENTWISTLE

CAMBRIDGE
UNIVERSITY PRESS

CAMBRIDGE UNIVERSITY PRESS
Cambridge, New York, Melbourne, Madrid, Cape Town, Singapore, São Paulo

Cambridge University Press
The Edinburgh Building, Cambridge CB2 2RU, UK

Published in the Unied States of America by Cambridge University Press, New York
www.cambridge.org
Information on this title: www.cambridge.org/9780521819466

First published 2005

Printed in the United Kingdom at the University Press, Cambridge

A catalogue record for this book is available from the British Library

Library of Congress Cataloguing in Publication data

Dowson, Jane
A history of twentieth-century British women's poetry / Jane Dowson and Alice Entwistle.
p. cm.
Includes bibliographical references and index.
ISBN 0 521 81946 6
1. English poetry – Women authors – History and criticism.   2. Women and literature –
Great Britian – History – 20th century.   3. English poetry – 20th century – History and criticism.
I. Entwistle, Alice. II. Title.
PR605.W6D68 2005
821′.91099287 – dc22   2004054647

ISBN-13 978-0-521-81946-6 hardback
ISBN-10 0-521-81946-6 hardback

For R. R. D (1931–2002) and R. H. W (1921–2004)

Contents

Preface

A proliferation of anthologies and reprinted works over the past twenty years has raised awareness of the number and variety of women publishing poetry in the twentieth century. At the same time, there is a sense that separatist treatments may have had their day. While this book is not intended to confine poets to a female-only tradition, reading position or audience, history tells us that without a distinct literary terminology, tradition and role models, women's poetry will continue to have uncertain status and fade from literary memory. The need to explore and chart the literary processes against which the woman poet defines herself and her art has led us to combine literary-historical survey with critical commentary. We have negotiated between recording reputations, largely based on critical reception, as they stand, and reassessing the significance of overlooked, as well as established, work. In wanting to present a near-exhaustive record of publications, we have erred on the side of comprehensiveness in the List of Published Works and in the 'Overview' to each of the three historical periods. The chapters develop critical readings which are pertinent to the period yet can also transfer to poetry in other historical or cultural frameworks. We envisage that some readers will enjoy the linear account of poets' writing in the context of women's social and literary environments. Others might already have an interest in particular names, or be moved to explore poets who have been brought to their attention for the first time. The breadth of styles dissolves any lingering assumption that the poetry of women is somehow formulaic and irrelevant to cultural or critical trends. At the same time, reading the works in context illuminates how a complicated gender-consciousness is frequently integral to their writing. In documenting and evaluating the publications and activities of well- and lesser-known poets, we want, primarily, to secure their future by stimulating new kinds of critical conversations about women and poetry.

Acknowledgements

This book was completed with the invaluable assistance of Research Leave Grants from the Arts and Humanities Research Board, and Small Research Grants from the British Academy, along with teaching relief granted by the Universities of De Montfort and the West of England, Bristol. We are grateful to Eavan Boland and Medbh McGuckian for their constructive dialogue and support. We have welcomed the knowledge and patience of Neil Astley, Ken Edwards, Peter Fallon, Peter Riley, Geoff Ward and the staff of the Poetry Library at the South Bank, London. Finally, we must thank the many friends and colleagues who have been involved in this project at different stages for their insight, tolerance and practical help, particularly Shelley Burch, Ruth Clarke, Nick Freeman, Jo Gill, Robin Jarvis, Victoria Stewart, Diana Wallace and, not least, Andy Mousley whose roles included fitting the final manuscript into a Jiffybag. The book is dedicated, for several reasons, to our fathers. Our love and special thanks go to Mark, Tom, Alf and our mothers.

The cover image 'Trilogy II' is by Eileen Cooper RA, represented by Art First Gallery London. Image © Eileen Cooper RA. Photography: Rodney Todd-White & Son, London.

Every effort has been made to clear rights on poetry extracts but some sources of copyright authority have been difficult to track down. Permission has been granted by the following:

Patience Agbabi/Edinburgh: Payback Press, for *R.A.W.* 1995; *Transformatrix*, 2000.

Allardyce, Barnett, Publishers, for quotations from poems by Veronica Forrest-Thomson from Veronica Forrest-Thomson, *Collected Poems and Translations*, ed. Anthony Barnett (Lewes: Allardyce, Barnett, Publishers, 1990), reprinted in *Selected Poems*, ed. Anthony Barnett (London: Invisible Books, 1999). Copyright © Jonathan Culler and the Estate of Veronica Forrest-Thomson 1990, 1999.

Anvil Press Poetry for extracts by Carol Ann Duffy: 'A Clear Note' and 'Lizzie Six' from *Standing Female Nude*, 1985; 'The Dummy' and 'Psychopath' from *Selling Manhattan*, 1987; 'Poet for Our Times' from *The Other Country*, 1990; 'Prayer' and 'Away and See' from *Mean Time*, 1993.

Bloodaxe Books for Fleur Adcock, *Poems: 1960–2000*, 2000; Moniza Alvi, *Carrying My Wife*, 2000; Annemarie Austin, *On the Border*, 1993; *The Flaying of Marsyas* 1995; Elizabeth Bartlett, *Two Women Dancing: New and Selected Poems*, 1995; Imtiaz Dharker, *Postcards from god*, 1997; Maura Dooley, *Sound Barrier: Poems 1982–2002*, 2002; Helen Dunmore, *Short Days, Long Nights: New and Selected Poems*, 1991; *Out of the Blue: Poems*, 2001; Linda France, *Red*, 1992; *The Gentleness of the Very Tall*, 1994; *Storyville*, 1997; Elizabeth Garrett, *A Two-Part Invention*, 1998; Lavinia Greenlaw, 'Hurting Small Animals', *New Women Poets*, ed. Carol Rumens, 1990; Maggie Hannan, *Liar, Jones*, 1995; Tracey Herd, *No Hiding Place*, 1996; Selima Hill, *Violet*, 1997; Kathleen Jamie, *The Queen of Sheba*, 1994; *Mr and Mrs Scotland are Dead: Poems 1980–1994*, 2002; Julie O'Callaghan, *What's What?*, 1991; Carol Rumens, *Thinking of Skins: New and Selected Poems*, 1993; Pauline Stainer, *The Lady and the Hare: New and Selected Poems*, 2003; Anne Stevenson, *Collected Poems 1955–1995*, 2000; *Granny Scarecrow*, 2000.

Valerie Bloom for 'Language Barrier' and 'Show Dem' from *Touch Mi Tell Mi* (Bogle-L'Ouverture Press, 1983) reprinted by permission of the author, c/o Eddison Pearson Ltd.

Eavan Boland for excerpts from 'Anna Liffey' and 'A Woman Painted on a Leaf' (from *In A Time of Violence*, © 1994 Eavan Boland); 'Suburban Woman', '6. The Muse Mother', 'The Journey' (© 1987 Eavan Boland) and 'Tirade for the Lyric Muse' (all from *An Origin Like Water: Collected Poems 1967–1987* © 1996 Eavan Boland) and 'The Harbour' (from *The Lost Land* © 1998 Eavan Boland). Used by permission of W. W. Norton & Company, Inc.

Carcanet Press Ltd for Patricia Beer, *Collected Poems*, 1988; Sujata Bhatt, *Point No Point: Selected Poems*, 1997; *Augatora*, 2000; Eavan Boland, *Collected Poems*, 1995; Gillian Clarke, *Collected Poems*, 1997; Anne Cluysenaar, *Timeslips: New and Selected Poems*, 1997; Elizabeth Daryush, *Selected Poems: Verses I–VI*, 1972; Elaine Feinstein, *Collected Poems and Translations*, 2002; Mimi Khalvati, *In White Ink*, 1991; Mina Loy, *The Lost Lunar Baedeker*, ed. Roger Conover, 1997; *Charlotte Mew: Collected Poems and Selected Prose*, ed. Val Warner, 1997; Anne Ridler, *Collected Poems*, 1994; E. J. Scovell, *Collected Poems*, 1988; Sylvia Townsend Warner, *Collected Poems*, ed. Claire Harman, 1982.

Harry Chambers/Peterloo Poets for Elma Mitchell, *People Et Cetera: Poems New and Selected*, 1987.

Wendy Cope for 'Poem Composed in Santa Barbara', *Serious Concerns*, Faber & Faber, 1992 © Wendy Cope. Reproduced by permission of PFD on behalf of Wendy Cope.

David Higham Associates for extracts from Elizabeth Jennings, *Recoveries*, 1964 and *New Collected Poems*, 2002; 'Colonel Fantock', 'The Sleeping Beauty' and 'Three Poems of the Atomic Age', in Edith Sitwell, *Collected Poems*, Macmillan, 1954.

The Estate of Hilda Doolittle for 'Euridyce' (excerpt), by H. D. from *Collected Poems, 1912–1944*, © 1982. Reprinted by permission of New Directions Publishing Corporation.

Carol Ann Duffy for extracts from 'William and the ex-Prime Minister', from *William and the ex-Prime Minister*, Anvil Press, 1992, and *The World's Wife* © Carol Ann Duffy, reprinted by permission of Faber & Faber Inc., an affiliate of Farrar, Straus and Giroux LLC, and Macmillan, London, UK.

Ruth Fainlight for extracts from *Sibyls and Others*, Hutchinson, 1980 and *Selected Poems*, Sinclair Stevenson, 1995.

Alison Fell for 'Women in the Cold War', 'Sail Away', 'Butterfingers' and extracts from *Kisses for Mayakovsky*, Virago Press, 1984.

Golgonooza Press/Brian Keeble on behalf of Kathleen Raine for extracts from 'Word Made Flesh', *Selected Poems*, 1998.

Lavinia Greenlaw for extracts from *Night Photograph*, Faber & Faber, 1993; *A World Where News Travelled Slowly*, Faber & Faber, 1997.

Oliver Hawkins, for the estate of Wilfred and Alice Meynell, for *The Poems of Alice Meynell*, Oxford University Press, 1940.

Margaret and George Hepburn for *The Writings of Anna Wickham*, Virago, 1984.

Jenny Joseph for 'The Lost Continent', *Selected Poems*, Carcanet, 1992.

Sylvia Kantaris for extracts from *Dirty Washing: New and Selected Poems*, Bloodaxe Books, 1989, and *Lad's Love*, Bloodaxe Books, 1993.

Jackie Kay for extracts from 'Kail and Callaloo'; *The Adoption Papers*, Bloodaxe Books, 1991; 'The Same Note' and 'In My Country', *Other Lovers*, Bloodaxe Books, 1993; 'Pride', *Off Colour*, Bloodaxe Books, 1998.

Denise Levertov for excerpts from 'Zest' and 'The Earthwoman and the Waterwoman' (*Collected Earlier Poems 1940–1960* © 1957, 1958, 1959, 1960, 1961, 1979 by Denise Levertov); from 'The Five-Day Rain' (*Collected Earlier Poems 1940–1960* © 1960 by Denise Levertov); from 'Abel's Bride' and 'Matins' (*Poems 1960–1967*, © 1966 by Denise Levertov); 'She and the Muse' (*Candles in Babylon*, © 1982 by Denise Levertov); and 'Wondering'

(*Sands of the Well*, © 1996 by Denise Levertov); all reprinted here by permission of New Directions Publishing Corporation and, where it appears in *Selected Poems* (Bloodaxe Books, 1994), Pollinger Ltd.

Hamish MacGibbon for extracts from Stevie Smith's *Collected Poems*, Allen Lane, 1985, and *Over the Frontier*, Virago, 1989.

Medbh McGuckian for extracts from *Marconi's Cottage* (1991), *Captain Lavender* (1994) and *Venus and the Rain* (1994), by kind permission of the author and The Gallery Press, Loughcrew, Oldcastle, Country Meath, Ireland.

Macmillan UK for Kathleen Jamie, *Jizzen*, Picador, 1999; Carol Ann Duffy, *The World's Wife*, 1999 and *Feminine Gospels*, Picador, 2002.

Wendy Mulford for extracts from *and suddenly supposing: selected poems*, Etruscan Press, 2002.

Nigel Nicolson on behalf of Vita Sackville-West for an extract from *The Garden*, 1946.

Mary O'Malley for 'The Shape of Saying', *Where the Rocks Float*, Salmon Publishing (Galway), 1993.

Grace Nichols for extracts from *i is a long-memoried woman*, Karnak, 1983 © 1983 by Grace Nichols (reproduced by permission of Karnak House Ltd); 'Spring', from *The Fat Black Woman's Poems*, Virago, 1984 © 1984 by Grace Nichols; and 'A Poem for Us' and 'On Poems and Crotches', from *Lazy Thoughts of a Lazy Woman and Other Poems*, Virago, 1989 © 1989 by Grace Nichols (all reproduced with permission of Curtis Brown Ltd, London, on behalf of Grace Nichols).

Mark Pitter on behalf of Ruth Pitter for extracts from *Ruth Pitter*: *Collected Poems*, Enitharmon Press, 1990.

The Random House Group Ltd for extracts from *The Handless Maiden* by Vicki Feaver, published by Jonathan Cape, 1994; Carol Rumens, 'Two Women', 'Houses by Day', *Selected Poems*, Chatto & Windus, 1987.

Denise Riley for extracts from *Mop Mop Georgette: New and Selected Poems 1986–1993*, Reality Street Editions, 1993.

Michèle Roberts for extracts from *The Mirror of the Mother*: *Selected Poems 1975–1985*, Methuen, 1986, reproduced by permission of Taylor & Francis Books.

Sheila Rowbotham for 'The Role of Women in the Revolution defined by some Socialist men'(1968).

Carol Rumens for extracts from 'In the Bedroom of the Page'.

Seren Books on behalf of Jean Earle for 'Jugged Hare', *Selected Poems*, 1990; and Sheenagh Pugh for extracts from 'Envying Owen Beattie', *Stonelight*, 1999, *and* 'Toast', *The Beautiful Lie*, 2002.

Elizabeth Stapleforth for Muriel Stuart, *Selected Poems*, Jonathan Cape, 1927.

Stephen Stuart Smith at Enitharmon Press for Frances Cornford, *Selected Poems*, ed. Jane Dowson, 1996.

Virago Press (Time Warner Book Group UK) for extracts from *Me Again: the Uncollected Writings of Stevie Smith*, 1981.

Michelene Wandor for 'Lullaby'.

His Grace The Duke of Wellington for 'Milk Boy' by Dorothy Wellesley.

The estate of Sheila Wingfield for extracts from *Beat Drum, Beat Heart* (1946), from *A Kite's Dinner: Poems 1938–54*, Cresset Press, 1954. Reproduced with kind permission from David Pryce-Jones.

Chronological Table of Selected Historical and Literary Events 1900–2000

Year	Historical events	Literary events
1901	Death of Queen Victoria.	
1903	Marie Curie wins Nobel Prize.	
1904	Founding of the WSPU in Manchester.	
1908	Women Writers Suffrage League founded by Cicely Hamilton and Bessie Hatton.	
1909		*Poetry Society* founded. Cicely Hamilton, *Marriage as a Trade.*
1910	Death of Edward VII. Suffragette March in Hyde Park.	
1911		*The Freewoman: A Weekly Feminist Review*, founded, ed. Dora Marsden (November); runs until October 1912.
1912		Carl Jung (1875–1961), *The Theory of Psychoanalysis.* Poetry Society formed; *Poetry Review* launched. Lady Margaret Sackville made first President.
1913	Royal Commission on Divorce.	Sigmund Freud's (1856–1939) *Interpretation of Dreams* (1900) translated into English. *The New Freewoman* founded, ed. Dora Marsden.
1914	First World War starts.	*The Egoist* (formerly *The New Freewoman*) founded, ed. Harriet Shaw Weaver, assisted by Richard Aldington and Dora Marsden; runs until 1918. May Sinclair, *Feminist Manifesto.*
1916		Carl Jung, *Psychology of the Unconscious.*
1918	First World War ends. Women over 30 get the vote. Countess Marckiewicz elected to Parliament.	
1919	Sex Disqualification Removal Act; all professions open except the church. Nancy Astor is first woman MP to take her seat in the House of Commons.	*The Egoist* becomes Egoist Press, London. Inauguration of *Vogue* in Britain.
1920		*Time and Tide* (1920–76) started by Lady Margaret Rhondda, London.
1921	Marie Stopes opens first birth control clinic in London.	

Year	Historical events	Literary events
1922		*Good Housekeeping* launched.
1923	BBC launches 'Woman's Hour'.	Carl Jung, *Psychological Types*.
1924	Workers' Birth Control Group.	
1927		*Close-Up* magazine founded by Winifred Bryher.
		Vita Sackville-West receives Hawthornden Prize for Poetry.
		Laura Riding and Robert Graves start Seizin Press (1927–39), Mallorca and London.
		Cheltenham Festival inaugurated.
1928	Women over 21 get the vote.	Nancy Cunard starts The Hours Press (1928–31), Paris.
		Ray Strachey, *The Cause*
1929		Virginia Woolf, *A Room of One's Own*.
1936	Spanish Civil War starts.	Penguin Books launched.
		Ray Strachey, *Our Freedom and Its Results*.
1937	The Matrimonial Causes Act.	*Woman* magazine launched.
1938	Inheritance Act.	
1939	Second World War starts.	
1942	Beveridge Report published.	
1944	Education Act.	*Outposts* magazine launched.
1945	Bombing of Hiroshima; war ends. Introduction of Family Allowance, state payment to mothers. BBC launches Home Service and Light programmes.	
1946	Royal Commission on Equality recommends equal pay for women teachers and civil servants.	Vita Sackville-West's 'The Garden' wins Heinemann Prize.
1947	India and Pakistan granted independence. Princess Elizabeth marries Lt. Philip Mountbatten.	
1948	NHS established. SS *Empire Windrush* lands in London. John Newsom report, *The Education of Girls*.	
1951	Festival of Britain (May–September).	National Poetry Competition flops.
1952	Death of George VI; accession of Elizabeth II.	
1953	Coronation. Kinsey Report: 'Sexual Behaviour in the Human Female'.	
1954	Rationing ends.	

Year	Historical events	Literary events
1955	National Council of Women, conference on single women.	Ruth Pitter awarded Queen's Medal for Poetry. Elizabeth Jennings wins Somerset Maugham Award.
1956	Report on Marriage and Divorce, the Morton Commission.	Outposts Press evolves from magazine. Elizabeth Jennings appears in Robert Conquest's Movement anthology *New Lines*.
1957		Claudia Jones founds *The West Indian Gazette*.
1958	First Aldermaston march. Notting Hill race riots. National Council of Women, conference on working mothers.	
1959	Obscene Publications Act.	Michael Horovitz founds *New Departures*. Frances Cornford awarded Queen's Medal for Poetry.
1960		R. D. Laing publishes *The Divided Self*. Jenny Joseph wins Eric Gregory Award.
1961	Contraceptive pill introduced in UK.	Penguin cleared of obscenity in *Lady Chatterley* trial. Simone de Beauvoir's *The Second Sex* published in Britain.
1962	Marilyn Monroe dies. National Housewives Register founded.	Doris Lessing, *The Golden Notebook*.
1963	Profumo Scandal breaks.	Stevie Smith 'Poet of the Year', Stratford-upon-Avon Festival. Sylvia Plath dies. Betty Friedan, *The Feminine Mystique*.
1965	Mary Quant opens Bazaar.	Approximately 7,000 people attend Royal Albert Hall Poetry reading featuring more than 40 poets.
1966		Juliet Mitchell, 'The Longest Revolution' in *New Left Review*.
1967	Abortion Law Reform. Family Planning Act.	Writers' Workshop formed.
1968	Martin Luther King assassinated. Enoch Powell's 'rivers of blood' speech. Anti-Vietnam War demonstrations.	Northern Poetry Library founded. Kathleen Raine fails to get Oxford Chair of Poetry.

Year	Historical events	Literary events
1969	First landing on the moon. Divorce Reform Act.	Enitharmon Press founded. Poetry Society's Poetry Gala, Royal Festival Hall. Stevie Smith awarded Queen's Medal for Poetry. Kate Millett, *Sexual Politics*. Sheila Rowbotham, *Women's Liberation and the New Politics*.
1970	First Conference of Women's Liberation Movement, Ruskin College, Oxford (February). Equal Pay Act.	Germaine Greer, *The Female Eunuch*. Kathleen Raine wins Cholmondeley Award.
1971	First International Women's Day (March); women march in London and Liverpool.	Stevie Smith dies. Phoebe Hesketh elected Fellow of the Royal Society of Literature. The Arvon Foundation Centre founded.
1972	First Women's Refuge set up in Chiswick, London.	*Spare Rib* launched. *PN Review* launched. Wendy Mulford founds Street Editions. Kathleen Raine receives WH Smith Literary Award. Molly Holden wins Cholmondeley Award. Liz Lochhead wins Scottish Arts Council Award. Penelope Shuttle wins Eric Gregory Award.
1973		Virago Press launched. International Cambridge Poetry Festival inaugurated.
1974		Jenny Joseph wins Cholmondeley Award.
1975	Sex Discrimination Act. Equal Opportunities Commission set up. National Abortion Campaign launched. Employment Protection Act introduces statutory maternity rights.	
1976	Domestic Violence Act. First rape crisis centre opens in North London. Mairead Maguire founds Community of Peace People movement later winning Nobel Peace Prize.	Onlywomen Press founded. Gillian Clarke edits *Anglo-Welsh Review*. Fleur Adcock wins Cholmondeley Award.

Year	Historical events	Literary events
1977		Elaine Showalter, *A Literature of their Own: British Women Novelists from Brontë to Lessing*.
1978	Hite Report. Organisation of Women of Asian and African Descent (OWAAD) formed.	The Women's Press launched. Anne Stevenson elected Fellow of the Royal Society of Literature.
1979	Margaret Thatcher becomes first woman Prime Minister; lowest number of women MPs (19) returned in 20 years.	Medbh McGuckian wins National Poetry Competition. Pamela Gillilan wins Cheltenham Literature Festival/*Sunday Telegraph* Poetry Competition. Anne Stevenson co-founds The Poetry Bookshop, Hay-on-Wye. Sandra M. Gilbert and Susan Gubar publish *The Madwoman in the Attic: The Woman Writer and the Nineteenth Century Imagination*. Denise Levertov elected to American Academy of Arts and Letters.
1980		Elaine Feinstein elected Fellow of the Royal Society of Literature. Medbh McGuckian wins Eric Gregory Award. Dale Spender, *Man Made Language*.
1981	The Prince of Wales marries Lady Diana Spencer. Brixton riots.	
1982	First Greenham Common Peace Camp. Channel Four launched.	April: Evening of International Poetry at the First International Fair of Radical Black and Third World Books.
1983		Grace Nichols's *i is a long-memoried woman* wins Commonwealth Poetry Prize. Carol Ann Duffy wins National Poetry Competition. Medbh McGuckian wins Alice Hunt Bartlett Award.
1984	Miners' strike prompts formation of Women Against Pit Closures.	Patricia Oxley edits the new *Acumen* poetry magazine. Alison Fell wins Alice Hunt Bartlett Award.
1985		*Women's Review* launched. Denise Levertov receives Shelley Memorial Award from Poetry Society of America. Jo Shapcott wins National Poetry Competition (joint award).

Year	Historical events	Literary events
1986		Carole Satyamurti wins National Poetry Competition. Jenny Joseph wins James Tait Black Memorial Prize. Helen Dunmore wins Alice Hunt Bartlett Prize. Poems on the Underground.
1987		Elizabeth Jennings wins WH Smith Literary Award. Wendy Cope wins Cholmondeley Award. U. A. Fanthorpe elected Fellow of the Royal Society of Literature.
1988	Berlin Wall comes down (November). Sian Edwards first woman conductor of Royal Opera House, Covent Garden.	The Poetry Library moves to South Bank, London. Carol Ann Duffy wins Somerset Maugham Award. Selima Hill wins Arvon/*Observer* International Poetry competition. Gwyneth Lewis wins Gregory Award.
1989		Carol Ann Duffy wins Dylan Thomas Award. E. J. Scovell wins Cholmondeley Award.
1990	Nelson Mandela released. Mary Robinson elected President of Ireland. Poll Tax riots (March). Mrs Thatcher resigns (November). Tracy Edwards captains first all-women crew to complete Whitbread Round the World Yacht Race.	Nicky Rice wins National Poetry Competition. Elaine Feinstein wins Cholmondeley Award. Helen Dunmore wins first prize in Cardiff International Poetry Competition.
1991	Helen Sharman first Briton in space.	Judith Wright awarded Queen's Medal for Poetry. Jo Shapcott's 'Phrase Book' is joint winner of National Poetry Competition.
1992	Ordination of first women deacons in Church of England. Betty Boothroyd becomes first female Speaker of the House of Commons.	Forward Poetry Prize set up. Kathleen Raine awarded Queen's Medal for Poetry. Elizabeth Jennings receives CBE.
1993		Carol Ann Duffy wins Whitbread Poetry Prize.
1994		First National Poetry Day. 'New Generation' Poets launched. Ruth Fainlight wins Cholmondeley Award. Alice Oswald wins Gregory Award.

Year	Historical events	Literary events
1995		Carol Ann Duffy awarded OBE. Wendy Cope wins American Academy of Letters Award. Kathleen Jamie wins Somerset Maugham Award.
1996	Prince and Princess of Wales divorce.	Orange Prize for Women's Fiction launched. Ruth Padel wins National Poetry Competition. Fleur Adcock awarded OBE.
1997	Labour party wins general election. Tony Blair becomes Prime Minister; 120 women MPs ('Blair's Babes') win seats. Death of Diana, Princess of Wales.	Jenny Joseph's 'When I am Old I shall Wear Purple' chosen as the Nation's Favourite Poem.
1998	Devolution in Scotland and Wales; 25 women elected to first Welsh National Assembly.	Poetry on the Buses.
1999	Devolution in Northern Ireland. Minimum wage introduced in UK.	Carol Ann Duffy elected Fellow of the Royal Society of Literature and nominated for Laureateship. Oxford University Press closes its poetry list.
2000		Kathleen Raine awarded CBE.

A History of Twentieth-Century British Women's Poetry

INTRODUCTION

'There aren't enough models of women writing poetry, so when we encounter the tradition we have to find a way to completely engage with what's gone before, a way to possess it.'

(Jo Shapcott, 2000)[1]

The chief impetus for this book has been to consolidate a sense of a separate 'tradition' unavailable to most twentieth-century British women poets: as Jo Shapcott suggests, the scarcity of positive female models both results from and conspires in women's uncertain relation to 'English' poetic history. Exploring how the cultural and socio-political circumstances of women's lives intersect with both their literary works and their critical reception, feminist critics before us have done much to explain how and why women's writing has been undervalued in the annals of literary history. Yet the twentieth-century British woman poet's struggle to stake a claim on the poetic map – against obstacles often highly specific to her literary profession – has never been properly contextualised.

In her introduction to *The World Split Open: Women's Poetry 1552–1950* (1979), Louise Bernikow remarks: 'The woman poet constantly pits herself against cultural expectations of "womanhood" and "women's writing"'.[2] In negotiating with (in Shapcott's words) 'what's gone before', British women poets have similarly been forced to work against both social and poetic grains. What often emerges in their work, especially in the early decades of the century, is a curious split between the strong egalitarian impulses manifest in their social action or private and non-fiction writing, and the self-concealment or self-dramatisation staged in their poetry. Partly for this reason, the gender-consciousness discernible in both familiar and lesser-known 'names' demands distinct critical frameworks.

Throughout the century, women write and publish poetry without critical recognition, hampered by the double bind which mocks them for

I

writing poetry as themselves, but castigates them for challenging their male counterparts on their own terms. Invariably, they end up torn between the political and cultural benefits of a gender-identification in which they find company and context, and portmanteau labels which threaten to obscure and devalue their variousness. Lady Margaret Sackville's Introduction to _A Book of Verse by Living Women_ (1910) provides an early account of the dilemma. Looking back to the predecessors she most admires, Elizabeth Barrett Browning, Christina Rossetti, Adelaide Proctor and Michael Field, Sackville considers how their work and status relates to her own: 'It is not a question of intellectual values – probably in this respect the women writers of then and now are equals – it is a question of the influences which have gone to the making of their work . . . women are not yet by any means quite free from the old (for poetry) disastrous influences . . . There is still in this country a perhaps healthy tendency to snub women for doing things because they are women.'[3] In 'Woman and Artist', Anna Wickham dismantles the debate poetically:

> If a woman is to be an expressor
> And avoid most desperate confusion,
> She, more than any, must compass Soul's exclusion.
> There's no excuse for expression from a woman
> Unless she be a representative human.
>
> If an artist must suppress sex too much is lost;
> The product, thought, is purchased at too high a cost.
> The singer must stand proud alone
> And claim a little eminence that is her own.
>
> Yet woman will confuse and vex
> If she is dominant in things of sex.
> The intellectual hermaphrodite
> Must stand unified and subject for delight.
>
> In this there is great strain
> And sore irreconcilables for one poor brain.[4]

With hindsight, Wickham's separatism is unusual; more poets resist an identification which, in harnessing craft to gender, seems to compromise rather than confirm the individuality on which their professionalism insists. In an article 'Some Observations on Women's Poetry' in 1925, Edith Sitwell reveals how acutely she felt the absence of helpful models when it came to finding the right form. She attempts to work through the difficulties of not identifying with the conventions associated with either masculine or supposedly feminine lines of poetry: 'Women poets will do best if they realise that male technique is not suitable to them. No woman writing in the English language has ever written a great sonnet, no woman has ever written great blank verse. Then again, speaking generally, as we cannot dispense with our rules, so we find free verse difficult.'[5] At the end of the century, Carol Rumens admits to a similar dilemma about women's appropriation of traditional forms, 'asking, each time I gave birth to a sonnet,/"Is it a boy?"' ('A Bookshop Revisited').[6] Ironically, she both maintains and mimics the debilitating preoccupation with whether to disguise or proclaim a gendered perspective:

> Women are often glad to be one of the crowd
> And not special cases.
> But some would argue there's still a place for proud
> Self-proclaimed poetesses.
> ...
> Poet or poetess, we've surely known times
> We sat up all night
> In our Yeatsian masks, like good little androgynes,
> And couldn't write.

The polished poem of course answers the concluding self-deprecation. This parodic repudiation of Kingsley Amis's 'A Bookshop Idyll' and John Keats's 'La Belle Dame Sans Merci' cleverly claims a creative territory which mediates between male-associated literary paradigms and female experience. In 1998 Rumens speaks for many in deconstructing, rather than explicitly denying, the gendering of poetic difference: 'Sometimes it doesn't worry me; sometimes I think perhaps I'm writing differently because I'm a woman, so I'm a woman poet – but so what? I'm also writing differently from any other poet, so it's not a very meaningful description.'[7] However, as Rumens, Sitwell and Wickham prove, the psychological and emotional tension involved in the persona of the 'woman poet' energises the imaginative and linguistic fabric of their compositions. Jane Holland's 'Pulse' signals the gender-negotiation and pluralism we emphasise: 'I'm not a woman poet./ I'm a woman and a poet./ The difference is in the eyes.' In the 'difference' on which Holland puns, the female 'eye'/'I' overwrites the disempowering effect of the male gaze traditionally inscribed in lyric poetry. Jackie Kay enforces the point: 'What [women poets] need is to be able to come together on the basis of our differences and not on the basis of our similarities.'[8]

The dynamic of 'difference' has much to do with our decision to include non-British poets who have settled, or have simply been published, in Britain, and whose work can be shown to have particular resonance in their contemporary literary-critical environment. Above all, this has enabled us to register the ways in which women's poetry contributes to the porosity and pluralism of twentieth-century so-called 'British' culture. For example, while the premise of the book has partly been to spotlight a company of writers overshadowed by their American contemporaries in critical discourse, nevertheless the richness of British/American cross-currencies and dialogues down the century is implicitly recognised throughout. We therefore integrate the prominent Anglo-Americans H.D., Laura Riding, Denise Levertov, Sylvia Plath and Anne Stevenson whose critical coverage in Britain often seems arbitrarily patchy. In this context, the still-compelling figure of Plath (whose posthumous lionisation, though suggestive of establishment support for women's poetry, deflects critical attention from a generation of deserving names and has arguably done Plath herself few favours) remains one among many. After the Second World War, the dynamics of cultural duality became increasingly relevant for the many black and Asian-British women poets. Along with their Welsh and Scottish counterparts, their opportunities for publishing in Britain noticeably opened up from the early 1980s. Towards the end of the century, the example of the Irish poets (Northern and Southern) who negotiate confidently with their complex literary history particularly infiltrates the British literary consciousness.[9] Although several poets can be positioned across crude social, as well as national, boundaries, Ethel Carnie at the beginning and Elizabeth Bartlett towards the end of the century are regrettably rare in their working-class origins.

The book's structure is designed to provide a comprehensive and evaluative critical record while orienting the more significant figures in relation both to each other and to the developments of British poetry. The Chronology emphasises how debates and legislation about gender equality characterise the century's social history and impact on its cultural forms. We indicate some of women's literary initiatives and include a suggestive, if far from exhaustive, register of formal awards. This gesture is not without the uneasy recognition that conservative literary establishments may prefer the innocuous and linguistically claustrophobic woman like Stevie Smith's 'Miss Snooks', who 'went on being awfully nice/And took a lot of prizes'.[10] To date, no woman has been offered the double-edged honour of Poet Laureate, although nominees and serious contenders have included Alice Meynell, Vita Sackville-West, Kathleen Raine and more recently Carol Ann Duffy. In an array of less controversial initiatives over the decades, women involved themselves energetically in publishing, setting up presses and literary magazines. From the Second World War on, increasing numbers edited anthologies, while most of the leading postwar names (Stevie Smith, Elizabeth Jennings, Patricia Beer, Anne Stevenson, Fleur Adcock, Carol Rumens, Gillian Clarke, Ruth Padel, Jo Shapcott, Deryn Rees-Jones, Kate Clanchy and Sheenagh Pugh, to name a broad cross-section) worked as reviewers and/or columnists on a range of mainstream and specialised publications. In the closing decades of the century, women poets became much more visible on an expanding circuit of literary festivals, competition panels and creative writing courses.

Our three chronological sections (1900–45, 1945–80, 1980–2000) can be identified with three major developments in the history of twentieth-century British poetry (modernism, the postwar Movement and postmodernism) and the three so-called waves of the women's movement (suffragism, Women's Liberation and 'power' feminism). Organised under loosely periodised headings, each part's Overview records and reviews the names which largely, but not exclusively, appeared in leading periodicals, key anthologies or other literary records. At the same time, we have necessarily reassessed existing or neglected critical treatments. We briefly indicate and suggest ways in which the chief figures positioned themselves in relation to the broader canonical norms inscribed in the mainstreams of British poetry.

Typically, we foreground the generative potential of women's poetic practice by drawing attention to works which investigate conventional poetic attitudes or vocabularies. Inevitably, there are many writers and works deserving of more consideration than we have been able to give.[11] The works we discuss can be cross-referenced against the List of Published Works (included at the end) which details the publishing records of almost all the writers mentioned. Dwelling on the major poets, the chapters explore the more period-specific issues or themes noted in each of the three introductions. Groupings are connected by literary or public context, such as modernism or war, by culturally relevant concerns, stretching from 'home' to social or sexual politics, or by practice, notably the ironic manipulation of voice in the dramatic monologue. Finally, the treatment of the lyric is returned to throughout.

If it is not possible to trace a neatly linear developmental path by women poets as a collective, we can, however, detect a shift from a limiting wariness of female affiliation at the turn of the century to the welcome sense of role models at the end. The four chapters of Part I circle and are inflected by the poets' deep-seated suspicion of a gendered voice. In quite distinct ways, some of the outstanding figures – Alice Meynell, Charlotte Mew and Sylvia Townsend Warner – move between ungendered pronouns and more woman-centred explorations of female psychology and experience. Highly gender-aware in their personal and critical documents, Mina Loy and Edith Sitwell only appear to evade the issue altogether by sinking their energies into a radical literary prospectus. Anna Wickham's subversion of modernism is highly expressive and dramatic, most happily in rhyming free-verse monologues. In Part II, war having served to sharpen debates about gender-relations, the tensions between women's enlarging public lives and unchanging private commitments are betrayed in their ambivalent treatment of domesticity and motherhood. Other poets' growing political purpose is manifest in the consciousness-raising feminist protests of the 1970s but the linguistically progressive work of a new avant-garde, represented by Veronica Forrest-Thomson, Wendy Mulford and Denise Riley, proves a more stimulatingly transgressive strand of activity. Stevie Smith, the only poet who has a chapter of her own, is a conduit between modernist and postmodernist principles of representation. Her crafty interplay between parody and pastiche draws attention to the socially loaded language of expression while the human drama of her poems insists upon the poet's role as cultural commentator. Notoriously unclassifiable, she exemplifies the ways in which women oscillate between high culture and their experiences; how they muddle or dispense with the oppositions between spoken and literary language; how they interrogate and revise stereotyping cultural myths.

Along with the Irish-born, English-educated Eavan Boland, Carol Ann Duffy is the major poet of Part III. In the century's last two decades, grouping the still-emerging number of published poets across four generations and diverse cultural locations has to be provisional and flexible. The complex interrelation of language, identity and 'place' helps to animate daring negotiations between expressive and closed linguistic strategies. Women most often participate poetically in the postmodern multiplicity of contemporary life, which takes them from global warfare to family breakdown, with dramatisation, dialogic personal testimony and ingeniously defamiliarising metaphors. The chapters appraise their restive use of voices and imagination; these voices present and exchange differing cultural perspectives in the colloquial, the vernacular and dialect. Distinctively in this period, many incorporate and scrutinise the dynamic vocabularies and forms of science, new technologies and media. Like the book's cover illustration, the final chapter on the 'renovated lyric' registers the freedom of women to articulate a pluralised, connected, but not fixed, female first person pronoun.

Overview

INTRODUCTION

During the first half of the twentieth century, two world wars, the culmination of women's suffrage in the vote and the widening of both literary and mass cultures reshape ideas about what it means to be masculine and feminine along with what it means to be British. In the early decades, one striking aspect of women's poetry is the disparity between the transformations concerning women's rights and the self-concealment in many poems. Stifled by iconographies of the 'poetess', diverse poets negotiate with the dual demands to write as distinctly 'Woman' while avoiding implications of the 'personal'. In order to win acceptance from male literary individuals and institutions, on whom they depend for publication and esteem, they frequently avoid gender identification by means of initials or pseudonyms and indeterminate pronouns. Avoiding charges of 'sentimentality', they prove their intellectual muscle with rigorous prosodic principles associated with the high literary forms of 'masculine' writing. As the century progresses, however, women with economic independence become producers of poetry, initiating printing presses, bookshops and literary journals. They write and deliver talks on literary criticism. They edit anthologies, pioneer poetry broadcasts, give readings and win prizes. Steadily, but not uniformly, women develop a more self-assertive colloquial voice, frequently through dramatised monologues and dialogues. They enforce the modernist concept of the 'persona', the masked identity of the poet on the page, in their dramatisations of male and female identities and relations. An outstanding few centralise women in their poems; they confront stereotyped femininity head on with parodic imitations and subversions. Drawing on the new terminology for exploring the unconscious, the boldest poets are distinctly twentieth-century in their depictions of complex female psychology.

Poetry by women both holds its own in and unsettles the terms of orthodox literary categories. This Introduction is organised chronologically to provide some notion of development in relation to women's literary negotiations with social imperatives. The three parts, 1900–15, 1916–29, 1930–45, accommodate the common stylistic classifications of Edwardian, Georgian, modernist, and 1930s 'movements' along with poetry of the two world wars. However, the stylistic and ideological associations of these groups are never straightforward. As for historical delineations, modernist practices can be taken back to at least 1910 with the Post-Impressionist exhibition or to the start of Imagism in 1912 and then forward into the 1930s and even the 1940s. Also, individual poets, most notably Edith Sitwell, cut across crude time delineations. What does come through in the anthology introductions, as in the burgeoning literary criticism of this period, is the sense of poetry's capacity to accelerate or counter cultural change. Camilla Doyle's 'The General Shop' poem encapsulates the kind of widely read poetry printed in conservative papers and popular anthologies: 'Yet smart new stores are dull compared/To this which always stays the same.'¹ This kind of 'general-shop' poem is relegated for the very reason that it leaves things unchanged.

If canons are largely set by contemporary anthologies and reinforced by subsequent ones, the period's leading poets are: Alice Meynell (1847–1922), Charlotte Mew (1869–1928), Anna Wickham (1884–1947), Frances Cornford (1886–1960), Edith Sitwell (1887–1964), Dorothy Wellesley (1889–1956), Vita Sackville-West (1892–1962), Sylvia Townsend Warner (1893–1978), Lilian Bowes Lyon (1895–1949), Ruth Pitter (1897–1992), Stevie Smith (1902–71), Kathleen Raine (1908–2003) and Anne Ridler (1912–2001). Retrospective literary criticism, such as it is, tends to concentrate on Smith, Mew and the native Americans Gertrude Stein (1874–1946), H. D. (1886–1961), Marianne Moore (1887–1972), Edna St Vincent Millay (1892–1950) and Laura (Riding) Jackson (1901–91). Notable among the overlooked poets are Margaret Sackville (1881–1963), Muriel Stuart (1885–1967), Elizabeth Daryush (1887–1977), Nancy Cunard (1896–1965), Mina Loy (1882–1966), Lynette Roberts (1909–95) and Sheila Wingfield (1906–95).

1900–15

The death of Queen Victoria and accession of King Edward VII in 1901, along with uncertainty about the effects of the new sciences and industrialisation created mixed moods of nostalgia, optimism and apprehension. The death of Edward in 1910 was followed by the reign of George V, which was overhung by the Great War (1914–18). This war, along with the influence of America through film, the radio and magazines, the impact of Carl Jung and Sigmund Freud when their translations became available, the first wave of feminism, the development of literary criticism and an increasingly literate public effected cultural transformations, particularly in relation to the concepts of nationalism and gender.[2] Inevitably, these transformations were accompanied by reactionary backlashes, especially against women's emancipation. Theories of innate sex difference, which continued to be validated by medical and scientific discourses, collided with literary women's preoccupation with the social and creative constructions of masculine and feminine natures and functions.

Looking back, W. B. Yeats saw 1900 as the year when poets got 'off their stilts'.[3] High diction was discarded in preference for colloquial idioms, albeit metrically regular and rhyming. While much poetry was formally conventional, whether based on classical forms or the more democratic ballad and narrative, the creeping vocabulary of psychoanalysis made way for the controversial *vers libre* and informed other modernist disruptions of linear syntax and narrative. The reaction against tenacious traditionalism was also manifested in the small but significant progressive groups of Vorticists, the English version of the Italian Futurists, who circulated their ideas and art in *Blast* (1914–15), and the Eiffel Tower group, who from 1909 met weekly in a Soho restaurant of that name. The newly literate public extended the market for books but inflamed concern about the erosion of literary standards. Advances in literacy were aided by increasing public libraries and printing. Literary papers shared a concern to safeguard value and taste from contamination by mass culture.[4] The *Times Literary Supplement* (*TLS*) was the major voice and particularly influential in establishing an atmosphere of the male club; it excluded women not only from its echelon but also from 'Poetry' by feminising their writing. The Poetry Society's *Poetry Review*, which started in January 1912, was also proudly reactionary and had a wide international readership.

Intellectual women who developed alongside suffragism more often than not stifled any directly personal perspective in their poetry, especially in the first fifteen years of the century when the concept and activity of emancipation was at its most intense. Some were active in the cause of equal rights or expressed their opinions in correspondence and journalism. Their participation in literary production also registers their emerging psychological, sexual and economic independence.[5] In June 1908 the Women Writers Suffrage League began and supported various suffrage journals. The literary paper *Freewoman: A Weekly Feminist Review* (1911–12), which became *The New Freewoman* (1913–14), circulated and strengthened women's resistance to universalising prescriptions about their nature and role. From 1914 *The New Freewoman* became *The Egoist,* subtitled 'an individual review', which was outspoken on issues such as women's sexual needs or how to be unmarried and happy.[6] Its stated aim, 'Our war is with words in every aspect: grammar, accidence, syntax', indicates the editors' recognition of the interdependence of remoulding literary conventions and achieving social liberation.[7]

Contradicting women's longed-for social equality, poets, editors and critics relentlessly enforced binary divides between male and female character and creativity. In a special edition of *Poetry Review* on 'Women-Poets', May 1912, the editor contrasted women's activities for emancipation in law with the essentialised female nature which was the substance of much traditional poetry:

It is a truism that the great poet is neither man nor woman, but partially each. He has represented Woman so adequately in poetry that there seemed scarcely any call for her to represent herself. Now at last, however, some change is taking place. Woman, late though it be, is becoming conscious of herself. Her awakening begins in a startled blinking of her eyes, an exclamation: 'What am I?' It proceeds in the helpless call: 'I am no worse than Man. I am no longer his slave'; then she throws up wild arms, and smashes windows. This is lively, but it is not logical; her call is 'I am a woman': she must reveal that she is Woman indeed. In the poetess, perhaps, chiefly, this revelation is becoming apparent. It begins with Christina Rossetti, and it continues to-day in many graceful lyrics of motherhood; charmingly turned, rare and intimate expressions of quiet thought, strength and courage. Despite all emancipation, Woman still lives in a garden and we must receive her verses gift-wise, as we might some fine broidery. She will play with a fancy as lovingly as with a child; she enjoys delicacy in her verse, and soft light shades: she loves especially a gentle hopefulness. Her poetry is the expression of personal moods, or of the mystical and apparently supernatural: it is remarkable how seldom she may be reckoned a whole poet.[8]

This lengthy extract indicates the acute gender consciousness initiated and maintained by the critics, even though, as here, they may seem to argue for artistic androgyny. The parodic portrayal of wildly smashing windows cunningly opposes both logic and a 'natural' womanhood which is rooted in the privacy of home, not the public domain. The universalising capitalisation of 'Woman' and the connection with her nineteenth-century predecessors homogenises women's poetry by the idealised qualities of gentleness and modesty. The editor is probably Harold Monro who in fact was a champion of women poets.[9] In this article he identifies the need to distinguish the literary poets from the 'delicate' feminine conformists who were the most readily published and promoted precisely because they offered no challenge. The editor also recognised that women's poetry was usually judged 'not only by Man, but also frequently by Woman herself, according to the severe tests of a masculine standard'.

To offset the generalities illuminated in the above editorial, Lady Margaret Sackville's *A Book of Verse by Living Women* (1910), which informed and provoked the *Poetry Review* special woman number, usefully documents writers and the mindset of literary women. It consists of twenty-five poets and one 'anonymous' with a bibliography of the writers' works. Some belong to the nineteenth century but Sackville's Introduction is a valuable articulation of women poets' self-consciousness and self-construction in the early twentieth century. She believed that Christina Rossetti and 'Mrs Browning' were yet to be equalled but 'Of women poets considered individually, Mrs Meynell of course is the recognised head ... Michael Field's is one of the strongest women's voices of the present day ... It is a shining answer to all those who say that women cannot write good poetry without the personal note.' Her main cry is for critical discrimination between the best and weakest writing:

There is still in this country a perhaps healthy tendency to snub women for doing things because they are women ... Yet women are not yet by any means quite free from the old (for poetry) disastrous influences. There is still too often the feeling that the poet is expressing, very admirably it may be, emotions and ideas which have been read and heard of, but which are often no more than vivid reflections. To some, women's poetry is a glass reflecting nothing but themselves, not a still pool of living water wherein the stars and skies are mirrored ... Certainly, every year brings proof that women's verse is a growing thing ... Always it becomes less imitative – its grasp on reality more sure, less trivial, more certain in its achievement.[10]

Sackville associates creative development with social emancipation: 'When women have fully proved their capacity for freedom, we can begin to estimate better their capacity for poetry.'

As documented in Sackville's anthology, Alice Meynell is the earliest significant figure in the twentieth century and epitomises the independent literary woman whose poetry is oddly restrained.[11] Although limited in evolving a more freely female creativity, she provided women with a highly regarded model of the 'woman poet'. She believed in feminist reforms and was a prolific journalist and essayist. Her literary criticism has a confident polemic and expresses an assertive personality which is muffled in her poems. *Later Poems* in 1902 was followed by a *Collected Poems* in 1913. *The Shepherdess and Other Verses* came out in 1914 and *Ten Poems 1913–15* the following year. *Poems on the War* (1915) and *A Father of Women* (1917) were privately printed by her son Francis, a socialist journalist and conscientious objector. She also edited anthologies and in 1911 produced poetry selections by Samuel Johnson and William Blake. She was variously constructed as embodying feminine ideals of spiritual intensity and maternal domesticity or as an honorary male writer.[12] On the publication of her posthumous *Last Poems* (1923), Alfred Noyes's eulogy in the *Bookman* emphasised the 'intellectual' quality of her work, defining it antithetically to the 'sentimental' poetry around.[13] He also claimed that she had written 'the three greatest sonnets ever written by a woman' – 'Renunciation', 'Thoughts on Separation' and 'The Young Neophyte'. S. Gertrude Ford's earlier two-page profile in the *Bookman* (1915), registers the suggestion that she be made Poet Laureate although Ford hints that she would need to be more 'topical'.[14] Her reputation in the United States is indicated in *Poetry: A Magazine of Verse*, which printed her poems: '[Meynell] needs no introduction in America . . . [where] her exquisite art is well-known.'[15] Meynell's centenary in 1947 produced some reevaluation but little feminist criticism.

Katherine Tynan (1861–1931), a close friend of Meynell, was also a respected literary woman. Along with Meynell and her Irish compatriot Eva Gore-Booth (1870–1926), she often exercised spiritual insights in verse. Although she produced little poetry in the 1900s, she published five books of poetry between 1911 and 1930. Mary Coleridge (1861–1907) published *Fancy's Garden* in 1901; *Poems of Mary Coleridge* (1907) was posthumous. She was a reviewer for the *Times Literary Supplement* and a strong essayist. 'Michael Field' (Katherine Bradley 1846–1914 and Edith Cooper 1862–1913) brought out *Wild Honey from Various Thyme* in 1908. *Poems of Adoration* (1912) and *Mystic Trees* (1913) register their conversion to Roman Catholicism and are considered less aesthetically stimulating than their other works. Altogether they published twenty-seven tragedies and eight volumes of lyrics.

In addition to poets already mentioned, Sackville's anthology includes Jane Barlow, Anna Bunston (whom she singles out for praise), Olive Custance (Lady Alfred Douglas), Harriet Eleanor Hamilton-King, Emily Hickey, Winifred Lucas, Eva M. Morton, Annie Matheson, Rosa Mulholland, Dollie Radford, Mary Robinson, Dora Sigerson Shorter, Cicely Fox Smith, Elinor Sweetman, Laurence Alma Tadema, Rachel Annand Taylor, The Hon. Grace Tollemache, Rosalind Travers, Rosamund Marriott Watson and Margaret L. Woods (who has an impressive list of publications spanning 1888 to 1921 with a *Collected Works* in 1914). Woods was counted among important contemporary poets by Monro, who ironically (she is now largely overlooked) predicted that '[her] dramas in lively exciting verse will probably be recognised as among the best specimens of the pure dramatic literature of the time'.[16]

1916–29

After a century of activism, this is the period when women won the vote: in 1918 for all married women over thirty who were on the local government electoral register, and in 1928 for all women over twenty-one. In 1919 Nancy Astor became the first woman MP to take her seat and the Sex Disqualification Act removed barriers to women becoming barristers, solicitors and magistrates and to other positions of power or learning. Oxford and Cambridge agreed to confer degrees on women (1920, 1921) and legislation in favour of women's rights continued throughout the 1920s. Changes in law reflected and generated altered ideas about domestic roles. In 1918 Marie Stopes (1880–1958) published *Wise Parenthood* and *Married Love* (selling 400,000 copies by 1923) which emphasised revised attitudes towards marriage, the nuclear family and women's sexuality. Her *Contraception* in 1923 registered their advances towards sexual autonomy. Stopes, whose poems appear in a number of anthologies, started Britain's first birth control clinic in 1921. The other seismic complication to traditional ideals of nation and gender was the First World War when, for the first time, women took over men's work and pay.

The binary rhetoric of Home and Front in 1914–18 did not correspond to women's experiences of war work. Furthermore, the conflation of 'Motherhood' with 'Patriotism' conflicted with many women's pacifist commitments. Postwar idealisations of domesticity eluded the bereaved and unmarried after a war that had wiped out actual or potential husbands, let alone fathers, brothers and sons. Married women had to be grateful for a mate but resented having to give up work since many had enjoyed employment and pay during the war. 'Old' Feminists believed that equality in legislation must remain central to women's activism whereas the 'New' Feminists began to champion segregated issues such as childcare and birth control. In 1916 *Vogue* arrived from the United States and fed women's appetite for more than the conventional role of homemaker which the English magazines had tended to support. *Peg's Paper*, aimed at working-class women, started in 1919.

The competing urges for both change and stability after the war energised mixed impulses about tradition and experiment in poetry and criticism. As seen in the prewar period, conservative critics used their reviews to play upon women's sense of womanly duty. Continuing from the early century, the critical double standard applauded discernible feminine ideals but downgraded them as literature. In his introduction to *A Book of Women's Verse* in 1921, J. C. Squire ostensibly observes the proliferation of women in literary places but accentuates their distinctively 'feminine' creativity.[17] Since most of Squire's poets were dead, his gesture at publishing women was actually retrograde to their release from outworn mythologies of poetesshood. John Pearson dramatises the battle between 'Squirearchy' and Bloomsbury which had acute implications for women, especially progressive poets: 'The Sitwells... were no match for the traditionalists who had the *London Mercury*, the *New Statesman* and the *Observer*, and most of the popular press behind them. Another area where the Squirearchy had power was in the awarding of the best-known prizes for literature and poetry, which had a curious habit of going to devoted members of the Squirearchy.'[18]

'The Poetry of Women', a review of three new books of poetry in the *Times Literary Supplement* in 1920, indicates how men's anxiety about women's new social freedoms after the war spilled over into the reception given to their poems:

Literature which answers to every change in the social life of a people, has already begun to register the fact of woman's emancipation. The ideal of self-expression, which has supplanted self-sacrifice as the aim of the modern woman, has possibly brought with it as many abuses as it has banished... Certainly, the result in literature may not at first seem very happy. As we contemplate the profusion of modern fiction with women's names on the title page, we may reasonably fear for the welfare of art smothered between the smatterings of science and the anarchy of instincts... But though we allow the novel to be abused in the interests of sex propaganda, lyrical poetry, by the very strict limits of its constitution, will permit no such transgression.[19]

The reviewer's resistance to professional women writers was partly a nostalgia for the prewar ideals of femininity (and presumably of masculinity): 'The poetry of women, then, has its basis in a sympathy with nature rather than art, and, as interpreters of the beauty and sanctity of *what is to so many of us almost a lost province,* they may contribute new truths to poetry and refresh it as its source, provided they can criticise more carefully the organism of which they remain a part.'[20] 'Woman', as a generic concept, was used paradigmatically for the mythical ideals of spirituality and traditionalism which were resurrected against postwar modernity. Thus even the seemingly genteel women who appear complicit with the applauded selflessness are transgressively self-expressive in the very act of writing.

The influential anthology series of this period indicate its literary cross-currents of innovation and conservatism. The Imagist anthologies ran from 1914–17 and broke some ground for the promotion of free verse. Edith Sitwell's controversial *Wheels* were annuals from 1916 to 1921 and stimulated considerable debate about the boundaries and morality of poetry. The move away from rural verse to the more intellectual and urban indices of Imagism and modernism was countered by the popularity of Edward Marsh's five *Georgian Poetry* anthologies which came out between 1912 and 1922. Georgian poetry was easily caricatured by the prevalence of sheep and country boots in the wholesome English countryside. This pastoralism was remote from a population where the majority lived in towns and agricultural work was in decline. The absence of human relations in Georgian poetry further removed it from the worlds of its general readers. The intellectuals were increasingly engaged with theories of psychoanalysis and T. S. Eliot's condemnation of Georgian poetry in *The Egoist* in 1918 fatally separated Georgian from 'modernist'.[21]

The broadening of mass culture through popular papers, magazines, fiction and the cinema propagated the division between high-, middle- and low brow which became a preoccupation of the literary papers. Male rivalry which excluded and inhibited women was aggravated during the 1920s by the growth industry of literary criticism. Critical debate was stimulated and sustained by the surge of highbrow periodicals and seminal critical works which rarely featured women. Vera Brittain recorded how she and Winifred Holtby 'were the first victims of that "discrimination" on which, with some justice, the *New Statesman* has prided itself ever since' when their names were omitted from a list of contributors which included practically everyone else who had written for it. She found the discrimination significant because during the 1920s and 1930s the *New Statesman and Nation* became known for its 'intellectual brilliance'.[22] Brittain's parenthetical phrase, 'with some justice', illustrates how even successful writers inhaled their inferiority. These cumulative exclusions entrenched 'femininity' and 'intellect' as binary opposites in a period which idolised literary intellectuality. In 1928 the Six Point Group, which was dedicated to social equalities in law, advertised a debate on 'Women in the Press', the motion being 'That the influence of the Daily Press is detrimental to the position of Women'.[23] It alluded to the growth of 'trash' weeklies aimed at women as consumers. Women's weeklies helped to give them identity as a subculture but they also perpetuated the equation between the 'popular' and the 'feminine'. This equation exacerbated literary women's urge to distance themselves from any appearance of femininity.

Barred from the major literary papers and belittled in the popular ones, many women were involved in the more inclusive new magazines which became channels of poetry and criticism between the United States and Europe. They set up journals which were progressive, and in keeping with their dominant goal of equality, published both men and women.[24] *Time and Tide*, inaugurated by Lady Rhondda, ran from 1920 and many intellectual women featured in its organisation, editing, writing or reviewing.[25] Of the poets, Holtby was a director, Scovell was among its editors and several others were published through it. Eliot's opinion that Harriet Shaw Weaver, editor of *The Egoist*, 'is the only woman connected with publishing whom it is really easy to get on with,' is a tribute but also reflects the sex war involved even in the progressive journals.[26] The personal records surrounding these activities are important documentaries of the cultural climate.[27]

Women promoted modern poetry not only through their journals and critical works, but also through bookshops and printing presses which mobilised the international network of artistic innovation in the 1920s. Sylvia Beach's famous Shakespeare and Company bookshop and lending library in Paris was an important venue for writers interested in modernism. In London Alida Monro became responsible for the Poetry Bookshop in Devonshire Street which was an international meeting place and eclectic in outlook.[28] It provided a platform for new poets, including Cornford, Mew, Sinclair and Wickham, by publishing their work and organising readings. Cunard's The Hours Press, in Réanville and then Paris, privileged experimental writing and printed twenty-four books between 1928 and 1931. Laura Riding, with Robert Graves, ran the Seizin Press (1927–39) to encourage new, mostly male, poets and later edited a critical review (*Epilogue* 1935–37). Ridler worked with Eliot at Faber. Less well-documented is the dependence of many men and women on the patronage of Dorothy Wellesley and Winifred Bryher. Wellesley put money into the Woolfs' Hogarth Press and edited the Hogarth Living Poets series; Bryher provided funds for Robert MacAlmon's avant-garde Contact Publishing Company in Paris, Beach's bookshop and the Egoist Press.[29] She also founded the progressive film magazine *Close-Up* in 1927.

For Meynell, this period until her death in 1922 was one of intense creativity. *A Father of Women*, her *Essays* (both 1917) and the posthumous *The Last Poems of Alice Meynell* (1923) were well received and individual poems were published in *London Mercury* and the *Observer*. Eva Gore-Booth published five books of prose, several newspaper articles and twelve books of poems including a *Complete Poems* (1929) and *Selected Poems*

(1933) which has a useful 'Biographical Note' by the social reformer Esther Roper. Although a vociferous suffragist, Gore-Booth tends to avoid gender distinctions in her poems. There are occasional references to Irish questions and the First World War but as an oeuvre they tend towards the mystical. Although rather universalising, there is some sense of a personal subjectivity at work in the imaginative spaces of spiritual perception. Conversely, the political agitator and commentator Cicely Hamilton (1872–1972), famous for *Marriage as a Trade* (1909), expressed herself in all genres except for poetry.

Without doubt, 1916 was a bumper year. It was the start of Sitwell's exciting *Wheels* anthologies and the second of the Imagist anthologies, this time edited by Amy Lowell. Mew brought out her first two books and Wickham published *The Man with a Hammer*. It was also the year of *The Sea Garden*, by H. D. and *The Pageant of War*, by Sackville (1881–1963) who was allegedly considered that rare combination of beauty and brains. In addition to her important anthology, *A Book of Verse by Living Women* (1910), she was in many anthologies although cited as an omission from Monro's *Some Contemporary Poets* (1920). A small section of her *Collected Poems* (1939) on war achieve her most contemporary idiom and the lengthy 'The Pageant of War' (1917) deserves inclusion in the canons of war poetry. Like many of her works, the multivocal dramatisations avoid a fixed authorial position while investigating political assumptions. War poetry books also came from Tynan (1861–1931), Brittain (1893–1970) and Jessie Pope (d. 1941) who was a formidably popular patriotic wartime versewriter.

Others who were notable during the First World War and due for more consideration than hitherto include May Wedderburn Cannan (1893–1973), although she tends towards male Edwardian clichéd patriotism and consolation.[30] The first person pronoun which dominates her slim volume *In War Time* (1917) tends to be universal and ungendered. The selection of her poems in Catherine Reilly's anthology *Scars Upon My Heart: Women's Poetry and Verse of the First World War* represent Cannan at her best. Margaret Postgate Cole (1893–1980), a Fabian socialist and prolific writer, produced only one poetry book (1918). The war poems, notably 'The Veteran' and 'Praematuri' which are in Reilly's collection, are outstanding and were printed in *An Anthology of War Poems* (1930).[31] Although Muriel Stuart's five books of poems, published between 1916 and 1927, were well reviewed in Britain and the United States, her work has mostly been forgotten. One reason for the oversight is the surprising scarcity of her poems in anthologies, probably because of their frankness about social injustices. In 1926 Henry Savage declared, 'there is no English woman poet living today who is Muriel Stuart's peer'. A new, though altered, edition of Stuart's *Selected Poems* (1927) in 2000 salvages some of the best and indicates her range. Her 1927 frontispiece, dedicated to Thomas Hardy who called her work '"superlatively good"', registers women's yearning for male validation.

Teresa Hooley (1888–1973) produced a *Collected Poems* in 1926, several volumes in the 1930s and three others. Helen Hamilton seems to have made her name from the hundred-page humorous but unsettling poetry pamphlet *The Compleat Schoolmarm: A Story of Promise and Fulfilment* (1917). She also wrote fiction and books of lyrics. The latter are remarkable for the contrast between their self-concealing, archaistic, devotional idiom and the directness and clarity of the satirical poems. In *Hope and Other Poems* (1924), it is as if she becomes creatively claustrophobic when trying to be 'literary'. Similarly, Eleanor Farjeon (1881–1965) hid her views beneath abstract lyricising in her literary collections (1911 and 1918) but assumed a satirical outspoken idiom in the guise of 'Tomfool' in the 1920s. These subversive comments on the news appeared serially in the socialist *Daily Herald* and were published in books by the Labour Publishing Company (1920, 1921). One line from her *Sonnets and Poems* (1918) is a giveaway of her radical spirit: 'Alas, that ever life's sleek counterfeit/Convention, should usurp life's very throne.'[32] S. Gertrude Ford published poems in periodicals and the two most outspoken of her four poetry books came out in 1917 and 1928. In addition, she wrote *Lessons in Verse Craft* and edited the *Little Books of Georgian Verse*. The poems of Winifred Letts (1882–1971) were circulated in various papers. Her popular *Songs from Leinster* (1913) was reprinted four times, followed by *More Songs from Leinster* (1926) and two other volumes (1916, 1917). Her poems ooze with human sympathy and provide models of loyalty, pity, courage and religious hope. She tends to use democratic forms like ballads and quatrains and presents herself as a genderless 'everyman' commentator. Her eponymous 'The Spires of Oxford', which was continually reproduced, typically expresses shared sentiments in literary form with consoling rhyme: 'But when the bugles sounded – War!/They put their games away.' Her stock responses to Irish scenery and culture also appealed to ever-abundant sentimental nationalism.

Rose Macaulay (1889–1958) was primarily a novelist and influential figure in the London literary scene until the 1950s. She made a reputation in the 1920s but her war poems were printed in various national and literary papers and make up half the poetry in *Three Days* (1919). They are confidently colloquial and the free-verse stream of consciousness indicates some modernist influences. She experimented with rhythm and her stance is decidedly unpatriotic and unsentimental. Nevertheless, it seems that poetry was too restricting for her imagination. According to her biographer, 'Friends say that Rose Macaulay had a haunting lifelong love of poetry: and, indeed, she wrote poems occasionally throughout her life. But her talent profited from a freer medium, where her thoughts could generate their own rhythms and develop unhindered their own curious, questioning forms.'[33] She was one of three nominees to Edward Marsh for his quest to include a woman in his *Georgian Poetry* anthologies – the other two were Mew and Sitwell. He chose Fredegonde Shove, whose appearance as the first female in *Georgian Poetry (1918–1919)* was registered in the *TLS*.[34] Shove, née Maitland, published three books of poems and a critical study, *Christina Rossetti* (1931). Both Shove and Macaulay are rated by Monro in *Some Contemporary Poets*.

Cornford, Pitter and Sackville-West had successful publishing histories and reputations but have been considered dull in retrospect.[35] This handed-down view is perhaps owing to the narrow representation of their poems in anthologies and the unavailability of their work. Sackville-West was connected by her social and amorous connections with the leading figures of both the conservative literary establishment and the Bloomsbury intellectuals. She qualifies as Georgian in all uses of the term: she was in Marsh's anthologies; she wrote within the historical timespan (1910–1936) – most of her poetry was written and published between 1918 and 1938, the best during the years 1926 to 1932 – and if Georgian means English pastoralism and a stylistic regularity, some of her poems conform to these characteristics. *The Land* (1926) was on its third reprint by the end of January 1927. Dedicated to Wellesley, it won Sackville-West fame as a poet, the Hawthornden Prize (1927), and a serious proposal for Poet Laureate in 1929 when Robert Bridges died. Although mocked by experimentalists like Sitwell, it reached a wide audience through the radio, public readings and newspapers, where it was initially published in extracts, and anthologies.

A figure hard to pin down is 'Susan Miles' (Ursula Roberts, née Wyllie, 1887–1975) who produced five collections, starting with *Dunch* (1918), then three in the 1920s and the novel-length *Lettice Delmer* which was probably written in the 1920s but not published until 1958.[36] She edited two poetry anthologies, as well as three novels and a biography of her husband, the Revd William Corbett Roberts (1873–1953), a radical egalitarian and pacifist. Her poetry is informed by wide literary reference and is confident in heroic, blank or free verse; she shifts between a first person persona and multivocality. Her poems were printed individually in papers ranging from the *Observer* to *Time and Tide*. The best are specific and the most authentic are the antiwar poems, including the highly dramatic and lengthy 'Grass Upon the Housetop' which seems to be stimulated by the death of her brother.[37] In the *Adventurers All* series, *Dunch* reads like a soap opera of provincial life. The episodes are ostensibly light-hearted but the satire can be topically poignant: 'I do not want to discuss the price of/flannelette with the doctor's wife', or:

> If only I would give up all that silly
>   Nonsense about the vote
> And turn my thoughts to duties
> That lie near home.[38]

Avoiding the consolation of rhyme, the situations remain open-ended. Several of Roberts's poems were in the Poetry Bookshop's *Recent Poetry 1923–33* and some appeared in other anthologies under 'Susan Miles'. Her name featured in *Some Contemporary Poets* but then disappeared.[39] Also overlooked is the remarkable collection of poems by the renowned suffragette and social historian Sylvia Pankhurst about her experiences in Holloway prison.

Although avant-garde modernism was strong throughout the period, cultural critics have tended to exaggerate the prevalence of radical poetics which was produced by and for a relatively small literary elite. The self-professed distance of high male modernism in the 1920s from 'the mass of humankind'[40] is evidenced by the rise of socialism culminating in the first Labour government in 1924 and the General Strike in 1926. However, several poets gained reputations as modernists in the 1920s. For women, one appeal of Imagist objectivity, avant-garde abstractions and Symbolist evocations was the chance to transcend gender affiliation. Edith Sitwell, Nancy Cunard and Iris Tree, who reacted against the traditions and privileges of their aristocratic families, had difficulty in identifying themselves with the biological and symbolised maternal function for women which arguably transferred to psychological conflicts with the concept of a female literary lineage. Their controversial *Wheels* anthologies were a launchpad for a new generation of poets where men and women were on equal terms.

In terms of publications, awards, works of criticism, innovations and reputation, Sitwell is the major woman poet of the twentieth century. Her work appears in most anthologies between 1925 and 1965. She is the subject of several portraits and literary and biographical studies, often tethered to the lives and work of her brothers Osbert and Sacheverell. Anecdotal references to the Sitwells relate to the first public performance of *Façade*, in the Aeolian Hall on 12 June 1923, which became 'part of the artistic history of the twenties, and central to the whole mythology of the Sitwells'.[41] Although given undue attention, *Façade* was Sitwell's break-through and for a time her London flat became a central meeting point for literary figures.

Cunard's poems are difficult to find and many remain uncollected.[42] Hugh Ford's commemorative anthology includes selections from all her published books and also from *Wheels*.[43] Her poetry was printed in journals including *The English Review* and *New Age* and she published four collections: *Outlaws* (1921), *Sublunary* (1923), *Parallax* (1925) and *Poems (Two) 1925* (1930). Meticulous as a translator, she also wrote poetry in French and Spanish. Her dominant form is the sonnet but her work after 1920 was more adventurous with free verse and more allusive, although she was still attentive to rhythm and often worked in iambics. In France, Cunard was influenced by the Dadaists and Surrealists whose distortions of images which signify the unconscious emerge in some of her poems. 'Simultaneous' and 'In Provins', which made up *Poems (Two) 1925*, originally published in 1930, mirror these new art forms in their free play of associated images.

As for Tree, apart from a reference in *The Trend of Modern Poetry* (Bullough, 1941), her poems have been largely ignored.[44] She produced four books of poems and they were printed in other anthologies and magazines such as *Vanity Fair*. Her difficulties with articulating a sceptical yet imaginative response to war and social injustice anticipate the artistic dilemmas of the 1930s poets. In exploring identity she drew on the terminology of psychoanalysis and moved towards a more natural idiom.

Helen Rootham did not have many poems in *Wheels* but was considered by the *Morning Post* to be the 'most profound and accomplished' of the contributors. Her poems indicate the influence of the French Symbolists Baudelaire and Verlaine, whom she translated and whom, along with some contemporary poets, she had introduced to Sitwell, when she became her governess. Mina Loy is a neglected modernist who has been appropriated by American histories but was British-born and lived in Europe before settling in New York in 1913. Sylvia Townsend Warner, who has been mostly recognised posthumously, helps to elasticise the canons of modernism. Some of May Sinclair's (1865–1946) poems were printed in literary journals and *The Dark Night* was published in 1924. A dialogic free-verse novel, it is a remarkable feat of psychological exploration which drew admiration for its ambitious experiments. Anglo-American connections were especially influential in the more avant-garde modernist developments where Moore, Lowell and Stein were powerful forces but cannot count as 'British' for this history. However, H. D., who became an emblematic 'Imagist', and the dynamic Laura (Riding) Jackson were expatriated from the United States and, as 'Anglo-Americans', are part of British literary history.

Modest, although contrasting, outputs came from Dorothy Wellesley and Sylvia Lynd (1888–1952). Harold Monro's often reprinted and revised *Twentieth Century Poetry* (1929) included Cornford and Parry Eden (b. 1885), whom Monro notes for her 'extraordinary intellect ... none trivial'.[45] She preferred the more popular forms of rhyming ballads and repetitive quatrains but the light-hearted humour tended towards satire and some of her work was published in *Punch*. Others were more reflective and Parry Eden's war poems had no trace of popular patriotism. Monro's anthology also promoted Field, Stella Gibbons, H. D., Mew, Meynell – along with her daughter Viola Meynell [46] – Shove, Sitwell, Warner and eight poems by Wickham, a number surpassed only by Siegfried Sassoon. *The Best Poetry* annual anthologies introduced several names who had one or more poems printed in daily or weekly papers but did not feature elsewhere. Of these, the recurring women's names omitted by Monro and not already mentioned are: Ethel Clifford, Rachel Annand Taylor, Margaret Maitland Radford, Evelyn Underhill, Irene Rutherford, Violet Jacob, Susan Mitchell, Stella Benson, Enid Bagnold, Nancy Campbell and Rose Fyleman.

1930–45

In this period especially, the competing demands and impulses which dogged educated women are frequently recorded. Many woman-centred poems are dramatic monologues or verse dialogues which allow for the dialectical representation of personal freedoms up against social constraints. The married and financially comfortable woman felt blessed, but the growing idealisation of the home brought pressures to find satisfaction within the secure yet stultifying family circle. Interwar legislation provided unmarried women with greater access to professions and public places but the 1931 census figures which recorded the drop in employment of women of marriageable age suggests that wives were discouraged from working.

Thanks to the work and public image of literary women in the first two decades of the twentieth century, by the 1930s reviewers were less able to draw upon the myths of feminine simplicity or conservatism but they still positioned poets in a literary sidestream. As Ridler recalled, 'It was difficult for women poets to achieve publication in the 1930s and still more difficult to be treated as a poet pure and simple, rather than as a woman poet.'[47] Several encountered resistance and found the atmosphere of competition to be inhibiting.[48] Sitwell concentrated on critical writing and a novel, partially because she was hard up. Her *Aspects of Modern Poetry* (1934), which is a useful document of contemporary trends and promotes progressive poets, has been overlooked, although it provoked personal quarrels with the leading critics, F. R. Leavis and Geoffrey Grigson. 'Souvenir de Monsieur Poop', from *Tender Only to One* (1938), is one of Stevie Smith's swipes at the literary establishment which made it so difficult for her to get her poems published and properly reviewed. It opens:

> I am the self-appointed guardian of English Literature,
> I believe tremendously in the significance of age;
> I believe that a writer is wise at 50,
> Ten years wiser at 60, at 70 a sage.
> I believe that juniors are lively, to be encouraged with
>   discretion and snubbed,
> I believe also that they are bouncing, communistic, ill
>   mannered and, of course, young.[49]

The repetition of 'I' and the exaggerated antipoetic versification indicates her lack of respect for the egocentricity and traditionalism of the publisher. In spite of obstacles, the 1930s saw women involved in poetry production and more acknowledged in the key journals and anthologies. Significantly, however, their political poems were not selected, except in liberal and left-wing publications and not always in these. The new edition of T. S. Eliot's *The Little Book of Modern Verse* (1934) was edited by Anne Ridler in 1941; Ridler also produced the supplement to the revised edition of Michael Roberts's influential *The Faber Book of Modern Verse* (1936) in 1951. Alida Monro, with Harold, edited *Recent Poetry 1923–1933* (1933) and Gwendolen Murphy's *The Modern Poet: An Anthology* (1938) has a useful Introduction. In the 1930s and 1940s, the radio provided opportunities for production and performance. The work of Hilda Matheson, as Head of Talks, and Janet Adam Smith, assistant editor on *The Listener*, testified to the conflicts between the progressive and reactionary forces within it. Smith was instrumental in the poetry programmes and edited the anthology of broadcast poems, *Poems of Tomorrow*, in 1935. Through her selection of poems and her implicit endorsement of the principles articulated by Eliot, she participated in the development of modernist ideas and practices. Furthermore, she achieved this against reactionary forces within the BBC and the listening and reading publics.

Women's poems represent the 1930s blend of modernist impersonality and social realism. In keeping with the decade's democratic principles, Cornford, Sackville-West, Pitter and Lynd aimed for colloquial diction without eschewing rhyme. They continued to reach wide audiences through the radio and anthologies. Wellesley was championed by Yeats, who in *The Oxford Book of English Verse* (1936) introduced her with a barbed compliment: 'at times facile and clumsy, at times magnificent in her masculine rhythm, in the precision of her style'.[50] In *Whether a Dove or a Seagull* (1934), the coded lesbian love poems presented under the dual authorship of Warner and Ackland belong to the countercurrent of 1930s personal lyricism. Poets who began to publish in the 1930s, but have been overlooked or sidelined because of what Adrian Caesar terms 'an inevitably ideological view of literary value'[51] include Daryush, Ridler and Bowes Lyon. Kathleen Raine was the most published in literary journals although her first book came out in 1943. A posthumous collection by Holtby (1898–1935) was printed although she had burned most of her earlier work. Stevie Smith broke into print with two poetry collections. Underrated poets whose work was circulated through papers, literary journals and anthologies include Stella Benson, Stella Gibbons,[52] Ada Jackson and Margaret Stanley Wrench, a Somerville graduate who won the Newdigate Prize for 1934. Brittain's *Poems of the War and After* (1934) responded to popular demand for her out-of-print *Verses of a VAD* (1918). She alleged no pretension to 'literary distinction' but claims some historical value in the poetry's record of war. It mainly resonates with collective grief although 'Lament for the Demobilised' registers postwar ironic detachment. The poem 'Married Love', dated 1926, articulates the new demands for equal partnership which are less explicit in other poems of that decade: 'Meek wifehood is no part of my profession,/I am your friend, but never your possession.'[53]

The political engagement of Warner, Ackland (1906–69), Mitchison (1897–1999), Holtby and Cunard challenged lingering assumptions that women's concerns are essentially personal not public. These poets were active in communist, socialist and feminist movements and attempted to write poetry of commitment which avoided propaganda. Tending to adopt the narrative and other verse forms associated with the period's realism, they also prove the inadequacy of aligning ideological and stylistic radicalism. Smith was not a political activist but her textual subversions went further than any other 1930s poet and were an aspect of her temperamental egalitarianism which was sympathetic to socialism and feminism. After 1939, when warwork dissolved lingering distinctions between women's and men's domains, women poets developed more confidence with a public voice.

In the 1940s the language of democracy, which had been coined more and more in the 1930s, developed widespread currency during the Second World War (1939–45) and was accompanied by significant social phenomena, notably a fifty per cent increase in trades unions' membership between 1938 and 1948. From December 1941 all women were conscripted to 'men's' jobs, many of which were available after the war, as Alice Coats records in 'The "Monstrous Regiment"':

> The newsboy and the boy who drives the plough:
> Postman and milkman – all are ladies now.
> Doctors and engineers – yes, even these –
> Poets and politicians, all are shes.[54]

As here, women's notion of sex equality still tended to be in terms of opportunity for work rather than segregated initiatives such as funding for childcare or even fair pay. Their egalitarian spirit was also driven by and directed at social responsibility such as classlessness and addressing poverty.

From 1940 E. J. Scovell (1907–99) and Frances Bellerby (1889–1975) emerged. Minor poets include Eva Dobell and Dorothy Ratcliffe (1894–1967), primarily a writer of plays. The Second World War nourished women writers with a gender-inclusive subject matter which validated their authority as cultural commentators. The allusions to legitimate and illicit liaisons in the Second World War poems indicate women's progress towards economic and sexual autonomy. The war exaggerated the return to realism associated with the 1940s when literature, not helped by a paper shortage, had to compete with the glut of cinemagoing. Ada Jackson published some of the most candid war verse and her prize-winning *Behold The Jew* (1943) brought her renewed attention. (A BBC broadcast of her poetry in 1933 had provoked an approach by Methuen.) The same programme also fanned some fame in the United States when the *New York Herald Tribune* bought rights to several of her poems.[55] Poetry about the Second World War was produced by many others, often principally prose writers such as Edith Nesbitt. Sheila Wingfield is a relatively unknown writer due for recognition; she produced seven books of poetry and her work was individually printed in prestigious papers from *The Dubliner* to *London Mercury, Time and Tide* and the *New Statesman*. Lynette Roberts is similarly experimental and overlooked. The poems of Olive Fraser (1909–77) remained uncollected until the 1980s. The work of influential Americans, Moore, Wylie, Riding and Millay, was reviewed in the British literary papers.

SUMMARY

The momentous changes to women's social freedom between 1900 and 1945 allowed them to become more involved with the production and criticism of poetry. Oppositionally, they encountered resistance to their legal and personal emancipation in the persistent feminising of their creativity by the conservative literary establishment. The potency of the abstracted womanly ideal is reinforced by the vehemence with which literary women distanced themselves from 'woman's poetry'. In an interesting coda to the article 'Women-Poets' (1912) the editor addresses a reader's enquiry about whether male love poems betray their delight '"in the act of praise rather than in the creature to whom their praise is offered. She is a kind of model, and ideal, an idol, if you will."' The editor agrees that:

Scarcely any poets have addressed verses of real fervour or beauty to their wives. This is perhaps as it should be, for both love and poetry can survive only in perfect freedom, and it is apparent that as we may expect greater poetry from a man while still unfettered by the bonds of domestic vexation, so with the growth of economic freedom, we may expect an even clearer and more gentle expression by woman of the inner mystery of her being, and delights and fears of love and motherhood.[56]

If the source and product of man's writing are fictional ideals, how can the woman take her inspiration from a tradition which ignores or mythologises her?

These poets' unconventional personalities and domestic arrangements further demonstrate that the ideals of femininity – marriage, motherhood and passive dependence – in the rhetoric of criticism and in the popular magazines were alien to them. Upper-class writers such as Cunard and Sitwell were distanced from the social snobbery and confining traditionalism of their families, particularly because, as women, they could not hold power or inherit property. Cooper and Bradley ('Field'), Sackville-West, Wellesley, Mew, Warner and Ackland can be identified within the lesbian continuum. Absconding from a marriage meant flouting the 'cult of femininity' which was especially propagated during and after each world war. Wellesley left her husband, Loy divorced her first husband and her second one died, Tree went through two unsuccessful marriages. Cornford and Wickham remained in the traditional nuclear family but Cornford suffered from severe depressions while Wickham separated from her husband for a time and eventually committed suicide, alleging that she felt a failure as a mother. Daryush was nearing forty when she married and did not have children. Coleridge, Farjeon, Mew, Sinclair, Sitwell, Cunard, Holtby, Smith and Pitter were single.

As they would have wished, women can be positioned within established literary categories but in the context of this history, the priority is to read their poetry for its negotiations with stereotyped femininity. In Chapter 1 we look at androgyny, whereby women try to combine received notions of male authorship with being female but find it an ideal hard to pin down. Meynell is the major figure, followed by the next generation of so-called Georgians, Cornford and Sackville-West. Daryush is hard to classify but important for her metrical experiments and achievements. Chapter 2 emphasises the challenge facing the woman who assumes a public voice for war and class politics. Not assuming an authority denied them socially, they frequently use dialogue to comment on public matters. Creative energy is generated when women experientially or imaginatively enter men's areas of experience. The best writing tends to depict the impact of institutional injustices on the individual or declare a gendered hand in women-centred poems. The egalitarianism manifested in socialist impulses often corresponds to their concerns about gender equalities. In Chapter 3 the avant-garde experimentalists are celebrated for their advances in confidence and contributions to poetic theories and practice. It has to be acknowledged that the more technically radical tended to come from the United States, but British-born Sitwell and Loy are significant innovators. By fracturing or displacing familiar syntax, forms, symbols and metres, they appear to evade authorial associations altogether. However, *The Sleeping Beauty* and *Anglo-Mongrels and the Rose* are reworkings of their respective personal histories. Their sometimes ostentatious intellectuality was fuelled by opposition to traditional British elitism which for them was tied up with becoming 'feminine'. H. D.'s Imagist clarity and Riding's rejection of conventional literary accessories refreshingly transcend gender imperatives while often scrutinising the processes of female self-realisation. In Chapter 4 dramatic monologues and dialogues about women's experiences and perspectives have the greater freedom from the negative mythologies of femininity. Through fictionalised personae women challenged gender stereotypes or explored the internal conflicts surrounding female autonomy. They can be read as context-specific but also access and create a shared female interiority which transcends the limitations of their social situations.

CHAPTER I

Lyrical androgyny

'Woman, so far as we can tell, from after Sappho to within our present epoch, has failed to represent herself through the belief that, in order to do so, she must become as Man' declared the editor of a *Poetry Review* on 'Women-Poets' in 1912. He hit upon women's central dilemma about adopting a male disguise for the sake of their credibility when literary men like this editor accentuated sex differences:

There is no eluding the fact that she is dependent, he independent. Her perpetual complaint of not being understood arises from the necessity to remain mysterious; when she chooses to flaunt herself before us in open and unrestrained language or action she only succeeds in appearing indecent. Briefly, Man hitherto has represented Woman in Art better than Woman has succeeded in representing herself.[1]

This chapter investigates the self-restraint which the becoming 'as Man' entails. Women's impersonations of male lyrics appear to liberate them from the self-denying aesthetic of the nineteenth-century 'poetess' but to limit their stylistic freedom. The most successful negotiations between the influence of the male tradition and the distinctly female perspective tend to be the implicitly or explicitly woman-centred poems. Thus the argument is the observation that the best do write as 'Woman', but in a manner which wrestles with the gender oppositions evoked in the *Poetry Review* article. The ideal of the androgynous imagination, as articulated in Virginia Woolf's *A Room of One's Own* (1929), was appealing to intellectual women: 'It is fatal for anyone who writes to think of their sex. Some collaboration has to take place in the mind between the woman and the man before the art of creation can be accomplished . . . Perhaps a mind that is purely masculine cannot create, any more than a mind that is purely feminine, I thought. But it would be well to test what one means by man-womanly.'[2] Like the poets, Woolf slides between synthesising and segregating the sexes.

29

Alice Meynell, 'Michael Field' (Katherine Bradley and Edith Cooper), Mary Coleridge, Eva Gore-Booth and Katherine Tynan, who started publishing in the nineteenth century, are sometimes classified as 'Victorian' but were respected literary women publishing into the twentieth century. Their conventional formalism positions them in their Edwardian or Georgian contexts and also places them in a line of women's poetry which evades gendered authorship. The next generation indicate the same avoidance of female distinctiveness but they can be distinguished from the former group by their reliance on psychological insights and a more contemporary diction.[3] Frances Cornford and Vita Sackville-West were the best known and Sackville-West was, like Meynell, potentially the first woman Poet Laureate. Other 'man-womanly' poets Elizabeth Daryush, Ruth Pitter, Dorothy Wellesley and Sylvia Lynd were popular between the wars. While acknowledging these poets' achievements and awards, we have to recognise that approval and prize-winning were marks of literary conformity. Woolf was sharply disparaging about Sackville-West's Hawthornden Prize (1927): 'the persistent voice [of male pedagogy] admonish[es] them [women] if they would be good and win, as I suppose, some shiny prize, to keep within certain limits which the gentleman in question thinks suitable'.[4] The result is a technical restraint which Woolf called the 'something muted' in Sackville-West's poetry. As Woolf suggests, the intrusive influence of male associations and literary fathers can be seen to stunt women's creativity. Theresa Whistler said of Mary Coleridge, who published anonymously or under a pseudonym, 'No-one so feminine can ever have longed more to be a man.'[5] Coleridge was absorbed by the work of Robert Browning and received technical instruction from Robert Bridges, yet her paradigmatic Victorian woman's poem 'The Other Side of the Mirror' (1882) evokes inexpressible female constraint which is absent from this later work. As for Bradley and Cooper, the male pseudonym 'Michael Field' is an obvious masking of their gender and the joint identity of their aunt-niece partnership. Their duality contradicts the unitary lyric 'I' of the masculine poetic tradition and upsets the assumption that traditional monographic authorship is sacrosanct. As Bradley explained to Browning in 1884:

The revelation of [the dual authorship] would indeed be utter ruin to us; but the report of lady authorship will dwarf and enfeeble our work at every turn. Like the poet Gray we shall never 'speak out'. And we have many things to say that the world will not tolerate from a woman's lips. We must be free as dramatists to work out in the open air of nature – exposed to her vicissitudes, witnessing her terrors: we cannot be stifled in drawing-room conventionalities.[6]

To assume masculine authority, they plundered their classical scholarship and reworked it to their own agendas which included female erotic lyricism.

In Freudian terms, these women turned away from their literary mothers and envied the male pen. In defending their stylistic conformity, we can argue that if these poets seem stale in retrospect, they used conventional forms in order to identify themselves with the male tradition which they sought to enter. In 'The English Metres', Meynell paid tribute to the tradition of British poetry which was stabilised by metrical conformity:

> The rooted liberty of flowers in breeze
>> Is theirs, by national luck impulsive, terse,
> Tethered, uncaptured, rules obeyed 'at ease',
>> Time-strengthened laws of verse.[7]

The militaristic language enforced the association between masculinity, Britishness and literary tradition. The three-column review of *Georgian Poetry 1916–17* demonstrates how the association between regular form and national stability became embedded during the First World War: 'If these young poets write in metre and rhyme and shape, it is because they want to, because expression urges them to form. And it is mighty comforting – in these days when the spirit is hungry for any scrap of permanence and continuity – to see the old friendly boots shaping themselves thus kindly to the proud young feet.'[8] While noting the masculine insinuation of 'boots', the point is that women cannot be made scapegoats for preferring 'metre, rhyme and shape'.

Although most poets in the early twentieth century were formally conventional, women tend to be pejoratively constructed as conservative in the hegemonic terms of a critical heritage which reveres stylistic modernism. *The Oxford Companion to Twentieth-Century Poetry*'s entry on Sackville-West points out that her reputation rests on *The Land*, which was 'deliberately anti-modernist and provincial, using regular iambic lines and archaic diction'.[9] Cornford was posthumously classified as 'Georgian' in a commemorative *Poetry Review* which further polarised her from modernism by stating that she 'declined to follow the Eliot-Pound fashion in her poetry'.[10] Daryush is said to have 'established herself as a traditionalist poet writing in conventional prosody but (like her father) willing to experiment in non-traditional forms'. Significantly, Donald Davie pointed out that Daryush's work on syllabic metres became more independent after her father died.[11] It was a no-win situation, when Woolf, although never a poet herself, coined the term 'Meynell claustrophobia' meaning 'no word not cut on Milton's tomb stone . . . and all that hard-boiled aridity'.

In her introduction to Meynell's *Poetry and Prose* (1947), Sackville-West was self-revealing about the burden of gendered affiliation: 'Most logically she abhorred such designations as *poetess, authoress* . . . in literature and the other arts she held that all creative artists should be regarded as mentally androgynous. It is difficult to find oneself more vehemently in agreement.'[12] Her long analysis indicates the extent and tortuousness of 'the woman question':

> Yet, with expected common sense, very much in line with the views later expressed by Virginia Woolf in *A Room of One's Own*, Mrs Meynell held that women had a particular contribution to make. She could also be sarcastic on the subject of those men who were themselves sarcastic on the subject of women; and when Mrs Meynell chose to be sarcastic she could carry it off as trenchantly as any Victorian husband . . . With all her balance, and the absence of fanaticism one would expect from so poised and controlled a character, she could put her finger very neatly on some of the fallacies involved in the argument; especially does she note, in her uninsistent way, one point too often overlooked – 'the habit by which some men reproach a silly woman through her sex, whereas a silly man is not reproached through his'.
>
> It seems inevitable, after these allusions to Mrs Meynell's attitude towards what is tiresomely called the woman question, to consider her own poems in the light of her femininity. Could a reader tell whether the writer was man or woman? I should not presume to decide. Nature produces virile (not necessarily mannish) women, and feminine (not necessarily effeminate) men; and generalisations take small account of the finer degrees on the sex thermometer where the mercury ascends or descends as in Hot and Cold, Maximum and Minimum, sometimes levelly balanced, sometimes disparate. On the whole, I should incline to attribute Mrs Meynell's poems to a woman; but in any case, to a highly conscious artist.
>
> This is the interesting point about her poems; she knew so exactly what she was about. From the technical point of view, every poet has much to learn from her.[13]

In addition to its insights into both Sackville-West and Meynell, this is a rare example of a woman poet connecting positively with a predecessor, albeit on the point of androgynous authorship.

ALICE MEYNELL

Frequently constructed as archetypally feminine – 'Mrs Meynell reveals herself a woman poet throughout her two small books of verse. It is subjective, not objective verse; its interest lies in what seems to be a sincere restrained, delicate and unvaried utterance of personal feeling and beyond this she rarely strays'[14] – Meynell's literary references, critical essays and male acquaintances assert connections with male writers. Her famed admirers Coventry Patmore, Francis Thompson and George Meredith constructively criticised her poems, as did her husband, the journalist Wilfred Meynell. She altered 'The Modern Mother' following Meredith's criticism and ironically obeyed her husband's guidance on a poem called 'Free Will'.[15] Also, her father's forceful Victorian personality endowed her with patriarchal principles. Angela Leighton astutely comments:

If one of the faults of Meynell's poetry is precisely its fastidiousness, certainly one of its strengths is its resonant resource of silence. The reserve of character which she shared with her father is turned, in the poems, into a language loaded with the 'significant negatives' of the unsaid. As she summarises in her essay: 'his personality made laws for me' (*Poetry and Prose* p. 227). Those laws, of metricality, impersonality, exactness, but also of a certain meagre and precious dispassionateness, became a lifelong poetic creed.[16]

As in 'The English Metres', in 'The Laws of Verse' Meynell professed to find freedom in the restraints which conventional rhyme and metre provided for her 'wildness'. The image of a man's embrace is ambiguously suffocating and energising:

> Dear laws, come to my breast!
> Take all my frame, and make your close arms meet
> Around me; and so ruled, so warmed, so pressed,
> I breathe, aware; I feel my wild heart beat.
>
> Dear laws, be wings to me!
> The feather merely floats. O be it heard
> Through weight of life – the skylark's gravity –
> That I am not a feather, but a bird.[17]

A bird is her favoured symbol of poetic inspiration and figures a yearning for creative liberty; presumably the difference between the feather and bird is autonomy and power. Jane Badeni also considers that the dichotomy between self-restraint and self-expression in 'The Laws of Verse' explains the blanks in Meynell's personal identity. In her notebook Meynell stated that 'All true poets love the bonds of prosody and, in lyrics, of rhythm; because all true poets have something of the wild at heart that looks for bonds. But those who have nothing to control, nothing to hold, are they who call for liberty. No quantity, no stress, no rhyme, no numbers.'[18] Other records allude to an undisclosed core similar to Christina Rossetti's elusive 'secret'. For Sackville-West, 'It is perhaps significant that the idea of "wildness" and the corrective symbol of the shepherd or shepherdess should occur so often in Meynell's prose and poetry. It is as though she desired the one, and then, alarmed, sought refuge in the other. Who knows what hidden turbulence may have torn her.'[19] The 'hidden turbulence' indicates the undertow in Sackville-West's poetry, too.

The locus of the spirit which imbues much of Meynell's writing tends to ungendered pronouns and avoids the binary sex restrictions of women's lived experience. In 'A General Communion' the vision is of men and women levelled under divine authority: 'I saw the throng, so deeply separate,/Fed at one only board –.'[20] Here, dreamstate implicitly rejects the status quo of material conditions while 'In Sleep' produces a devotional vista of Christ inhabiting those who champion the oppressed. Although help for the poor is a shared human concern, taking the part of the downtrodden is a common projection of women's standpoint at the margins.[21] In these poems, the dramatic dialogue avoids personal or gender imperatives but validates a woman's public commentary on social evils.

The self-concealment in Meynell's poetry seems at odds with the free articulation of her opinions in essays and criticism. An active member of the Women Writers Suffrage League and a respected voice for women's emancipation, she walked in processions of the militant suffragette movement and became president of the Society of Women Journalists from 1897. Even Sackville-West asserted that 'this mother, this journalist, this hostess, this poet, held strong views about the position of women in a world controlled by men'.[22] As a mother of eight children, trying to have a successful professional literary career, Meynell neither belittles nor idealises mothering. Her essay 'Mary, the mother of Jesus' (1912) quietly challenges the still - life image of the Madonna. The popular 'Maternity' on a still-born child is one of her most successful:

> Ten years ago was born in pain
> A child, not now forlorn.
> But oh, ten years ago, in vain,
> A mother, a mother was born.[23]

In this second and concluding stanza, the conversational declaration avoids an omniscient authorial lyric voice. In the famous 'A Father of Women', she addresses the postwar reality of superfluous women to argue for their new status: 'Approve, accept, know them daughters of men,/Now that your sons are dust.'[24] Like these, 'The Modern Mother' could be certified as 'woman-manly' in that it prioritises female experience:

Oh, what a kiss
With filial passion overcharged is this!
To this misgiving breast
This child runs, as a child ne'er ran to rest
Upon the light heart and the unoppressed.

Unhoped, unsought!
A little tenderness, this mother thought
The utmost of her meed.
She looked for gratitude; content indeed
With this much that her nine years' love had bought.

Nay, even with less.
This mother, giver of life, death, peace, distress,
Desired ah! not so much
Thanks as forgiveness; and the passing touch
Expected, and the slight, the brief caress.[25]

In these three (out of four) stanzas, we find regular rhyme, literary archaisms – 'ne'er', 'meed', 'Nay' –, elliptical markers of the unsaid or unsayable – 'Oh', 'ah!' – and intrusive exclamation marks. As Leighton points out in her commentary on 'The Modern Mother', Meynell brings a complex psychology to the subject which in 1900 was rare in 'serious literature':

Meynell, here, expresses something about motherhood which seems entirely new: its guilt. Motherhood gives, not only life and peace and love but, logically, their opposites as well. The mother is a giver of 'distress' and 'death', and in return for those terrible gifts the best she can expect from her child is 'forgiveness'. The shock of that word after a century of uplifting mother-morality is profound. Instead of bearing the ultimate protector and guardian, the source and sign of virtue itself, the mother kills, and in a reversal of values which strikes at the very sanctuary of the Victorian home, deals mortality to her own child ... The screen of verbal simplicity in these poems cunningly disguised notions which are far from acceptable commonplaces of women's poetry.[26]

Albeit cramped by overconformity, Meynell did a good job of gaining respect in the British literary establishment. She was elected to the committee of the Royal Society of Literature in 1914 and gave readings and lectures on English literature in the United States. The high public profile and strong influence of the males close to her may explain the limitation to her output and creative development. Meynell believed vehemently in artistic inclusiveness but was at her best when writing 'woman-manly' poetry rather than disguising herself as a man through imitative formalism, impersonal pronouns and male literary references.

FRANCES CORNFORD

Cornford's private writings indicate an acute problem with female authorship which is not immediately obvious in her poems. It is clear from her
literary papers and correspondence that, like Sackville-West and Meynell,
she was attracted by Woolf's solution to gendered writing:

People will think that poetry is just the words you write, but really it's a state of
mind. And I believe that when writers enter into that state of mind they are neither
male nor female, they are androgynous, though fortunately the voice in which they
describe the regions from which they return will be either a man's or a woman's.[27]

Here, Cornford echoes Woolf's slippages between sexlessness and androgyny. She wrote to Woolf that she was conscious of writing back 'through
one's fathers'[28] and looking back in the 1950s recorded her lack of sympathy
with anthologies of women's poetry, 'due to the horror in which all right-
thinking people must hold the word "poetess". She, we all feel, is somebody
with far too much fervent, personal emotion per square yard, so to speak.
A woman poetess was "never gay".'[29]

Cornford published eight poetry books (plus two of translated poetry) and
was well-known to both intellectual and 'middlebrow' readers.[30] She aimed
to break from Edwardian 'faded poeticisms and lolloping turgid metres',
adding, 'I long to write much more in the stresses of my natural speaking
voice though I think I only occasionally succeed at doing this'.[31] This frustrated yearning for a freely colloquial idiom chimes with Meynell's dynamic
between self-containment and creative freedom. In her words, Cornford
studiously avoided the 'embarrassingly personal' and Sylvia Townsend
Warner used her as an example of women writers who were adept at 'vanish-
ing' – 'the writing is no longer propelled by the author's anxious hand, the
reader is no longer conscious of the author's chaperoning presence'.[32] However, superficially agreeable poems resonate with a struggling self-realisation
when read in the context of Cornford's life. They are thus 'woman-manly'
rather than ungendered. 'A Glimpse' suggests alienation from the male-
dominated university territory where, as Woolf recorded in *A Room of One's
Own*, women were trespassers: 'This was the turf; there was the path. Only the
Fellows and Scholars are allowed here; the gravel is the place for me.'[33] 'The
Scholar', written after her husband's death, similarly depicts his self-contained
remoteness as it impinges on the poet-wife's consciousness:

> You often went to breathe a timeless air
> And walk with those you loved, perhaps the most
> You spoke to Plato. You were native there.[34]

Cornford's preferred rhyming is usually the cohering pattern and, as here, loosened up by enjambment and uneven line lengths it can be convincingly colloquial. The poem parallels the oppositional public and private voices of her personal papers; the correspondence constructs a cheerful compliance with the competing demands of family life and forays into the world of publishing, but her journal entries illuminate the 'not-waving-but-drowning' undercurrent.[35] Her depressions, her sense of failure as a mother and her frustrations as a woman writer point to a level of unverbalised experience in poems which have often been mistaken as simplistic or 'genteel', such as 'Ode on the Whole Duty of Parents', which was one of the most frequently anthologised.[36] Here again, the stylistic regularity is through rhyme while the line variability and fluidity achieve a conversational idiom, albeit a rather highly cultured one. In the epigrammatic 'She Warns Him', a series of metaphors signify the emotional deadness recorded in her diaries: 'a lamp that is out', 'a star that is dead', a 'shallow stream' and an empty book.[37]

'The Sick Queen' is among Cornford's best. Exploring the ideal of maternal self-negation, it can be read as the most autobiographical. Through extended metaphor it potently dramatises the poet's confinement during the 'rest cure' prescribed for her severe depressions:

> I hear my children come. They trample with their feet,
> Fetched from their play to kiss my thin-boned hands lying on the sheet,
> Fresh as young colts with every field before them,
> With gazing apple-faces. Can it be this body bore them?
> (This poor body like an outworn glove,
> That yet subdues a spirit which no more knows that it can love.)
> All day is theirs. I belong to night,
> The brown surrounding caverns made of dream. The long failing fight,
> On and on with pain. Theirs is sweet sleep
> And morning breakfast with bright yellow butter. They can laugh and weep
> Over a tiny thing – a toy, a crumb, a letter.
> Tomorrow they will come again and say: '*Now* are you better?'
> 'Better, my lords, today', the Chamberlain replies;
> And I shall be too tired and too afraid to cry out that he lies.[38]

Emotional and intellectual drowning are encoded in the parenthesis and extended symbolism but contained by the rhyming couplets. The effort to appear well for the sake of her family is projected through the ragged line lengths. The distortion of the fairytale persona accords with Woolf's injunction to kill the mythical domestic angel. In a letter to Cornford in 1929, Woolf said that her poems had struck a personal chord.[39] The concealed weariness of the sick queen was a condition familiar to both writers and may largely account for their affinity.

We see that, like Meynell, Cornford achieves her desired natural diction in the more female-centred poems. 'Constant' alludes to the altruism and silent grief of women suffering from 'the pain unknown' of loss. 'Mother and Child Asleep' reflects on the requirement for women to give all to their families and then to let them go. 'A Peasant Woman', included in *Twentieth-Century Poetry* (1929), edited by Monro,[40] objectifies the isolation and waiting which such women endure at every stage of their lives.[41] As in several poems, the urge for freedom is in tension with duty or the conservative impulse to keep things as they are. Cornford's 'woman-manly' poems indicate women's quest for a poetic language to express female perspectives and experience without appearing feminine.

VITA SACKVILLE-WEST

The influence of, or like-mindedness with, Woolf is also evident in Sackville-West's unpublished autobiography where she advanced her theory of the dual personality 'in which the feminine and masculine elements alternately predominate'.[42] The notion of androgyny provided Sackville-West with a means of containing her 'duality', her term for her bisexuality. It is possible to detect greater psychological realism, freer versification and less forced rhyme schemes after her connection with Woolf and Bloomsbury in 1922, although *The Land* was already in draft and little influenced by Woolf's advice to free up her technique: 'the danger for you with your sense of tradition and all those words'.[43] The Woolfs encouraged Sackville-West in what she wanted to be most of all, a 'good poet', by publishing her work. In April 1926 she wrote, 'all I can say is, that rhythm and I are out of gear', and in December 1928 she considered 'going into mourning for my dead muse'.[44] She wanted her poetry to be well received – 'I mind about that poem [*The Land*], never having minded about any other book.'[45] She was, however, disillusioned with *The Land* for being 'damned bad. Not a spark in it anywhere. Respectable but stodgy.'[46] In later letters she was similarly self-deprecating about her *Collected Poems*, although it is likely that she was seeking reassurance – 'all that tripe ... I can't rid myself of the idea that it is all a little pretentious' ... '[*Collected Poems*] is the only book of mine I shall ever have minded about – (i.e. I don't give a damn for my novels, but I do give 1/2 a damn for my poems, which is not saying much).'[47] Sackville-West's adherence to rhyme, metrical rigidity and formal diction corresponded to the public persona of a traditional home and country lover which she constructed through her correspondence with Nicolson, her gardening columns and talks. Behind these impersonations of respectability lurked the nonconformist adventurer who is glimpsed in the ambiguities and coded passions of her poetry.

Adcock disparages Sackville-West's 'Miltonic or Virgilian imitations' but does not recognise that her recourse to these writers was a means of both entering into the British literary tradition and of exploring the ambiguity of her sexual orientation.[48] In its easy metre and country settings, *The Land* was ultimately 'agreeable' poetry but, as she recorded in her autobiography, 'secrecy was my passion', and her affair with Violet Trefusis was 'that little undercurrent'.[49] Sackville-West carefully researched and documented the skills, processes and landscapes which were being modified by mechanisation. She is alleged to have denied knowledge of Virgil's *Georgics* but Nicolson noted that she conceived a kind of 'English Georgics' in 1921 when she first started on *The Land*.[50] *King's Daughter* (1929), number eleven of the Woolfs' *Hogarth Living Poets*, is a pastiche of sixteenth-century courtly love sequences. The persona of the male courtier allowed Sackville-West to dramatise her fantasies with her female lovers: 'Put on your smock, Princess; let satins lie./ Put all your plumes and all your velvets by.'[51] Although biography illuminates the personal situation of the poems, she frequently alluded to masks; the switches between male and female speakers allowed her to try out different identities. Given that Sackville-West depicts fictional personae in her poems, the solitary writer self-dramatised in *Solitude*, published in 1938 but begun in 1927, can be taken as one of her fantasy images. The book-length poem gives the impression of a 'worldly-sick' recluse exploring the liberties of her youth.[52] Although it appeared to be autobiographical, Hilda Matheson wrote to say that she 'found no clue, in this self-communing poem, to the things in you which I have failed to understand in the last few years. I am puzzled by your attitude to love – cheap and easy.'[53] Matheson echoed Woolf's earlier reference to the 'something muted' which limited Sackville-West's writing. In 1926 she acknowledged it in a letter to her husband:

There *is* something muted ... Something that doesn't vibrate, something that doesn't come alive ... It makes everything I do (i.e. write) a little unreal; gives the effect of having been done from the outside. It is the thing which spoils me as a writer; destroys me as poet. But how did V. discover it? I have never owned it to anybody, scarcely even to myself. It is what spoils my human relationships too, but I mind less.[54]

Again, we see how the attempt to be gender-neutral liberated her from the self-negating aesthetic of the conventional poetess but muffled her creativity.

ELIZABETH DARYUSH

Another significant formalist who concealed female authorship, Daryush became more assured in the 1930s after the death of her father, the Poet Laureate Robert Bridges. As Yvor Winters concludes, 'Her talent then, although it was obviously formed by her father's influence, appears only to have borne fruit after his death, and to have developed very rapidly within a very short period, after a long period of stagnation.'[55] Interestingly, she did not marry until 1926 and so was based at home until the age of thirty-nine. She experimented with syllabic sonnets where she used the 'stress laws as partly worked out by my father'. Daryush was actually more adventurous than Bridges in trying to achieve a rhythm of natural speech within technical straitjackets. She used many five- and sometimes four-syllabled lines as well as blank verse. It is now commonplace to alternate between stressed and syllabic metres but it can be argued that Daryush paved the way for the metrical ranges of W. H. Auden and other poets who popularised syllabic metres after 1939. There are three *Selected Poems* (1935, 1948, 1972) and the last contains what she most wished to preserve from the books of *Verses I–VI*. It also includes her explanation of syllabic metre, given originally in the Preface to *Verses: Fourth Book* (1934):

By [syllabic metres] I mean metres governed only by the number of syllables to the line, and in which the number and position of the stresses may be varied at will and are so printed as a reminder to the reader to follow strictly the natural speech-rhythm, and not to look for stresses where none are intended ... I have long thought that on some such system as this for a base, it should be possible to build up subtler and more freely-followed accentual patterns than can be obtained either by stress-verse proper, or by the traditional so-called syllabic metres.[56]

Interestingly, a review of this collection noted a marked development: 'Readers of Mrs Daryush's previous books know that she often feels cramped by traditional metres. Her new book contains an experimental element, marked as such by having the lines printed without capitals.'[57]

'Still Life' is considered by Donald Davie to be her greatest success with the ten-syllabled line:

> She comes over the lawn, the young heiress,
> from her early walk in her garden-wood
> feeling that life's a table set to bless
> her delicate desires with all that's good.[58]

The poise of the lines and visual stasis both invoke and undermine the ideal; the metaphor of a love letter for the 'unopened future' hangs tantalisingly in the air, suggesting both closure and promise. Whether free choice is a genuine possibility for all within a class-ridden convention-bound society is the dilemma of 'You who are Blest'. Daryush's sensitivity to class differences is also suggested in 'Children of Wealth' where the metrical dexterity involving enjambment constructs a sense of urgency.[59] As here, the voice in the poems often uses the vocative but both the speaker and addressee are usually ungendered, unnamed and elusive: 'If your love prove unworthy, why then,/by this much you're the freer.' This poem dares to name the concept of a 'mistaken marriage' and by doing so further challenges assumptions about duty.[60] The disciplined form of the sonnet supports the rhetoric of conformity versus individual freedom.

Daryush seems most imaginative with woman-centred subjects but the most direct poems about female nature and sex relations are rarely printed. One of her most experimental and successfully colloquial is a dramatic monologue by Persephone:

> the sometime fair Hope-maiden who roamed free
> Among the flowers, till Hell's arch-lord, Default
> Swept me down, down to the dark antevault.[61]

Again, we have the motif of freedom denied. 'Default'/'antevault' demonstrates how syllabic verse allows the rhyming of accented with unaccented syllables. 'Off Duty' (1938), not included in *Selected* or *Collected Poems*, scrutinises the magnetic force of self-giving service which both attracts and repels a nurse:

> She goes slowly to the door –
> Feels at each freeing step a check, a wrench … What chain
> Still binds her, draws her spirit back, back, to the place of strain?[62]

Among the few poems which hint at women's rights, 'The woman I'd revere' surprisingly colludes with binary polarities of sex difference. Similarly, 'Woman, dweller in the heart' reinforces the traditional oppositions between private female and public masculine spheres, although the line 'Woman, pent within the home' indicates some resistance to an ideal of domestic contentment, as does the wish for a meeting-up between men and women.[63] The nearest to an explicit feminist impulse comes in 'Well, what of it? What if you are beautiful?'[64] In the sonnet 'When your work's done, banish it behind you', Daryush advised women to become themselves after sacrificing all to their children.[65]

Other formalists who are more 'woman-manly' than they first appear include Ruth Pitter, whose poetry is described as 'usually but not always written in conventional prosody' in *The Oxford Companion to Twentieth-Century Poetry*. In *Ruth Pitter: Homage to a Poet*, her verse forms are commended as 'those of the mainstream English poetic tradition' and consequently, 'It would be possible to argue that Ruth Pitter is a man's poet.'[66] The link between the tradition and male writing identified here gave these poets validity as intellectual writers but thwarted their freedom. The notion of psychological androgyny was a theoretical resolution to the oppositional pulls of a patriarchal professional environment and the distinctly female roles of their personal lives. High regard often involved the cost of a freely female creativity.

If 'androgyny' is used synonymously for sexless authorship, it allows male models of writing and constructions of women to perpetuate. As Elaine Showalter points out, 'androgyny, the sexual ethic of Bloomsbury, and an important concept of the period, provided an escape from the confrontation with the body'.[67] She believes that, 'at some level, Woolf is aware that androgyny is another form of repression':

The androgynous mind is finally, a utopian projection of the ideal artist: calm, stable, unimpeded by consciousness of sex. Woolf meant it to be a luminous and fulfilling idea; but, like their utopian projections, her vision is inhuman. Whatever else one may say of androgyny, it represents an escape from the confrontation with femaleness or maleness. Her ideal artist mystically transcends sex and has none.[68]

Implicitly, Woolf's proverbial room-of-her-own is a metaphor for the imaginative freedom of female-specific creativity. However, Woolf's avoidance of writing poems suggests her awareness of an irresolvable bind: 'Women have had less intellectual freedom than the sons of Athenian slaves. Women, then, have not had a dog's chance of writing poetry.'[69] Her more constructive 'Poets ought to have a mother as well as a father'[70] gestures towards 'woman-manly' writing. As seen in this selection, the more overtly woman-centred poems appear to be the most imaginatively liberated and best achieve the colloquial register for which the writers strained.

CHAPTER 2

A public voice: war, class and women's rights

This chapter addresses women's negotiations with a public voice when they had scanty literary models and limited opportunities to speak out on political matters. Their activities, journalism and personal records demonstrate the extent of their drive for democratic causes, whether the suffragette movement, pacifism or social reforms. In May 1940 Virginia Woolf gave a paper to the Workers' Educational Association in Brighton which looks towards a postwar egalitarian future and its benefit to the writer who aimed for both realism and utopian democracy:

The novel of a classless and towerless world should be a better novel than the old novel. The novels will have more interesting people to describe – ... The poet's gain is less obvious; for he has not been under the dominion of hedges. But he should gain words; when we have pooled all the different dialects, the clipped and chained vocabulary which is all that he uses now should be enriched. Further, there might then be a common belief which he could accept, and thus shift from his shoulders the burden of didacticism, of propaganda. These then are a few reasons, hastily snatched, why we can look forward hopefully to a stronger, a more varied literature and towerless society of the future.[1]

She refers to the social consciousness inflicted on writers in 1914 and the 'tower-dwelling' privileged poets in the 1930s who were challenged to write of a classless ideal which was beyond their experience. The difference for women in this period is that they viewed hierarchies and hedges from ground level. They usually avoided the polemic of their nonfiction in their poetry but sometimes voiced collective experience or resisted injustice with unambiguous didacticism. There are choric texts, verse dramas and other lengthy dramatic poems which are due for resurrection. The implicitly inclusive audience often raids the ready distinction between poetry and verse. More often, their preferred monologues and dialogues confront received wisdoms. The frequent multivocality avoids fixed ideological positions or authorial assumptions, but allows an interrogation of power. Women also drew upon the structural privacy of the lyric but implicitly for the world to hear. Sylvia Townsend Warner is the most accomplished literary political commentator, while Stevie Smith is the most potent on the individual's struggle with institutional oppression.[2] Additionally, some of the most striking poems on public affairs are the strongest of less well-known poets' work.

Conservative critics entrenched the association of women with the personal life; a rhetoric of innate female patriotism, maternity and sentimental love undercut the goals of women's suffrage. The myth that women eschew national or global topics is perpetuated by the excision of their political work from anthologies and other literary records. There are too few critical studies on the overlooked poetry of war.[3] The available biographies of influential reformers are inspiring records. Irish-born Eva Gore-Booth moved in 1897 to Manchester where she supported movements for economic and political reform and for the enfranchisement of women.[4] In 1913 illness forced her to London where she worked 'ceaselessly' in the Women's Peace Crusade. According to Esther Roper, she had 'a passionate sympathy for suffering and injustice and a strange feeling of responsibility for life's inequalities'.[5] Like Gore-Booth, Naomi Mitchison and Winifred Holtby promoted socialist and feminist ideals through journalism and the women's, peace and labour movements. They were both known as antifascist writers involved in *Left Review*. In the 1920s Holtby spent three months in Central Europe and went to South Africa to fight for civil liberty. In the 1930s she supported the Six Point Group which was working with the Equal Rights International. Mitchison joined the Labour Party in 1930 and stood for the Scottish Universities parliamentary seat in 1935. She went to Vienna in 1934 to provide aid to the social democrats. Jill Benton describes the Mitchisons' home in Hammersmith during the 1920s and 1930s as a 'class melting pot', where working-class neighbours mixed with their social circle of politicians and artists. At the onset of the Second World War, she settled in Kintyre and introduced her political ideals into the feudal traditions of the small Scottish community. Margaret Cole has a prolific list of fiction and political writings on democracy and social reform, specialising in marriage, women and children, education and Soviet Russia. She and her husband were pillars of the Fabian Society, which was dedicated to 'equality of opportunity' and the abolition of 'economic power and privileges of individuals and classes'.[6]

Sylvia Townsend Warner and Valentine Ackland became tireless in their activities connected with the British Communist Party, which they joined in 1935. They subscribed to the *Daily Worker*; they belonged to the Left Book Club,[7] the Congress of Writers and the Association of Writers for Intellectual Liberty; they attended the International Peace Congress in

Brussels and the Congress of the International Association in Defence of Culture in Madrid and Valencia. This latter organisation aimed for an international exchange of literature and to fight against war, fascism and 'everything that menaces culture'.[8] In September 1936 they volunteered to help the Spanish Republicans and gave assistance to the Red Cross Unit in Barcelona. Their concern for the exploitation of the rural poor is dramatised in Warner's long satirical narrative poem *Opus 7* (1931) and Ackland's newspaper column *Country Dealings*. During the 1930s, Nancy Cunard became mythologised as a rebel for her 'almost frenetic involvement in social and political affairs',[9] and she became a good friend of Warner from 1942. She championed black identity and power in the face of 'imperialist British aristocracy'[10] in *Black Man and White Ladyship* (1931) and *Negro: an anthology* (1934),[11] and by working for the Associated Negro Press of the United States. During the Spanish Civil War she was a reporter on the republican side and in the Second World War she was 'a convinced believer in French and Spanish spirit and culture'.[12] Her *Poems for France*, 'written by British poets since the war' (1944), consists of vibrant poems by men and women, including Ackland, Warner, Sackville-West, Jackson and Spalding, as well as Cunard's own.

These and other writers consciously negotiated between the revolution of the word of high modernism and the polemic required by their sensitivity to injustices. The competing demands of the aesthetic and democracy were voiced by Stephen Spender:

If it is conceded that this is possible – that the destruction of the values of living, and their supercession by machinery, aims of power, and materialism, might make life meaningless – is the poet justified in stepping out of his poetry, as it were, and taking a hand in altering the world? Is he justified in using poetry as a means of propaganda for traditional values which may, in fact, be revolutionary?

Most contemporary poets seem to have been faced by these questions. Some have replied by abandoning poetry altogether and joining revolutionary movements.[13]

In 1941 Spender was partly responding to Cyril Connolly's influential 'Comment' the year before which stated that 'The moment we live in is archaistic, conservative and irresponsible, for the war is separating culture from life and driving it back on itself, the impetus given by Left Wing politics is for the time exhausted.'[14] The schism between creativity and politics was particularly acute for women, who were not expected to be politically informed nor to be poets. Holtby confessed to experiencing a lifelong conflict between art and social reform,[15] whereas Warner reconciled the tension in her 'discovery that the pen could be used as a sword'.[16]

The arena of social politics is the most challenging for women to speak in as themselves. Eleanor Farjeon chose to comment on contemporary life in the guise of a jester; her 'Tomfool' books, published by the Labour Publishing Co., do not bear her name at all and presumably she did not identify herself in the socialist *Daily Herald* where the poems first appeared. This anonymity provided a freedom of speech and the fool's mask allowed for satirical ventriloquism of social types, from the cricket fan to the drunkard or harassed employee. The poems are based on snippets from newspaper columns and government white papers as well as new fashions. 'A Prayer' parodies both institutional and individual avoidance of human responsibility for social action: 'O God, what shall we do/If Thou Who feedest the sparrows/Feed not the children too.'[17] Although seemingly sexless in its male disguise, the voice has the distinctly female approach to poverty which looks on from ground level.

WAR

The published poets involved in war activity and social reform represent the common impulse of many women for human rights and political democracy; they display little English nationalism and some tackle the oppressions of British imperialism. The biographical notes in Catherine Reilly's *Women's War Poetry and Verse* (1997) record the social and literary involvement of a huge array of writers through both world wars.[18] Poetry by women extends the canons of war poetry which have been dominated by the English trench poets. Retrospective poems transgress strict periodisation and there is a significant scattering of European – including German – and American poets, although oddly not H. D.

During the First World War, it was hard to compete with the universal voice of the soldier poet. Some poetry simply assumes the uniform of prescribed female patriotism or domestic preoccupation. Jessie Pope, who published three volumes during the war and who articulated the official recruiting propaganda, was promoted by the popular press and subsequently taken to be more representative than she was. When she and other women impersonated contemporary male combat poems, as in 'From a Trench' or 'Over the Top', they tended towards clichés and stock responses.[19] The homilies of Katherine Tynan and Teresa Hooley seem uncritically reliant on official discourses. Their hostility to war's damage and loss is offset by abstract patriotism or spiritual solace. Grief poems, as in May Wedderburn Cannan's popular *In War Time* (1916), can be claustrophobic in their personal intensity and the closure of trite generalisations which are glossed with consoling rhythm and rhyme. Nevertheless, some refute the 'tinsel platitudes' offered to the bereaved.[20]

Margaret Sackville, a pacifist, suggests in 'Nostra Culpa' that women were guilty of keeping quiet because of their need for male approval:

> We knew that Force the world has deified,
> How weak it is. We spoke not, so men died.
> Upon a world down-trampled, blood defiled,
> Fearing that men should praise us less, we smiled.[21]

As depicted here, unspoken resistance often lay beneath women's superficial acquiescence in the nationalistic outlook prescribed for them. Although it is a short poem, Sackville's manipulation of the rhyming iambic pentameter indicates the gravity of her revelation. Since the expression of antiwar sentiment was suppressed, much poetry can be read as an instrument for women 'having their say' when they had no other outlet against the war machinery. Taking a 'towerless' perspective, several poets spoke for noncombatants, the deserter and the demobilised. Vibrant poems register their excitement at doing 'things they've never done before' and getting paid for it: 'Earning high wages? – Yus,/Five quid a week./A woman, too, mind you.'[22]

These poems are crucial documents of women's consciousness about the 1914–18 war, although they often lack contextual specificity. For example, S. Gertrude Ford treats the euphemistic rhetoric of newspaper language with the satire of Sassoon. In 'A Fight to a Finish' she parodies the rhyming couplets associated with popular jingoism: '"Fight on!" the Armament-kings besought:/*Nobody asked what the women thought.*'[23] This emphasised, almost parenthetical, sentence conveys the silencing of their opposition. Dramatisation enables her to shoot the invectives not expected of women. Ford was an energetic socialist, feminist and writer. Her concern for economic equality above warfare is expressed in 'The Tenth Armistice Day': '"Flowers for the dead? Bread for the living rather!"'[24] Arguably, war fever had been quickened to distract from the social and economic crises in Britain. Many in Ford's *Poems of War and Peace* (1915) stir up women to counter warring instincts: 'Men make the war; mere women we, /Born to accept and acquiesce./But how long, Lord, shall these things be?'[25] In a similarly satiric tone, Helen Hamilton's aggressively advertised *Napoo!: A Book of War Bêtes Noires* (1918) consists of dramatic monologues like 'The Super-Patriot' which topple heroic ideals and indicate the antiwar appetites of general readers. 'The writer of Patriotic "Ad"' (pp. 56–58) subverts the 'pompous platitudes' of poster campaigns. 'Jingo-Woman' bravely attacks those who collude with recruiting propaganda, and in 'The

Romancing Poet' Hamilton complains, 'I wish you would refrain/From making glad romance/Of this most hideous war' and asks the war poet for 'Fit words ... /Not your usual stock-in-trade,/Of tags and *clichés* –'.[26] As she points out, traditional literary resources ill-fitted women's experiences of war work, leave-taking, loss or alienation from male militarism. In 'The Father', Muriel Stuart stages a domestic situation to interrogate the assumptions of war:

> I said
> 'My son shall be no coward of his line
> Because his mother fears!' You turned your head
> And your eyes grew implacable on mine.
> And like a trodden snake you turned to meet
> The foe with sudden hissing ... then you smiled
> And broke our life in pieces at my feet.
> 'Your child?' you said. '*Your* child?'[27]

She exposes the authority of the male voice which quarrels with the mother over whether their child shall be educated into warfare. The contemporary idiom of rhyming iambic pentameter is characteristic of Stuart's dramatic monologues.

From these samples it is evident that, as with most realist and protest writing, the poetry is formally conventional but its flexed metres and rhyme produce the conversational idioms. We see how women avoid propaganda through dramatisation and dialogue. Some confront modernism's undermining of didacticism or social documentary. Of these, May Sinclair, Charlotte Mew, Nancy Cunard, Edith Sitwell and Iris Tree characteristically experiment with rhymed and unrhymed free verse. Memorable poems operate like snapshots. Sinclair's 'Field Ambulance in Retreat' and Mew's 'The Cenotaph' utilise Imagist clarity. Lynette Roberts's 'The Cenotaph' is also an unexpected perspective in free verse – 'The Man in the Trilby hat has furtively shifted it' – and her polyphonic verse novel *Lettice Delmer* (composition undated) dramatises a family saga during the First World War.[28]

There is little appeal to abstract values, fewer sonnets and greater stylistic variety in the poetry of the Second World War. Again, women are more concerned with the impact and psychology of war than with victory. Since all men and women were involved, there was less scope for rhetorical and imaginative juxtapositions between Home and Front or between recruiting euphemisms and the fates of the dead and wounded. Warner's 'Road 1940' voices the lament of a woman landed with someone else's sick child. She questions the future for which it is saved:

Why did I lift it, she said,
Out of its cradle in the wheel-tracks?
On the dusty road burdens have melted like wax,
Soldiers have thrown down their rifles, misers slipped their packs:
Yes, and the woman who left it there has sped
With a lighter tread.[29]

Typically Warner, it compresses and dramatises the powerlessness and the strength of spirit which such women demonstrate in the context of warmongering and social injustice. In a diary entry in 1929, musing on the publication of *A Room of One's Own*, Warner pondered: 'Sex in literature, *pace* Virginia's new book. The moment you say how women are to write well, you've given away your case, as a feminist. It should be how people are to write well. And personally I mistrust the ambivalence of sex idea. The best male authors are undoubtedly the most male, great writing seems to establish itself in periods of marked sexual distinction, periods of sexual fusion produce only good writing. So why aren't the best female authors to be the most female?'[30] In her lecture 'Women as Writers' (1959), Warner distinguished women's literature by a 'pantry window' outlook which is akin to a 'kind of workaday democracy, an ease and appreciativeness in low company' and 'a willing ear for the native tongue'. Accordingly, the colloquial variations of dialogue and monologue admit the underdog perspective.[31]

Mitchison's dramatic monologue 'The Farm Woman 1942' combines female and economic suffering, characteristically shifting between the local and the global. The subject is covered with bruises which she protests are from her work but which suggest marital violence:

The tractor is ill to start, a great heaving and jerking,
The gear lever jars through palm and bone,
But I saw in a film the Russian women working
On the land they had made their own,
And so and so,
Said the farm woman:
And I bruise easy.[32]

An echoing story set in the same year, 'Milk Boy', is one of Dorothy Wellesley's best in its particularity:

There are no more tears for the body to weep with.
Early this morning at the break of day,
A boy of sixteen went out for the milking
Up on the white farm alone on the hill,
With a single white candle upheld by his hand,
Carrying his pail through the air so still.

> Then came the Nazi, knowing the white farm there,
>
> The hour of milking white heifers of morning.
>
> There lay the red pools, with the milk pools mingling
> O there in the sun – in the red sun arising,
> The white boy, the white candle, the white heifer
> Dying . . .[33]

This single clip of the war's devastation is enhanced by the starkly elegiac voiceover. E. J. Scovell's 'A Wartime Story' tells how a woman burns her dead baby which had been conceived with an airman while her husband was overseas: 'agent of fate/Like a stone dropped in the pool of grosser lives'.[34] It evokes the ever-rippling tragedy of war through a typically unseen personal trauma. Other memorable sideshows of the war's atrocities, notably Hiroshima and the concentration camps, include Karen Gershon's 'A Jew's Calendar'.[35] The colloquial understatement and disconcerting detachment are characteristic of this war's antiheroic poetry. Ada Jackson's collection *World in Labour* (1942) is one of the most original. 'Maimed baby' is a shocking cameo of the effects of 'the Fuehrer' which she confronts in the monologue 'Hitler Youth' where a duped young Nazi disciple has been run over:

> Now all my bones are powder-fine;
> The stones are grouted with my blood;
> I am become the road – the way –
> I thank thee, Fuehrer. It is good.[36]

Of the poetry on the Spanish Civil War, in which British class politics were played out on the international scale, Cunard's 'To Eat Today' is an evocative episode of a family recovering from a bomb striking their home.[37] Cunard is alleged to have instigated the letter 'To the Writers and Poets of England, Scotland, Ireland and Wales', requesting a statement of their position; the replies were published by *Left Review* in 1937 and it sold more than three thousand copies.[38] After helping the Spanish republicans in 1936 and 1939, she continued to campaign for them in the *Manchester Guardian*, *News Chronicle* and *Daily Herald*.[39] Regrettably, her planned volume of poems on Spain was never completed. More available, Warner's poems on the Spanish war are characteristically conversational yet detached. 'Benicasim' depicts the town on the east coast of Spain where the wounded from the Spanish People's Army went to convalesce: 'For along the strand/ in bleached cotton pyjamas, on rope-soled tread,/wander the risen-from the dead'.[40]

So far, we find a female political aesthetic achieved through a micro-cosmic scenario, often from a topographical or psychological sideline. It defies the pervasive myth of women's ignorance of or accord with mascu-line politics. In his Foreword to *Poems by Contemporary Women* (1944), Hugh Lyon makes familiar comments about feminine gentility:

But here is a fresh claimant to favour, a chorus of voices, speaking to him not only of war, but of home, of the dreams of his heart and the ardours of his soul; songs to drown for a moment the urgent tumult into which he is thrust. For the quieter the voice of the poet, the more powerful its spell; and the reader will find quiet voices here – 'soft, gentle and low, an excellent thing in a woman'.[41]

He selects poems which fit this conservative restraining model of the housebound mute, which has to be refuted by the number and quality of their neglected proclamatory poems. These can only be surveyed here but warrant further attention. Margaret Sackville's modernised classical verse dramas demonstrate supreme confidence with poetry as a public medium. 'The Pageant of War' dated 1914 is an astounding antiwar vision. The setting is a dazzlingly white road whose fabric is history's war dead: 'The bones which make it are so light/(Children's bones weigh very little)'. The figure of War is repelling:

> He had to wear a mask, lest seeing
> That obscene countenance too near,
> The heart of every human being
> Should shrink in loathing and slay it there.[42]

Sackville's poetry had good and lengthy reviews in the *TLS*. Mary Borden's prose poetry in *The Forbidden Zone* (1929) is exemplary in its journalistic realism about her time in a hospital unit at the Front nursing French soldiers:

> This is the hymn of mud – the obscene, the filthy, the putrid,
> The vast liquid grave of our armies.
> It has drowned our men.
> Its monstrous distended belly reeks with the undigested dead.[43]

The pluralised pronouns and choric collage conflate the personal with the collective. Muriel Stuart's strikingly dramatic dream narrative 'Christ in Carnival' (1917) appeals to a shared spiritual nature in its compassion for the underclass and in its agitation for social change. Inspired by the hunger marches, the insistent rhythm, longer lines and despair at human barbarity in Sitwell's *Gold Coast Customs* (1929) anticipate the style of her famous 'Still Falls the Rain – The Raids, 1940. Night and Dawn', which registers the widespread negotiation between modernist fragmentation and the expressive when responding to war.

Lynette Roberts's *Gods with Stainless Ears*, dedicated to Sitwell, was explicitly written for filming. Subtitled 'a heroic poem', it maintains classical blank verse throughout the fifty pages. Consisting of five parts, each is prefaced with an 'Argument' to set the scene. Roberts uniquely directs an apocalyptic vision of monstrous war which includes close-ups of personal anguish which culminate in the gunner entering a 'Mental Home for Poets'. Wingfield's *Beat Drum, Beat Heart* (1946, composed by 1944), is a neglected oratorio on war. Pushing home the prejudices against women as public commentators, G. S. Fraser announced: 'Sheila Wingfield is something rather unusual in women poets, an objectivist . . . The emotions get expressed indirectly through her grasp on the outer world.'[44] Ada Jackson's candid opposition to Hitler's regime is strikingly realised in the nineteen-page prize-winning pamphlet poem *Behold the Jew* (1943). She mixes celebration of Jewish identity and major talents with compassion for the race's history of suffering, repeated for each individual in quotidian experiences. Although based on rhyming iambic quatrameter which is varied for changes of mood, the poem has epic stature. H. D.'s *Trilogy* (1944–46) is considered a masterpiece of war writing and of her career in its evocation of personal and collective subconscious drives.

SOCIAL INJUSTICE

In this time we repeatedly find versions of Woolf's vision for 'a world without classes or towers'.[45] For Naomi Mitchison, for example, 'I call it war when people are being physically and mentally crippled, deprived of life either suddenly or gradually.'[46] Apart from two publications, many of Mitchison's poems are uncollected from journals or from her drawers at home. Although not bothered about uniform rhyme or distracting imagery, her changes of rhythmic pace accompany her cunning shifts between easy personal diction or more rhetorical political commentary. *The Alban Goes Out* is a long narrative preserving the Scottish fishing community which was threatened by English colonialism. *The Cleansing of the Knife 1941–7* is a ballad of epic length told by 'A woman of Scotland' who speaks out 'with the voice of Scotland' because the 'stories and poems and songs' of dead writers have not prevented further wrongs. She laments Highland clearances but ends with the redemption of Scottish identity in localities like Mitchison's Carradale. She proposes the superiority of women's impulse for socialist democracy: 'It was, after all, the peasant women rather than the peasant men who so liked the idea of communal farms under the Plan, who should so cheerfully forsake the traditions that women are supposed to like so much.'[47] She was unashamed in her feminist and socialist drives and in her conflict between the two. 'To Some Young Communists from an Older Socialist', printed in *New Verse*, January 1933, registers her interest in building bridges between communism and socialism.[48] The idiom is both intimate and outspoken. Elsewhere, Mitchison produces the incantatory rhythms associated with public ritual or mythology:

> To us the dams and the pylons, the fields plowed with tractors,
> To us anode and cathode, to us dyes and test tubes,
> All delicate adjustments, all new parts,
> The pressing and battering of the half-formed idea,
> To us in silent creation, to us at last
> After centuries freedom. You cannot chain us now,
> You have lost your power, young men. Young men,
>   with freedom we take
> The future also.[49]

Sylvia Townsend Warner's *Opus 7* (1931), a pastiche of eighteenth-century antipastoral narrative, is one of her most ambitious and achieved negotiations between the didactic and aesthetic:

It was towards the end of this decade [1920s] that I bethought me that it was about time to try to do for this date what Crabbe had done for his: write a truthful pastoral in the jog-trot English couplet. And I wrote a narrative poem called 'Opus 7' about a comfortless old woman in a village who turned a random flower patch into a commercial success in order to buy drink to warm her old bones. I wrote it in London, but by the time it was published I was cockney no more.[50]

Although her diction is stilted in places, Warner animates the formal requirements of heroic couplets with the 'native dialects' which she observes women write particularly well. The backdrop of wartime austerity extends the scope. Planted in a rural community, the elderly Rebecca Random attempts to make do by selling flowers to buy gin. An Anzac soldier, who has a drink with her, voices a disillusion similar to that of the woman in 'The Road, 1940':

> When I was a pup
> I felt to come to England I'd give up
> all I could ever have – and here I am,
> her soldier. Now, I wouldn't give a damn

> for England. She's as rotten as a cheese,
> her women bitches, and her men C3's.
> This silly sloppy landscape–what's the use
> of all this beauty and no bloody juice?[51]

More obliquely, Stevie Smith topples class towers by undermining patriarchal stereotypes. 'Lord Barrenstock' is a 'seducer of a hundred little boys' and cheats individuals of their status and property. In 'The Bishops of the Church of England', 'Major Macroo' and 'Lord Mope' the tragicomic caricatures of patriarchal oppression are more vitriolic: 'Such men as these, such selfish cruel men.'[52] Her distaste for oppressive institutions extends to blind patriotism: 'England, you have been here too long,/And the songs you sing are the songs you sung/On a braver day. Now they are wrong.'[53] The lectures at the back of Anna Wickham's *Writings* indicate her involvement in social welfare and class warfare.[54] Her verse epitaph, 'Laura Grey: died June 1914, in Jermyn Street', published in the *Daily Herald*, 16 June 1914, commemorated the suicide of a pregnant woman at the mercy of an unequal legal system, complaining 'where was the man?'[55] In her lecture 'School for Mothers' (probably written 1909–1910), she crusaded for such abused women.[56] 'The Town Dirge', which dramatises the inexorable death of a child born into poverty, operates as a political tract to incite civil protection for 'the weak'.[57] According to Richard Aldington, Wickham's *The Contemplative Quarry* (1915) 'registers the revolt of the human sort of mind from the exasperating pretensions and limitations of English Middle Class life'.[58] S. Gertrude Ford's 'Houseless by Night – May 1911' is prefaced by '(A recent inquiry revealed the fact that, for thirteen rescue homes in one area, not one shelter was provided for the respectable and destitute)'.[59] 'The Pageant of Women – June 17 1910', also from her *Lyric Leaves* (1912), is a rousing cry for sex equality: 'Way, Make way, for the marching troops of justice.' Ford's commitment to democracy is epitomised in the title-poem of *The England of My Dream and Other Poems* (1928):

> There woman, owned man's comrade and his equal,
> May stand erect, freed from her fettering past,
>   By justice, and by liberty its sequel,
> To the fullness of her stature risen at last.   (pp. 11–12).

In Ford's utopia all stand under the flag of peace and equality, which Heaven applauds and poets celebrate. The poem is dedicated to Nina Alice Hutteman Hume, 'a queen of reformers and my dearest friend'. Ford's individual poems were printed in journals ranging from *Christian Commonwealth* and *Missionary Echo* to the *Daily News* and the *Westminster Gazette*. Like her poetry, her *Lessons in Versecraft* (1919 and reprinted) mediates between literary tradition and formulaic popular verse.

WOMEN'S RIGHTS

In various ways women negotiated between the high diction or forms which would give their work literary credibility and the democratic themes which were the personal impulses to the poems. Cora Kaplan rightly argues that 'The emphasis on women's imagination relating to the private realm can be understood as the control of high language which is a crucial part of the power of dominant groups, and the refusal of access to public language is one of the major forms of the oppression of women.'[60] As addressed in the previous chapter, literary women involved in campaigns often distanced themselves from suffragism in particular to maintain their credibility as poets acceptable to a male-dominated establishment. Few poems which imply a public hearing focus solely on female roles and identity but Helen Hamilton's *The Compleat Schoolmarm: A Story of Promise and Fulfilment* (1917) is an extraordinary document of how female education could be emotionally crippling: 'To those women who, striving to make education more human than it at present is, nobly, and despite its drawbacks, remain in the teaching profession, this book is dedicated (without their permissions) in respectful sympathy and admiration.' Like Hamilton's *Napoo!* (1918), it consists of satirical free verse characterisations. Taking a 'heroine' through school, training college and then her career as a teacher condemned to spinsterhood for her noble profession, the potency is the tragic subterranean loneliness and exhaustion which parallels the narrative of events that the public perceive as glorious opportunities – graduation, Old Girls' Day, summer vacations. Take the passage where the girl receives her degree:

> The long-deferred break-down takes place,
> Deferred with difficulty,
> When you reach your boring home,
> And you are ill, my heroine,
> Quite seriously, for some long time.
> Common thing, it is for graduates,
> 'Sweet girl graduates',
> To smash up when they've done their time
> Or shortly after.

> Proof at least, they've made the most
> Of chances educational
> And earned their parents' money's worth!   (p. 17).

It exposes questions about the much-hailed privilege of education for girls, not suggesting that they would be better off in domesticity but that the system which reinforces female segregation is abusive.

The paucity of poetry on suffragism is disappointing. There are a few remarkable choruses written to the tunes of hymns and popular folk-songs, with Ethel Smyth's 'March of the Women' as the best known. In *The Suffragette,* the official organ of the WSPU, the only poetry in the 1915 editions is stirring canonical men's war poems. The most absorbing records are *Holloway Jingles* and Sylvia Pankhurst's *Writ on Cold Slate.* Both document life inside Holloway Prison during the suffragette militancy, and the difference between them helps to distinguish women's political poetry from 'verse'. *Holloway Jingles, 'written in Holloway Prison during March and April 1912',* strengthened the spirit of the writers and readers suffering for their ideal. The Foreword by Theresa Gough, 'Holloway Jail, 28 April, 1912', is addressed to the Comrades who provide and feed on 'that omniscient love which is the very basis of our movement'. The verses are designed to benefit the collective spirit with cheery metres and generalised anecdotes in popular forms such as hymns, ballads or limericks. Syntax tends to be forced for the sake of rhyme. They have tremendous historical interest but lack the imaginative, linguistic and metrical versatility of Pankhurst's. Her sonnet 'Writ on cold slate' refers to the paper deprivation of prisoners:

> Only this age that loudly boasts Reform,
> hath set its seal of vengeance 'gainst the mind,
> decreeing nought in prison shall be writ,
> save on cold slate, and swiftly washed away.[61]

The pastiche of bygone diction corresponds to the primitive conditions in jail and the antiquated laws of the country. Like this one, most of the poems are written in blank verse without intrusive rhyme. They have the immediacy of the present tense and the artist's keen eye for nuance and detail. Some, like 'In Brooding Depths of Night', present episodes which combine the narrative quality of a short story with wider implications: 'born of the "Have Nots",/Those numerous hordes who toil no wealth to win' (p. 28). 'A Wreck' (pp. 40–45) is a mini-epic of a woman on the edge of insanity which is the cause and effect of violent treatment by prison officers, themselves captive to 'the Power beyond' – the national government. It evocatively combines Pankhurst's talents as historian, storyteller and painter:

> to her doth no-one speak
> in that cold cell, close-locked, where now she lies
> till with a tube, at last, the crowd will come,
> to force it into the resisting frame;

The iambic pentameter is meticulous yet sufficiently elastic for natural diction. In these poems Pankhurst speaks out for those who could or did not. As Warner notes:

A working-class woman may be as gifted as all the women writers I have spoken of today, all rolled into one; but it is no part of her duty to write a masterpiece. Her brain may be teeming, but it is not the fertility of her brain she must attend to, perishable citizens is what her country expects of her, not imperishable Falstaffs and Don Quixotes. The Lord himself may long have wished for her books to be written; but leave has yet to be granted ... Women writers have come from the middle class, and their writing carries a heritage of middle-class virtues; good taste, prudence, acceptance of limitations, compliance with standards, and that typically middle-class merit of making the most of what one's got.[62]

Ethel Carnie [Holdsworth] (1886–1962) is the only 'working-class' poet. A South Lancashire 'ex-mill girl' who contributed to *Woman Worker*, which she edited for a while, she also wrote militant propaganda, novels and children's stories. Her as yet uncollected poems from various papers such as *Freedom* are the most assertive, perhaps because confident of a likeminded audience. Some of the most revolutionary in sentiment are the most formal, frequently in sonnet form or rhyming quatrains. However, 'A Marching Tune' from *Songs of a Factory Girl* (pp. 32–34) is a stirring chorus of workers' solidarity: 'We have waited so long/We can wait no more./And we march forth our freedom to meet.' *Voices of Womanhood* (1914) resounds with work-weariness and the double oppression of seemingly inexorable working-class womanly identity: 'But I must stay pot-bound in place of birth.'[63] However, 'A Vision' is a quiet exhortation to women. They must overcome their station and make their voices public. The pluralised conversational blank verse is typical of Carnie's best:

> When she shall speak, ah, then the world will hear,
> Will listen as she listened all this while,
> For as her strength was in this little house
> So strong will be her presence in the world.[64]

CHAPTER 3

Modernism, memory and masking:
Mina Loy and Edith Sitwell

While elasticising modernism to recognise the impetus of less ostentatious poetry, women must be situated within the avant-garde continuum because of its association with intellectuality and because their involvement has been understated. Just as the male high modernist luminaries, Ezra Pound and T. S. Eliot, emanated from the United States, so the most radical females, Gertrude Stein, Marianne Moore and Amy Lowell, were native Americans. H. D. and Laura Riding moved to Britain and Mina Loy moved from England to the United States. All experimentalists were in touch with the international network of artists and writers in London, Paris and New York and many women were involved in its progressive literary journals which proliferated during the 1920s. Imagism, which reinvigorated literary language and broke some ground for avant-garde innovation, was an Anglo-American current animated by Lowell, H. D. and May Sinclair, largely in Britain through *The Egoist.* Iris Tree and Nancy Cunard also developed the Imagist trend towards more abstract visual linguistics. Their esoteric metaphors, vocabulary and verbal play have the 'difficulty' which notoriously characterised modernist poetry and which was at odds with women's democratic orientation. While supporting the objective clarity and compression of the Imagist and Ezra Pound's 'Make-it-New' credos, poets were rescripting gender representation which avoids fixity. The impetus for fracturing conventions often came from their personal experiences of tragedy and restraint.

The complex symbolism of female modernists benefits from but moves beyond the clarity of Imagist compression. Describing 'Modern Poetry' in *The Faber Book of Modern Verse* (1936), Michael Roberts notes that 'the Imagists themselves sometimes confused the image, the clear evocation of a material thing, with the symbol, the word which stirs subconscious memories. Such, indeed, was their intention: their poetry was meant to widen outwards like the ripples from a stone dropped in clear water.'[1] Roberts further specifies the unconscious resonances of childhood development which this poetry accesses:

In the near future we may see greater emphasis placed on poetry as a means of appealing directly to the subconscious mind, and less on poetry as a conscious criticism of life . . .

Sometimes the reason for the order of the images of such poems and the cause of their effectiveness are fairly obvious. Their power and order may come from casual memory, or from the make-up of the mind, from the deep impressions of early childhood, or from the influence of the birth trauma, or from the structure of the language itself.[2]

We certainly see a concentration on childhood impressions in the work of many women whose lexical applications of psychoanalytical concepts are well-worn to twenty-first-century readers but were refreshing cultural forms in the 1920s. H. D. noted, as if for the first time, that Sigmund Freud 'opened up the field of the knowledge of the unconscious mind' and 'brought the past into the present'.[3] Key techniques are revisionary mythmaking, metapoetic symbols frequently involving colour, strong rhythmic shifts and elliptical typography. H. D.'s *Notes on Thought and Vision* record her version of the interchanges between levels of consciousness which she called 'over-mind' – or 'super-mind' – and 'sub-conscious mind'.[4] In *Tribute to Freud*, she recognised the significance of redeploying symbols in order to 'strike oil' in the unconscious: 'There are all these shapes, lines, graphs, the *hieroglyph of the unconscious*, and the Professor had first opened the field to the study of this vast unexplored region. He himself – at least to me personally – deplored the tendency to fix ideas too firmly, to set symbols, or to weld them inexorably.'[5] Part of that renewal is liberation from conventional gender imperatives. In her *Notes*, H. D. confronts and overrides the dualisms which 'split experience at all levels'.[6]

Female modernist poets frequently rewrite mythical or historical characters, such as Eurydice, who is marvellously and lengthily dramatised by H. D.:

> so for your arrogance
> I am broken at last,
> I who had lived unconscious,
> who was almost forgot;
>
> if you had let me wait
> I had grown from listlessness
> into peace,
> if you had let me rest with the dead,

I had forgot you
and the past.[7]

Here, we see a specifically female avant-gardist maintenance of human
identity and relations which combines with the self-masking recom-
mended for high modernist impersonality. In the Eurydice myth, the levels
of the ordinary human world and underworld usefully mirror different
levels of consciousness. In H. D.'s poem, Eurydice's pain is the awakening
of the buried mind which parallels the process of psychoanalysis. Similarly,
Riding's dramatic monologue of Helen of Troy investigates the power and
fragility of her paradigmatic female beauty. These poems correspond to
Roberts's recognition that, 'If the poet turns to an existing myth or legend,
however shop-soiled, and sees in it a profound significance, he will see the
legend itself exemplified and symbolised in the world about him.'[8]

Mina Loy's *Anglo-Mongrels and the Rose* and Edith Sitwell's *The Sleeping
Beauty* and *Troy Park*, which rework their early development, were all
written around 1923–25. They are neglected texts: hard to get hold of, hard
to comprehend and hard to pin down as feminist. Both poets aimed to
enlarge their readers' consciousness by defamiliarisation. Their experiments were driven by their alienation from the constraints of English
traditionalism associated with their upbringing. In 1914 Sitwell severed
family ties to live on soup and buns in Bayswater and during the 1920s she
and her brothers were synonymous with progressive poetics.[9] She became a
public literary figure through her poetry performances, lectures and criticism. Searching the poetic equivalent of music and abstract art bypassed
the troubling bind of writing as either a man or a woman, which was no
doubt aggravated by experiencing rejection from both her father and her
mother. Mina Loy abandoned her English roots and settled in the United
States, via periods in Europe. Her striking typography was inspired by
contemporary art and music and the empty textual spaces expose both the
potency and limits of language in the complex processes of female subjectivity and sex relations.

EDITH SITWELL

In her public performances, controversial criticism, tea-party entertainment of major writers and audacious attempts to discard traditionalism in
her poetry, Sitwell was a much-needed model. However, her antipathy to
several women, the absence of obviously feminist subject matter and the
oddness of the poems have deterred feminist scholarship. Like other

literary women who became gossiped about, such as Millay and Moore, Sitwell cultivated a protective public image of self-fashioned eccentricity which parodied stereotyped femininity. She also channelled her sense of social exclusion into witty but acerbic criticism such as *The English Eccentrics* (1933) or *Aspects of Modern Poetry* (1934). The unsatisfactory relationship with her parents converges with her tricky ideas about distinct male and female literary practices. Her reviews of women's books and her frequent references to the nature of women's poetry illustrate her preoccupation with the gendering of poetic techniques which she confronted in the rhetoric of male criticism. In a letter to Robert Nichols, she complained about her poems being called 'trivial' in the *New Statesman*:

Damn them, – oh damn them! If they only knew the amount of concentration I put into these things, the amount of hard work and the frayed nerves it entails. They grumble because they say women will try to write like men and can't – then if a woman tries to invent a female poetry, and uses every feminine characteristic for the making of it, she is called trivial. It has made me furious, not because it is myself, but because it is unjust.[10]

Sitwell voices her vexed gender awareness in 'Some Observations on Women's Poetry' printed in *Vogue* (1925): 'Women's poetry should, above all things, be elegant as a peacock, and there should be a fantastic element, a certain strangeness in its beauty. But above all, let us avoid sentimentality ... we cannot hope to write a poem more perfect in its own way than "Goblin Market".'[11] Like Christina Rossetti's *Goblin Market*, Sitwell's long poems often operate on the simultaneous levels of dream-state allegory and personal psychology. Both poets' shifting between memory and fantasy depends upon symbols which can only partially be decoded. They both tease the boundary between nonsense verse or nursery rhyme and high literary ambiguity, largely through exaggerated rhythm, which for Sitwell was 'one of the principal translators between dream and reality'.[12]

Façade, *The Sleeping Beauty* and *Troy Park* transmute the misery of her childhood into her aimed-for 'strangeness'. Sitwell continually quipped about her parents' rejection and cruelty over her appearance; they put her in an iron brace, allegedly to strengthen her long spine. In a letter to John Lehmann, she connected the suppressed suffering with her writing: 'I can't tell the truth about my sainted mother. If I had been a slum child, I would have been taken away from her. But I wasn't a slum child, and motherhood is a *very* beautiful thing! I often wonder what my poetry would be like if I had had a normal childhood.'[13] In 'Colonel Fantock', from *Troy Park* (1925), dedicated to Osbert and Sacheverell, images of loneliness, such as 'I think that only winged ones know the eyrie is so lonely', are woven into the tapestry of memory's associative details. Another profession of alienation – 'I always was a little outside life' – reads simultaneously as a tormented recollection and a means of psychic rehabilitation by aestheticising the emotional scars. In the imaginary locus of the poem, the adult can be reconciled with her childhood wounds:

> All day within the sweet and ancient gardens
> He had my childish self for audience –
> Whose body flat and strange, whose pale straight hair
> Made me appear as though I had been drowned –
> (We all have the remote air of a legend) –.[14]

Parenthetical statements alert us to the most suppressed emotion. 'Colonel Fantock' is typically both representational and mystifying. Sitwell uses regular blank or rhyming verse and recognisable syntax but the imagery is often obscure. As Cora Kaplan states of Rossetti, dream-form could 'exempt her poems from the demands of clarity'... 'In "Goblin Market" ... the images can no more be made to fit a coherent psychic schema than translated into social or autobiographical narrative.'[15] Although quite different in the contexts of their poems, the most useful connection between Rossetti and Sitwell is their capacity to evoke multiple but elusive associations – the stirring of subconscious memories. A passage from Part 16 in Sitwell's *The Sleeping Beauty* refracts Rossetti's evocation of goblin fruit which are both enticing and sinister:

> The fruits are cold as that sweet music's time –
> Yet all those fruits like the bright snow will fade.
>
> The country bumpkins travel to the Fair,
> For Night and Day and Hell and Heaven, seem
> Only a clown's booth seen in some bad dream,
> Wherefrom we watch the movements of our life
> Growing and ripening like summer fruits
> And dwindling into dust, a mirage lie:[16]

Paradoxically, the poetry seems to demand a decoding of symbols which cannot be fully translated, a process akin to psychoanalysis, as H. D. recorded from her treatment: '[Freud] unravelled from the mixed conditions and contacts of the ordinary affairs of life the particular thread that went on spinning its length through the substance of the mind, the buried mind, the sleeping, the unconscious or subconscious mind.'[17]

The Sleeping Beauty (1924) potently explores the 'buried mind' of Sitwell's childhood 'hell' through symbols, frequently drawn from the house and gardens at Renishaw Hall.[18] Published just prior to the article on women's poetry, it was well received and the first of her works to appear simultaneously in an edition in the United States. It opens:

> But far from snow-soft sleep, the country Fair
> Spangled like planets the bucolic air
> Under hot Capricorn, with gold goat-legs,
> Rough satyr hands, that in the sunburnt hay
> Pulled the long wind-blown hair of Susans, Megs,
> And under great trees dark as water lay.
>
> It seemed a low-hung country of the blind, –
> A sensual touch upon the heart and mind.
> Like crazy creaking chalets hanging low
> From the dark hairiness of bestial skies
> The clouds seem, like a potting-shed where grow
> The flower-like planets for the gay flower show.[19]

We could paint this more easily than explain it. Sitwell's experiments with the discordant effect of adjacent rhymes partly accounts for the bleak mood. Assonance ('spangled', 'planets', 'air'), and particularly dissonance ('bestial skies'), are meant to produce 'a sense of menace'.[20] Sitwell's favourite jaunty rhyming couplets clash with the mental unease evoked by distorting pleasant images; thus chalets, potting sheds and flower shows seem decidedly sinister. The associative sequences construct the dream or nightmare vision for which there is no easy Freudian analysis nor compensatory recourse to a familiar world. The second section above was picked up by one of the most astute write-ups in the *TLS* (3 April 1924): 'The most sensitive poets often construct masks for their emotions rather than expose their keenest feelings. We may have every respect for such a course in its relation to character while regretting its effect on art. In some of the verses which compose this poem Miss Sitwell shows that beyond her notable satiric gift and power of fantastic description she possesses an emotional potentiality which is not only more widely appreciable but more poetically valuable.'[21] For Roberts, this is an aspect of a 'good poem': 'It is possible, therefore, for a poem to be professedly realistic and yet to have the vigour and insistence of a dream or nightmare. Good poetry always has something of this quality, but the nightmare may be directly verbal, rather than visual ... In some poems the dream-quality is exaggerated and the structure, which is believed to characterise the fantasies of the deeper levels of sleep is deliberately made the model for the structure of the poem.'[22]

As magnified in Sitwell's work, the symbol is particularly significant in women's experimental writing in that it addresses conventional assumptions upon which familiar mythology depends. The stifling effect of her conventional upbringing is depicted in the recurring image of her stuffed parrot in a cage.[23] A parrot, of course, only repeats others' words. Later on in Part 16 of *The Sleeping Beauty*, Sitwell reiterates the mitigated, but continuing, atrophy of her personality due to the social conditioning experienced through her family:

> But age has brought a little subtle change
> Like the withdrawal caused by the slow dropping
> Of cold sad water on some vast stone image:
> A slow withdrawal, a sad, gradual change
> O'er tragic masks through which strange gods have cried –[24]

The rhythm's insistence mediates between the remembered world and the moment of writing, while the dissonances of 'cold sad water' and 'slow dropping' depict the intended 'menace'. Although the adult self is more resilient, the tragic mask conceals hopelessness:

> And there are terrible and quick drum-taps
> That seem the anguished beat of our own heart
> Making an endless battle without hope
> Against materialism and the world.[25]

The quickening then slowed rhythmic alterations indicate hope running dry and the mental disorientation of nightmare. The strong musicality of repeated rhyme both aggravates and alleviates the stings of the past: 'When we were young, how beautiful life seemed! –/The boundless bright horizons that we dreamed.'[26] The rhyme-dependent rhythm was a self-confessed principle. While affording some auditory or visual coherence, it maintains a sense of psychological *in*coherence:

Most modernist poets are keenly interested in developing technique along the lines laid down for us by our predecessors. For myself, I spend much of my time in experimenting in the effects that rhyme and texture have on rhythm. Many of the violent rhythms which I obtained in *Bucolic Comedies* were got largely by the use of rhymes, internal and external . . . All great art contains an element of the irrational.[27]

Like the above article 'Modern Poetry', Sitwell's 'Some Notes on My Own Poetry' which introduce her *Collected Poems* (1947), her reviews and her critical works such as *A Poet's Notebook* (1943) illuminate her ambitions. In the latter her notes 'On texture' state her emphasis on 'sound and light' which point towards an invisible dimension.[28] She writes of rhythm as 'the executive sense of soul' in that it translates between the material and

spiritual worlds, which include the untapped regions of the unconscious.[29]
In 'Some Notes', she expands on the purpose of her experiments:

In many poems [in *Bucolic Comedies*] the subject is the growth of consciousness.
Sometimes it is like that of a person who has always been blind and who, suddenly
endowed with sight, must *learn* to see; or it is the cry of that waiting, watching
world, where everything we see is a symbol of something beyond, to the consciousness that is yet buried in this earth-sleep.[30]

In 'The Little Ghost who died for Love', the first of three *Rustic Elegies*
(1927), Sitwell gives voice to a woman unjustly hanged in the seventeenth
century; the law made her die in proxy for her husband who absconded
after killing an opponent against whom his devoted wife had protected
him:

> ... he fled
> And I was strung and hung upon the tree.
> It is so cold now that my heart is dead
> And drops through time ... night is too dark to see[31]

The dramatic monologue conflates the broken-heartedness of the histor-
icised speaker with any woman's, including Sitwell's. She suffered from
unrequited love for the homosexual painter Pavell Tcheltichew, to whom
the second dialogic elegy, 'The Hambone and the Heart', is dedicated. Thus
the impersonality of modernist principles ostensibly provided a legitimate
sortie from experience and from identifying herself as a woman but the
problematic process of masking is also the subject of Sitwell's poetry.

MINA LOY

She wore femininity as a mask, sometimes to disguise what she often called her
'masculine side', sometimes to draw the masculine to her side and sometimes to
make her feminism less threatening. Loy wore mask upon mask; she was a poet of
sophistication, in the word's true sense. She knew something about constructing
myth and she knew something about violating the rules of heterosexual
discourse.[32]

As Roger Conover indicates here, Loy also operated in public via various
masks which allowed her to try out different roles. Unlike Sitwell, however,
partly thanks to the freedom of living abroad, Loy upturned feminine
restrictions by exaggerating female sexuality.[33] She was publicly identified
as the emblematic 'Modern Woman' by the *New York Evening Sun* (13 Feb.
1917), but her involvement in the development of experimental poetry will
have indirectly influenced poets in Britain, particularly those who met her

in Europe or New York. Her writing was available in Beach's bookshop in Paris, which was visited by Wickham and Sitwell. Her verse portrait 'Nancy Cunard' registers a degree of acquaintance and admiration.[34]

Whereas Sitwell parodied English metrical rigidity, most famously in 'Sir Beelzebub' from *Façade*, Loy preferred the up-to-dateness and cultural distinctiveness of American jazz:

This unexpectedly realized valuation of American jazz and American poetry is endorsed by two publics; the one universal, the other infinitesimal in comparison.

And why has the collective spirit of the modern world, of which both are the reflection, recognized itself unanimously in the new music of unprecedented instruments, and so rarely in the new poetry of unprecedented verse? It is because the sound of music capturing our involuntary attention is so easy to get in touch with, while the silent sound of poetry requires our voluntary attention to obliterate the cold barrier of print with the whole "intelligence of our senses".[35]

In the above article 'Modern Poetry' (1925), Mina Loy identified herself as American because she was self-consciously avant-garde in her manipulation of colonising English language and poetic conventions: 'The new poetry of the English language has proceeded out of America ... For the true American appears to be ashamed to say anything in the way it has been said before.'[36] As indicated here, Loy's commitment to renovating the versification of the English tradition was fuelled by her antipathy towards her English background. Loy would have been brought up on British literature, and in July 1915 she remarked, "'I don't believe the men in England have got any of the new consciousness about things that is beginning to formulate in some of us – they cannot evaluate a reaction to any stimulus except through juggling with standard poetical phrases – if only they would realise that art always begins with a man's being quite simply honest with himself.'"[37] Like her American and British contemporaries, Loy's verbal experiments drew upon the techniques and structures of modern European visual art, especially Futurism and Cubism. In 1899 she studied art in Munich; she then moved to Paris where she found artists and writers immersed in Impressionism. In Paris she knew writers such as the Symbolists Apollinaire and Stein. Her first husband was the English painter Stephen Haweis whom she met there in 1903. She also went to Florence, and she finally settled in New York in 1916.

Like Sitwell's *The Sleeping Beauty*, Loy's 'Anglo-Mongrels and the Rose 1923–1925' vehemently opposes imperial Britain whose chief instrument of domination is language. It first appeared in unsequenced parts in various journals. The typography resembles that of the English Vorticists whose distorted and enlarged fonts appear in *Blast*, and it makes the poem appear to be more linguistically radical than it is. Like Sitwell, Loy plunders traditional symbolism and denies its conventional associations but she is even more innovative than Sitwell in her free verse. As denoted in the title, 'Anglo-Mongrels' is particularly concerned with the alienation of cultural duality, namely the half-Jewishness of Loy's own identity. It examines the formative processes of English culture, especially its educational and family systems. The sequence 'English Rose', which first appeared in *Lunar Baedecker* [*sic*] (1923), manipulates the flower, high emblem of English heritage, to satirise nationalism. The lives and coming together of her parents are depicted by the transparent pseudonyms, 'Exodus' and 'Ada', her Jewish father and English mother who is the Rose. Further on in 'Anglo-Mongrels', Loy traces her early development in the persona of 'Ova' who finds, 'only words/mysterious'.[38] Typically, image and sound tend to replace metre and rhyme as the controlling devices of the poem. The foundational limitation of language is its binary formulations: 'Two years of her initiation/to light and darkness' (ibid.). The individual needs linguistic armoury against the template prepared 'by the family/reflection/ of national construction' (p. 153):

> Lacking dictionaries
> of inner consciousness
> unmentionable stigmata
> is stamped
> by the parent's solar-plexus
> in disequilibrium
> on the offspring's
> intuition (p. 148).

Between 1914 and 1920 Loy suffered a mental breakdown which is likely to have stemmed from the collapse of her first marriage and been accelerated by her father's opposition to divorce and the death of her second husband. The section 'Marriage Boxes' laments the sex war which cripples 'the personal':

> Oh God
> that men and women
> having undertaken to vanquish one another
> should be allowed
> to shut themselves up in hot boxes and breed (p. 143).

The textual spaces and absence of punctuation or capital letters go some way towards fracturing the constricting binaries which result in the conflicts evoked here and in other poems. We can see the influence of the

Futurists' aesthetic principles which can be detected early on in Loy's work and in the 'Technical Manifesto of Futurist Literature' (1913).[39] It is believed that Loy had affairs with the Futurist pioneers, Carlo Carrà, Filippo Marinetti and Giovanni Papini, whom she met in Florence. Marinetti advocated radical departures from conventional literary form and image, such as 'One must destroy syntax and scatter one's nouns at random', 'abolish the adjective', 'abolish the adverb' and 'Every noun should have its double: that is, the noun should be followed, with no conjunction, by the noun to which it is related by analogy.'[40] Loy was also influenced by the French philosopher Henri Bergson who advocated that a poem should be an uninterrupted sequence of images. In this way the interpretative distance between reader and text is reduced. Their influence can be seen most directly in her doctrinaire 'Aphorisms of Futurism' (1914), fifty-one prescriptions for self-liberation. The agenda of the doctrine is to achieve total consciousness by escaping from the psychic restraints of tradition and convention which forge 'the mechanical re-actions of the subconsciousness, that rubbish heap of race-tradition'.[41]

Loy is the most adventurous woman poet to examine sexual relations, notably in 'The Love Songs'(1923) or 'Songs of Joannes' (1917) which can be read as a satire on gender roles, or as a more tragic exploration of the failure of love and the violence and anger of sexual conflict.[42] In the haunting long poem 'The Effectual Marriage' (1915), the characters Gina and Miovanni are thinly disguised inversions of Mina Loy and Giovanni Papini.[43] The poem appears to be primarily about the oppression of women within a marriage, but it explores the restraints of the social institution on both partners. The typographic gaps are acute pointers to the inaccessible areas of the unconscious which stunt both the individual and the partnership:

> While Miovanni thought alone in the dark
> Gina supposed that peeping   she might see
> A round light   shining   where his mind was
> She never opened the door
> Fearing that this might blind her
> Or even
> That she should see   Nothing at all[44]

The injunctions concerning mutual sexual relations arguably pick up or contradict the principles of Loy's 'Feminist Manifesto' which urge women not to depend on a man, to desire or to be jealous of him. Loy's thirty-four part sequence 'The Love Songs' or 'Songs of Joannes' is difficult to interpret and to position, although 'Joannes' represents Papini. While in free verse and unstitching normal syntax, these poems are still expressive. The *dramatis personae* and dialogue are recognisable and the textual spaces indicate tortuous mental processes.

The textual spaces also point to a self-fulfilment which Loy's characters rarely achieve. According to Bergson, humans need a moment of self-comprehension to save them from wasting their lives. In Loy's 'Parturition', childbirth is this moment of self-awareness for the female subject. The lines 'For consciousness in crises   races/through the subliminal deposits of evolutionary processes' (p.6) correspond to the urgency of 'Aphorisms on Futurism' where she announced, 'TODAY is the crisis in consciousness' (p.151).[45] In 'Anglo-Mongrels' the sequence 'Ova, Among the Neighbours' on unravelling consciousness is the most energetic: 'This consciousness within her/uncurled itself upon the rollers of objective experience' (p.152). Loy's verse portrait 'Gertrude Stein' indicates her understanding of the contingency between revived language and full self-realisation.[46] Her admiration for Stein is also evident in her prepublication review of *The Making of Americans* for *Transatlantic Review*, 1924. Loy indicated her understanding of the 'logopoeia' which she applied to her own poetry and made the case that by destabilising high cultural norms, modernism worked on democratic principles: 'through cubism the newspaper has assumed an aesthetic quality, through Cézanne a plate has become more than something to put an apple upon, Brancusi has given an evangelistic import to eggs, and Gertrude Stein has given us the Word, in and for itself'.[47]

The goal of H. D., Sitwell and Loy to access the unconscious and expand consciousness is part of a commitment to renovating contemporary culture made by other female modernists, notably Laura Riding. Like *The Sleeping Beauty* or 'Anglo-Mongrels', Riding's 'Memories of Mortalities' draws upon her childhood to examine her development as a woman: 'I had learnt to be silent/And yet to be./I had learnt how the world speaks.'[48] Unlike the others, Riding refuses to use symbols. Her prose treatise *The Word 'Woman'* (1933) was intended to 'strip literature of its mythologies of ludicrous pieties' and looks at the alienation of women in language.[49] Riding left the United States in 1926 and became known in Europe and Britain, partly through her Seizin Press and through her relationship with Robert Graves. Their collaborative *A Survey of Modernist Poetry* (1927) was the first to coin and define the term 'modernist'. Like Sitwell's introductory 'Notes on My Own Poetry', Riding includes in her *Collected Poems* a 'Preface' where she explains that her experiments with shedding 'literary conventionalities of poetic idiom' – rhyme, image, symbol or form – were aimed at achieving the diction of uncontaminated thought.[50] She was, however, hampered by her belief in absolute and essential 'meaning': 'Where language is converted into the mere instrument of an art, it loses its virtue as the expressive instrument of humanity.'[51] Riding's ideal of cultural sanctification through linguistic purity is also illustrated in *A Pamphlet against Anthologies* (1928).

If we look from Riding's dismissal of all poetic accessories or the spatial free verse of Loy to Sitwell's and H. D.'s centralising of symbol, we can suggest that a female modernist aesthetic is achieved through maintaining but distorting the inherited myths, forms and syntax of British literary tradition. Amid the collage of psychic conflicts and unexpressed desires, there is often a yearning for emancipation which a poem partly fulfils in its licence to be experimental.

CHAPTER 4

"*I will put myself, and everything I see, upon the page*": *Charlotte Mew, Sylvia Townsend Warner, Anna Wickham and the dramatic monologue*

While not linguistically avant-garde, women's appropriations of the Victorian dramatic monologue negotiated between high modernism's trumpeted 'impersonality' and their yearning for self-realisation. The constructed persona inherent in the form affords authorial self-concealment while liberating the writer's expressive creativity. It enables the woman writer to direct the reader's sympathy and judgement from 'behind the scenes' while involving him or her as confidante. Sometimes the fictional subject and context provide a cathartic evasion of the poet's condition but more often they can be directly construed with biographical details. Isobel Armstrong argues for restoring a tradition of this more 'affective' but studiedly antisentimental poetry, the 'impersonal self-exposure which occurs through the negotiations with expressive structures'.[1] The vibrancy frequently comes from the dialogic scrutiny of personal and social power relations. Collectively, they contradict essentialising assumptions about the nature and roles of men and women. One distinctly twentieth-century feature of all the poems is the psychological concept of repression as newly informed by Freud and Jung. Also twentieth-century is the idiomatic colloquial diction on which monologue is contingent. Formally, they range from the tight structure of the sonnet to ventures with *vers libre,* although rhyming still proliferates. The majority of poems were published in the 1920s and 1930s. Charlotte Mew, Sylvia Townsend Warner and Anna Wickham are the outstanding writers of monologue but ingenious examples come from Naomi Mitchison, Winifred Holtby and several little-known poets. Since this book is based on British-born or naturalised poets, Edna St Vincent Millay (1892–1950) whose dramatic monologues paradigmatically satirised idealised love, frequently in sonnet form, although well-known in Britain, is not looked at; nor are other Americans who dramatised constructions of female identity, such as Dorothy Parker (1893–1967), Louise Bogan (1897–1970), Elinor Wylie (1885–1928) or Sara Teasdale (1884–1933).

CHARLOTTE MEW

Mew's psychological alienation is commonly transferred to social outsiders and outcasts, whether the nun, the prostitute, the changeling or the mentally ill. 'At the Convent Gate', the first of her 'Early Poems', is Browningesque in implicating an audience within the poem: "'Why do you shrink away and start and stare?"'[2] Typically Mew, it evokes a yearning for what is not there, whether God, a lover or, in the absence of these, death. The dilemma between the free spirit and religious discipline is supported by the structural irony of the colloquial sonnet. 'In Nunhead Cemetery', 'Asylum Road' and 'Ken'[3] become more harrowing if read with reference to her brother Henry and sister Freda; they developed schizophrenia around 1890 and were confined in mental hospitals until their deaths, Henry's in 1901 and Freda's after Charlotte herself.

'The Quiet House' rearranges aspects of Mew's family, home and history as they register in her memory; the childlike voice indicates how the formative experiences of abandonment impinge on the adult: 'Since Ted and Janey and then Mother died/And Tom crossed Father and was sent away.' Three out of the seven Mew children died as babies or in early childhood – two in 1876 – and her father, not mother, had died in 1898. The overwhelming sensations are cumulative losses, broken relationships and shame, partly due to her nurse's severe doctrines of divine retribution. (She had died in 1893.) Unuttered grief and guilt are projected through distorting feel-good images like the rose and through colour symbolism:

> A Rose can stab you across the street
> Deeper than any knife:
> And the crimson haunts you everywhere –
> Thin shafts of sunlight, like the ghosts of reddened swords have
>   struck our stair
> As if, coming down you had spilt your life.
>
>   I think that my soul is red
> Like the soul of a sword or a scarlet flower:
>   . . .
> I am burned and stabbed half through,
>   And the pain is deadly sweet.[4]

Rhyming provides some linguistic, and implicitly psychological, coherence but is overridden by the fluctuating line lengths and sentences continuing across the end-of-line rhymes. This textual tension between linguistic containment and spillage enacts a mind on the brink of breakdown. The textual absence so typical of women's poetry is marvellously manipulated by Mew. What is the unsayable pain marked by the elusive 'everywhere' and the ensuing ellipsis? Earlier, an unexplained act by 'my cousin's friend' is similarly encoded by a dash: 'He frightened me before he smiled –/He did not ask me if he might –.' The oxymoronic 'deadly sweet' and the torment of half-done burning and stabbing are peculiarly disconcerting. Assonance ('strangest pain', 'can stab') alongside dissonance ('burned and stabbed') is haunting auditory rhetoric for unresolved emotions.

Written in 1913, 'The Quiet House' was in Mew's words 'perhaps the most subjective to me of the lot',[5] and it exemplifies 'impersonal self-exposure'.[6] Its strong symbolism and typographical markers of the unsaid also correspond to Armstrong's demarcation of twentieth-century female expressive poetry by a Freudian sense of the '*unknowable* unconscious'. Her explanation of Victorian expressive theory is necessary to her rehabilitation of the 'affective':

People have noticed the superficial resemblance of this theory to Freud's account of repression, but it is radically different because it assumes a consciously *known* experience which is inexpressible because the verbal forms of language are inadequate, ineffable. Freud, on the contrary, assumed that representation is part of a symbolic structure of displacement which is a manifestation of the *unknowable* unconscious. Thus he places emphasis on the importance of the material sign or symbol where Victorian expressive theory does not.[7]

Women codify their as yet ungrasped subjectivity with the 'unsaid' of symbolism and textual spaces.

Mew's hallmark is summoning felt absence through obscuring symbolism, textual gaps and expanding and retracting line lengths. Whereas the first person pronoun in 'The Quiet House' is implicitly autobiographical, the personal resonances in Mew's seven-page 'Madeleine in Church' are more covert. Both poems succeed in telling a woman's entire emotional history. The persona is a heart-torn divorced woman and her audience a 'plaster saint'. As Mew intended, it also captures an intense *cri du cœur*, 'the moment when the emotion unmistakably concentrates itself into a few words'.[8] The unsettling colour symbolism and tamed wild line variations contribute to the powerful evocations of screwed-up fear and pain:

> But this place is grey.
> And much too quiet. No one here,
> Why, this is awful, this is fear!
> Nothing to see, no face,
> Nothing to hear except your heart beating in space
> As if the world was ended. Dead at last!

> Dead soul, dead body, tied together fast.
> These to go on with and alone, to the slow end:
> No one to sit with, really, or to speak to, friend to friend:[9]

Although she is addressing an icon, the last line, especially the confiding 'really', beckons the reader. At the end we painfully overhear Madeleine crying out in empathy to the crucified but unresponsive Christ figure. In the extract above absence is most intensely present, through the 'nothings' and 'no one's'. In the opening lines of 'On the Road to the Sea', the interpretative space created by the end-of-line elliptical dash and the enigmatic 'hard thing' potently appeal to the reader as well as the unspecified intimate in the poem:

> We passed each other, turned and stopped for half an hour, then
>   went our way,
>   I who make other women smile did not make you –
> But no man can move mountains in a day
>   So this hard thing is yet to do.[10]

Typically for Mew, the treatment of emotions is the core and the subject is tormented by what she cannot have: 'But I want your life before mine bleeds away –/Here – not in heavenly hereafters – soon, –'. The elusive identities of lover and loved one codify the same-sex passion. As Armstrong notes of Rossetti's 'Winter, My Secret', 'A poem about telling a secret becomes a poem about the conditions under which the sexuality of the speaking subject is created and bound.'[11] Mew's biographers agree that her secret love for women remained unresolved and is projected on to her representations of mental conflict.

Male or gender-indeterminate monologues enabled Mew to express her repressed sexuality. 'The Farmer's Bride' articulates unbearable longing for union with a woman who is close but unattainable. First published in *Nation* in 1912, when the Royal Commission on Divorce and Matrimonial Causes was approaching the end of its deliberations, the poem attracted correspondence over the farmer's lack of condemnation for his runaway bride.[12] As tragic 'hero', structurally the farmer appeals for the reader's sympathy, but we are propelled towards the silent bride-in-hiding through the dominant symbol of a small scared mouse, rabbit or leveret on the run. The multivocality of his monologue further unfixes moral certainties:

> "Not near, not near!" her eyes beseech
> When one of us comes within reach.
>   The women say that beasts at stall
>   Look round like children at her call
>   *I've* hardly heard her speak at all.[13]

Such verbal simplicity in the face of social imperatives contributes to the tragic effect.

The immediacy of the dramatic monologue coupled with associational evocations of unfathomable emotion are admirably achieved in 'Saturday Market', 'one of the most successful things Charlotte Mew ever wrote', according to Penelope Fitzgerald.[14] Local detail is reminiscent of the family's experiences of the Saturday market in Newport on the Isle of Wight where they took an annual holiday. The poem warrants a place in a modernism which admits representational experimentalism. Not just the title, but the playful yet sinister mystification also connect with Christina Rossetti's *Goblin Market*. Both set a dark deed against a background of festival and are morally ambivalent by dispensing with authorial direction. Mew's tale, however, merges external and internal narratives, as in 'Bury your heart in some deep green hollow.' Like 'The Farmer's Bride', the tragic plot and rural setting echo the fiction of Hardy whom Mew greatly admired and met in 1918. The secret 'murder' is not named but is implicitly an abortion or baby-killing:

> What were you showing in Saturday Market
>   That set it grinning from end to end
> Girls and gaffers and boys of twenty –?
>   Cover it close with your shawl, my friend –
> Hasten you home with the laugh behind you,
>   Over the down –, out of sight,
> Fasten your door, though no one will find you
>   No one will look on a Market night.
>
> See, you, the shawl is wet, take out from under
>   The red dead thing –. In the white of the moon
> On the flags does it stir again? Well, and no wonder!
>   Best make an end of it; bury it soon.
> If there is blood on the hearth who'll know it?
>   Or blood on the stairs,
> When a murder is over and done why show it?
>   In Saturday market nobody cares.
>
> Then lie you straight on your bed for a short, short weeping
>   And still, for a long, long rest,
> There's never a one in the town so sure of sleeping
>   As you, in the house on the down with a hole in your breast.[15]

The rhyming at odds with the untidy line lengths produces the freely colloquial expression which Mew so effectively achieves. Typically, compassion is directed to the 'criminal' for being a victim of social proprieties. Illegitimacy was socially shameful and abortion was difficult because of the state's promotion of motherhood, especially when the birth rate was low. The Abortion Law Reform Association was set up in 1936, eight years after Mew's death. The 'hole in the breast' indicates a sentence of lifelong mourning and repentance. It may also symbolise the child which Mew would not have because of the mental weakness in her mother's family and because of her desire for women: 'If there were fifty heavens God could not give us back the child who went or never came', she wrote in 'Madeleine in Church'. She and her sister Anne were privy to new eugenics about congenital mental illness leading to social decay. The simple vocabulary, rhyme and imagery, as in 'the red dead thing', draw attention to a simple, country person's mask of naïveté and innocence, forced by the collision between moral laws and her hidden guilt. Since the commentator seems both separate from and also subsumed into the conscience of the woman, it is as if she moves between subjective and objective verdicts on her 'crime' and its life sentence. Such personal internalisation of social condemnation by the marginalised is, of course, the point and acutely pertinent to Mew.

Monro's verdict indicates Mew's skill at imaginatively transforming personal experience through dramatisation: 'One of the peculiarities of the authoress of these poems is a projection of herself outside herself, so that a kindred personality seems to align with her through life; her own yet not her own ... she only half-surrenders the magic of her personality ... the best [poetry] is the nearest to ordinary speech.' He also recognises that 'the best poetry is the least *poetical* ... we are often least conscious of it as *poetry* when we are most moved ... No argument, or quotation, can prove that the poetry of Charlotte Mew is above the average of our day.'[16] Her achievement with colloquial expression is especially notable given the prevalence of her rhyming. Mew's reputation was largely established by *The Farmer's Bride* in 1916 which was reprinted in 1921 with new poems and simultaneously published with an American edition notably titled *Saturday Market*. *The Rambling Sailor* (1929) covers the happier years 1924–25 which followed her mother's death. She did not leave a large oeuvre but she was a major poet in a tradition of women's expressive poetry.

SYLVIA TOWNSEND WARNER

Like Mew, Warner interrogates the self-renunciation to which nineteenth-century texts often capitulated. The carefree independence of 'The Absence' reverses romantic myths: 'How happy I can be with my love away!'[17] Her dialogic monologues often dramatise internal conflicts and contemporary debates. 'The Rival' is ostensibly a down-to-earth reported monologue by a farmer's wife about her husband's emotional detachment, but it depicts her sense of confinement and neglect which is typical of women's interwar writing:

> The farmer's wife looked out of the dairy:
> She saw her husband in the yard;
> She said: 'A woman's lot is hard,
> The chimney smokes, the churn's contrary.'
> She said:
> 'I of all women am the most ill-starred.
>
> Five sons I've borne and seven daughters,
> And the last of them is on my knee.
> Finer children you could not see.
> Twelve times I've put my neck into the halter:
> You'd think
> So much might knit my husband's love to me.'[18]

The startling symbol of motherhood as a noose operates as a *cri du coeur* which undercuts the mundane vernacular. The register of the reporter is detached but the 'you' requires a response from the reader. As a reviewer observed in *Time and Tide*, Warner's poems bridge nineteenth-century Romanticism and twentieth-century modernist innovation in their combination of pastoral and stream-of-consciousness: 'There is no doubt that Miss Warner is a poet, but there are epitaphs and ironic tragedies on the roads of Wessex and psychoanalysis.'[19] As here, her sexual and social politics were rarely acknowledged in contemporary reviews, which centred on her formalism.

As seen in Chapter 2, Warner's urgency for the underdog was expressed in her socialist writing and activities which culminated in joining the Communist Party. Her poems were printed in literary journals and anthologies, and she contributed articles on contemporary literature to *Time and Tide*. She published *The Espalier* in 1925 and in 1928 published *Time Importuned* which provoked J. G. Fletcher to proclaim in *The Criterion*, 'Now that Miss Charlotte Mew is dead, I think Miss Warner should be proclaimed the best poetess in England.'[20] She was unmarried, like Mew, but unlike her in a settled lesbian partnership, and thus even more distant from contemporary ideals of marriage and motherhood. The disjunction between unarticulated expression, that is the semiotic, and the official symbolic formulation is most clearly manifested in the

coded love poems between Warner and Ackland, published in their com-
bined volume *Whether a Dove or a Seagull* in 1934.[21] It contains much of
their best work yet is woefully scarce. Not all are love poems, but their
conversational lyrics indicate the double restraints of the lesbian existence
disguised by gender neutral pronouns. In Ackland's quasi-sonnet, 'What
must we do if we cannot do this', the evocation of the unspeakable love
depends upon symbols – 'our tightened cord, our secret tether'. In
'Drawing You Heavy with Sleep', the metaphors of fluidity and liquidity
are paradigmatic representations of female sexuality, albeit masked by
ungendered pronouns.[22] Even such coded representation of female desire
was brave in a cultural climate which expected women, particularly poets,
to model sexless femininity. *Whether a Dove or a Seagull* is part of a body
of lesbian modernist poetry which includes lyrics and experimental pieces
by Mew, H. D., Sackville-West and the Americans Lowell, Stein and
Barnes.[23]

ANNA WICKHAM

In her investigation of gender constructions, Wickham exemplifies the
expressive female modernist. The publication of *The Writings of Anna
Wickham* in 1984 brought out her poetry from obscurity. She was well
known in Britain, Paris and the United States where her reputation was at
its height after the First World War. Born in Britain, she grew up in
Australia, returned to Britain in 1904 and married Patrick Hepburn in
1906. She held soirées at their home in London, with music, entertainment
and lectures on women's suffrage. Her literary acquaintances included
Nancy Cunard, the Poetry Bookshop crowd, such as the Monros and
David Garnett, and the bohemian writers in London associated with
D. H. Lawrence.[24] She spent five months in Paris in 1922, during which
she met Ezra Pound as well as Natalie Barney, Sylvia Beach, Robert
MacAlmon, Edna St Vincent Millay, and Djuna Barnes. Temporarily,
she became part of the circle of women who lived on the Left Bank and
Natalie Barney became an emotional centre. Domestically, she felt a failure: she had a stillborn child and a miscarriage before her first son James
was born; he was followed by three more children but her third son died of
scarlet fever in 1921. She had a stormy marriage; when her husband died in a
climbing accident in 1929, she was freed from the bonds of marriage but
not from those of motherhood.

For Wickham, creative freedom involves reworking and publicising her
experience and perspective:

I thought there was no pleasure in the world
Because of my fears.
Then I remembered life and all the words in my language.
And I had courage even to despise form.
I thought, 'I have skill to make words dance,
To clap hands and to shake feet,
But I will put myself, and everything I see, upon the page.'[25]

'Return of Pleasure' is in the free verse which she associates with psychological and aesthetic liberty. The speaker in dialogue with herself typifies the internal conflict which is Wickham's signature. Here, Wickham conflates the speaker with the poet, but most often she exploits the distancing allowed by a fictional character to investigate female, and sometimes male, psychology. Nevertheless, much of the poetry illuminates and can be illuminated by her autobiography. Her boldness in refuting self-renunciation as a womanly ideal provoked her husband to certify her as insane on hearing that her poems were to be published.[26]

Although female identity is usually projected as unfulfilled, women in her poems are oppressed by social laws rather than the essentialising inferiority prescribed by Freud. In the loose sonnet 'Examination', the colloquialisms and divergence from iambic pentameter in relation to the sonnet framework combine her ever-competing impulses for freedom and conformity: 'I write my thought in this most ragged way/That being baulked of beauty, I am stung to pray.'[27] The strict parental regime of her childhood and severe Roman Catholic education had instilled the principle of obedience but also provoked rebellion against discipline. She felt an outsider in Australia and particularly in the convent where it was known that her father was antireligious.

The coexistence of tenses and voices essential to dramatic monologues allows her fictional women to explore and expose her multiple roles. In 'Definition' Wickham questions whether a wife's identity is anything more than a mother and bed partner. Internal tension between liberty and loyalty is replicated in 'The Wife':

> My brain dies
> For want of exercise,
> I dare not speak
> For I am weak.
>
> 'Twere better for my man and me,
> If I were free,
> Not to be done by, but to be.
> But I am tied[28]

The 'I dare not speak' again allocates the privilege and responsibility of confidante to the reader and accounts for the weighty significance of otherwise light-hearted rhyming verse. In his review of *The Contemplative Quarry* (1915) in *The Egoist*, Richard Aldington picked out the last line as an example of Wickham's tendency to ruin a perfectly good poem with 'doggerel'. Apart from this flaw, however, he admired her manipulation of rhyme and conceded the logic of her argument:

[It is] the humorous protest of a sane woman observing the insane things which are excited from her sex by bourgeois rules. She manages to say bitter and satiric and true things with a good deal of humour (she runs the eighteenth-century trick of antithetical rhyme) ... You get the impression of a woman (you seldom get the impression of femininity from a woman's book) who is very interested in life and especially in her own life. She wants to know what the devil women are to do with their lives.[29]

The parenthetical generalisation '(you seldom get the impression of femininity from a woman's book)' exemplifies how the majority of women writers were preoccupied with avoiding negative gender identification.

Wickham's dramatic monologues of female infidelity and free will, such as 'Divorce', seem rare.[30] In the context of the emphasis on women's duty as homemakers during and after the First World War, even more shocking would have been 'The Revolt of Wives', which contradicted the essentialised maternal instinct which patriarchal discourses took for granted:

> Nor for my very pleasure will I vex
> My whole long life away in things of sex,
> As in those good Victorian days
> When teeming women lived in stays.
> . . .
> Show us the contract plain, that we may prove
> If we are loved for children, or are loved for love.[31]

The shifting between first person singular and plural disperses the private/public polarity and makes the apparently individual complaint universal. The silent vocative 'show us' is a direct challenge. The coupled rhymes in tension with the colloquial voice structurally support the subject who is wracked by the competing demands of individual choice and social propriety. 'The Marriage' is free verse and freely examines the complex psychology at work in domestic conflict.[32] This poem asks whether such apparently inevitable strife is down to the sex war or a shared human desire for both security and freedom. Although the poems operate in conjunction with *Fragment of an Autobiography* (reprinted in *Writings*), they are not confessional. One of her most haunting, an implicitly male monologue 'The Sick Assailant', demonstrates her skill as a storyteller: 'I hit her in the face because she loved me./It was the challenge of her faithfulness that moved me –'.[33] It brilliantly exemplifies Freud's theory of masculine submission to and domination of the mother/son bond in all male/female relations. The numerous uses of 'me' and 'she' reconstruct the egocentric object-ification of the woman. 'The Sportsman', 'The Pugilist' and 'The Happy Mathematician' are more humorous jibes at stereotyped masculinity.

'The Angry Woman' is a lengthy disclosure of Wickham's fluctuations about gender differences. The speaker questions the value of marriage for women: 'If sex is a criterion for power, and never strength,/What do we gain by union?' But her ideal is human equality: 'In many things are you and I apart/But there are regions where we coincide/Where law for one is a law for both.' The concept of mental androgyny parallels other women's search to transcend seemingly inexorable laws of binary gender difference–'There is the sexless part of me that is my mind'[34] – particularly in creativity. It is clear from poems like 'Suppression' – 'If you deny her right to think,/If you deny her pride of ink' – and 'Woman and Artist' – 'There's no excuse for expression from a woman/Unless she be representa-tive human' (both undated) that writing was an act of freedom.[35] Freedom of expression is her central preoccupation in *Fragment of an Autobiography*:

The relief of writing will give me nervous and physical energy to continue with my task. I write also because I am a woman artist and the story of my failure should be known. I have a European reputation: my poetry is mentioned with honour in the *Encyclopaedia Britannica*: that should give me the right to live. I have very little newspaper reputation. I have always avoided it as a part of my phobia.[36]

Confronting her internal sense of failure, Wickham noted the lack of positive role models – 'there have been few women poets of distinction' – and the high suicide rate among her predecessors, which she increased by hanging herself in 1947. The guilt attached to the tension between writing and fulfilling the womanly duties which society prescribed is what finally shrouded her.[37]

The directness of Wickham's poems suggests neither a Freudian unknowability nor the deficiency in available language which delineate twentieth- and nineteenth-century expressive theories. She sets up a model of female control of language for the purpose of communicating 'myself, and everything I see'. Her lyrics blast the divide between personal and public realms which all monologues implicitly transgress. Increasingly, we find women uncritically harnessing language to their worlds.

'MINOR' POETS

The impulse for freedom which strained against the reins of convention is the subtext of many of Mitchison's poems, which correspondingly tend towards free verse. 'Woman Alone' depicts a woman going through the motions of lovemaking when psychically remote from her partner. 'Dick and Colin at the Salmon Nets' is more personal (Dick was her husband) and more resigned to the apparent inevitability of sexual segregation.[38] It echoes Mitchison's assertion in 1930 that 'Apparently, all the feminist battles are gained, or almost all. Actually nothing is settled, and the question of baby or not baby is at the bottom of almost everything.'[39] Holtby's rhyming dramatic monologue 'Beauty the Lovers Gift' dramatises the contradictory expectations for women to be like ornaments and companions. It is addressed to a man or men in general, whereas 'Boats in the Bay', also uncollected from *Time and Tide*, appeals to an empathetic woman reader: 'I will take my trouble and drop it into the water/It is heavy as stone and smooth as a sea-washed pebble.'[40] The symbolised emotional 'drowning' may be unnecessarily obvious but its particularity remains open for the reader.

As seen in the previous chapter, women modernists rewrite cultural myths, taking figures such as Helen of Troy or Euridyce. The distance of a historical or classical character offers greater freedom for exposing current perspectives as well as 'writing back' the versions of the past through a female eye. 'Artemis Married' by Stella Gibbons is a rather evocative dramatic monologue in the much-reprinted anthology *Twentieth-Century Poetry* (1929). The mythical goddess who is charged with care for women's sexual development and childbirth is visited by a male hunter:

> Shame . . . He played with my crying children,
> Yawned, and spat in the ashy fire,
> Stared at my yellowing shoulders in homespun
> Without the stare of desire.
> Shame . . . even then, I sang as I spun,
> But the fool, with a finger above his head,
> Must point to my unstrung, dusty bow
> And: 'Is that your husband's bow?' he said.[41]

The assonance is what Gibbons admired in Mitchison, writing to her in the 1920s: 'I am sending you my poems – I've just had the first copies. Do discount all the *vers libre* ones – I've got through that now! Since then I've written one or two with your vowel rhymes but they are all rather intime . . .'[42] She expressed gratitude for a book of T. S. Eliot's poems which presumably

fuelled her wish for the more personal distance which the dramatic monologue enables.

Ada Jackson is an overlooked out-of-print poet whose monologues
match the scope of the more widely known writers. They tell a story and
take the masks off the public versions of womanhood. 'Anne Shakespeare'
is the complaint of the great dramatist's wife about his absorption in work
and his relationship with the dark lady:

> Not all the grief of earth can heal
> The wounds of lonely sleep,
> The hurt of years when he came not[43]

Although specifically contextual, the worlds of the speaker and the contemporary reader are conflated. Jackson's 'The Farmer's Mother', written
in convincing rural dialect, strips off the façade of tranquillity surrounding
a picture-book ideal of rural living in an extended family. A grim alternative to marital conflict, Sylvia Lynd's 'The Solitary' hauntingly evokes
the vacuity of spinsterhood in a society which centralises the marriage
ideal.[44] It also records the actuality of singleness for many women after the
First World War. Sometimes the single woman was depicted as having a
mental freedom which seemed enviable to the married one.[45] The dramatic
monologues of Muriel Stuart (1885–1967), such as 'Mrs Effingham's Swan
Song' or 'Mrs Hamilton', are reminiscent of the Victorian Augusta
Webster's witty exposures of incarcerating socialisation, particularly for
women: 'I am sorry for women who are growing old, /I do not blame them
holding Youth with shameful hold –/Of doing desperate things to lips and
eyes.'[46] In 'The Bastard', an ostracised victim of man's desire addresses her
unborn child:

> But thou wilt lie no longer than love lay,
> Thou wilt weary of my body, even as he;
> And I again with body and blood shall pay
> To the last farthing's ruthless penalty
> The nights with love, the days, the hours with thee.[47]

Like this, several tend to be cynical, antisentimental dramatisations of or
about relationships between men and women. See, for example, 'In the
Orchard' – '"I/thought you loved me," "No it was only fun"' – or 'Gay
Girl to Good Girl' where the idiom and debate on sexual difference are
remarkably contemporary.[48]

The numerous dramatic monologues by these poets, and others represented in anthologies and journals, interrogate prescribed gender imperatives

and relations. Like the short story, they operate as snapshots and potently indicate a context beyond the single speaker's. They fracture the authority of the masculine Romantic unitary lyric 'I' while maintaining the self as a literary source; although not yielding to the antireferential impersonality demanded by high modernism, the monologues allow self-concealment for the poet. They explore and provoke, rather than escape from, emotion. Their narratives are associative, rather than linear, and they manoeuvre symbolism, rhyme, line lengths and verse forms to reconstruct the individual's negotiations between self-denial and self-realisation. Collectively, they subvert the idealisations of romantic love and feminine identity perpetuated in literary tradition, social conventions and women's popular culture, although in this period there is still a restraint about female desire. Luce Irigaray sees such impersonations of fictionalised women and social relations as a consequence of women being 'exiled from themselves'.[49] More positively, we see that by dramatising the disjunctions between how they are supposed to be and their struggling subjectivity, women overcame gender prescriptions which had blocked a specifically female creativity. Their openness to personal and professional female alliances indicates their readiness to identify themselves as women writers unfettered by the strangling codes of femininity.

Overview

INTRODUCTION

The first thirty-five years of the postwar period encompass considerable socio-cultural change. In an uneasy peace haunted by the atom bomb and the Cold War, and amid intensive economic and socio-political restructuring, the position of women remains contentious. Divisions over the reentrenching of gender roles in the 1950s and 1960s only deepen with the emergence of Women's Liberation. Lacking any coherent political outlook, women's poems veer between the conservative and the radical, between adopting or negotiating with the traditional principles and values of the literary academy, and developing new experimental modes to undermine it. As debates grow about what the state can or should do in the name of the individual, this poetry, in all its contradictions, bespeaks women's struggle to secure the personal and public freedoms which society denies them. The poets' mining of the personal is not especially unusual in postwar poetics; their often subversive (rather than self-indulgent) use of it to illuminate women's domestic, spiritual and political lives is more significant. The most radical use it to question lyric expression itself.

For most, chief among those freedoms is the opportunity to write and publish, and compete for critical recognition. The 'poetess' tag, used less freely as the years pass, takes a long time to disappear. As late as 1977, when the literary historian Robert Hewison makes passing reference to Lady Emerald Cunard, '(mother of the poetess Nancy Cunard)', he not only relegates her daughter to parentheses but omits her from the index.[1] Scepticism towards women's poetry is famously articulated by the American Theodore Roethke, who denounces it for 'lack of range – in subject matter, in emotional tone – and lack of sense of humour ...; the embroidering of trivial themes; a concern with the mere surfaces of life ...; refusing to face up to what existence is, lyric or religious posturing; running between the boudoir and the altar, stamping a tiny foot against God; ...

sententiousness[;] carrying on excessively about Fate, about time; lamenting the lot of women; caterwauling ... and so on.'[2] Equally notorious is Geoffrey Summerfield's exclusion of women from his 1974 Penguin anthology *Worlds*: 'Britain in the last fifteen years has not produced a woman poet of real stature.'[3] In response, women make their presence felt outside the avenues favoured by the academy, through the small presses and little magazines which many start up and run, and in self-edited anthologies. At the same time, they learn to foreground and examine the full extent of their experiences, private and public, female-centred or not. With radical feminist critics like Julia Kristeva and Hélène Cixous theorising a buoyantly female language, against the backdrop of Women's Liberation women poets begin deploying and deconstructing the lyric 'I', often but not always gender-identified, in more confidently innovative ways. As class structures change, the influence of modernism gives way to the postmodern, and as the widening of mass culture further erodes boundaries between highbrow and lowbrow, their poetry increasingly becomes a site of socio-political as well as aesthetic negotiation.

The story of women poets' struggle for professional credibility is partly told in the anthologies of the period. In 1982 Blake Morrison and Andrew Motion belittle the 'stretch, occupying much of the 60s and 70s ... ' since 'the last serious anthology of British poetry', as a 'spell of lethargy'.[4] The claim is disingenuous. Besides 'serious' surveys of the period supplied by Cecil Day Lewis and John Lehmann (1959), Kenneth Allott (1962), Edward Lucie-Smith (1970), Philip Larkin (1973), and D. J. Enright (1980), 'niche' anthologies such as *A Group Anthology* (1963), *Children of Albion* (1969) and *Eight Contemporary Poets* (1974) counter Al Alvarez's influential but highly selective *The New Poetry*, which Morrison and Motion emulate.[5] Yet the latter's 'manifesto-making' ambitions find them stolidly endorsing a limiting elitism which, by 1982, is insecure and, despite a worthy-seeming 1:4 male to female ratio, partisan.[6]

No mainstream anthology reflects the contribution of women to British poetry between 1945 and 1980. In 1949 the earliest postwar women-only anthology, *The Distaff Muse*, edited by Clifford Bax and Meum Stewart, advertises the 'impressive number of poets of quality [thirty-five] ... in [its] large modern section'.[7] In the same year, Kenneth Rexroth, uncomfortably aware that 'it seems somewhat false to discuss a writer on the basis of her sex, as a woman poet, or worse, poetess,' notices from the United States that 'the war years produced a number of remarkable women poets ...'[8] In 1950 Hermann Peschmann hails 'the emergence of a considerable body of women poets of distinction ... [as] something new. I think it beyond question that at no previous point in our literary history – not even twenty-five or thirty years ago – have there been so many women poets writing at such a consistently high level.'[9] These three anthologies feature most of the significant figures of the first generation of postwar women poets, many of them – Bellerby, Sitwell, Cornford, Daryush, H. D., Stevie Smith and Sylvia Townsend Warner – established before the war. *The Distaff Muse*, its editors anxious 'to scrape off some of the absurd associations [which] cluster like barnacles round the melodious word "feminine"', but inclined to overvalue the 'twinkle in the eye', partly explains why names such as Wrenne Jarman, Olga Katzin ('Sagittarius'), Helen Spalding, Helen Waddell, Margaret Willy and Ursula Wood (later Vaughan Williams) appear in later retrospectives.[10] Other names from this generation include Susan Miles (Ursula Roberts), Joan Barton and Sheila Wingfield.

Peschmann puts Edith Sitwell at the centre of 'a group of genuine poets diverse in temperament, outlook, technique and appeal' including Sackville-West, Anne Ridler, E. J. Scovell, Ruth Pitter and Kathleen Raine. Despite the absence of Stevie Smith, his list seems farsighted (Jennings's first collection appeared in 1953). Most commentators count Ridler, Raine, Scovell and Pitter as key figures of the period. Focusing on younger poets, Rexroth adds Lynette Roberts, Brenda Chamberlain and Denise Levertov among others. Besides the American Sylvia Plath – whose contribution to British poetry, although too powerful to be overlooked, takes effect only gradually after her death in 1963 – other names which start appearing in anthologies, periodicals and broadcasts are Anna Adams, Gerda Mayer, Anne Beresford, Patricia Beer, Molly Holden, Gladys Mary Coles, Phoebe Hesketh, Anne Cluysenaar, Jean Earle, Lotte Kramer, Maureen Duffy, Jenny Joseph, the Polish emigré Karen Gershon, Freda Downie, Elma Mitchell, Elizabeth Bartlett, Jean Overton Fuller, Rosemary Tonks and New Zealander Fleur Adcock. As the 1960s give way to the more politicised idiom of the 1970s, such names as Veronica Forrest-Thomson, Penelope Shuttle, Ruth Fainlight, Frances Horovitz, Nicki Jackowska, Judith Kazantzis, Michelene Wandor, Michèle Roberts, Sylvia Kantaris, Libby Houston, Jeni Couzyn, Gillian Allnutt, Alison Fell, Sheenagh Pugh, Sally Purcell, Geraldine Monk and Elaine Randell join those which dominate the last decades of the century: Anne Stevenson, Elaine Feinstein, U. A. Fanthorpe, Carol Rumens, Liz Lochhead, Wendy Mulford, Medbh McGuckian and Eiléan ní Chuilleanáin, Denise Riley, Gillian Clarke, Wendy Cope, Eavan Boland and Carol Ann Duffy. Some engage more actively than others with the difficulties of writing poetry as a woman, while growing interest in the looseness of identity and the construction of female selfhood is reflected in the use of masks and dialogue.

In 1959 Sylvia Townsend Warner observes of women as writers, 'we must bear in mind that we have not very much to go on, and that it is too early to assess what they may be capable of.'[11] By 1980 the capabilities of women poets are much clearer.

1946–55

In Britain the decade bridged the gulf between a receding prewar existence and the uncertainties which followed. In poetry these were years of quiet adjustment, when continuity, both formal and thematic, was only gradually prized less than change and challenge. Few women poets resumed the prewar struggle for critical recognition and status, or openly tackled traditional gender roles.

Ambivalence distinguishes this period from the affluent, optimistic later 1950s. Despite the programme of economic, political and social repairs proposed by Beveridge, rebuilding the nation's battered infrastructure proved slow and expensive, and ongoing rationing did not help the public mood. Scepticism became dissatisfaction, returning the conservatives to power in 1951. Domestic nervousness was framed on an international scale by frantic efforts to prevent another world war, but diplomatic manoeuvres could not ease the fears about the atom bomb, sharpened in Britain by the Korean conflict in 1950, and tensions over Eygpt and Suez, which hastened the emergence of the peace movement.

As many observers note, postwar social reforms disarmed feminism: rising numbers of female MPs, welfare state reforms and increased female employment opportunities helped to dissipate its energies. After the upheaval of war, too, conventional domestic life must have seemed deeply attractive: demobilisation was accompanied by a surge in marriage and soaring birth rates. Wider recognition of the housewife's workload brought rapid development of labour-saving gadgets, all conspiring in 'the broader theme of homemaking as a career'.[12] If the pomp of the coronation, witnessed by thousands on a rainy day in June 1953 and greeted as the dawning of a new 'Elizabethan Age', cheered the public, the accession of an iconic young Queen, a very visible working wife and mother of two children, failed to alter conservative attitudes to gender roles.

In terms of poetry, the decade has tended to be seen as a lull between what Howard Sergeant calls the 'wartime boom' of the early 1940s and the Revival which Eric Mottram dates from the 1960s.[13] It covered the eclipsing of neo-Romanticism, associated with Dylan Thomas, by Philip Larkin and what Anthony Hartley pronounced, in a review in the *Spectator* in 1954, 'the only considerable movement in English poetry since the Thirties'. Stylistically, a highly symbolic rhetoric gives way to the rigour, wit and irony of what duly becomes 'The Movement', Larkin at its centre.

For women, the transition was chiefly thematic, formal consistency suggesting determination to prove themselves technically in an unforgiving critical milieu.[14] The many writers of nostalgic wartime lyrics are gradually overshadowed by a smaller field of poets whose prosodic techniques are beyond reproach. Initially, poems hover between relief that war has ended and concern about the future. Rexroth notices that the probing of history, landscape, nation and selfhood becomes a general 'reorientation towards personal expression, and away from construction and political rhetoric . . .'; this perhaps registers female cultural alienation: as professionals from a society in pursuit of economic confidence, and as writers from rational language and critical discourse. Increasing spirituality inflects the personal focus which he also remarks: 'women have written about the things that matter, not about current delusions – lovers and husbands . . . babies, death, birth . . . all subjects frowned upon in earlier years'.[15]

Formally speaking, in the period preceding the arrival of Sylvia Plath in 1956, the gender-shy lyricism favoured by prewar writers such as Wellesley, Bowes Lyon, Cornford and Bellerby continued. A clutch of longer poems published soon after the war reveals how others joined the effort to reconceive historical, spiritual and moral landscapes. The book-length pastoral *The Garden* by Vita Sackville-West supports the theory that war prompts women to turn to history in order to imagine and face the future. Written in the manner and spirit of *The Land*, *The Garden* won the Heinemann Prize in 1946 but was never well reviewed; it marks the end of Sackville-West's poetry-writing career.[16] 'Daring to find a world in a lost world', the poem advises that collective recovery depends on retrieving an equilibrium revived in its neo-Augustan formality:

>   . . . The civil
> Ever opposed the rude, as centuries'
> Slow progress laboured forward, then the check,
> Then the slow uphill climb again, the slide
> Back to the pit, the climb out of the pit,
> Advance, relapse, advance, relapse, advance,
> Regular as the measure of a dance;[17]

Scarcely acknowledging the vagaries of its own moment, linking national wellbeing with private horticultural 'endeavour', *The Garden* idealises the interdependence of man and nature. It implies that only this ancient relationship can safeguard the future. Nigel Nicolson observes that 'a profounder commentary than *The Land*, [it] was her attempt to reconcile the known with the unknowable, probing ever deeper and never reaching the bottom of the well'.[18] Where Sackville-West discovers consolation in history, Edith Sitwell's *The Shadow of Cain* blames the past for recent wrongs. By the mid 1940s, Sitwell was enjoying a reputation as a literary impresario, critic and public personality which endured until her death in 1968. For Peschmann, in 1950, 'new certitude, courage and power' makes her the 'pre-eminent' woman poet of the period.[19] Written in 1946, after an eyewitness account appeared in a newspaper report about Hiroshima, and published the following year as the second of *Three Poems of the Atomic Age*, 'The Shadow' is an intensely spiritual work, tracing the ancient 'separation of brother and brother, of Cain and Abel, of nation and nation'. The city's destruction is figured apocalyptically:[20]

> ... there came a roar as if the Sun and
> Earth had come together –
> The Sun descending and the Earth ascending
> To take its place above ... the Primal Matter
> Was broken, the womb from which all life began.[21]

Sitwell contemplates a catastrophe foreshadowed by Abel's murder, finding hope only in the unrealised potential of the future.

Like Lynette Roberts and Anne Ridler, both of whom had long poems published by Faber in 1951, Sackville-West and Sitwell refrain from writing in an explicitly female voice. Written 1942–43, Roberts's *Gods with Stainless Ears* (a highly self-conscious 'Heroic Poem' dedicated to Sitwell) is a modernist epic of cultural protest; its charged recuperation of Welsh myth, history and language refracts the postwar preoccupation with lost or threatened identity. Ridler's fable of spiritual recovery, *The Golden Bird*, (reminiscent of *The Waste Land*) blends Arthurian romance, fairytale and a Morris-like Utopian socialism (the Bird's pursuer, youngest son of the court gardener, ends up in the suburbs where 'there is only one class/And one design for living'). In this playlike text, the voices are all male; the demure and dutiful 'Lady' whom the hero finally claims never speaks.

Other poets use war to contextualise gender. H. D.'s monumental wartime sequence only appeared as *Trilogy* in 1973, having been written and published separately as *The Walls Do Not Fall* (1944), *Tribute to the Angels* (1945) and *The Flowering of the Rod* (1945). In this work the articulate woman gradually asserts herself in a cultural matrix which, having been violated, is positively transformed by war. Set against a backdrop in which Christian and classical mythological narratives converse, in the closing section the 'unmaidenly' and subversively 'unpredictable' figure of Mary Magdalene contests the three biblical versions of womanhood in the Christian story of birth, death and resurrection. H. D. avoids triumphalism; a letter quoted by Georgina Taylor confirms: 'I had started making it a Victory poem but Victory is such a problem . . . I mean, there is the devastation everywhere. So I just thought the best thing was resurreuction [sic]–a rising out or above all the dreary waste and sorrow.'[22] In the light of the breakdown H. D. suffered at the end of the war, *Trilogy*'s slow centralisation of the woman poet seems reflexive; Taylor speculates that H. D. found in writing 'a way through the war, a means of survival . . . a healing vision for herself and others'.[23]

Once well respected, Sheila Wingfield is hardly known today. Her most significant work, *Beat Drum, Beat Heart*, written before the war but published in 1946, foregrounds gender.[24] The implicit contrasts of four apparently gendered sections dissolve in the apposing of the private, emotional, spiritual sphere (the 'heart') and its public, politically emblematic counterpart (the 'drum'), partly in the 'beating' which connotes both pleasure and anguish, excitement and dread. 'Men at War' waver between resignation and triumph; 'Men At Peace' are disheartened. 'Women in Love' answer by eliding love and conflict but 'Women in Peace' remain divided by wealth, class and differing experiences of motherhood. The equivocal mood is distilled in a female voice: 'Angel and beast in me are one: . . ./. . . Through me/All contraries of grief and joy are strung:/I am rage and mercy, impulse and slow patience,/Folly and wisdom . . .' The 'contraries' coalesce in the isolated and self-consciously 'crazy' figure of the woman poet:

> Aloof from others, I still speak for them
> And must fulfil them. Bending my ear to catch
> The oracle, at the same time it's I,
> Fume-crazy croaking sibyl, who predict it.[25]

The ambiguously realised, 'fume-crazy croaking' sibyl revises familiar anxieties about the role and function of the woman poet. Laden with self-deprecation, the image affirms the sibyl's inherently public powers, even as it distils the subjective 'I' which gives the oracle voice.

The English landscape and country life are vividly rendered by four of the period's chief poets: Pitter, Raine, Scovell and Ridler. The early 1950s found Pitter, the eldest, roughly halfway through her long writing life: her final collection appeared in 1987. While her popularity peaked during the war, there were later critical successes: *The Ermine* won the Heinemann Award in 1953 and, in 1955, she became the first woman to earn the Queen's Medal for Poetry. Pitter's prosody can seem dated but hers is a wry and edgy poetry. What Peschmann calls her 'deeply felt and exactly observed nature poetry' rarely occludes the human: she makes a witty but unsentimental diarist of rural life.[26] She has been read in a tradition of English poetry linked, via Hardy and Edward Thomas, with the Romantics. The fine bird sketches of *The Bridge* (1945) and portraiture of village life and customs recall John Clare, and at times William Blake. The title-poem in *The Ermine* comes closer to Robert Frost in its half-teasing simplicity:

> Royal he is. What makes him so?
> Why, that too is a thing I know:
>
> It is his blame, his black, his blot;
> The badge of kings, the sable spot.
>
> O subtle, royal Ermine, tell
> Me how to wear my black as well.[27]

These taut couplets obliquely utter the class-consciousness of the daughter of (her words) 'intelligent, idealistic' schoolteachers.[28] Moreover, 'The Ermine' hovers between the documentary and the visionary, pondering the uncertain relationship between the concrete, rational world, and the unknowable realms which frame it. Introducing Pitter's *Collected Poems*, Jennings notes her stated desire to 'express something of the secret meanings which haunt life and language . . . to find words for what seems inexpressible'.[29] In this Pitter finds affinity with Raine, Smith, Ridler, Scovell and Jennings herself. Some argue that the spirituality which frequently colours women's nature poetry confirms the return of poetic language to the private sphere, yet Isobel Armstrong argues that – as a branch of the 'ambiguous, alternating force' she terms 'the affective' – the language of spiritual quest allows women writers to signal and contest their alienation.[30]

Like Pitter, Kathleen Raine was acclaimed in the 1930s, before her first collection *Stone and Flower* appeared in 1943. A *Collected Poems* followed in 1956. Having begun writing while studying natural science, Raine's 'first poems were written . . . to impose some sort of order on the world in which I found myself, and to which I was socially ill-adjusted. Poetry was the straw at which I clutched, that fragile identity the only one I had.'[31] Assuming that, 'insofar as we are human, we are spiritual beings', the process of self-scrutiny led Raine into the neoplatonic studies for which she became renowned.[32] In the natural 'grammar' celebrated in 'Word

Made Flesh', the concrete and the visionary, the verifiable and the speculative, illumine and complicate each other:

> Grammar of five-fold rose and six-fold lily,
> Spiral of leaves upon a bough, helix of shells,
> Rotation of twining plants on axes of darkness and light,
>
> Instinctive wisdom of fish and lion and ram,
> Rhythm of generation in flagellate and fern,
> Flash of fin, beat of wing, heartbeat, beat of the dance,
>
> Hieroglyph in whose exact precision is defined
> Feather and insect-wing, refraction of multiple eyes,
> Eyes of the creatures, oh myriadfold vision of the world,
>
> Statement of mystery, how shall we name
> A spirit clothed in world, a world made man?[33]

Here, the scientist's precision mingles with the more hermetic, visionary instincts which would colour and were themselves informed by Raine's scholarly work on Blake and Yeats in later years, and inflected virtually everything that this rigorous, and in some quarters very influential, figure wrote.[34]

By the early 1950s, both Ridler and Scovell were established names. Married to an ecologist, whom she frequently accompanied on field trips, Scovell focuses on plant and animal life with a naturalist's attention, detailing plumage and foliage attentively. Her discovery of visual and aural resonance in park or garden, river bank or sea cliffs, is no less precise for the meditative conflation of cerebral and sensory which Scupham admires: 'That sense of the slight thing closing over its own mystery, the chancy bit of life which waits for interpretation.'[35] Scovell's friend Ridler is acutely aware of spiritual mystery, brought to silence in attempt after attempt to articulate the divine mysteries inscribed in land and seascapes, flora and fauna. In 'Bathing in the Windrush', language and water are likened for dividing opacity and clarity, potential from actual. The unsaid proves more resonant, as the dimly lustrous submerged limbs of the swimmers 'are like symbols, where half-seen/The meaning swims, and drawn to the surface, dies.'[36] More orthodox than Raine's, Ridler's spirituality is also bound up with the natural world; for John Williams, her 'very English religious experience [can be] firmly located in an English garden'.[37] However, both Ridler and Scovell address, more directly than Raine or Pitter, the personal, often domestic, female experience which underpins much postwar women's poetry.

For two of the most important postwar poets, the period was one of consolidation. For Stevie Smith, the publication of *Harold's Leap* (1950), containing such gems as 'The River God' and 'Do Take Muriel Out', anticipates the success of *Not Waving but Drowning* in 1957. In 1946 the Oxford-based Elizabeth Jennings began the English degree which brought her into contact with Larkin and, later, the other 'Movement' poets. Six poems were anthologized by Kingsley Amis in his 1949 edition of *Oxford Poetry* before a first collection, *Poems*, appeared in 1953. The period ended in acclaim: *A Way of Looking* won the Somerset Maugham Award in 1955. The material anthologised in Robert Conquest's *New Lines* (1956) comes from these first two books.

In *Poetry Today*, Jennings acknowledges a preoccupation with the dialectic of isolation and connection which recurs in women's poetry all century.[38] 'The Island' ponders the relationship between place and individual, and the conjunction of strange and familiar; in this self-sufficient place visitors become 'Seekers who are their own discovery'.[39] Formal discipline can help to contain the disruptive force of desire – sometimes sexual, sometimes not – which distinguishes human experience. In both 'The Climber' ('Every man/Tied to the rope constructs himself alone') and 'Fishermen' ('Learning themselves in this uncertainty'), individual endeavour is given shape by shared desire.[40] For Jennings, poetry is a valve: utterance requires an order of language which clarifies and validates the search for answers. While gender does not always signify, both 'The Climber' and 'Fishermen' are located outside the female – plainly domestic – experience. The fishermen's mutinous wives and the climbers' 'careful women/(Who watching children climbing into dreams/Go dispossessed at home)' are alike in their exclusion but, tied to the isolating imperatives of children and home, remain disconnected from each other. Sometimes, then, the impulse to find what she calls 'a way to lose the loneliness' reveals Jennings's empathetic sense of female isolation: her ideal community is often female, and many of her portraits are of women.

1956–70

This period introduces what Jonathon Green memorably describes as 'Years of revolt, years of carefree, sinless excess, of drugs, music, revolution and fucking in the streets, of Swinging London, of the ever-exciting tomorrow ... when to be young was not only very heaven but mandatory too.'[41] However, with the flashpoints of Suez, Cuba and Vietnam fuelling the civil rights and peace movements in the mid 1950s, the effects of what became a postwar culture of public protest only gradually animated women's poetry. Despite the politicisation of gender issues, sexism was rife, even in the apparently democratic counterculture. As the writer 'Miles' recalls, the underground magazine '*IT* was originally run on the classic sexist role divisions. That was the way Sue and I lived: I went to work and she stayed at home.' His wife echoes, 'as the only woman, my job was to make the tea and the sandwiches and whenever they were going to actually make decisions I was asked to go out of the room. And I did.'[42] Against this backdrop, alongside Smith, Jennings and Raine, writers such as Patricia Beer, Fleur Adcock, Anne Stevenson and, most notoriously now, Sylvia Plath provided an ambivalent base from which a number of their contemporaries launched the more politicised, if sometimes crudely wrought, poetry of the final decade of the period.

There were signs of change long before the emergence of Women's Liberation in 1970. An English translation of Simone de Beauvoir's *The Second Sex* appeared in 1961, while Hannah Gavron's *The Captive Wife* (1966) paralleled Betty Friedan's epoch-making study of American women's domestic life *The Feminine Mystique* (1963). Mary Stott, editor of the *Guardian*'s 'Mainly for Women' page from 1957 to 1972, remembers debating the page's label in the same year: 'Out of that ferment of ideas came, for example, the Pre-School Playgroups Association, the National Association for the Welfare of Children in Hospital, the Disablement Incomes Group, the National Council for the Single Woman and her Dependents, the Association for the Improvement of the Maternity Services and many others.'[43] Patricia Waugh detects in the appearance of Juliet Mitchell's 'The Longest Revolution' in *New Left Review* (1966) the roots of what convened in Oxford, in early 1970, as the Women's Liberation Movement.[44] Denise Riley concurs: 'I read *The Second Sex* and *A Room of One's Own* at the same age, and thought of myself as a feminist, although this had to remain a privately held conviction for several years more. In this spirit I joined the Abortion Law Reform Association while still at school; this was just before the passage of the 1967 Abortion Act.'[45] Yet Mitchell says her piece was 'written before there was a women's movement ... and before I was aware of feminist stirrings in the States following Friedan's work'.[46]

These years saw women benefit from the growth of little magazines and various small-press publishing initiatives, like the pamphlets produced by Howard Sergeant's *Outposts* from 1956 and Harry Chambers's Phoenix imprint, which begins in 1959; the influential Penguin *Modern Poets* series; and annual anthologies like P.E.N. *New Poems*. However, of the highbrow anthologies sparked by Conquest's *New Lines* (1956), neither *Mavericks* (edited by Howard Sergeant and Dannie Abse in 1957) nor Alvarez's *The New Poetry* (1962) feature any women. Edward Lucie-Smith and Philip Hobsbaum's answer to Alvarez, *A Group Anthology* (1963), includes three but only two – Adcock and Shirley Toulson – produced collections. Michael Horovitz's 1969 *Children of Albion* was ignored by a squabbling academy. The founder of the nationwide 'Live New Departures' performances, running from 1961, Horovitz undoubtedly strengthened links between poetry, popular culture and politics. The chaotic reading at the Albert Hall in 1965, featuring some forty poets and attended by an audience of more than seven thousand, led to other events such as the Poetry Society's three-week-long Poetry Gala at the Royal Festival Hall in early 1969. However, Horovitz's anti-establishment school was no less exclusive: even Libby Houston, one of the five women included in *Children of Albion* (beside Frances Horovitz, Carlyle Reedy, Anna Lovell and Tina Morris), and involved with Live New Departures, felt herself 'an oddity ... a woman; a poet'. Houston says, 'I thought of myself as a person and a poet; never as a woman poet, seldom as a woman.'[47] Such tensions colour the main all-women anthology of the period. Joan Murray Simpson, introducing *Without Adam: The Femina Anthology of Poetry* (1968) warns, 'these poems are not specifically feminine in outlook'. Interestingly, Stevie Smith is as irked by the book's overt gendering ('awkward, very awkward indeed') as by the foreword urging women 'to take heart and prove that they are poets notwithstanding the fact that the greatest poets are men'.[48]

Overall, the period links, by publication, prewar voices such as Cornford, who died just before the appearance of her final collection, *On A Calm Shore* (1960), Bellerby (who published collections in 1957 and 1970), H. D. (*Helen in Egypt* appeared in 1961), Warner and Pitter (1968) and Wingfield (1964), with Scovell, Ridler (whose *A Matter of Life and Death* won acclaim in 1959) and the indefatigable Raine. Names such as Margaret Willy, Erica Marx, Kathleen Nott, Elizabeth Bartlett (who started writing in 1942) and Elma Mitchell are also anthologised in mainstream annuals although their activity is neglected in the critical discourse. Reviewing 1957–60, Jennings, for example, claims: 'There never seem to be many good women poets at any given time.' As well as Cornford, Bellerby and H. D., Jennings herself overlooks Plath's *The Colossus* (1960), Smith's *Not Waving but Drowning* (1957) and Karen Gershon's *The Relentless Year,* included in Edwin Muir's trio *New Poets 1959*. She approves just two new poets: Patricia Beer for *The Loss of the Magyar* (1959) and Jenny Joseph for *The Unlooked-for Season* (1960).[49] Anthony Thwaite's survey of 1960–73 registers neither Plath's death in 1963, nor Sitwell's in 1964, ignoring the appearance of *Ariel* and Plath's *Collected Poems*, as well as the six works produced by Raine. He adds only Smith, Plath and Molly Holden to coverage of Ridler, Jennings and Beer (who produces collections in 1963 and 1967).[50]

Written in the early 1970s, Margaret Byers's survey of 'Recent Poetry by Women' is more comprehensive.[51] Although 'always disappointed to see how few women are included in anthologies', Byers does not herself provide exhaustive coverage. Beer (who has published three collections by 1970), Elaine Feinstein (two) and Fleur Adcock (who, having been educated in England during the war, emigrates to Britain in 1963, publishing collections in 1964 and 1967) are warmly approved. Holden is criticised for 'limited use of irony', along with Beresford, Couzyn and Houston. Horovitz (the first of whose four collections appeared in 1970) and Rosemary Tonks both command circumspect interest. All three surveys occlude a range of noteworthy poets including Phoebe Hesketh, Susanne Knowles, Brenda Chamberlain and Jean Overton Fuller. First collections from Eavan Boland and Anna Adams are also overlooked. None notes the continuing interchange between British and American poetry of which Plath remains the most obvious (if not very representative) example, and from which Feinstein and the English ex-patriate Denise Levertov, publishing in the United States throughout the period, and American émigrés Anne Stevenson and Ruth Fainlight, all benefited.

Overall, women poets gradually registered what Michael Woods interprets as a shared postwar 'dream of freedom: freedom from other people and from ethics'.[52] For many, the language and formality valued by the academy could not answer their increasing psychological and economic independence. While few wholly reject traditional models, the mining of personal, often female-centred experience intensifies the scrutiny of voice and identity. Although Beer's first three collections testify to the pull of the canon (Wordsworth, Gray, Donne, Drayton and Eliot are all references), poems such as 'Vampire', 'Witch', 'Beatrice-Joanna', 'Four Years After' and 'In A Country Museum' reflect or treat a female perspective.[53] For Beer, the retreat into history sometimes permits liberating self-transformation; she confides that she 'started by taking refuge in myth, . . . using it like a pair of sunglasses behind which to feel embarrassed, timid or angry without drawing attention to myself'.[54] By contrast, the mythic presences of Joseph's first collection, moving equably between male and female worlds, seem relaxed. In the diverse voices of 'Eurydice to Orpheus,' 'Danaë' and 'Persephone returns', Joseph weighs the reality of authentic experience and its construction in poetic language: '"Art" and "artificial" are words that to me are closely allied'.[55] Otherwise, the widely anthologised 'The lost continent' seems the best of a series of semi-Freudian dreamscapes in which language, place and (in this case plainly female) identity are subsumed: 'Sleeping deep like a child within the womb/The curled-up figure of the woman lies/And lost within that passive sea my words'.[56]

The seven collections of what might be called Jennings's 'middle period' converse with the essays in *Every Changing Shape: Mystical experience and the making of poems* (1961).[57] As the only woman in *New Lines*, Jennings found her association with the Movement 'positively unhelpful, because I tended to be grouped and criticised rather than be grouped and praised'.[58] In 1961, by now widely recognised as one of the leading poets of her generation, she registers a determination to 'ransack all the technical resources at [her] disposal' and extend her work 'beyond the purely personal either to examine ideas such as power and authority'.[59] This prepares for the abstracted mood of *A Sense of the World* (1958) and *Song for a Birth or a Death* (1961), in poems such as 'World I Have Not Made':

> I live in a world I have not created
> inward or outward. There is a sweetness
> in willing surrender: I trail my ideas
> behind great truths.[60]

The idealisation of a world 'I could inhabit freely' is balanced by the 'sweetness' of the 'willing' concession to 'great truths'. By the 1960s the trope of sacrifice, the universally patriotic wartime virtue reinforced for women in the postwar patriarchy of the 1950s home, was coming to validate the dissolving of independent female selfhood in the spiritual and domestic ideal, the loss of private identity in the public – or publicly determined – sphere. And yet, in an interesting sleight of hand, Jennings's voluntary self-surrender slyly reappropriates the authority which it appears to cede.

The thinking sensate self frequents Jennings's poems. In *A Sense of the World*, a powerful current of isolation, often prompted by the absence of a loved one, stems from failure ('Choices', 'In a Foreign City') or reluctance ('Her Garden') to connect with an uncomprehending world. 'At Noon' dejectedly weighs

> A world that has no need of me.
> The poems stride against the strain
> Of complex rhythms. Separately
> I lie and struggle to become
> More than a centre to this room.[61]

The complexity of selfhood underpins the six-part sequence 'The Clown', 'gay/And terrible at once' for his carnivalesque disruption of the relation of performer and audience, conflating actual and enacted tragedy. A sense of social and emotional isolation is confirmed in the disintegrating language of 'About These Things', which seems to hint at the onset of the psychological difficulties which Jennings's next collections chart.[62]

An entry in Sylvia Plath's diary, dated 1 April 1956, presciently glosses women's poetry of this period. As if foretelling her own influence on postwar poetry in general, particularly women's, Plath commands herself: 'Be stoic when necessary and write – you have seen a lot, felt deeply, and your problems are universal enough to be made meaningful – WRITE'.[63] Uncannily, she seems here to foresee the aesthetic potential of the 'problems' which if they prove tragically self-destructive in her own case, resonate elsewhere. Amid women's interest in health issues (Holden's courageous charting of the effects of multiple sclerosis springs to mind), perhaps because physical incapacitation recalls other forms of female disempowerment, a distinct strand of what might be called neurotic poetry emerges with surprising force in this period. Observing that both Plath and Sexton, two of the nine female poets she discusses, have killed themselves, the American critic Suzanne Juhasz contends that the 'peculiar tension' of the woman poet's position 'can lead to destruction as well as creation', and boldly links their 'madness and ultimate suicide . . . to the conflict and strain experienced in trying to be both woman and artist'.[64] John Brannigan suggests that 'tropes of breakdown, suicide, displacement, madness, dissolution and death [in women's fiction] . . . represent an important dispute with the cultural politics of consensus and consolidation'.[65]

Plath's early death echoes a note sounded by Smith, who attempted suicide in 1953, Bartlett, whose poem 'Neurosis' appears in P.E.N. *New Poems 1954*, and sometimes by Stevenson (who suffered a breakdown in the 1960s). In *Recoveries* (1964), *The Mind Has Mountains* (1966), *The Animals' Arrival* (1969) and *Lucidities* (1970), Jennings probes the bouts of psychological illness which periodically hospitalised her in the 1960s. They make her 1960 assertion that 'Poetry has become a gesture of defiance, a plea for order in a universe of confession and man-made chaos' seem poignant.[66] Jennings's nervous state seems to tell in her poems' formalities. In the shrunken world of *Recoveries*, childhood its central reference point, simple stanza-forms are regulated by painstaking rhyme schemes, lineation holding disorder at bay. A more confessional mode develops only slowly. In 'Still Life and Observer', what might be self-scrutiny is deflected on to the (male) observer 'whose gaze balances the objects'/. . ./(Himself almost a still life) … '.[67] *The Mind Has Mountains* is more female-centred and overtly disempowered; despite the clear colloquial idiom of gems such as 'A Depression' and 'One Flesh', Jennings's voice remains self-distancing. This is perhaps why, in the context of psychiatric treatment, dialogue proves generative (see 'The Interrogator', 'Lisa', 'Questions' and 'Suicides'). When inhibitions fall away with linguistic control, the effect is powerfully unsettling.

Various other poets also explore the debilitating effects of psychological illness, breakdown and depression in poetry, including some deft and sensitive individual studies of the effect of neurosis on identity and relationship from Hesketh ('She Knows Me Not') and the self-conscious, Clare-like lyrics of the little-known Scottish poet Olive Fraser, virtually unrecognised in her lifetime despite early prizes. Although neither publishes a main collection before the mid 1970s, the work of Freda Downie and Elma Mitchell also belongs here.

1971–80

Amid social and economic malaise, growing numbers of women poets emerged, fostering new alliances and rifts. Although what became known as feminist poetry was dismissed by an academy as hysterically partisan, in openly tackling sexuality, and taboos like lesbianism, abortion and the physical and emotional abuse of women, feminism helped to change what British women wrote poetry about, if not necessarily how it was written. However, political and literary differences between radical and liberal, formalist and experimentalist, proved as divisive among poets as in society at large; remaining silent about the social tensions of the moment, writers such as Raine, Pitter and Jennings arguably protested their discomfort at the summoning of the personal in the name of the political. This does not seem, in retrospect, to have affected them adversely; nor, however, can it be said to have been much of a benefit.

In retrospect, the death of Stevie Smith in 1971 seems a touchstone. The establishment's faintly mystified affection for Smith colours Beer's tribute in *The Estuary*:

> A heroine is someone who does what you cannot do
> For yourself and so is this poet. She discovered
> Marvels: a cat that sings, a corpse that comes in
> Out of the rain. She struck compassion
> In strange places …[68]

For Jeni Couzyn, by contrast, Smith emphatically offers personal and professional inspiration:

whenever I doubt my own identity as a poet and as a human being, I am able to find in her work, in all its nakedness and pain, the humour and courage that reaffirms for me the validity of poetry. Although in a sense she is dead, Stevie Smith is for me the most accurate, relevant and poignant woman alive.[69]

Weighing strangeness against the validation of poetic identity, these tributes mark out two loose groupings, one conservative, the other more radical, which develop over this decade. Like many leading critics, Beer elevates Smith partly for peculiarity, implicitly amused by the ambiguities of her idiom. For the younger, more feminist, more partisan Couzyn, who illustrated her own work with whimsical Smith-like sketches, there seems nothing ambiguous about so 'relevant and poignant' a presence.

Unexamined tensions between established poets like Jennings, Raine and Beer, and younger writers (often associated with the rise of feminism) like Couzyn reflect those between the poetic mainstream and the margins. This mirrors the divisions between establishment-funded enterprises like the Poetry Society and self-funded small presses and little magazines. Jennings or Beer tend to complain about a changing cultural environment obliquely, whereas newer voices engage head-on with the threat of nuclear war, gender inequality, civil rights, and altering paradigms of sexual identity and behaviour.[70] After the marches and demonstrations of the 1950s and 1960s, freedom – of opportunity and language, in public and personal life – becomes the refrain of protest. Peace activist Pat Arrowsmith, repeatedly imprisoned for campaigns ranging from the Liverpool Dockers to the Cambodian War, insists (from Holloway prison) in 1974 that, 'freedom isn't in the heart or head:/It's in the deed, the choosing.'[71]

With poetry enjoying increasing cultural space, partly through radio and television, middlebrow annuals like P.E.N. *New Poems* and the Arts Council's *New Poetry* series helped to render women's poetry more visible, along with feminist publishers like Virago (founded in 1973), Onlywomen Press (1976–77), the more internationalist Women's Press (1978) and Sheba (1979–80), although experimental writers were forced to rely on small specialist presses. In addition to initiatives like the Cambridge Poetry Festival, review pages in mainstream and niche publications multiplied (*Time Out*'s poetry column was started by Wandor in 1971; *Spare Rib* first appeared in 1972). For formal, thematic and political reasons, poets appearing in self-published journals, or in the pamphlets and anthologies produced by feminist presses, sit uneasily beside more 'literary' names, yet Wendy Mulford, Denise Riley, Alison Fell, Michèle Roberts, Judith Kazantzis, Gillian Allnutt, Jeni Couzyn and Liz Lochhead all unsettle assumptions about feminist writing.

The decade which witnessed revived interest in Daryush, whose *Collected Poems* (1976) appeared the year before her death, was quietly productive for Wingfield, Pitter, Ridler, and Jennings, who published some five volumes each, while Tonks and Scovell fell silent. Hesketh and the increasingly woman-centred Beresford produced three collections, Raine four. *The State of Poetry Today*, a survey sponsored by *New Poetry* magazine in 1978, reveals that of the six women among 194 contenders for the best five living poets named by its readers, Raine outstripped Jennings, coming ninth of fifteen poets mentioned twenty times or more.[72] This confirms the visibility and status of both poets among informed readers. The survey reflects little awareness of the activities of other women. Arrowsmith, Downie, Kantaris, Kazantzis, Bartlett, Earle and McGuckian all produced first collections, while works from Boland, Shuttle, Adams, Joseph, Holden, Mitchell and Horovitz were greeted warmly.

From the academy's perspective, the success of *The Estuary* (1971), followed by *Driving West* (1975) and *Poems* (1979), make this Beer's decade: she edits and reviews energetically. Though just as productive, Beresford, Fainlight, Feinstein, Couzyn, Forrest-Thomson, Adcock and Stevenson enjoy less attention. Important newer names include the Irish Eiléan ní Chuilleanáin (1972, 1975 and 1977), Liz Lochhead (1972), Carol Rumens (1973), U. A. Fanthorpe (1978), Gillian Clarke (1978), Jean Earle and Sheenagh Pugh, while writers such as Carlyle Reedy, Mulford, Riley, Elaine Randell, Glenda George and Geraldine Monk contribute to Mottram's 'British Poetry Revival'. Black poets such as Valerie Bloom and Grace Nichols (who arrived in the UK in 1977) have yet to make their particular voices heard.[73]

Amid patchy critical coverage, a steady flow of all-women anthologies, starting with Trevor Kneale's modestly eclectic *Contemporary Women Poets* (1975) and gathering pace with feminist volumes, like Lilian Mohin's *One Foot on the Mountain* (1979), helped to sharpen debates about separatist publishing.[74] Traditionalists like Beer argue that 'to single women out as a race apart does not really do them a service'.[75] In 1974, insisting 'that women can be poets in the fullest sense: they have proved that they can', Adcock accepts that 'we are not after all trying to pretend that we are not women', but remarks: 'The problem is less that of writer as woman than that of writer as social being with conflicting responsibilities – which, unlike the status of women, cannot be expected to alter much.'[76] Mohin is left urging that 'Feminists ... must continuously see and say that what the world/men has declared invisible or invalid is real and important ... our poems have force because they run counter to prevailing views and because we know they do.'[77]

Despite an absence of poetic consensus, women merge socio-political discussion with 'personal matters of birth and bereavement, childhood and topography, love, domestic living and old age', as Alan Brownjohn and Maureen Duffy note in 1977.[78] With Levertov by now an international figurehead of the peace movement, the protesting mode of her *To Stay Alive* (1971), *Footprints* (1972) and *The Freeing of the Dust* (1975) reflected the growth of antinuclear feeling; meanwhile Levertov, Feinstein, Gershon, Kramer, Fainlight and Rumens begin to offer a strand of Jewish female poetics contributing to the general investigation of women's cultural place. As anxieties about class, race and social inequities feed into dissatisfaction with the treatment of women by society at large, this restiveness is articulated in the recourse to myth and other transforming narratives, in a reasonably broad reflection of the decentring of subjectivity. Besides emblematic figures of subversive female power, like witches, priestesses and other female performers, deities or classical characters like Penelope, Persephone and Eurydice are favourite ways of signalling the potential of the female imagination.

In this context, 'senior' poets like Raine and Jennings remain gender-evasive. With Raine continuing to refine her antimaterialist, Symbolist leanings, after the self-exposure of the previous decade, Jennings's becomes a highly deflective poetry. In spiritual but still uncertain mood, a succession of sonnets dealing with love, faith and a sense of loss rarely confronted directly, are varied chiefly by self-effacing tributes to other writers, painters and musicians. Beer is more engaged than Jennings, but despite the toughness noted by Wes Magee escapes the pressures of the present through the historical.[79] Even so, Beer's edition of P.E.N. *New Poems 1975* incorporates discussions of race, class, Northern Ireland and prison; while *New Poetry 2* (edited with Kevin Crossley-Holland in 1976) includes Valerie Sinason's streetwise accounts of ethnic tensions and youthful social deprivation.[80] The feminist agenda increasingly pervades the annual anthologies, while studies of female role models (Gillian Allnutt's 'East Anglian Progenitor' and Medbh McGuckian's 'Aunts' in *New Poetry 5*) and domesticity are frequent.[81]

The influence of place on the imagination, identity and self-perception interests women amid post-Freudian awareness of the multiplicity of subjectivity. For Feinstein, landscape often frames the transfiguring effect of art on personal reality. Elected in 1980 as Fellow of the Royal Society of Literature, Feinstein produced three major collections during this period. Influenced by the 'open form' poetry of Charles Olson's 'PRO-jective Verse', for Feinstein the poetic construct itself transforms experience, wherever it is lived out: in a Leicester air-raid shelter or a car parked above Jerusalem.[82] An idiom which is neither gender-shy nor explicitly feminist democratically insists that 'every day/we rise new creatures'.[83]

Expatriate Adcock views her 'cultural displacement' with equanimity: 'It is no bad thing to be an outsider, if one wants to see places and events clearly enough to write about them.'[84] Her self-distancing idiom is under-pinned by her rediscovery of the country and people she knew first as a child; in the Lake District poems published as *Below Loughrigg* (1979), selfhood coheres, paradoxically, in the liminal and in between:

> . . . . I am the track to the top
> skirting and scaling rocks. I am the cairn.
>
> Here on the brow of the world I stop,
> set my stone face to the wind, and turn
> to each wide quarter. I am that I am.[85]

Adcock is less interested in the complexities of a multiple, fragmenting subject than some of her peers. A fractured lyric 'I' links the low-key, philosophical romantic impulse of Joseph and the young Clarke with the poems Elizabeth Bartlett belatedly collects in her first collection, *A Lifetime of Dying* (1979). Bartlett says that her own psychoanalysis sparked her humane, uncompromising if not obviously radical poetry: 'I am drawn to people with maimed personalities because I know I am one myself'.[86] Bartlett's perceptive example connects with a spectrum of woman-centred writing ranging from Mitchell's acerbic tones (widely noticed in 'Thoughts After Ruskin'), through the fluid symbolism favoured by Shuttle and Jackowska, to the work of feminists like Couzyn and Kazantzis. In Mitchell's 'The Knitter in Bed 14', 'womanly webwork' traps the knitter in the 'heartless repetitions' of the pattern, 'chain-mail against the escape of ideas'. Of the 'Seven persons . . ./Sex, female; ages, various' listed in 'Census Return', only the young have any agency; the self-absorbed adults seem unaware that all 'have been, all the time, the same one'.[87] This resonates with the 'imminence' of Couzyn's pluralistic self-construction, as 'a wide house/a commune/of bickering women'.[88]

Gaining two awards in the period, Shuttle wins interest for mapping the creative dreamworld of the female psyche against the biological imperatives of sexual function in an intensely personal way. Writing candidly about menstruation, pregnancy and maternity, she explores the fluidity of gender difference and the interdependence of male-female relations, turning sexual difference into 'dialogue'.[89] Almost all the poets discussed here make use of myth, ancient history, fairytale and folklore; as Shuttle says, 'Poems remind us of the transformative possibilities of our lives'.[90] From the modern myths of advertising, television and cinema in Feinstein's work to Wandor's summoning of Lilith, in dances, ballad, songs and even incantations, women poets, self-consciously witchlike (Beer, Shuttle, Roberts and Boland), possess themselves of subversive powers. In the sequences 'The Spell' and 'The Dance', Couzyn directs the instinctive knowledge of Jean Earle's 'The Healing Woman – Of Her Gift' to decisive ends.[91] Where Lochhead offers fairytales of the Grimm Sisters and Kazantzis's *The Wicked Queen* (1980) reworks the classical stories of Leda, Circe, Penelope, Clytemnestra and Electra, Jackowska's *Incubus* (1981) turns to diabolism, its epigraph warning, 'The only way to disarm the devil is to mate with him'.[92]

Such reworkings are not exclusively feminist; Lochhead explains hers as 'just tales told from one woman's point of view'.[93] Yet they push the figure of the woman poet centre-stage, perhaps most powerfully in Stevenson's epistolary sequence *Correspondences* and Fainlight's 1980 work *Sibyls and Others*.[94] Framed by *Travelling Behind Glass* (1974), and *Enough of Green* (1977), the three-part *Correspondences* blends female history and culture through the nuanced transatlantic exchanges of several generations of one family. The tensions and power relations between different correspondents (stern husband or father to loyal or errant wife or daughter, or sister to sister) span geographical and generational distances, contrasts and parallels emerging between different voices. Since the 'dialogue' between addressor and addressee corresponds with that of poet and reader, we are complicit in the difficult process of voicing women's experience, whether this is enabling (as for Kay Boyd, the poet whose mother's death in the Vermont town of Clearfield opens the work) or disempowering (as for her maternal ancestor, Abigail Chandler). Stevenson remains an equivocal presence behind a work which contests its own authenticity; at once Muse and Scribe, she manages reflexively both to celebrate and call into question her own compromised powers of utterance.[95]

Fainlight uses the suggestively manifold figure of the Sibyl to signify the reach of the legendary priestess-seer, mythologised across the globe, and the difficult legacy of the powers for which she is both feared and venerated. As the poems emphasise, the sibylline gift empowers and disables: it gains the oracle status and respect only on male terms, and at the expense of youth, beauty and freedom. Sometimes Fainlight seems to envy the simplicities of the sibyl's existence, 'no longer forced to make/a choice between two worlds'.[96] Other poems stress the sense of predicament while hinting that those powers are not, after all, wholly compromised. Leaving the impression of exploiting an ambiguous role to the full, Fainlight's sibyls show that the only authority they can wield on their own terms is subversive. Ironically, they escape a preordained, formulaic and overdetermined existence by taking refuge in its rule-bound unrealities. In *The Region's Violence* (1973), a woman who daubs her body with paint is 'released by this disguise/From everything . . .'; elsewhere, another voice insists:

> I escape through speech:
> Which has no dimensions,
> Demands no local habitation
> Or allegiance, which sets me free
> From whomsoever's definition:
> Jew. Woman. Poet.[97]

SUMMARY

The survivors of a productive prewar generation, figures such as Raine, Pitter, Ridler, Scovell and Jennings remain quietly authoritative throughout the period; unlike growing numbers of younger poets, they mostly skirt topical literary, political and cultural debates. In general, the poetry discovers the postwar woman positioned equivocally between public and private spheres. The impinging of the gendered exterior world on female experience and imagination is countered by the examinations of female subjectivity which register the enfranchising force of poetic utterance politically, spiritually and/or aesthetically. Amid ideological debates and artistic controversy, perhaps the most exciting evidence of women poets' refusing of the cultural status quo lies in the lyric experiments being practised out of sight of the mainstream.

Despite an apparent movement away from the individuality of the early postwar years towards the self-aware sense of community encouraged by feminists, there is too much diversity to make for tidying generalisations of the sort that prevail in readings of postwar British women's poetry. In the years since her death, the critical establishment seems to have satisfied itself that Plath's provocative, highly coloured poetics can stand for postwar

British women's poetry in general. However, if her visibility, aided by the potent theatre of her biography, has made her influential among younger readers (some of them poets), the extent of Plath's impact on the leading names of her own generation is certainly debatable. Moreover, it might be argued that the Plath 'circus' has deflected attention from other equally deserving names, while helping to mythologise various unhelpful assumptions about the tormented, 'unstable' figure of the woman poet to damaging effect. This is partly why we centralise the more understated but deeply equivocal figure of Stevie Smith. Smith's literally inimitable example distils most of the chief characteristics and concerns of women's postwar poetic practice; from the farsightedly duplicitous language use and ironic refashioning of formal tradition, to the range and wit of a thematic palette often slyly manipulating the personal for political ends. When Smith, frequently read as an outsider, is positioned in a female history of the poetic century, her work illuminates a series of perspectives common among her peers, not least in questioning and destabilising the hegemony of modernism. In its detailed portrait of Smith's mediation between oral and literary registers, Chapter 5 figures the enlivening conversation between form, voice and theme which marks the period.

The remainder of the chapters examine this from various angles. As society at large wrestles with the changing expectations of women busily overhauling their cultural status, Chapter 6 finds a broad cross-section of poets inscribing the ambivalence with which they experience the conflicted but generative space of the home, intimately associated with the bearing and raising of children. In contrast, Chapter 7 examines the collaborative impulse and initiatives of a band of openly activist writers, whose poetry controversially enacts the interpenetration of 'personal' and 'political' for radical ideological ends. Showcasing the oeuvres of Virginia Forrest-Thomson, Wendy Mulford and Denise Riley, Chapter 8 explores the self-conscious determination of a well-established female neo-avant-garde to resolve the problematic, even contradictory, conjunction of lyric expression and late modernist poetic experiment.

CHAPTER 5

Stevie Smith

Stevie Smith (1902–1971) is a pivotal figure in the century's female poetry. Her publications span the three historical phases of this *History*, starting with *A Good Time Was Had By All* (1937) – and many of these poems had been written during the previous ten years – to the present. However, the nature of her largely posthumous fame continues to be elusive. Although any attempt to pin down a technical, cultural or gendered specificity is unsatisfactory, taken as a whole her work exemplifies the diverse ways in which women poets before and after her negotiated with British literary traditions. Her multivocal dramatisations go further than her predecessors and anticipate the energetic dialogism which is widespread at the end of the century. Her orientation towards democracy is a postwar period feature but accords with women's empathy with social marginality throughout the century. Like all literary women, she is antisentimental but revalidates personal emotion as an artistic source. Autobiography and fantasy are one of the many oppositions which she conflates, often through the dramatic monologue. Unlike the universalising and static persona of orthodox lyricism, her dramatisations recognise and displace the social luggage of linguistic expression and interaction. She subverts and disempowers the syntax and symbolism of respectable discourses, from the ancient to the journalistic. We see her reworking of cultural myths, ranging from classical tragedies and legends to popular fairytales, as a longstanding and continuing strategy of women writers which exposes and invigorates outworn and self-fulfilling stereotyping. Although unstitching familiar linguistic and literary tapestries, she retains language's representational function. This holding together of the experimental and expressive is one strong strand of female writing, which historically can be stretched from interwar modernist movements through to postmodernism and its aftermath of alternative realism.

Since her uncompromising individuality made it difficult for Smith[1] to get published, the coincidence of composition and publication is more than usually erratic. After her first three collections (1937, 1938, 1942), she struggled to get her poems in journals, let alone in book form, until *Harold's Leap* (1950). This was followed by another vacuum before *Not Waving but Drowning* (1957), although there were always plenty of poems. The positive reception to *Selected Poems* (1962) helped her most successful period and her final collections, *The Frog Prince* (1966) and *Scorpion and Other Poems* (1972), can be considered the most untethered in terms of literary conformity. The 1980s brought fresh editions (*Uncollected Writings*, 1981; *A Selection*, ed. Hermione Lee, 1983), critical biographies (Barbera/McBrien, eds., 1985; Spalding 1988) and some serious articles. In 1993 Linda France took Smith as the launchpad for new generations in her anthology of sixty contemporary women poets.

Her defiance of conventional literary classifications cost Smith proper critical acclaim. In 1966 George Hartley, editor of a new *Selected Poems* and for whom she was 'almost unclassifiable', observed, 'I am not aware that Stevie Smith's poems have ever received serious critical assessment though recently I have seen signs that this may not be far off.'[2] To some extent she can be positioned around contemporary trends but typically crosses boundaries. Her strong impulse for social equality and the conversational lyrics – what Auden coined 'memorable speech' – align her with the 1930s. The inclusivity of her narrative verse, ballads, children's tunes, folk songs and hymns also fit with the return to more oral and communal traditions in the 1930s which continued into the 1940s. The interplay of voices which construct shifting levels of consciousness negotiate between the modernist psychologising of human character and the postwar neo-Romantic return to a fixed lyric personality, albeit unheroic. At times her self-conscious commentary, her addresses to the reader and her absurdist manipulations of habitual meaning-making apparatus anticipate the metalinguistics of postmodern play.

Ultimately, the pulse of her writing presses upon the borders of definable poetics. Her comment, 'There is no very great distinction between what is poetry and what is prose', indicates her irreverence for strict delineations on which the fundamental origins and assumptions of genre rely.[3] The visual sketches, which only obliquely match particular poems, add a third dimension to a simple poetry/prose binary; their ambiguity and suggestiveness produce further indeterminacy, not just about the single poem but about the very processes of determining meaning. The personalised creatures in her light-hearted sketchbook *Some are More Human than Others* (1958) confront assumptions about the linear evolution of human civilisation from the animal kingdom. Emptying binary logic of its

signifying power frees up the referents for fresh constructions of consciousness. As Martin Pumphrey (1986) puts it in his probing analysis: 'To single
out as important simply those poems that can be read most easily as
"serious literature" is to evade the critical challenge of Smith's full poetic
performance.'⁴ One fundamental polarity which she unfixes is the lit-
erary/oral in favour of a stage/page conjunction associated with theatre
and performance poetry. By removing ready differentiation between
spoken and written English, she flattens social hierarchies which
are demarcated by regional and class variations of accent and dialect.
Furthermore, she pushes the boundary of linguistic and nonverbal
constructions through her drawings, her recourse to paintings, her
musicality and her aural renditions of actions or moods, such as 'yippity
yap', 'pad pad' or 'bog is dood'; these also blur the line between adults
and children or people and animals. In her highly conscious choice and
rejection of speech registers, this poet continually scrutinises the contingency
between language, the instrument of socialisation, and what it feels like to be
human.

Read in conjunction with her letters, essays or novels, Smith's poems
often refract the human significance of current affairs, such as suburban
development, the hydrogen bomb, colonialism, or the removal of the
death sentence. 'Valuable', composed after 'reading two paragraphs in a
newspaper', confronts the low self-esteem in the girls who 'cheapen'
themselves in conceiving illegitimate babies.⁵ Here, as often, she scrutinises the psychological processes of power-play in the abusers as well as
their victims. 'Angel Boley', based on the 1966 Myra Hindley child
murder case, typically mimics and unsettles the range of available
narratives about its horror. These explorations of unvoiced, unseen and
often unrealised impulses potently confront readers with their own. The
narrative condensation of Smith's best-known 'Not Waving but Drowning'
is a satisfactory emblem of her attention to undisclosed emotional undertow which is also a recurring ensign of women's poems. The onlookers
(who include poet and reader) and the sinking subject are all implicated in
the states of both watching and being 'too far out'. Where we position
ourselves determines our sense of being either part of the crowd – 'they
said' – or the outsider – 'oh no no no!'. This dialogic is central to how the
poetry dislodges certainty and invites as many connections as readers. Yet
Smith confessed to the personal origin of the piece: '"I felt too low for
words (eh??) last weekend but worked it all off in a poem . . . called 'Not
Waving but Drowning'".'⁶ The figurative and elliptical '(eh??)' evokes
unsayable feelings.

Rescuing emotion from the bin of denigrated 'sentimentality' is one of Smith's major achievements:

> Full well I know the flinty heart
> That beats beneath these gentle airs
> That asks the people to her hearth
> But for a writer's cares
> That asks them from below above
> But only to observe, not love.
>
> Then also as a writer she must fail
> Since art without compassion don't avail?[7]

Her use of the female pronoun in the penultimate line is unobtrusive but remarkable. The scarcity of punctuation and the mix of regular, irregular and half-rhyme along with the question mark, oddly superfluous here, are among her frequent devices and arguably typical of a renovated 'feminine' language. The switch from first to third person both synthesises and distances the poet and the subject.

The provocation of feeling which is the pleasure and power of lyrical poetry had been pejoratively feminised by modernism's reaction against excessive Victorian sentimentality. In *Over the Frontier*, Smith challenges the dismissive essentialising of feminine emotionalism:

> Even manly hearts may swell
> At the moment of farewell . . .

How true the poet's sentiment, benign, how *noble*. And if the manly heart, what of the heart feminine, may not that swell and fail and tear and burst for the sadness of a mismanaged love-situation, that is so much the situation between my departed Freddy and myself.[8]

Freddy is her fictional name for an ex-fiancé, Eric Armitage; the broken engagement, due partly to her aversion to the prospective confines of suburban conventionality and partly to her problem with an 'à deux' model of sex relations, provoked the troubled poem 'Freddy': 'Nobody knows what I feel about Freddy/I cannot make anyone understand.'[9] Difficulty with male intimacy is easily attributable to her rage against her 'absconding and very absent pa'[10] and to the lack of any other close male family relations. 'The heart had gone out of us' is a recurring sentiment and the continually voiced deathwish in her tragedies of loss, loneliness and longing knit together a huge untidy oeuvre: 'Poor human race that must feed/on pain'.[11] For Smith, the human heart is, of course, made of interdependent opposing tendencies: 'I think a human being is a complex organism. Human beings are not consistent, are they? I think that they are consistently what they are. They can be consistently inconsistent. But people are such a mixture of different qualities. You can have such good and bad qualities in the same person.'[12] Her pastiche and parody of literary diction, coupled with prosaic commentary, investigate how much the complexity of human beings is down to the variety of languages which constitute them. Her strategic interplay of voices matches M. M. Bakhtin's observation that language is never neutral but comes from 'other people's mouths, in other people's contexts, serving other people's intentions'.[13] She exploits the power of parody to seize the authority of centralising discourses which erode all other voices. Thus her poetry 'talks back' against social hegemony. The application of Bakhtin's ideas on textual politics to Smith's poetry may be hardening into some kind of orthodoxy but they do provide a sufficiently flexible terminology for her multivocality.

Smith foregrounds the intrinsically dialogic nature of writing, that is, the artistic organisation of diverse speech types. The speakers may be placed in opposition or parallel to each other but they always refer to an ideologically laden dominant discourse, drawing attention to how minority voices are silenced.[14] 'Childe Rolandine' articulates the heartfelt cry against injustice which is missing from canonical poets:

> But then she sang, Ah why not? tell all, speak, speak,
> Silence is vanity, speak for the whole truth's sake.
>
> And rising she took the bugle and put it to her lips, crying:
> There is a spirit feeds on our tears, I give him mine,
> Mighty human feelings are his food
> Passion and grief and joy his flesh and blood[15]

The secretary typist bored with her job is a thin gloss of the poet's actual routine work at Newnes publishers. The feminising of Robert Browning's 'Childe Rolande' may suggest that women are more constrained than men by the tacit injunction against defying cultural codes. Like the tears, the bugle's note is nonverbal. Smith's poems sometimes invoke an audience within the text, as in the Browningesque dramatic monologue, but more often the frequent questions, as in the above 'why not?', make demands on the reader. The heightened dynamic between writer, speaker and reader conforms to what Bakhtin terms 'literary-verbal performance' and fore-grounds how 'every word is directed toward an answer and cannot escape the profound influence of the answering word that it anticipates'.[16]

In lifting the barricade between writer and reader, a device exaggerated in her novels, they share authorial power: 'Read on, Reader, read on and work it out for yourself.'[17] Knowledge is thus empirical not absolute. She goes as far as is possible to remove the deadening barrier of print from the greater authenticity of talk, as she declared in *Novel on Yellow Paper*: 'The talking voice that runs on, and the thoughts come, the way I said, and the people come too, and come and go, to illustrate the thoughts, to point the moral, to adorn the tale./Oh talking voice that is so sweet, how hold you alive in captivity, how point you with commas, semi-colons, dashes, pauses and paragraphs?'.[18] Accordingly, avoidance of the demands of literary standardisation is Smith's hallmark. We see again and again two parallel narratives, the spoken and the unsaid, representing acceptably prescribed speech in tension with censored sensations and thoughts. The conversational idioms deflate high literary diction and open up the unconscious processes of socialisation.

The concomitant voices in her poetry pave new pathways of antidualistic conceptualisation which avoids the endless war for supremacy between genders and other polarised groups. 'The Word' both enforces and defies the high modernist dismissal of Romantic emotional spontaneity:

> My heart leaps up with streams of joy,
> My lips tell of drouth;
> Why should my heart be full of joy
> And not my mouth?
>
> I fear the Word, to speak or write it down,
> I fear all that is brought to birth and born;
> This fear has turned my joy into a frown.[19]

Directly alluding to William Wordsworth's lyric, Smith here retains the expressive function of poetry but undercuts the notion of untransformed spontaneous feeling. She contemporises Wordsworth's ambition to speak in 'the language of men' but dispenses with the poet's supposedly superior insight. While raising the status of oral speech, the whole poem forces awareness that some diminishing mutation happens when speech is fixed by writing.

In 'The Word', the exaggeration of the personal pronoun ('My'/'I') through repetition both asserts and parodies the personal centre of the poem. The confiding rhetoric combines the intimate with the proclamatory and removes the misleading distinction between private and public which has been invoked to relegate women's lyrics to the attic of literary activity. The distinction between autobiography and imagination is another central binary which women's female monologues particularly complicate. Self-deprecating about the narrowness of her social territory,

Smith defends the personal origin of her reading and relationships: 'You will say: But your poems are all story poems, you keep yourself hidden. Yes. But all the same, my whole life is in these poems . . . everything I have lived through, and done, and seen, and read and imagined and thought and argued. Then why do I turn them all upon other people, imaginary people, the people I create? It is because . . . it gives proportion and eases the pressure, puts the feelings at one remove.'[20] In her novels, interviews and correspondence, Smith freely referred to the lived circumstances of her writing, such as 'The Deserter' about her ill-health, or 'The Stroke' in response to her aunt's fatal affliction, or the recurring invitations to death.[21] Self-confessedly direct reworkings of her past inform 'A House of Mercy' in which the poet is both narrator – 'It was a house of female habitation' – and the central character:

> I was the younger of the feeble babes
> And when I was a child my mother died
> And later Great Aunt Martha Hearn Clode died
> And later still my sister went away.
>
> Now I am old I tend my mother's sister
> The noble aunt who so long tended us,
> Faithful and True her name is. Tranquil.
> Also sardonic. And I tend the house.[22]

The childlike aggregative 'and' accentuates the ever-present past which the dramatic monologue potently reconstructs.

Smith's monologues are markedly twentieth-century in her investigation of unvoiced imperatives which accord with the Freudian concept of repression and the concealed unconscious. 'I Rode with My Darling' reverberates with the unspeakable losses of her mother, sister and aunt along with the illusory 'darling'.[23] The frequent riding and other travelling metaphors denote journeys into the unknown or towards alternative psychological states. They also interrogate nineteenth-century realist 'cradle-to-the grave novels that never let you out under three volumes'. Whereas the child comes good in these novels, in Smith's poems the complex perpetuation of the child-in-the-adult is dramatised and denoted through childlike phrases. In 'To Carry the Child' the entire debate about the debilitating force of unresolved childhood conflict is presented conversationally to an undefined audience.[24] Arguably, the lack of a father's ruling presence freed Smith from the chains of patriarchal language.

Like 'Childe Rolandine', 'Deeply Morbid' indirectly promotes the normality of women in the workplace while exposing the humdrum nature of their occupations. In the harrowing story of Joan, the faceless office girl who goes missing, the figures in the drama, including the narrator, are interdependent through the merging of their commentaries. Thus Smith implies the power dynamic of dialogic interdependence – Joan against a corporate office culture:

> Deeply morbid deeply morbid was the girl who typed the letters
> Always out of office hours running with her social betters
> But when daylight and the darkness of the office closed about her
> Not for those ah not for this her office colleagues came to doubt her
> It was that look within her eye
> Why did it always seem to say goodbye?[25]

The rhetorical question involves the reader as an addressee. Joan's numbed brain (implicitly resulting from tediously routine work as well as from loneliness) is seized by a Turner painting in the National Gallery where the visual canvases succeed in awakening her senses, which verbal intercourse had killed. Notably, social aspiration – endemic in the suburban culture which so alienated Smith – is soul-destroying. For the office girl, the mediators of cultural norms shape self-apprehension but strangle self-realisation. As Bakhtin observed in novels, this poem dramatises how voices in conflicting, consensual or competitive dialogue mirror the dynamics of self-in-relation:

For any individual consciousness living in it, language is not an abstract system of normative forms but rather a concrete heteroglot conception of the world. All words have the 'taste' of a profession, a genre, a tendency, a party, a particular work, a particular person, a generation, an age group, the day and hour. Each word tastes of the context and contexts in which it has lived its socially charged life; all words and forms are populated by intentions.[26]

Smith's poems scrutinise the rhetoric of Religion, Education, Science, Patriotism and Law. Her famously eclectic intertextual allusions endow nursery rhymes, Grimms' fairytales, ancient legends, popular proverbial wisdom, classical and Shakespearean tragedies, biblical doctrine, Milton, William Blake and a Renoir painting with the same status.

Like any category, 'woman poet' is too limiting (and notably rarely used of her); however, although ambivalent about feminist, along with any, polemic, Smith was undoubtedly conscious of gendered authorship. 'Miss Snooks, Poetess' dramatises the tendency to applaud women's unchallenging literary conformity and thus perpetuate it:

> Miss Snooks was really awfully nice
> And never wrote a poem

That was not really awfully nice
And fitted to a woman,

She therefore made no enemies
And gave no sad surprises
But went on being awfully nice
And took a lot of prizes.[27]

Here we see her distinctive stamp of idiomatic characterisation and remarkable compression. The voice belongs simultaneously to the poet, the subject and literary authority. The parodic intonation of exaggeratedly sanitised speech introduces an inherent criticism of its inbuilt assumptions about feminine creativity. The repetitions mimic the meaninglessness of 'nice' and the syntax of the second line differentiates bland verse derivations from proper poetry. The vehemence of her stand against parrotlike mediocrity in 'Pretty' is a clue to the verve of her refusal to be acceptable by compromising artistic individuality: 'Cry pretty, pretty, pretty and you'll be able/Very soon not even to cry pretty.' Associationally, she satirises agreeable but undemanding nature poetry: 'There is frost coming from the ground, in the air mist/All this is pretty, it could not be prettier.'[28] Likewise, she is merciless with unthinking vernacular clichés which veil any subconscious resistance to social prescriptions:

Cool as a cucumber calm as a millpond sound as a bell
Was Mary
When she went to the Wishing Well[29]

Mary runs away from marrying the miller's son and so subverts the expectations set up by the archetypal story. Whether a children's tale or Greek drama, a girl is supposed to wish for a mate. The happy ending to 'Votaries of Both Sexes Cry First to Venus' both feeds and parodies readers' desires for compensatory perfection. It is an extraordinary mélange of a hymn tune, a lover's impassioned contradiction of romantic fantasies and a detached voiceover.[30]

Although vulnerable to institutional oppressors, her subjects are also casualties of their network of family, friends and colleagues and many poems are open-ended tragedies of male/female relations. The dramatic irony in 'Drugs Made Pauline Vague' makes it one of her most poignant condensations of infidelity and deception, albeit with a complicit 'other woman'.[31] Such fractured family set-ups undo notions of cultural stability so yearned for after the Second World War. Her essay 'A London Suburb'

(1949) characteristically cracks the protective shell of British decency: '. . . And behind the fishnet curtains in the windows of the houses is the family life – father's chair, uproar, dogs, babies and radio.'[32] The narrator's measured assertion of social order over the implicit chaos and distress undermines the sanitised or prejudiced versions of respectable English routine. Smith poked fun at both the stereotyping and the stereotype of Englishness in 'The Hostage', 'Parents', 'The English', 'The English Visitor' and 'A British Song'.

Smith delights in taking her characters and readers to territories previously uncharted in literary representations. The ideal swiftly set up in the title of 'The Wedding Photograph' is ripped apart by the bride's hidden resistance to a prescribed route with which she is only colluding with her public face. The reader as confidante is required to adjudicate between her game and the social pressures which send her to it – pressures known, of course, to the poet who broke an engagement. Like a short story which begins and ends *in media res*, the poem is enjoyable for summoning a life through a snapshot, literally here:

> Goodbye Harry I must have you by me for a time
> But once in the jungle you must go off to a higher clime
> The old lion on his slow toe
> Will eat you up, that is the way you will go.
>
> Oh how I shall like to be alone on the jungle path
> But you are all right now for the photograph
> So smile Harry smile and I will smile too
> Thinking what is going to happen to you,
> It is the death wish lights my beautiful eyes
> But people think you are lucky to go off with such a pretty prize.
>
> Ah feeble me that only wishes alone to roam
> Yet dared not without marrying leave home
> Ah woe, burn fire, burn in eyes' sheathing
> Fan bright fear, fan fire in Harry's breathing.[33]

Many of her favourite ploys are in this poem: the frequent 'goodbye', which here is amusing in its incongruity; the poetic rhyming alongside a line of sheer prose (l. 10); the blurring of differences between animals and humans ('roam'); the interdependency of public and personal experience; the yearning to be away and alone; the notion of driving unconscious desires ('eyes' sheathing'); the tragicomic tone which teases us with uncertainty about how playful and how serious are the wife's intentions, largely due to her childlike renditions of jungle danger and the whole situation of rejecting conventional prescriptions, especially for women. As audience, we are made unnervingly complicit with the wife's deception, figured by the smile, repeated three times in one line for dramatic impact and to imitate the endlessness of the photos. The absence of condemnation for the murderous hypocritical wife was morally radical. Instead, Smith's habitual vocal shifts indicate women's struggles against external imperatives: 'Yet dared not without marrying leave home' is the reference point of the dominant social order which she is inwardly transgressing.

Textually, coexisting voices equally validate the characters they construct so that female causes have no greater claim than any other. However, much of Smith's oeuvre investigates the constitution of women's natures and function. She tends not to simply reverse power relations between men and women but scrutinises the origins of power and violence. 'How cruel is the story of Eve' questions whether male domination is essentially or historically fashioned:

> He must make woman lower then
> So he can be higher then.
>
> Oh what cruelty,
> In history what misery.[34]

The almost throwaway lament is a refrain which punctures patriarchal aspirations. The lines of the early poem 'Girls! although I am a woman/ I always try to appear human' is typically ambiguous about whether women can be counted as equals in terms of human nature and rights or whether they should segregate. The diction implicitly satirises the culture of girls' schools, where Smith found it hard to fit in.[35]

Smith's dialogism can be read in Woolf's terms of 'breaking the sequence' of masculine binary logic which inexorably relegates the feminine to the weaker 'other'.[36] In *Over the Frontier* (1938), we find the radical assertion that, 'never again in England I think shall we breed exclusively masculine and exclusively feminine types at any high level of intelligence, but there will always be much of one in the other'.[37] In fact, Smith's poems usually maintain gender difference but contradict unifying prescriptions of female identity or function. Take the variety of her women and then the emphasis on friendship above marriage. In 'A Dream of Comparison: after reading Book Ten of *Paradise Lost*', the conversation between Eve and Mary presents opposing female types — 'the difference between them was radical' — who thus contradict homogenising femininity. She ruptures the Miltonic blank verse and the didactisim of classical epic in favour of dialectical thought.

Since Mary celebrates life and Eve prefers the oblivion associated with prebirth, they also externalise Smith's unresolved conflicts: "'Oh to be Nothing", said Eve, "oh for a/Cessation of consciousness'" ... "'Mary laughed: "I love Life, /I would fight to the death for it"'.[38] The quest both to extend and lose consciousness dominates her work and a phase of acute depression culminated in a suicide attempt on 1 July 1953. As an unmarried poet who developed in a female household, then the female community of Palmers Green High School, Smith, like Mew or Jennings, was particularly alienated from the idealisations of marriage and motherhood. 'A Mother's Hearse' (1950) controversially illuminates the overinflation of maternal self-lessness. Indulgence produces a child monster so that the family become immured from their friends and the outside world. Although it appears as an indictment, typically, the observer's critical spirit is also examined:

> Oh wretched they and wretched the friend
> And this will continue without end
> And all for a mother's love it was,
> I say it were better a mother's hearse.[39]

Rhyming, repetition and word order are the dramatic props; the casually confessional 'it was' and 'I say' appeal to an audience so that the intonation, a key to interpretation, becomes a shared activity between writer and reader.

Like many twentieth-century women writers, Smith revises cultural stereotypes often to portray disappointment and entrapment. She encapsulates the space between desire and completion by avoiding compensatory closure:

> In front of the mighty washing machine
> The small lady stood in a beautiful dream,
> 'That these clothes so clean (oh what a relief)
>   Must still be ironed, is my only grief.'
>
> But then came a great witch passing on the air
> Who said, 'What is it you still wish for, my pretty dear?'[40]

This rare allusion to comfortable but restricting domesticity is set in the borderzone between the recognisable and the fantastic; this imaginative space masks the profound and acute dilemma between security and escape which proliferates in women's representations of women. In cleverly making the witch, not a fairy, the rescuer, Smith makes us 'work out for ourselves' which is the better choice. We also have to reassess received assumptions about the moral wisdom of fairytale. The final comment is, as often, suspect and demands turning over: 'Heart of my heart, is a mournful song, /Never will this poor lady come home.'

This longing to be elsewhere is everywhere in Smith's people, often figured highly symbolically. Freud explained these sensations of loss and desire as nostalgia for the pre-Oedipal mother/child union. Fantasy woods and rivers, typical of book illustrations, are frequently entered to flee the grimness of circumstances or psychological states but are never utopian depictions of freedom or fulfilment. As Steven Wade puts it, 'Naturally, Smith's explorations of myth have a playful side, as in her "River God of the river Mimran" poem, but, as always, she uses common fairytale or legend to inspect or dissect received ideas, ranging from dogma to allegory . . . In a way, it is all a teasing of our literary and religious heritage in the sphere of folk-tale and myth, but it also provokes as it entertains.'[41] In 'Fafnir and the Knights', we readily switch allegiance from the chivalric knight to the dragon he is supposed to slay, as if we have always wanted to.[42] 'The After-thought', which consists of inner dialogue between Rapunzel and her lover, demystifies the archetypal heroism of the fairytale, ending enigmatically with a recognisable problem of communication between men and women: 'What is that darling? You cannot hear me?/ That's odd. I can hear you quite distinctly.'[43] As in unglossed folktales, there is usually something unresolved, often sinister, but the situations are unexpected and contemporary.

Although conflating the past with the present, fantasies offer a distance from women's constraints and conditions, albeit for closer scrutiny. They provide alternatives to limiting cultural prescriptions and interrogate repressed collective desires as embodied in an individual. As already seen, the Freudian significance of dream is exploited in the appropriations of epic, legend and fairytale to tell the 'other' story, that is, of some kind of marginality. In 'I had a dream . . .', the contemporary speaker becomes Helen of Troy:

> But what I did not know,
> And I could not get Cassandra to say either,
> Was which of the Helen legends I was,
> The phantom, with the real Helen in Egypt,
> Or the flesh-and-blood one here
> That Menelaus would take back to Sparta.[44]

The unleashed discourse of a silenced classical feminine icon is transmuted to a contemporary woman's chat which counters the phallocentrism of both classic characterisation and psychoanalytical principles. Other monologues by representatives of corporate female mythology include ones by Dido, Persephone and 'The Queen and the Princess'. The latter two are as much concerned with exploring mother/daughter feelings as with catching men. A long poem, printed near the end of Smith's final collection, confronts all mediations of idealism and untruth. It ends:

> I do not think we shall be able to bear much longer the dishonesty
> Of clinging for comfort to beliefs we do not believe in,
> For comfort, and to be comfortably free of the fear
> Of diminishing good, as if truth were a convenience.
> I think if we do not learn quickly, and learn to teach children,
> To be good without enchantment, without the help
> Of beautiful painted fairy stories pretending to be true,
> Then I think it will be too much for us, the dishonesty,
> And, armed as we are now, we shall kill everybody,
> It will be too much for us, we shall kill everybody.[45]

Echoing Eliot's sense that 'human kind/Cannot bear very much reality',[46] the poem was decidedly public because it was commissioned by the *Guardian* for Whitsun.[47] Although it is hard to identify any familiar credentials of 'poetry' here, Larkin picked out this as one of her 'firmest endings'.

Through many dramas and commentaries, Smith dealt with the forces of socialisation, particularly false ideals fed to children. The knight whose heroic mask conceals how he is haunted by Care is a metaphor for the stripping away of surfaces throughout her work.[48] In her manipulation of nursery rhyme, myth and fairytale, we experience their potential to either reinforce or subvert mainstream cultural codes. The baby in 'Childhood and Interruption' is enviably not 'properly awake', so is free of social contrivances:

>   no arrangement they make
> For him can touch him at all, he is alone,
> For a little while yet, it is as if he had not been born
> Rest in infancy, brother Jake; childhood and interruption come swiftly on.[49]

Thus speaks the young sibling, defying the rosy unrealism of the children's Christmas carol 'Away in a Manger' with a prosy line. The atemporality and linguistic mélange in these poems mediate between material and transcendental existence. The alternative consciousness offered through this mediation is more accessible to the outsider – whether insane or a child – who is not at home in respectable standard English.

Some poems point to sensations which paradoxically depend on yet evade the strictures of language: 'It is better to see the grass than write about it/Better to see the water than write a water-song.'⁵⁰ 'The Passing Cloud', subheaded 'From the Royal Bethlehem Hospital', attributes visionary power to the mad who are favoured with extralinguistic apprehension:

> I will laugh and sing, or be dumb if they please, and await at the
>   Lord's discretion
> The day I'll be one, as one I'll be, in an infinite regression
> One, ha ha, with a merry ha ha, skip the fish and amoeba
>   where are we now?
> We are very far out, in a rarefied place, with the thin thin dust
>   in a giddy chase,
> The dust of Continuous Creation, and how is that for identification?
> You'll like it; you must, you know,
> That merry dust does jig so.⁵¹

The stretched lines typographically point beyond their textual limits, while exaggerated rhyme and repetition arbitrate between the irrational and rationality. The anchorless pronouns which switch between singular and plural, first and second person, model the processes of self-realisation. Interestingly, 'far out', means mental despair in the later 'Not Waving but Drowning' but here it denotes the happiness associated with pre-linguistic and nonverbal emancipation, indicated in the 'ha ha', 'ding-dong', skipping, jigging and piping:

> And in the ding-dong of the universe I pipe my innocent voice
> I pipe my innocent voice I pipe, I pipe and I also sing
> Till I'd sung too loud and woke myself up and that is another thing

She harnesses marvellously the antipoetic patterns of Edward Lear's non-sense verse with Gertrude Stein's exaggerated repetitions and severed signifiers, thus bridging popular and avant-garde evasions of documentary realism which confine women to the moulds of received verbal uniforms.

Literary 'development' seems an irrelevant lens for analysis when throughout her writing Smith plays the wise fool with paradox and complicates enclosing binary oppositions. As Mark Storey concludes, '[Smith] stands outside any tradition of the day; in so doing [she] acts as a comment on what is happening elsewhere; she becomes a touchstone.'⁵² As he points out, her contrived carelessness and ostentatious simplicity were a risk which produce the 'critical problem'. In blotting out distinctions between speech and writing, she craftily robs literary criticism of its evaluative vocabulary which relies on concepts of comparison and contrast.

The best accessories are her other writings, novels, correspondence, note-books and interviews. Hence the discerning selection by Hermione Lee, the treasury *Me Again* and Frances Spalding's illuminating critical biography integrate extracts from all her writings. Smith's prosy poems and poetic fictions accompany the thematic correspondences between traditional opposites: the irrationality of logic and, of course, the commixture of masculine and feminine human characteristics.

The emotive power of human tragedy which Smith dramatises means that to treat this extraordinary oeuvre as 'woman's poetry' is overly reduc-tive of her technical and psychological complexity. Yet we have seen how she is exceptionally 'antifeminine' in her detached antisentimentality but also takes features associated with *'écriture féminine'* further than women before her. As Martin Pumphrey so astutely observes, 'a reading of her poetry that takes account of her as a woman writing seems to clarify precisely those difficulties that have taxed most critics. Approached in this way, Smith's "oddness" identifies her with other women writers whose poetic strategies have been directed not towards the construction of an authoritative and consistent poetic persona or self but towards disruption, discontinuity and indirection.'[53] She subverts the struts of masculine literary symbolic discourse with adventurous rhyming and polyphony. She psychologises human behaviour, sometimes implicitly or explicitly in terms of socially constructed sex differences. She disables stereotyping mythologies yet invigorates poetry's representational func-tion. Sylvia Plath called herself a 'desperate Smith addict' and she was cordially reviewed by Naomi Mitchison and Elizabeth Jennings. Patricia Beer's poem 'Stevie Goodbye' and Linda France's tribute in *Sixty Women Poets* testify to her relevance to women poets after her.[54] The dearth of critical analysis, however, indicates the lag in responding to her demands for new formulations of poetic value which especially attend to the specifics of women's experimental expressive poetry.

CHAPTER 6

The postwar generation and the paradox of home

> ... that four-walled chrysalis
> and impediment, home;
> that lamp and hearth, that easy fit
> of bed to bone;
> those children, too, sharp witnesses
> of all I've done.
> ...
> the walls that crush us
> keep us from the cold.
> I know the price and still
> I pay it, pay it:
>
> Words, their furtive kiss,
> illicit gold.[1]

Maura Dooley recollects a time 'when the word "domestic" occurred ...
like a reflex, in any review of a new collection by a woman, thereby relegating
both scope of book and scope of ambition to the kitchen. Write about blood,
babies, the moon and jam-making and be a "Woman Poet"; or, cut out half
of your experience of life and get taken seriously. Maybe.'[2] The ancient
association of women and domesticity has always haunted women writers,
torn between daily routine and creative fulfilment. In their relentless domesticating of women's poetics, commentators fail to grasp that, as Kathleen
Raine puts it, 'No kitchen sink, however glossy, can tether the imagination
...'[3] In describing it as both 'chrysalis/and impediment', Anne Stevenson
refuses to simplify the part played by the home, as well as motherhood, in
literary creativity. Her phrasing signals instead the ambivalence with which
she and others view its circumscribing but curiously generative influence.

What Diana Wallace terms the 'coercive domestic ideology' of the early
postwar period in Britain had significant implications for women's poetry.[4]
By the early 1950s, for working women and housewives alike, the demands of
family and home remained as urgent as ever. The American poet Adrienne

Rich remembers how 'middle-class women were making careers of domestic perfection ... People were moving out to the suburbs, technology was going to be the answer to everything, even sex; the family was in its glory. Life was extremely private; women were isolated from each other by the loyalties of marriage.'[5] Social and economic marginalisation does not lessen their sense of duty to the home.[6]

Many feminist literary critics have explored the different ways in which women novelists narrate, as Juliet Mitchell puts it, 'the story of their own domesticity, the story of their own seclusion within the home and the possibilities and impossibilities provided by that'.[7] The same conflicts resound in poems tackling the often fraught relationship between a woman's aesthetic and domestic lives, and the changes wrought on female identity by marriage, household duties and children. As time passes and cultural conditions alter, an increasingly politicised set of tensions nuance what might be called the British woman poet's 'domestic Muse'.

Gender complicates the relationship between the woman poet and the Muse. Germaine Greer explains that the nine female classical Muses were all expert poets, yet the 'rhetoric of musedom' excluded women writers from the delicate intercourse (to inspire and to be inspired in both cases being at once penetrative and passive) between a conventionally male poet and his conventionally female Muse. As Greer notes, 'conscious efforts to weaken this gender-specificity seem to be ineffectual ... Either [women poets] must impersonate the muse herself or impersonate the male poet.' Her very existence distorts and subverts the traditional working partnership between author and source of inspiration. Greer thus finds the female poet condemned to

subject-matter [which] seems in some limiting and stifling way to be herself. Whereas the male poet might be thought to be projecting a separate identity (the work), the female poet is invariably seen to be projecting herself in an unavoidably immodest way.[8]

Although Greer does not concede it, domesticating the Muse offers a way round this impasse. Her hybrid figure blurs the distinction between life and art, linking and dividing the world of the creative imagination and humdrum reality. Authorising the aesthetic value of the traditionally feminised domestic sphere, a Domestic Muse oversees the construction of a pragmatic, exclusively female and highly self-aware creative dynamic. When she makes an early appearance in English poetry, in Anna Laetitia Barbauld's 1797 mock-heroic 'Washing Day' (cited by Greer), it is with conspicuous lack of ceremony:

> ... Come then, domestic Muse,
> In slip-shod measure loosely prattling on,
> Of farm or orchard, pleasant curds and cream ...
> ...
> Come, Muse, and sing the dreaded washing day.[9]

Summoned by an unapologetically female voice, this Muse is an understanding companion, implicated by gender in the domestic grind she is asked to oversee. Her cheerful legitimation of the weekly wash as creative activity converts tedious labour into imaginative resource. In this way Barbauld reproaches the masculine literary traditions which trivialise her choice of subject: men do not know how to value Wash Day; it is excluded from the discourse of inspiration, despite the suggestively beautiful bubbles that Barbauld's speaker is left contemplating. In contrast, the domestic Muse belongs amid the dispiriting labour of 'red-armed washers'; her presence sanctifies the task as well as supplying relief from it. Even laundering can inspire: in doing so it offers freedom from itself; drudgery, deflected, is transformed. Women poets down the centuries have taken comfort from this idea. Jennifer Breen finds Barbauld and her Romantic peers 'often wittily subvert[ing] the masculine notion of a female Muse by humorously invoking her help in writing about housewifely and culinary arts'.[10] Angela Leighton (invoking Freud) notices the Victorians attesting to 'the double meaning of home which runs through women's poetry: home may be unhomely, the woman's place may have shut her out, it may not be the woman's place at all'.[11] In 1948 Bax and Stewart 'salute ... the brains, the sensibility and the fine artistry of women poets' by choosing a spinning metaphor for the title of their anthology *The Distaff Muse*.

In the transitional mid 1940s the joys of home must have been heightened by fears still too raw after the war for physical and emotional closeness, and the nuclear family unit, to be taken for granted. Phyllis Lassner finds women writers of the Second World War using the domestic novel to question 'the political ideology of war and its relation to domestic ideology'.[12] To some extent, this is true of the poetry, too. In Sheila Wingfield's *Beat Drum, Beat Heart*, housework engenders the 'pride'

> That any woman has felt who's putting a room to rights,
> Scrubbing as if herself were being scrubbed,
> Scouring as if her soul were being scoured,
> Straightening up and sorting as if in her own mind[13]

Wingfield's conflation of housewife and house in linen tidying might reprove, or aim to inspire, a nation plainly failing to set itself 'to rights'.

Although, as Lassner notes, 'the roles of housewife and hostess became noticeably frustrating and constraining', they were hard to escape.[14] Two decades later a letter to the *Sunday Times* (1963) could still demand: 'Do today's women know what they want? They abandon a career in favour of marriage and children, and once having achieved both they don't seem to be able to wait to get back to work.'[15] Like the novelists Lassner finds contesting the 'assumption that the family home was an inviolate sanctuary preserving universally held values', many postwar women poets reflect equivocally on domesticity and the web of tensions and loyalties it comprises.[16]

The appearance of a domestic Muse amid the conflicted gender constructions of the 1950s and 1960s is unsurprising. Betty Friedan's work contextualises the appearance of '[a] mystique of feminine fulfillment' in the postwar United States:

By the end of the nineteen-fifties . . . fourteen million girls were engaged by 17 . . . Women who had once wanted careers were now making careers out of having babies . . . They baked their own bread, sewed their own and their children's clothes, kept their new washing machines and dryers running all day . . . and pitied their poor frustrated mothers, who had dreamed of having a career.[17]

As Friedan implies, the drift into domesticity is given impetus by marriage: a time-honoured process of female self-transformation, from girlhood to wife and womanhood, begins in betrothal. Eavan Boland 'stumbled, almost without knowing it, into the life of a woman. I married. I moved to a suburb. Gradually it all looked different.'[18] Marriage remains a touchstone for poets writing throughout the period, although views alter with the rise of Women's Liberation. In the apologetic voice of an inexperienced young wife looking back on her first year of married life, E. J. Scovell constructs herself in subserviently domestic terms:

> I am not used to the house linen yet,
> The sheets still folded clouds; your china still
> On the top shelf shows faces new to me;
> And I am still a stranger and
> The youngest in your house.
>
> I was born here a second time, to learn
> Slowly like a child, by heart and touch,[19]

Figured as both stranger and infant, Scovell's speaker could hardly seem more disempowered by married life: the linen and china do not just belong to her husband; they seem to *be* him. It is difficult to hear regret or irony in the tone. Such self-effacement is not unusual. An early poem finds Denise

Levertov (who married in 1948) echoing: 'It is you who make/a world to speak of.'[20] Plath, writing in 1956, expects to relish a benign, self-sacrificing domesticity in which the emotional and intellectual extend and illuminate each other:

I am inclined to babies and bed and brilliant friends and a magnificent stimulating home where geniuses drink gin in the kitchen after a delectable dinner and read their own novels ... this is what I was meant to make for a man, and to give him this colossal reservoir of faith and love for him to swim in daily, and to give him children; lots of them, in great pain and pride.[21]

As Jeni Couzyn drily observes, Plath's 'expectations for her emotional life came straight from glossy magazines'.[22] Al Alvarez, recalling when he first met Plath in 1960, remembers her as 'effaced, the poet taking a back seat to the young mother and housewife ... bright, clean, competent, like a young woman in a cookery advertisement'. Only then does he record, unironically, the academic and intellectual achievements which 'belied her housewifely air'.[23]

Despite her hopes, the closest Plath's poetry comes to her vision of domesticity is the steely grandmother of the inhospitable 'Point Shirley', who 'Kept house against/What the sluttish, rutted sea could do'.[24] Here, housework is purposeful, a matter of survival. Other poems are more deeply riven by the competing claims of domestic perfection and literary success. In 'Lesbos' and 'Kindness', the home – always a site of emotional and intellectual turbulence – enshrines an intensely personal struggle against stifling domestic routine.[25] The Bee sequence has been read as an oblique investigation of the same dilemma. If, as Janice Markey claims, the bees are 'role-models for women who in the 1950s were denied power and position and as such were subordinate and passive', their precedent is troubling.[26] In 'The Bee Meeting', their ceaseless, confident productivity induces more anxiety than admiration. The bees' relentless fecundity – dependent on their imprisonment – makes a nervy speaker (finding them perhaps, virginally, naïve) envious or disdainful. Their self-sufficiency is reexamined in 'The Arrival of the Bee Box'.[27] The coffinlike box compels but 'appalls'; the speaker longs to 'be sweet God, I will set them free'. Christina Britzolakis finds the bees' 'hierarchically ordered, industrious collectivity' matriarchal and yet 'authoritarian'. As poems such as 'Stings' and 'The Swarm' confirm, their productivity depends on 'a highly structured division of labour' ultimately 'overseen by the male bee keeper'.[28] According to Britzolakis, the ambiguities allow Plath to shift between different role identifications. She can insist that, 'I am no drudge' while blaming domesticity ('the engine that killed her – /The mausoleum, the wax house') for her extinguished creativity.[29]

Plath's example reiterates that for women who sought an independent working existence amid the gender stereotyping of the 1950s and 1960s, the 'impediment' of domesticity is at best draining. If, chrysalislike, home and family reward time and effort with emotional sustenance, the grind of housework inevitably compromises, if not effectively denies, a woman's separate intellectual development and creative freedom. Levertov's 'The Five-Day Rain' echoes Plath in voicing, as Geoffrey Thurley says, 'the predicament of the woman who wants to accept the role of mother and wife, with all the curtailments and sacrifices it involves, without losing contact with that other self that writes poetry and lives intensely':[30]

> Wear scarlet! Tear the green lemons
> off the tree! I don't want
> to forget who I am, what has burned in me,
> and hang limp and clean, an empty dress –[31]

Thurley observes of this poem that each self is a version of the other: 'the poetry comes out of the conflict of the two roles'.[32] Boland again: 'Once I began to live my own life – a life with a husband, a home, small children – I could see at first hand how remote it was from the life of the poet as I had understood it. I began to realize that a subtle oppression could result from this fracture between the instinctive but unexpressed life I lived every day and the expressive poetic manners I had inherited.'[33] She begins to sharpen her consciousness of this in *The War Horse* (1975) – in advance of the profoundly woman-centred poems of *In Her Own Image* (1980) and *Night Feed* (1982) – for example, in poems like 'Ode to Suburbia' and 'Suburban Woman', summoned by the poet ('courtesan to the lethal/rapine of routine') in solidarity: 'Defeated we survive, we two, housed//together in my compromise, my craft – '.[34]

By the 1960s if anything cuts across generational and social boundaries to link women poets, it is the 'subtle oppression' Boland senses, intensified in the crowded interior of the home itself. Published in 1967, Levertov's 'Abel's Bride' seems to consider domestic incarceration anachronistic but unavoidable:

> She thinks herself
> lucky. But sad. When she goes out
> she looks in the glass, she remembers
> herself. Stones, coal,
> the hiss of water upon the kindled

branches – her being
is a cave, there are bones at the hearth.[35]

In Elma Mitchell's 'Recreation', the oppressive 'bitty/Ripples of domesticity' constantly interrupt but never prevent 'the quiet tugging' of the embroidery in which a long-suffering wife and mother works out a persisting creativity.[36] By the 1970s more openly feminist poets, especially those associated with the Women's Movement such as Denise Riley, Wendy Mulford and Michèle Roberts, were radicalising Plath's angry lead. However, as Mitchell's poem hints, and Stevenson's well-known essay 'Writing as a Woman' reveals, resistance is not restricted to committed feminists. Couzyn says that Patricia Beer is favoured by anthologists 'in the sixties and seventies for token woman, because she can be relied on never to embarrass the reader with anything too "female"'.[37] Yet in 'Summer Song for me and my Aunts', Beer (who subsequently defines herself as 'a rather wonky feminist') urges 'Never . . . /Let being a woman/Or the baking of bread/Keep you off the heath.'[38] In Carol Rumens's 'Houses by Day' (from her first, according to Lyn Pykett 'proto-feminist,' collection *A Strange Girl in Bright Colours*), the self-silencing prompted by 'The trauma of marriage' is grown in domesticity, symptom not cause of the entrenched social construction of women as housemaids and sex objects.[39] The speaker must adjust to a sterile housebound solitude she cannot escape, even after her marriage ends. In Ruth Fainlight's 'Domestical', the home frames a self-sacrificial performance defined chiefly by frustration:

> Because I will not admit what I think, I have
> no opinions; never admit what I want,
> have forgotten my needs; never admit who I am,
> have lost my name and freedom
>
> Until this huge discomfort constitutes
> my whole existence – called to act a part
> for which I'm completely unsuitable.[40]

Poets do not have to be married to register the confining effect of domesticity. Ruth Pitter's 'The Ploughboy's Plea' (*A Heaven To Find* 1987) notices the dependence of masculinity on domestic support, while the tight couplets of 'Pot-Bound' (*Still By Choice* 1966) figure how home constricts creative growth. However, other women treat the 'subtle oppression' of domestic life more positively. If Gillian Clarke's 'Letter From a Far Country' 'is my small contribution towards feminist protest,' it also '[celebrates] life's good things – clean sheets, the smell of baking, orderliness – with which my mother and grandmother surrounded me'.[41] Jenny Joseph 'used my own life only because it is material we have unique access to'.[42] Indeed, as Simone de Beauvoir argues in *The Second Sex*, the self-determined reconceiving of home as workplace can seem liberating:

confined within the conjugal sphere[,] it is for [woman] to change that prison into a realm. Her attitude towards her home is dictated by the same dialectic that defines her situation in general: she takes by becoming prey, she finds freedom by giving it up: by renouncing the world she aims to conquer a world.

More specifically, 'With her fire going, woman becomes a sorceress; by a simple movement, as in beating eggs, or through the magic of fire, she effects the transmutation of substances: matter becomes food. There is enchantment in these alchemies, there is poetry in making preserves; the housewife has caught duration in the snare of sugar, she has enclosed life in jars.'[43]

In some respects, these activities recall the oppressive expectations of *The Feminine Mystique*, picked up in the claustrophobia of Plath's 'Wintering': 'the rancid jam' of 'the room I could never breathe in'.[44] Partly in the heavy assonance of 'jam' and 'room', 'Wintering' implies that domesticity is a double-jointed term, signifying both the workspace of the home and the 'work' by which that space is defined. Writing candidly about the depression which followed the birth of her first child, Stevenson admits that she assumed that domestic life would render her 'a writer with a handicap':

I dread, and have always dreaded, that marriage, a home and family would sap my creative energies, that they would devour my time and my personality, that they would in a venomous way that I can't easily explain, use me up.[45]

Joseph found that 'The use of dailiness got me dubbed as a "domestic" poet which I not only resent but disagree with.'[46] Yet de Beauvoir, conceding that often 'writers who lyrically exalt [domestic work] are persons who are seldom or never engaged in actual housework', maintains that if 'the individual who does such work is also a producer, a creative worker, it is as naturally integrated in life as are the organic functions'.[47] Acknowledging that 'Any writer has to keep his or her imagination alive, and that means he or she can't happily live a lie or write well in an alien role', Stevenson comments that she 'blamed too much on the marriage and my role as a woman in it. I should have written in spite of everything that seemed against me.'[48]

Certainly, 'The Price' perhaps provocatively suggests that, as 'chrysalis', embodying the relationships and resources from which a woman draws, joyfully or resentfully, material and spiritual inspiration, domesticity can stimulate as much as 'impede' self-expression. In doing so the home paradoxically offers a way of escaping its own confines, much like Barbauld's 'Washing Day'. Levertov openly connects housework, intellectual activity and imaginative freedom:

> work by a strong light
> scour the pots
> destroy old letters
>
> finally before sleep
> walk on the roof where
> the smell of soot recalls a
> snowfall.
>
>   Up
> over the red darkness dolphins
> roll, roll, and tumble, flashing the
> spray of a green sky.[49]

'Zest' suggests that it is only in the aesthetic that the fruitful tensions inherent in the so-called 'Domestic Muse' can be fully staged. The puritanical regime seems intended to nourish not suppress the alternative sensual existence attending (or following) the 'walk on the roof'. The yoking of work and play, industry and 'inspiration', evokes the interdependence of the apparently opposed worlds of the imagination and reality in the (implicitly female) creative experience. As James Breslin notes, 'Levertov locates her muse within the domestic world, but without domesticating her. The muse in fact manifests the presence of the mysterious within the house, "within you", within a newly conceived domestic order.'[50] 'Matins' glories in the mundane details (knocking pipes, a broken hairbrush, breakfast) of a 'new day', only conceding the friction between mythic and quotidian in a final oxymoron:

> Marvelous Truth, confront us
> . . .
>
> dwell
> in our crowded hearts
> our steaming bathrooms, kitchens full of
> things to be done, the
> ordinary streets.
>
> Thrust close your smile
> that we know you, terrible joy.[51]

Various poets consciously invoke a subversive domestic Muse, transforming the 'dailiness' of house and home into a creative resource. Scovell, whom Geoffrey Grigson calls 'the purest of woman poets of our time', is characterised by Kenneth Allott as 'very much a woman poet in the domesticity of her muse'.[52] Domesticity provides a fertile context for much of Scovell's work, especially 'Poems On Infancy'; in fact, for Peter Scupham, 'Home, house and household, the domus, are where her imagination starts.'[53] Its influence is most subtly realised in the refined, self-aware poems of *The Space Between* (1982) and *Listening to Collared Doves* (1986), where quiet evenings spent in easy separateness, 'In our two bodies, in our lives as parallel,/Reading, or I sewing' seem enchanted.[54] Where Levertov is perhaps inclined to emphasise the connection between household tasks and creative work, Scovell underplays it. More significant is the intersection of, and play between, inside and outside. The balance she typically strikes between interior and exterior is altered and surreptitiously gendered in 'Domestic'. Made inviting by the 'first fire of autumn', the house ('Used carelessly in the good days, a shed or shelter;/A half-way house, indoors to out . . .') comforts where before it confined: 'impregnated/With dark and cold, with warmth, warm voices, curtains drawn,/It comes into its own.'[55] In 'A Short Night', house and garden converge in a nurturing effect mediated by womanhood:

> She is in the garden weeding almost in darkness.
> Indoors we say it is quite dark. Fetch her in.
> . . .
>   . . . Get her to come.
> Call your wife, our hostess, home.
>
> So she comes in, tranquil, grubby and vague
> With gardening, bringing the scent of stock through the door,
> . . .
> And makes us tea and puts the tray on the floor,
> And the talk flourishes more than before.[56]

Scovell is not unusual in exploring the relation of exterior and interior. Sylvia Townsend Warner, Phoebe Hesketh, Pitter, Molly Holden, Beer and Boland are among many who construct the garden, requiring and rewarding cultivation, nurture and time, as an ambiguous site of female agency which enfranchises but encloses. For the terminally ill woman of Jennings's 'Her Garden', the 'high walls' distance the passers-by she can hear, while the space they enclose brightens the 'sudden shade' of the interior, and ventilates 'her old rooms'. 'Bridg[ing] the pause/between fruition and decay', the garden becomes a subversive extension of the 'infected' interior; its protective perimeters concentrate its healing (but not curative) effect just as the borders focus the fertility which eases the approach of death.[57]

Many poets find aesthetic, socio-political and psychological significance in the liminal. The female speaker in Levertov's 'From the Roof', wrestling with 'playful rebellious linen' on a 'wild night', delights in a task which suspends her, literally and liberatingly, between earth and sky, interior and exterior, domesticity and commerce.[58] For Pitter, a gale dramatises both the strength and the flexing edifice of 'The New House', rendered 'nothing but desire and fear forming and dissolving/With the wind streaming, with the world revolving'.[59]

The 'gradual' differences reported by Boland multiply when a woman's ties to husband and home are deepened and complicated by the woman-centred experiences of pregnancy, childbirth and childcare. More than any other facet of home and family life, the bearing and raising of children affects not only the daily practicalities of running the home, but a woman's emotional relationships, ideological beliefs and developing sense of self. As Tess Cosslett explains, 'motherhood puts into question a woman's sense of identity, as her body changes shape and splits apart, and a new social role is thrust upon her. Discontinuities between her self before and after birth, and in her relationship to the foetus/baby inside and then outside her, force reformulations of her sense of [identity].'[60] From the 1950s onwards poets grow relaxed about detailing and exploring the familiar-strange experiences of pregnancy and birth.[61] They write about maternity with insight and toughness, compassion and comedy. The rewarding burden of children, the unpredictable anxieties and pleasures they bring, only heighten the dilemmas of their domestic circumstances.

In *Of Woman Born*, Rich notes that 'Out of her body the woman created man, created woman, created continuing existence. In biological mother-hood . . . [she] was not merely a producer and stabilizer of life [but] a *transformer.*' Historically, these transformative powers were culturally influential: 'in creating a situation in which they could nurture and rear infants safely and effectively, women became the civilizers, the inventors of agriculture, of community, some maintain of language itself'.[62] Rich accepts that this paradigm overlooks how maternity affects the mother herself: 'The woman who has long wanted and awaited a child can anticipate becoming a mother with imaginative eagerness; but she too must move from the familiar to the strange.'[63] The witty, end-stopped epigrams of Plath's earliest pregnancy poem, 'Metaphors' ('Money's new-minted in this fat purse./I'm a means, a stage, a cow in calf.') foresees the im/potency of physical transformation; the 'difficult borning' anticipated in 'The Manor Garden' – written when Plath was some six months pregnant – is already burdened by a history outside the expectant mother's control.[64] Each poem betrays the 'drama' which de Beauvoir senses 'acted out within the woman herself. She feels it as at once an enrichment and an injury; the foetus is a part of her body, and it is a parasite that feeds on it; she possesses it, and she is possessed by it; it represents the future and carrying it, she feels herself vast as the world; but this very opulence annihilates her, she feels that she herself is no longer anything . . . a conscious and free individual, who has become life's passive instrument.'[65]

As de Beauvoir suggests, on one hand maternity intensifies a sense of female empowerment; an important critique by Nina Baym quotes an essay which resees the mother 'as metaphor for the sources of our own creative powers[;] . . . in which the mother is no longer the necessary comfort but the seed of a new being, and in which we are no longer the protected child but the carriers of the new woman whose birth is our own.'[66] However, as Rich also says, 'Pregnancy may be experienced as the extinguishing of an earlier self'; parturition only heightens this.[67] In 'Calliope in the Labour ward', Feinstein, who recalls using poetry to recapture 'the exultation of childbirth', summons the epic Muse ('she who has no love for women/married and housekeeping') to honour the nerve and endurance of those who 'sail to a/ darkness without self/where no will reaches'.[68]

Accordingly, women poets render the emotional and psychological effects of childbirth ambiguously; as a separation which is not, a physical and psychological self-negation which is also intensely affirming, a climax which is only a prelude. Mitchell's 'At First, My Daughter' conflates a shared lifetime in the multiply equivocal 'first and last moments/Of being together and separate/Indissoluble – till we are split'.[69] The sober pun embedded in the title of Plath's 'Morning Song' achieves a graver mixture of instinctive understanding and dismay:

> I'm no more your mother
> Than the cloud that distills a mirror to reflect its own slow
> Effacement at the wind's hand.[70]

Anne Ridler's 'A Matter of Life and Death' poises a newly delivered mother on an experiential cusp which equates with the position of the baby: 'till this moment what was he to me?/Conjecture and analogy/Conceived and yet unknown[.]'[71]

There is no doubt that children inspire their poet-mothers: as works by Mitchell, Ridler, Scovell, Hesketh, Stevenson, Feinstein, Fainlight, Clarke,

Beer, Couzyn, Rumens, Boland (signally, in the 1982 collection *Night Feed*) Raine, Elizabeth Bartlett, Frances Horovitz (whose son Adam appears throughout *Water Over Stone*, 1980), Holden, Fleur Adcock, Sheenagh Pugh and Penelope Shuttle testify. Even the childless Elizabeth Jennings finds in maternity both theme and analogue for literary creativity. While Stevenson's speaker is awestruck by the newborn's 'intricate/exacting particulars: the tiny/blind bones ... distinct eyelashes and sharp crescent/fingernails', the opening poem of Scovell's 'Poems on Infancy' contemplates the innate potency of the sleeping infant.[72] Elsewhere, Levertov's 'The Earthwoman and the Waterwoman' contrasts two versions of maternal creativity. The Earthwoman's 'cakes of good grain' complement the 'gay songs' of her counterpart; the former's slow-fermenting powers, realised in her hearty offspring, parallel and invert the fey, whimsical talents and 'spindle thin' progeny of her alter ego 'dancing in the misty lit-up town/in dragonfly dresses and blue shoes'.[73]

However, the aligning of motherhood and creativity is neither practically nor imaginatively straightforward. As Tillie Olsen warns, creativity and maternity share 'more than toil and patience. The calling upon total capacities; the re-living and new using of the past; the comprehensions; the fascination, absorption, intensity.' Childrearing proscribes writing: 'It is distraction, not meditation, that becomes habitual; interruption, not continuity; spasmodic not constant toil.' She concludes, 'Work interrupted, deferred, postponed, makes blockage.'[74] While Plath never seems to have blamed her children for compromising her work, she produced few poems in the first year of her first child's life. 'Stillborn' is especially poignant: 'These poems do not live. It's a sad diagnosis./... and their mother near dead of distraction.'[75] Other poets dramatise the price of the perspective-altering condition of motherhood. In Stevenson's 'The Victory', maternity lacerates ('I thought you were my victory/though you cut me like a knife'):

> You barb the air. You sting
> with bladed cries.

It concludes, in bafflement, 'Why do I have to love you?/How have you won?'[76] The same intellectual and emotional disempowerment inflects the truncated lines of Feinstein's 'Mother Love', as the speaker surrenders to physical and mental exhaustion: 'You eat me, your/nights eat me/Once you took/haemoglobin and bone/out of my blood; /Now my head/sleeps forward on my neck/holding you'.[77] Both texts ironise the 'mother tongue' which, Ursula Le Guin observes, 'spoken or written, expects an answer. It is conversation ... It connects ... its power is not in dividing but in binding.'[78]

Moreover, as the tenor of the critical discourse makes clear, the aligning of maternity and creativity is not necessarily attractive to the embattled woman poet; the more she employs the metonym, the greater the risk to her professional identity. In one of those axiomatic assertions which (since they can never be disproved) persist in the Plath mythology he helped to create, Alvarez assumes that having a baby 'liberated her into her real self . . . her most creative period followed the birth of her son'.[79] Beside this, the punning equivocation of 'Morning Song' makes political as well as emotional sense.

The conflicted nature of the domestic sphere is doubled and distilled in the maternal figure who inhabits it; Nancy Chodorow argues that 'Mothering . . . involves a double identification for women, both as mother *and* as child.'[80] In such a moment of self-recognition between baby and mother, Ridler's 'The Gaze' reprises the ambivalence explored in this chapter. Interestingly, Ridler decided to exclude poems about infancy from her *Collected Poems* 'in order not to be typecast as a poet of domesticity':[81]

> Mirrors return the image which we show them,
> But like a thinker, when you reflect on me
> You take me in.[82]

Discussing the problems facing the woman poet who tackles domestic subjects, Stevenson remarks, 'Tension is a mainspring of the imagination. And something has to be sacrificed – the satisfaction of a role, the satisfaction of a cause, . . . even, of a sense of guilt.'[83] In many ways this explains why the domestic sphere represents a dangerous but often fertile locus of self-inspection and self-reconfiguration, just as maternity and maternal responsibilities intensify questions about the relationship between a writer's private and public lives. Repeatedly, the postwar woman poet affirms that the problematic of 'home' underwrites and charges her aesthetic as profoundly as her conflicted, multiple identity.

CHAPTER 7

The poetry of consciousness-raising[1]

Louise Bernikow explains that 'Woman's place in literary life . . . has been a place from which men grant her leave to write about either love or religion. Everything else threatens male turf . . . When women move into the area of political consciousness, particularly feminism . . . we move out of place.'[2] Arguably, women poets have been 'moving out of place' in the name of feminism all century but, prompted by Women's Liberation, they do so most concertedly in the late 1960s and 1970s. As feminists, the poets associated with this period share a starting place: 'Our window on the world is looked through with our hands in the sink and we've begun to hate that sink and all it implies – so begins our consciousness.'[3] Enshrining the view that 'art [is] only valuable when . . . it [goes] out to find a mass audience, raise[s] their political consciousness, rouse[s] them to political action', they frequently write to and for each other, reifying and contesting the biologically determined and socially constructed realities of their bodies and lives for openly political reasons.[4] The sense of concert is as important to their poetics as their politics; it proves equally contentious.

It is partly for apparently valuing content (expressing commonly held views) over formal craft that 'Feminist poetry' has become a term of almost universal critical derision, energetically avoided by most poets.[5] And yet, as the central essays of a fairly limited discourse convince, the term encompasses too broad a spectrum of positions to be so simply dismissed.[6] There is no doubting the importance of an ideology linking, at different times and to varying degrees, names such as Carol Rumens, Carol Ann Duffy, Fleur Adcock, Gillian Clarke, U. A. Fanthorpe, Liz Lochhead, Eavan Boland, Elaine Feinstein and Elma Mitchell with (once) more obviously political writers such as Jeni Couzyn, Nicki Jackowska and Gillian Allnutt. However, by the end of the century Rumens speaks for many in arguing, 'My personal, social ideas are certainly feminist, but my poetry is not their handmaid . . . Feminism helped reinforce the sense of my own and other women's worth, but ... poetry [should not] be seen as a way of serving those social or political rights.'[7]

While several critics have examined how Rumens and others converse with feminism, few have pursued the early development of what Claire Buck calls 'British feminist poetry' in any detail.[8] This chapter explores the origins of a body of work that everyone accepts is difficult to identify precisely. Mostly written or first published in magazines, pamphlets and anthologies soon after 1968,[9] the poetry treated here was – in Buck's words – 'presented as such, at the time, by the poets themselves', partly in being published by feminist publishers like Sheba or the Only women Press, in collectively published (women-only) anthologies, or in other 'identifiably feminist contexts such as *Spare Rib*, *Red Rag*, *Writing Women* and *Distaff*'.[10] Such contexts frame and reinscribe its unapologetically political outlook. Often acknowledging the collective nature of their writing process, these poets stress their strong sense of community. Typically, they utter their ideological principles, especially the process of consciousness-raising, as much through their prosodic practice as through voice or theme.

In large part, feminist poetry of the 1970s can be read as a collective protest against aesthetic and social isolation: many of its central literary figures have described how participation in their local Women's Liberation groups shaped their poetic development.[11] In the crop of women-only anthologies where most were first published, as Michelene Wandor explains, a sense of common enterprise generates the 'confidence to home in critically on subject matter that has been taboo or shadowed in the canons of twentieth-century poetry'.[12] Understandably reluctant to overdetermine feminist poetry, Buck takes Lilian Mohin's *One Foot on the Mountain* as her focus. Drawing its title from a poem by Alison Fell, this generous 252-page selection, containing the work of fifty-five poets, showcases the feminist poetry which emerged from the first decade of the British women's movement. It remains definitive. However, two narrower anthologies which preceded Mohin's help to illuminate this work.[13] If Mohin's sprawling collection maps out the territory, in all its breadth and diversity, *Cutlasses and Earrings* (1977) and *Licking the Bed Clean* (1978), featuring five poets each, provide a route through it.

Published in consecutive years, the two pamphlets chart the growing self-confidence of the feminist voice. The earlier publication, *Cutlasses* is obviously less adventurous, its ideology announced by the word 'feminist' as an angled flash over the word 'poetry' on an unillustrated front cover. Beside later anthologies, especially given the theatrical potential of its title, this seems understated. *Licking* immediately appears more untidily self-assured, an impression confirmed by the rapid sketchy style of the line drawings (by Pixner and Fell) which decorate the front and back jacket, and are scattered through the text. A less structured, nonhierarchical approach is advertised by the sketch of a group of five female figures, clasping each other's shoulders, at the head of a preface which takes the unusual form of an anonymised informal conversation between the authors. The change suggested by such visual differences is confirmed in the contents of the two books.

Distinguishing itself from other women-only anthologies (such as Trevor Kneale's 1975 *Contemporary Women Poets*, which includes feminists like Harriet Rose and Valerie Sinason while avoiding an ideological stance) *Cutlasses* declares itself 'an extension in literature of political feminism' and proclaims 'a new subject matter ... which challenges conventional love poetry in particular and also asserts the presence of women as writers with a new militancy'. The editors are firm: 'The message or dilemma of each poem is as important as the rhythm, the imagery, the language we use ...'[14] Apparently more informal, *Licking* is also more self-conscious. It advertises itself as a collective enterprise, born of weekly meetings: 'the group helped us ... to develop confidence in our identity as writers'.[15] The introduction is framed, significantly, as an open 'discussion' of issues ranging from the definition of a feminist poem to '*The women we "ought" to be*', as if we are witnessing a kind of literary 'consciousness-raising', the process behind the devolved structure of the women's movement. As Coote and Campbell explain, consciousness-raising

stresses the need for every participant to work out her politics for herself, in a supportive context ... It fosters solidarity. It makes personal experience the base on which theory and strategy are built. It ... is the process of bringing into awareness deeper levels of female experience – by naming and affirming individual feelings and experience and finding out how far they are common to women in general.[16]

While many of these ideas are evoked in the poems themselves, they also inform the anthology's preface, underlining its difference from Fell and Wandor's approach. For example, it is quickly admitted that 'Lack of confidence runs deep in us' although one voice explains, 'We agreed that it's vital as feminists and writers to express what we are, even if it isn't what we would like to be, and to try and honestly grasp the tension of that contradiction.'[17] Differences of view are neither disguised nor excused in the collective process of 'naming and affirming individual feelings and experience[s]'.

Both anthologies demonstrate their radical ideals in poems which never lack political inflection without necessarily being overtly political. Fell and Sheila Rowbotham engage most directly with topical events and debates: in *Cutlasses*, Fell's 'Women in the Cold War' and Rowbotham's 'The Role of Women in the Revolution defined by some Socialist men (1968)' and 'Harry McShane', are obvious examples, while *Licking* includes Fell's 'The Victors October 18 1977' and 'For Maria Burke'. Despite the ironic, half-amused air of its 'Let us' refrain, 'The Role of Women ...' is a furiously unsubtle critique of masculine politics by one of the leading figures of Women's Liberation:

> Let us wank into Revolution
>
> Let us find girls to make the tea
> Let us explain to them
> The nature and limits of emancipation
>
> Let us stick cunts
> On our projecting egos
> Calling this comradeship[18]

Although she can achieve it more delicately (as in the Stevie Smith-like lyric 'The sad tale of nobody me' in *One Foot*), Rowbotham's argumentative poetry is less successful than Fell's, whose 'Women in the Cold War' and 'For Maria Burke' are among her best work, or that of Michèle Roberts', whose lesbian love song 'Klefshaven' ('Cleft haven' in Norwegian) overwrites male literary tradition without reenacting its exclusivity. Although this poem is charged with erotic feeling, rendered in a richly suggestive language ('I wanted to slide further into you, klevshaven/and to suck your forest and hear your waters/crash'), its conclusion looks to a unified future: 'women/have landscapes to build, men and women/have landscapes to build, to build'.[19]

The only poets to appear in both pamphlets (and in *Licking*'s 1980 sequel, *Smile, Smile, Smile, Smile*), Fell and Roberts remain among the most respected writers to have emerged out of the feminist movement. The elder of the two, Fell became involved with the women's movement in Leeds in 1970. A biographical note explains that, 'it was as a result of her feminist commitment that she left Leeds for London' the same year, where she co-founded the Women's Street Theatre Group and began writing for underground papers like *INK, Islington Gutter Press* and *Red Rag*.[20] She joined the editorial board of *Spare Rib* in 1975. Among various books, Fell has published three full collections, and edited several women-only antholo-gies, of prose as well as poetry. Fell's manner can seem blunt, but compassion colours poems which are rooted in (often Scottish) places associated with war or struggle, as well as those confronting the construction of the female (often sexual) identity, or female-centred experience. Her upbringing in the Scottish Borders haunts the much-anthologised 'Women in the Cold War'. Here, a clearly female voice is dismayed by a rural community apparently unmoved by international crisis. Impatient of her peers, 'smooth/and full-blown dreaming of marriage' the speaker pityingly realizes the narrowing effect (figured in the present participles) of family life on female potential. When she airs her intention to become 'an artist':

> their eyes scaled and their good sense
> bunched against me.
> 'That's no' for the likes o' us.'
> Elizabeth, Elaine, Rhoda of the long legs,
> all matrons, mothering, hurrying
> their men to work at 7am.[21]

Fell's example warns against underestimating a poetics which draws without apology on her own life, in particular close family relationships. The portrait of the grandmother which emerges from the intricacies of 'Girl's gifts' (thoughtfully unpacked by Buck) is delicately handled, while the sister who shared her experiences of childhood is depicted with affection.[22] However, 'Butterfingers' is both admiring and critical of her mother: 'these hands slippery from not/holding have let me crash'.[23] 'Sail away' is a more reflective account of this relationship:

> We never suited each other
> and we don't fit yet.
> I rattle at the stones you
> won't look under;
> you see a queer stick,
> odd daughter,
> a questioning thing.[24]

The use of such personal experience underlines how the self-critiquing habit of consciousness-raising informs a poetics rooted in the same process. 'Sail Away' suggests a straining of relations between generations which Wandor's 'Lullaby' implicitly elaborates:

> She sang me to sleep
> made sure I had her dreams
> and then protested
> when I awoke
> from her nightmare[25]

Wandor suggests that Fell is not unusual in filtering her relationship with her mother in the effort to understand the social inequalities she contests. An uneasy relationship with the French Roman Catholic mother who 'found my writing an attack on her', often returns Fell's co-contributor Michèle Roberts to the tensions associated with the role and experience of motherhood.[26]

Roberts's poetic self-confidence grew with, and to some extent out of, her political experiences: 'In adolescence, increasing alienation from myself and from the view of feminity purveyed by the late 1950s/early 1960s culture drove me and my writing underground ... I came out as a poet when I found the Women's Liberation Movement in 1970 and realised that I wasn't mad so much as confused and angry.'[27] 'Klevshaven' apart, the poems in *Cutlasses* (its title from Roberts's 'The wanderer and The seafarer revisited') are immature but reveal a bilingual's sensitivity to language. The selection included in *Licking* ranges from the well-known critique of masculinity (reported in a baffled male voice) of 'Women's entry into culture is experienced as lack', to the explicitly sexual 'Go away: For Pam'. The poems in the follow-up anthology *Smile, Smile, Smile, Smile* evince a maturing dexterity (in the tongue-twisting phraseology of 'Civilisation's Acrobat') and Roberts's sharpened interest in the multiplicity of selfhood ('The Amazon's Song', 'The Vicar's Wife's Song', 'The Mistresses' Song to Husbands').

Uneven as they are, Roberts's early poems confirm her psychoanalytical interest in the relationship between language, form and female (sexual as well as social) identity, in contrast to Fell's more pragmatic, more self-sufficient idiom. *The Mirror of the Mother*, her first collection, finds in motherhood a reflexive metaphor for the female experience; neither the Demeter and Persephone poems, nor precursors like 'Then I have been wanting to mourn', spare the emotional complexities of mothering. Roberts remarks that 'I know I write out of the experience of loss; the earliest experience of that is the loss of my mother.'[28] Since her mother is clearly still alive (at the time she is writing), her 'loss' seems to have been psychological. 'Then I have been wanting to mourn' warns that a woman's understanding of her relationship with her mother is profoundly and hopelessly affected at the moment of puberty; the young woman first confronting the biological imperatives of motherhood realises how her displaced childhood has taken with it the mothering which defined it.[29]

Roberts does not limit herself to the metaphor of motherhood: 'I'm female: I use female images to describe the various processes involved in creating a poem or novel. The nun contemplates in silence. The housewife creates order out of chaos. The sibyl is possessed by the goddess. The priestess declaims to the listening people. The mother conceives an idea. The midwife aids the birth.' Monologue allows her to adopt the guise of various female archetypes, while probing the culturally influenced divisions which complicate femaleness. She warns, that 'for a long time I have been preoccupied with the fragmentation and splits I feel . . .: whore/madonna, you've got a body or a soul . . . brains or beauty, you can't be a mother and an artist.' This might explain why those metaphors are not always present in earlier poems; 'I struggled to find them. I needed to name myself in a way that connected female-powerful-creator.'[30]

Exploring fracture and creative connection together, 'Memories of trees' is a resonant moment in Roberts's early poetics. Conjuring the voice of a hybrid myth-like creature which is both woman and tree, this poem celebrates – in densely lyrical language – the tensile strength and plasticity of female power. The conceit marries the material, creative functionality of wood with the more ambiguous potential of its 'passages, and gaps'. In tracing an enabling transformation of womanhood, the poem performatively nourishes a sense of collective female identity:

> we are the hedges around farms
> the milking-stool, the cradle
> we furnish ships, and boxes
> brooms, coffins, desks, and paper
> we are your floors, your windows
> our roots nourish us, twinned
> labyrinthine memories, between us
> passages, and gaps, . . .[31]

In the second half of the poem, the slippage to another myth ('I am not only/heroine, but also/minotaur, she too') figures not only the 'labyrinthine' nature of both myth and memory but also the dualities, both exciting and problematic, awaiting women who contest their conventional role. As Wandor – to whom myth is equally important – puts it, 'we are both explorer and explored'.[32]

Despite differences of stance and style, Fell and Roberts broach most of the concerns uttered by other feminist poets, especially the determination to be heard or read in a communal context. Given the practical, political and philosophical significance of the collective to their lives and sense of identity as writers, they and their peers repay consideration as a group. As Mohin's selection demonstrates, common concerns emerge in themes which endorse the principles and preoccupations of feminist ideology, and a relaxed approach to language and the mechanics of poetic form. Most obviously, feminist poets tackle political issues in ways which justify or illustrate the campaign for women's rights. Examples like Fell's 'For Maria Burke', 'November, '77' (Caroline Halliday), 'For a Housewife' (Gill Hague), Janet Dubé's 'it'll take a long time', and Diana Scott's 'Of the Children of Other People', 'Six poems for hospital workers' and 'Social Security visiting inspector semi-blues' all boldly protest the position of women, their daily lives governed by economic and domestic inequity. Relatively few poems feature men directly, although they make appearances as lovers, fathers, brothers, and – more tenderly – sons. They are most likely to be vilified for conspiring in or condoning domestic and sexual abuse, like the husband of 'Maryse' by Jane Holiday; the rapist and policeman in Wendy Harrison's 'Night Encounter'; the high court judge addressed in Valerie Sinason's 'Dressed to be killed' and the creepy priest in Halliday's 'Confession'.

Throughout, the writers in *One Foot* 'move out of place' by daring to expose, examine and revalue woman-centred experience, reiterating both the complex forces at work in the construction of female identity, and the heterogeneity of the female perspective. It is where singular and plural intersect that poets such as Kazantzis (who finds it 'impossible to write against the grain of my continuing experiences') translate the personal into the political domain.[33] As the original (New York) *Redstockings Manifesto* puts it: 'We regard our personal experiences, and our feelings about that experience, as the basis for an analysis of our common situation ... We question every generalization and accept none that is not confirmed by our experience. We identify with all women.'[34] In so-called 'feminist' poetry, deconstruction of the private reaches of (female) selfhood becomes the starting point of the collective struggle for women's political and cultural rights. Accordingly, in an enfranchising process of self-validation, the poets repeatedly write to and about other women, and not only as lovers or friends. Like Fell, Roberts and Wandor, several revive and retell ancient narratives from a previously unheard perspective (Mrs Noah in Kazantzis's 'No room in the ark'). Others turn female-centred mythical or legendary material to political use. Sooner or later most write to and about themselves, as mothers, daughters, sisters and lovers, even sometimes as poets. However, Kazantzis speaks for many in aiming to write poetry 'where topical events can be allied without falsity to my own inner life and both can mirror something more universal'.[35]

This remark both underlines and throws into question the assumption that this strand of poetry is so self-interested as to be narcissistic. If the voice of the first person singular resounds in feminist poetry, it is not necessarily the poet's own. Fell's 'For Maria Burke' (subtitled 'who knocked at the door while I was writing about the alienation of life in the cities under capitalism') encourages us to identify with both the speaker who confides it, and the authenticating poet who recounts their encounter.[36] This sophisticated text layers the orphan's narrative, the powerlessness of her poverty and homelessness doubled by drug dependency and gender, with that of the narrator-witness startled into deeper political awareness. The poem offers the unwitting Maria a voice (a kind of cultural, as well as actual, shelter) and context in which to piece her tale together. However, the account also embeds the story of the narrator's privileged lifestyle and language. The speaker's awareness of the collision between the political and personal which Maria represents (replayed in the textual interleaving of the third and dialogic first person narratives, and the accompanying commentary) makes her gravely and pointedly self-critical. The intrusion of outer on inner experience moves the poem beyond the self-centred dynamic of narcissism.

The monologue is favoured by Mohin's poets to the point where this anthology sometimes seems reflexively to stage as well as perform the function of consciousness-raising. In Scott's 'A Love Poem to Myself', singularity multiplies with the voices 'working with power//The great voice of one filling the hall and/stairwell'.[37] Here the persistence of the third person pronoun ventilates more apparent narcissism with the broader perspective which always fuelled feminist ideology. In 'the long-haired woman', Kazantzis deconstructs this collective speech, finding its power in a kind of underground communication system which defiantly uses public places and channels to cut through the isolation of female life, allowing women surreptitiously to 'move out of place' both as individuals and in concert:

> listening from woman to woman
> from house to pub to flat to café to house
> on the phone
> to the next woman[38]

While poems like this gesture at female diversity, they also reflect the fact that it makes political sense not to pursue it. Kazantzis is not unusual in signalling an individuality she fails to explore in any depth before subsuming it in the plural. To some extent, the 'feminist' poetry of the 1970s is weakened by its politically driven sacrificing of individuality in the name of the common cause. On the other hand, as Buck and Bertram demonstrate, if this at times clumsily universalising writing (what Buck calls 'a sustained form of cry') has generated critical hostility, it has also been paid little close attention. For Buck, the neglect – an aspect of the marginalisation of women's poetry as a whole – helps to explain its political ineffectuality by comparison with that of American feminist poets like Adrienne Rich. For Bertram, it confirms the stranglehold of a dominant liberal humanist aesthetic over postwar British poetry. However, while Bertram and Buck both scrutinise the workings of feminist poetry, neither weighs the *literary aims* outlined by Mohin: 'the conceptual restrictions of what it is appropriate for women to be, to think, to write are being carefully eroded . . . we have begun to do really new work, feminist work . . . and, by doing so, are redefining poetry as well'.[39]

Mohin's declaration opens up critical debates about the status and value of feminist poetry. If, as recent scholarship suggests, 'the conceptual restrictions' she describes have been 'eroded' by women poets for several centuries, to what extent, and in what ways, is the work of a group of feminist poets published at the end of the 1970s 'new'? How does it achieve the kind of poetic redefinition that Mohin asserts? For in some senses, *One Foot* is hardly novel: the use of personal experience is widespread in postwar poetry, while women poets have long distinguished themselves from their male peers by reworking myth, for example. Its privileging of the female voice, woman-centred experience, and the construction of female identity is not exclusive to the feminist community. Yet Mohin proves the lengths to which women are prepared to go in order to challenge 'what it is appropriate for women to be, to think, to write'.

Many of these poems seem intended to shock readers into political awareness. They tackle subjects like physical and sexual abuse, rarely before treated openly in poetic history, exploring women's sexual and imaginative experience in disconcertingly graphic detail. Caroline Gilfillan's 'Blood that we are taught to hate' and Halliday's 'Turkish Bath' celebrate the female form and physiology; Kazantzis's courageously circumspect 'Towards an abortion' is one of many to view female biological function more ambivalently, while in 'Lesbian' and 'Dressed to kill', Paula Jennings challenges the socio-cultural expectations which conspire in defining an acceptable version of female sexuality in a different but equally blatant way. Materially, then, this poetry deals forcefully with discomfiting subjects; thematically, as Scott warns, it 'charts new territory'.[40]

It can also alienate. This is partly to be expected, as Bernikow warns: 'Rage and anger, particularly aimed at men, meet resistance in the male reader. Homosexual love between women may meet indulgence but certainly not understanding. Nor have the guardians of tradition taken kindly to the sound of a woman's voice, alive or on the page, chanting anarchy, chaos, or revolution.'[41] On the question of form, however, the women join in the disapproval. Introducing *The Faber Book of Twentieth-Century Women's Poetry*, Fleur Adcock roundly dismisses '"primal scream" writing: slabs of raw experience untransformed by any attempt at ordering and selection'.[42] The complaint compresses the three main reasons for critical exception to feminist poetry: its choice of material, its tone and its refusing of formal discipline. Firstly, Adcock implies that feminist poetry is an embarrassing offshoot of the confessional poetry written by Anne Sexton and Plath. While both are presences in *One Foot* and other anthologies (and poems like Halliday's resonantly titled 'Confession' and Kazantzis's 'Towards an abortion' are plainly confessional in mode and manner), the charge fails to acknowledge the transforming nuances of consciousness-raising at work in these and other poems.[43] Buck argues that feminist poetry reformulates '[the confessional model] as a poetics of consciousness-raising in which women's personal experience becomes central to the poetry, but only insofar as its status as private and individual experience is challenged by means of a feminist political perspective'.[44]

The tonal range of this poetry – less inclined to unrestrained complaint than usually supposed – is also broader than Adcock suggests. While irritation runs through many poems, grief, pity and humour (deployed most effectively by Kazantzis, Pixner and Sinason) also play their part. Even the anger directed at the judge of Sinason's 'Dressed to be killed' and at the men in Rowbotham's 'The Role of Women . . .' is the sharper for its self-control. However, the related charge, that a general failure to 'order . . . and select' denies such work the status of poetry, is more serious, especially in the light of feminist efforts to redefine poetry. In part, the 'accessible language and form' of feminist poetry, especially the prevalence of free verse, distracts from what can be deeply self-conscious prosody. In 'and mother why did you tell me', Stephanie Markman eschews capital letters and punctuation, giving her phraseology a frantic edge:

> mother why did you tell me
> tell me
> tell me why did you lie
> mother why did you teach me
> teach me[45]

In the dry triads of 'Uncertainty', Hague's panic 'wants to rise and can't/ because of solid discipline,/of old poetic ways'.[46] Pauline Long's self-referential meditation on female utterance, 'If women could speak what language

would they use?' is closely wrought, its stanzas gradually contracting
from four or five lines into couplets, its flexing lines accommodating the
naturally rhythmic inflections and internal rhymes of a flaring rhetoric:

> Who are those women, standing there and laughing,
> Those women standing there, dancing,
> Those women, singing, talking, speaking, shouting,
>
> Speaking in some language that some understand
> Speaking with eyes and tongue and head and body
> Speaking.[47]

In a poem threaded through by rhetorical questions, the use of punctuation
is interesting. Its presence here signals the (imprecise) diversity of the
female community, its self-affirming energies captured in the participles
which the commas separate; its absence suggests how this community, in
all its disparateness, unites in uttering its common purpose, and conveys
the excitement triumphantly affirmed in the repetition of 'Speaking'.

Such examples suggest that this poetry is less 'unordered' than it might
seem. However, feminist poets' determination to challenge what they
consider the patriarchal apparatus of poetic evaluation fuelled critical
antipathy. The preface to *Licking* flaunts its disdain: ' – Standards are
irrelevant to us, a bogey ... We should be suspicious of the elitism implied
in them.'[48] Defending literary elitism in the *Everyman Book of English Verse*
(1981), John Wain retraces these remarks, with fastidious horror, to 'a
collection of work by five feminist poets; I will not give its name because
I do not want to hand it a free advertisement.'[49] His disdain is shared by an
academy antagonistic to a poetry which, it assumes, 'tries to overturn the
whole notion of quality, to reject all criteria or what makes a poem"a
poem"'.[50] Here, Rumens spells out what Wain and Adcock imply: refusing
to play by the rules, feminist poetry defeats its own literary ambitions and
sacrifices any claim to aesthetic worth.

Although many feminist poets admit to dissatisfaction with critical
standards, Rumens's charge remains unfair.[51] In context, the comment
Wain lifts from *Licking* helps to clarify the innovations Mohin promises:

– But we already have standards; we revise our own poems, we criticise each
other's work, we think we might not be good enough ... it's liberalism to
pretend we don't. Standards are about how we get our experience across.
About finding language that's appropriate, alive ... We owe it to ourselves
and whoever reads the poems to write as well as we can and to develop and
assert our own standards.[52]

The emphasis on the right of the collective to evolve its own aesthetic, in 'appropriate' language, lies at the heart of feminist redefinitions of poetry. Gillian Allnutt defines a feminist poem as 'one that is written by a woman with respect not only for her own truth, her own way of seeing and feeling the world, but also for the language – "man-made" but not, given a little loving attention, unmalleable – which she uses to express that truth.'[53] However, the foregrounding of a female subjectivity which is by definition embattled is less straightforward than Allnutt, let alone many of the poets themselves, suggests. In an interesting theoretical leap, Buck argues that the prevalence of 'the lowercase first-person pronoun' in feminist poetry figures the equivalence of poetic and political, moving 'beyond the assertion of an autonomous and individualist model of subjectivity to an exploration of the way identity emerges from within a linguistic and social nexus ... [T]he "self" is distinguished and specified in terms of a particular feminist agenda of self and liberation ... that opposes a masculine and individualist model of selfhood with a model conceived in terms of relationship and a feminist political community.'[54] On the other hand, the gap between the unapologetically subjective 'voice' of the poem, and the ideological context/community in which it is often submerged is not always managed as effectively as Buck implies. Arguably, the strenuously self-critical counterpoint charging 'For Maria Burke' is that poem's most resonant feature; in other poems, frequently, too much seems to be presumed poetically of a relationship between individual and group which is neither self-evident, nor leaves room for political and ideological growth.

The anthologies discussed here reveal a shaping poetics innovative if not unproblematic in its self-interestedly collective purpose. Feminist poems are informed by the communal on every level; their collaborative method and practice, their choice of content and idiom. Individual poets repeatedly emphasise the extent to which their literary identity is bound up with the companionship and confidence supplied by other feminist writers: by 1982 Roberts has published four collaborative collections, but none on her own.[55] Fell, Roberts and Wandor are not the only ones to extend this sense of community in literary activities disseminating or connected with feminism: as well as editing anthologies, many of their peers also research, write and find ways to publish books about women's issues as well as novels, short stories, plays and poetry; they edit and contribute to review pages; they form and join artistic initiatives like feminist publishing collectives, poetry magazines, visual art projects, and theatre, writing and study groups. In this context, the poems of self-proclaimingly feminist anthologies like *One Foot*, whether they critique poetic tradition (Wandor's 'Some Male Poets' or Mohin's 'Radical Feminist Poem'), or erode its gender-specific conventions (Scott's 'Love Poem to Myself', Allnutt's 'The Talking Princess', Sinason's 'Passing the test', or Hague's 'Three/One Women') make aesthetic and political sense of each other. This interdependence charges the process, even if it can appear cliquish in ways that succeeding generations are careful to avoid. The partisan mood of Ann Oosthuizen's 'Bulletins from the front line' (honouring her four co-editors on *Licking*) is imbued with personal responsibility:

> Here it is, the war
> In me, start here.[56]

CHAPTER 8

Disruptive lyrics:
Veronica Forrest-Thomson, Wendy Mulford and Denise Riley

The linguistically disruptive work of writers like Veronica Forrest-Thomson, Wendy Mulford and Denise Riley resists easy categorisation. These poets, like their peers and successors (Carlyle Reedy, Elaine Randell, Glenda George, Geraldine Monk and Maggie O'Sullivan, for example) write openly from a position of difference: from the formal lyric expectations of postwar, Movement-influenced British mainstream traditions; from the postwar American poetics and L = A = N = G = U = A = G = E poetry with which most converse; from the work of other women poets, even the prewar precursors they learn from rather than emulate; from male peers and, ultimately, from each other. It is tempting to situate them, as Mulford once located herself, in a 'place of recalcitrance' yet recent criticism finds for them unsettling markers like 'expressive', 'experimental', 'feminist', 'lyric' and 'modernist', each with its own contested discourse.[1] The terminologies seem only to confine a poetry which calls the nature of difference itself into question.

Comparing such writers with Edith Sitwell or Mina Loy suggests how the landscape of British poetics has changed for women over the century. Primarily, what survives the passage of time are the links with an intellectual elite (located, for several of those treated here, in and around Cambridge), the role of progressive publishing outlets – especially the responsive medium of the little magazine – and an internationalist (not exclusively American) perspective prompting new directions in poetic practice and linguistic and sociological theory, as well as translation. They renovate, update and complicate the textually dynamic, impersonal example of their modernist predecessors, as Freud gives way to Lacan and the political inflections of Kristevan semiotics. Once again, the inscrutable Stevie Smith hinges the two generations; her playfully antirepresentational example offers a poetic (and to some extent chronological) departure point for a 'neo-avant-garde' taxed less by the constraints of family and class than by the struggle to utter, against the grain of the poetic mainstream, the contingencies of its own cultural moment.

Reedy maintains that 'No model adapted from a previous culture is likely to be adequate in permitting the poet to meet the challenges of . . . her own time and place.'[2] O'Sullivan clarifies her own purposes as 'Activated, closely, broadly, introspectively – Charting ambiguity,/tending the possibilities in language.'[3]

Mulford was among the first to try to clarify the radical aims of an emergent poetics in which, as poet, editor and founder of the small press Street Editions, she was instrumental:

> With what voices do women poets speak? In avant-garde, experimental or Language Poetry (to throw in three assorted and not particularly helpful labels), there is no unified lyric voice – its claims are exploded . . . In its place, we . . . follow the text in all its provisionality, its multiple meanings, its erasures, silences, chora. Into the darkness, along the glass-sliver edge between consequentiality and inconsequentiality, abandoning narrative, assuming a poetics of play and gesture.[4]

For the Marxist-feminist Mulford, the will to undo the male hierarchies of lyric tradition is political; an earlier essay confides, that 'I want to join my voice with the voices of other *women* struggling to destruct [sic] the lie of culture.'[5] Various critics agree that it is in exploring the textual interstices enjoyed by Mulford that she and her peers have discreetly animated British poetry since the 1970s. Clair Wills, Linda Kinnahan and Romana Huk reproach the neglect of such work and have helped to open it up literally and theoretically.[6] All three insist that feminists can write experimental poetry without defeating their own ideological convictions, primarily by (to adapt Mulford) 'de[con]struct[ing]' the lyric 'I' at the centre of the 'lie of [poetic] culture'.[7] For Wills, the twentieth-century's 'transformation of the relations between the public . . . and private sphere' explains women's fusing of traditional (expressive, subjective, lyric) and experimental (exteriorised, anti-representative, metalinguistic) modes; their work proves 'not the absence of a sphere of privacy but the ways in which that . . . realm of experience is constructed through the public . . . Interiority then, but without the representation.'[8] Huk also refutes the opposition of 'traditional' and 'disruptive': 'what we must redefine as "radical poetry" . . . would be a practice that works more self-reflexively from within as well as without the conventional/historical/discursive boundaries that locate its project to critique or explode those limits'.[9] Kinnahan offers a detailed account of the ways in which Monk, Mulford and Riley each tackle 'the task of rethinking the lyric self while retaining the potential for subject constitution that the speaking "I" opens'.[10]

Arguably, the reticent figure of Rosemary Tonks mediates between Smith and the 'linguistically innovative' poets gathered together by O'Sullivan in

1996.[11] Admired in certain critical circles – she was anthologised by Philip Larkin (1973) and latterly by Sean O'Brien (1998) – Tonks fell silent after the appearance of her second collection *Iliad of Broken Sentences* (Bodley Head, 1967). Her spirited satirical idiom is still regarded as something of an acquired taste in critical circles; emphasising the continental air and metropolitan settings of her poems, Simon Jarvis contends that her 'two volumes of poetry stand entirely outside any of the main or even marginal currents of post-war English writing'.[12] Yet the overwrought voice of 'The Sofas, Fogs and Cinemas' (*Notes on Cafés and Bedrooms*, 1963) also sounds mischievously Prufrockian:

> I have lived it, and lived it,
> My nervous, luxury civilisation
> My sugar-loving nerves have battered me to pieces.[13]

As well as recalling Eliot, Tonks's theatrical, self-interrupting style, its fractured and repetitive phraseology textured by exclamations, italics and ellipses, tests the limits of dramatic monologue. In an account which ranges an agitated (ungendered) speaker against an apparently overbearing, self-centred (male) interlocutor, the tensions between speech and thought, inner and outer worlds are reengaged in the opposing of low (cinema) and high (opera) culture, of self-knowing neurosis and implacable self-confidence, as the tone veers between accusation and mockery with Plath-like urgency:

> The screen is spread out like a thundercloud – that bangs
> And splashes you with acid . . . or lies derelict, with lighted waters in it,
> And in the silence, drips and crackles – taciturn, luxurious.
> . . . The drugged and battered Philistines
> Are all around you in the auditorium . . .
>
> And he . . . is somewhere else, in his dead bedroom clothes,
> He wants to make me think his thoughts
> And they will be *enormous*, dull – (just the sort
> To keep away from).
> . . . when I see that cigarillo, when I see it . . . smoking
> And he wants to face the international situation . . .
> Lunatic rages! Blackness! Suffocation!
>
> – All this sitting about in cafés to calm down
> Simply wears me out. And their idea of literature!
> The idiotic cut of the stanzas; the novels, full up, gross.
>
> I have lived it, and I know too much.
> My café nerves are breaking me
> With black, exhausting information.[14]

However, while the cosmopolitanism harks back to high modernism, other elements (partly in turning away from 'black, exhausting information') point beyond that *'enormous'* Eliot-like presence. Unseaming the cultural and political binaries it describes, the poem utters the speaker's 'exhausting' effort to find a language with which to argue alterity and resist the assault of environs and relationship on the lyric 'I'. The fraught, explosive manner of an apparently interior monologue captures the speaker's wavering self-control, and hints at its psychological effects. Much is left unsaid.

Many poets apart from Tonks renovate modernist assumptions about lyric form and content: Frances Horovitz, Penelope Shuttle, Jeni Couzyn or even the self-professedly experimental Welsh poet Alison Bielski ('exploring the area where different art forms meet') might be summoned alongside Tonks here.[15] In none, however, is the relationship between the architecture and materials of the lyric poetic construct, its speaker, and the elusive, duplicitous nature of its meaning called so archly and actively into question as it is by writers like Reedy, Randell, Monk and George who contribute to Mottram's British Poetry Revival in the 1960s and 1970s. All repay scrutiny; pressure of space has required us, reluctantly, to be more selective than any of them deserve.

'TO GET THE BETTER/OF *WORDS*': VERONICA
FOREST-THOMSON

> to Humpty Dumpty, who said
> that we could only learn to get the better
> of *words*, for the thing which.[16]

When she died unexpectedly, aged only 27, during the 1975 Cambridge Poetry Festival, Veronica Forrest-Thomson was already a considerable presence in academic circles. Her contemporary, poet-critic Geoffrey Ward, says that 'She was the biggest loss to English as a discipline in my lifetime, without any doubt whatsoever.'[17] Two women have helped, in mitigation, to ensure that Forrest-Thomson's name survives: Mulford, who oversaw the publication of her posthumous collection *On the Periphery* in 1976 and, more recently, Alison Mark, whose critical work has reignited interest in a remarkable poetics.[18]

Forrest-Thomson's scientific and often very funny poetics is theorised in her criticism, chiefly *Poetic Artifice*, published posthumously in 1977.[19] She blends the disjunctive character of postwar American poetry with European linguistic philosophy (Wittgenstein), Dada and Unrealism, psychoanalytical theory and structuralism. If, as G. S. Fraser recalls, 'What she looked for in poetry was a critical clash and juxtaposition of conventions', it was in order to interrogate them.[20] Her ideas are difficult to summarise here, but an overriding interest in language – its sources, intrinsic features, operation and referentiality – impels the central self-reflexive refrain: what does the language of a poem do, to the poem itself, author and reader? Mark summons Forrest-Thomson's words: '"The question always is: how do poems work?" Always how they work, rather than what they mean.'[21] Vigilant attention to the poem's self-conscious process ('artifice') fosters the kind of reading that Forrest-Thomson calls, approvingly, 'suspended naturalisation'. This 'allows the constraints imposed by the formal patterning of the poem to govern the range of interpretation applicable, resisting the tendency to a premature narrative assimilation of the poem'.[22]

Assimilation, like 'naturalisation', resounds in a poetry which, like Humpty Dumpty, encourages and frustrates the effort to 'learn to get the better/of *words*'. The term is applied in what Forrest-Thomson calls the 'image-complex' ('a level of coherence which helps us to assimilate features of various kinds', among which might be metaphor, for example).[23] Honouring Lewis Carroll's antiexegetical 'nonsense verse' (and the reading of 'Jabberwocky' which Humpty Dumpty offers in *Through The Looking-Glass*), to some extent the opening lines of 'The Further-Off-From' depend on assimilation. To read this poem is to recognise in reading, like learning, the effort to assimilate an assimilation (the poem) of an assimilation (its borrowed language). It argues that getting 'the better/of *words*' means grasping, paradoxically, the task's impossibility. The poem functions just as its title promises: in the attempt to learn, knowledge (comprehension of what Humpty, or what the poem itself 'means') draws nearer only as it is proved to be 'the further-off-from'. As well as 'mak[ing] explicit the dialectical relationship between the reader's interpretation and the words on the page', this inner dynamic helps to complicate the poem's account of subject/object relations.[24] Whether or not the preposition and hyphen-heavy title is read into the first line, Humpty becomes addressee as well as addressor; the line ending calls who said what into question.[25] Centralised on the line, 'only' is ambiguous; depending on where the stress falls, either we have no choice *but* to 'learn to get the better/of *words*', or we should never expect fully to know *how* 'to get the better/of *words*'. Barely three lines in, the poem has turned into a highly compressed riddle. Despite the full stop, the last half-finished clause, like the title, condenses and replays all the tensions: the clearer Humpty's remark (suspended formally and semantically) begins to seem, the 'further-off' both it, and the possibility of acting on his advice, seems.

The choice of Humpty Dumpty as the focus for this lesson does not, given his fate, seem coincidental; in a note appended to *Language-Games* (1971), Forrest-Thomson promises that 'the new kind of subject will be one that can be approached and even defined in terms of formal experimentation. The process is one of smashing and rebuilding the forms of thought'.[26] Humpty's soon-to-be-shattered shape literally prefigures the elision, in 'formal experimentation,' of destruction and construction, subject and object. The poem goes on, elliptically (and suggestively free of punctuation):

> And is the oyster also the pearl,
>   then what about the oyster
>   catcher

The movement from Humpty to oyster to pearl to bird/man generates the 'thematic synthesis' elicited by suspended naturalisation. Such terminology seems as modernist as the often Imagistic air of Forrest-Thomson's first collection, *Identi-Kit* (1967). Poems such as 'Clown (by Paul Klee)' wield a Sitwellian rhetoric (although she was no admirer of Sitwell, Forrest-Thomson shared the former's interest in French Symbolism and Surrealism); the self-censoring sonnet 'Contours – Homage to Cezanne' recalls Loy's taut lexical logic; the rhyming couplets of 'Through the Looking-Glass' seem Smith-like in their chastening of fairytale into prayer:

> Mirror, mirror on the wall
> show me in succession all
> my faces, that I may view
> and choose which I would like as true.[27]

'Through The Looking-Glass' is among the first poems which, disentangling desire, language and self-projection, speak to the subject's 'several identities' (a phrase used in 'Antiphrasis', and 'Antiquities'); Alison Mark reads other early examples, such as 'Gemini', the titular 'Identi-Kit' and 'Sagittarius' astutely.[28] Like Suzanne Raitt's appreciative review of the *Collected Poems and Translations*, Mark's accounts are only faintly nuanced by gender.[29] This respects a poet who, maturing in the insular patriarchy of Cambridge, shows little interest in other women poets and hardly mentions gender in her critical work. Yet 'An Impersonal Statement' (1967) warns how 'a, perhaps exaggerated, respect for impersonality' gradually achieves, in the 'exploration of language-possibilities [which] extend man's capacity to articulate and experience . . . a more personal level, by showing what can be done with an experience or subject to, perhaps, help others to live their own experiences more fully and richly'.[30] Accordingly, Ian Gregson finds Forrest-Thomson paradoxically 'combin[ing] the talents of a linguistic analyst with those of a love-poet'.[31]

Gender plays more part in *On the Periphery* than in earlier books, especially in 'The Lady of Shalott: Ode', 'The Garden of Proserpine' and 'Cordelia: or, "A Poem Should not Mean but Be"' (published as a pamphlet in 1974; Raitt calls it 'the crown' of the *Collected Poems*).[32] Both argue with the canonical writings which frame them. The silence of Tennyson's enigmatic Lady, revived as a female Ancient Mariner kneeling in snow, is as menacing as the sight of her 'who thicks men's blood with cold'.[33] The dialectic of love and death, passion and frigidity, hope and knowledge returns in Persephone, addressing her 'many-toned' alter ego Aphrodite ('goddess of tight corners'). Persephone may 'know better' than her readers that 'Love is hellish' but, helplessly contracted to Zeus and 'gloomy Dis', she can only point out the further trap within the trap:

> Of all follies that is the penultimate:
> To let our own inventions destroy us,
> The ultimate folly, of course, is not to let them destroy us.[34]

In 'Cordelia', the parallels between emotional experience and aesthetic (poetic) enterprise, both refracting the dialectic of destruction and construction, are made plainer and more gendered still. Stealing openly from Milton, Pound, Swinburne, Shakespeare, Joyce, her friend J. H. Prynne and, most obviously, Eliot (chiefly *The Waste Land*), Forrest-Thomson stands (almost literally, naming herself at line 110 of a 214-line text) at the core of a poem built, antithetically, out of the example of 'bullying men' traced to 'The infernal Odyssos . . . whose bile/Stirred up by envy and revenge destroyed/The mother of womankind.' Impudently subduing Eliot, Milton and Shakespeare, 'Cordelia' conjures itself out of the same destructive energies as those of history, in turn predicated upon emotional conflict. This is how 'there is a point where incest becomes/Tradition' and the subjective 'I' dilates: 'I, Helen, I Iseult, I Guenevere, /I Clytemnestra and many more to come./I did it, I myself, killing the King my father./ Killing the King my mother, joining the King my brother/. . . I, Veronica did it, truth-finding, truth-seeking/Muck-raking.'[35] The poet identifies herself with women whose strength is realised in the endurance of defeat. However, the (now poignant) insistence that 'you can't do anything when you are dead' ironises their example; the mood remains farsightedly equivocal.

'A WRITING OF THE SELF?': WENDY MULFORD

> is a writing of the self a writing of writing?
> and is a writing of writing a writing of the self?
> double u one.
> mark one.[36]

As the epigraph hints, Mulford's poetry is neither very far from Forrest-Thomson's, nor very close to it. Her manner is more down to earth, but she, too, pays close attention to the interplay of syntactic units and textual arrangement. It is often in refrain that Mulford's idiom exposes the cultural or political frameworks of language. Like all her best work, 'l.' conflates the philosophical and aesthetic implications of a self-consciously metalinguistic deconstruction of (female) subjectivity, in which both expression and experience are repeatedly turned literally inside-out in order to explore the (punningly) 'double [yo]u', or rather, 'mark one'.

Six years older than Forrest-Thomson, Mulford grew up in Wales; she moved to Cambridge in the 1960s, founding Street Editions in 1972. The press (renamed Reality Street Editions when it merged with Ken Edwards's Reality Studios) was to become a leading outlet for experimental literature, helping to shape Mulford's own work: 'I started to discover what I was doing about 1974–5, at the time that I was publishing some key "modernist" texts by contemporaries.'[37] These included Prynne, Andrew Crozier and John James (whom she married); she approached Forrest-Thomson about a collection just before her death in 1975. However, Mulford has always maintained her distance from the academic world in which both women moved; as 'Notes on Writing' warns, 'If I write inevitably from the place of being an "intellectual" through my education and profession, that place is shot through with arrows of resistance and doubt, unease and disbelief.'[38]

Politically, Mulford is dismayed by an 'intellectual' poetry unaware of, or unmoved by, the cultural elitism it inscribes. In engaging the same contingencies of language and self as Forrest-Thomson, she subsumes the latter's highly theoretical emphases in a more socially responsible perspective, as in this unusually linear moment in 'ABC of Writing':

> the child lived outside the house
> and grew up ignorantly. she grew up in dreams. later she learned to see. she
> saw where the workpeople lived who worked inside the house and on the
> land. she watched and listened and so she learned.
> later she read and began to see
> why her people would never understand

that there over there they could not see
nor their own part in shaping that reality[39]

Describing this poet as one 'whose language is always a spoken language, never remote nor artificial ... always language with a purpose', Lee Harwood condenses Mulford's response to Forrest-Thomson's more 'remote' artifice.[40] For Mulford, the cultural divisions embedded in terms such as 'inside' and 'outside' (like presence and absence or, equivalently, private and public) can be bridged by 'understanding'; awareness of how interiority intrudes on and mediates external experience. The child's place among 'her people' compels both the interest which removes her from their cultural 'reality', and the sense of recognition with which she learns to understand it by reading herself into it. The child's gender reminds that Mulford's 'purpose' is female-centred and political: 'What in practice does it mean for [the woman writer] to talk about the revolutionary violation of the Law?' 'Against the cold: two she's and a he' demands, 'you inside what do you want?'[41]

Given her politics, Mulford (who is sometimes called a 'contemporary modernist') views modernism with scepticism: 'for me there is always a barrier, a sense of otherness about this tradition ...'[42] Yet aspects of her practice seem distinctly modernist in disposition. Early poems place a painterly emphasis on the visual, and sometimes find an economic intensity which is both surrealist and Imagistic (like Horovitz, she enjoys haiku). This accents the linguistic disruptions by which (in line with Pound) poetic language is made 'new'. In 'The meaning of blue', a crisply realised foreground yields to the opaque breadth of the semantic:

> the feathering touch of highwater nudging the estuary grass –
> taking my mind beyond image
> in to silence

> Through density dictator language must be
> indefinitely in absence we uncover the
> real meaning of blue[43]

The words themselves attest to and challenge a 'dictator language' briefly, here, in abeyance; clarity is 'uncovered', ironically, 'in absence'. The generative agency of such syntactic disarrangement is confirmed in 'Trawls':

> small in
> tense sur
> rounds sur
> renders I, she each little

> noun apart their cargoes
> quarrels the slipway un-
> coiling cables a quick
> haul into the lee losing a
> kind of repeated, gentle
> humiliation[44]

In this poem, pared-down formality disciplines an elliptical, involving idiom reminiscent of Stein. Sundered by their foreshortened lines, the first words stage the estranging effect of syntax which rolls 'I, she each little/noun apart' together. The working language of boats (slipway, cables, haul, lee) is both abstracted by the absence of connectives and made more immediate. Semi-realised verbal gestures like 'slip', 'un-/coil', 'haul' and 'losing' obliquely connect the activity of trawling with the desire for understanding, while denying any overdetermination. At the same time, the two pronouns standing at the centre of the text invite us to read this as a poem which literally trawls the buoyantly multiple, unruly ('quarrel[ling]') character of female identity, the hiatus separating and linking self/other. Outside any obviously human context, if this is a depiction of subjectivity, it is free of the cultural constructions informing the repressive regime of 'The Ancrene Riwle', for example.[45]

Dedicated to the French psychoanalytical theorist Hélène Cixous ('who gave me the question'), 'How do you live?' finds Mulford moving more plainly into the realm of poststructuralism:

> no clear answer, ambivalently.
> reciprocally.   in
> oscillation. lurching in surprise &
> wonder.[46]

Obtrusive punctuation, apparently intent on closing down linguistic suggestion, is undone by unexpected spacings flaunting themselves as aporia. To borrow the language of feminism, the poem foregrounds a 'lack' which is also fullness and presence. In part, the effect of the spaces is to intrude on and interrupt the reader in the act of reading, bringing home the intrinsic possibilities of language and silence. In a revealing moment, Mulford recalls:

When I was a child at school in Wales, our teachers would point with long rulers at the letters and words we were supposed to read and understand on the blackboard. The pointers annoyed me. They slowed up the process of reading when I wanted to race ahead. Now I can see the value of their slow material intrusions, waylaying my attention, prodding into visible existence the baffling abstraction of the word.[47]

Ironically, the full stops imbue this opening section with a certainty absent, semantically, from the words themselves. The mood is countered in the nervously energetic direct speech of a conclusion in which limitations and qualifications crowd together in expressive disarray:

> "a woman's place behind the home
> everywhere & nowhere fear
> of placeness, hold on
> for what we can, cradling
> cuddling care. home love
> tucked body refuge will satisfy what part?"[48]

For Kinnahan, this excerpt 'seems to ask what parts of a woman's subjectivity the experience of body as refuge will "satisfy," a question dually directed toward patriarchy's use of women's bodies and toward Cixous' identification of the female body as source for subjectivity'.[49] Yet the dilemma is anchored in the push-pull dynamic of the home, locus not so much for the kind of fixed, culturally proscribed sense of female identity which Mulford's work has resisted from the outset (the 'fear/of placeness'), as for the mutually sustaining emotional relationships (rather than bodily transactions) in which the competing claims of public and private, inner and outer life finally meet and converge, 'hold[ing] on for what we can, cradling/cuddling care'. Kinnahan rightly notes that the restorative effects of an emotional balance which cannot be protected from the socio-economic injustices of daily life must be limited; in the process of the poem, the demand 'how do you live?' eases into the more self-aware complexity of 'how can we live?'. As 's' later hints, the move from determinacy to indeterminacy opens up the limits of both language and world for the dissolving, desiring subject: 'hoping apart a substance, these politics of impossible/convergence, into gaps, presenting absence'.[50] In Mulford's work, the dismemberment of the subject is an act of linguistic and lyric renovation which, if it violates poetic convention, does so enquiringly, unassumingly and constructively.

'WHICHEVER/PIECE IS GLIMPSED, THAT BIT IS WHAT I AM': DENISE RILEY

> right through this tracery, voices leap up, slip side-
> long, all faces split to angled facets: whichever
> piece is glimpsed, that bit is what I am, held
>
> in a look[51]

Aesthetically if not chronologically, Riley's poetics opens up a dialogue between Forrest-Thomson's anatomising of 'artifice' and Mulford's interrogating of language and subjectivity, although she holds that 'to assess an individual writer *exhaustively* via a real or imaginary social alignment is to prefer a . . . sociogeography to an examination of the work . . . it wraps up a package; it elides'.[52] Her self-fragmenting, daringly lyric poetry resists 'wrap[ping] up'.

Born the year after Forrest-Thomson, Riley arrived in Cambridge in the late 1960s as an undergraduate and returned there in 1975. A respected social historian, philosopher, editor and literary commentator, she is probably a better-known poet than either Forrest-Thomson or Mulford but owes much to the latter, who published Riley's *Marxism for Infants* in 1977), and collaborated on *No Fee: A line or two for free* (Street Editions, 1978). Riley's closeness to Mulford (the authorship of the poems in *No Fee* is left unspecified), and shared political beliefs explains the ideological stance of her earlier poetry, although a maturing idiom gradually alters course. In the first poem of *Marxism for Infants*, the 'Savage' who returns 'home from the New Country/in native-style dress' brings a new set of ideals with her:

> The work is
> e.g. to write "she" and for that to be a statement
> of fact only and not a strong image
> of everything which is not-you, which sees you[53]

However, framing gender politics in cultural (especially capitalist) terms, the poem ironises the compromised figure of the returning (colonised) exile. Arguably, the 'Savage' herself never fully perceives the extent of her own economic and ideological subjection, encoded in the 'native-*style* dress' (an implicitly naive, even insulting, attempt at cultural identification) and confirmed in the poem's final lines: 'The Savage weeps as landing at the airport/she is asked to buy wood carvings, which represent herself.' This is deliberately impersonal, deeply political writing; the doubly estranged figure of the (in one wry sense, 'noble') 'Savage,' her natural voice lost in the explanatory rhetoric of 'the work', holds representation firmly at bay. Here, whether seen to operate linguistically or behaviourally, language is revealed to dictate how 'to write' rather than to express '"she"'.

Riley's use of the third person is an interesting aspect of her defamiliarising scrutiny of female experience. Her memoir 'Waiting' explains that 'When I say "I" and add the past-tense verb, I am at once in the realm of untruth. "I" was never a child. I use this as the voice of synthesising adulthood, oiling the disjointed, making an easy tolerability out of the unbearable.'[54] In response, the narrative of 'Waiting' shifts focus from 'I' to 'she,' reifying the untruthful space between actual and remembered experience, and, paradoxically, authenticating itself at the same time. Riley makes similarly suggestive use of the dialectical distance and intimacy of 'she' and 'I' in her poetry; 'she has ingested her wife . . .' confides, in an elision which isn't, '"She" is I.'[55]

The equation reveals a lyric instinct stronger than in Mulford. After all, to assume that the 'Savage' weeps only in disappointment and political frustration is to devalue the emotion of a homecoming in which the estranged and the familiar clash and blend in an epiphanic instant of self-distancing but also perhaps self-recognition. Conversely, however, the formula also affords the text a newly antilyrical edge. When 'I' is also 'she', the authoritative, universal voice of the (conventionally male) lyric poet is both enlarged and destabilised:

> such face bones honeycombed sockets
> of strained eyes outlined in warm
>
> light aching wrapped in impermeable
> coating of pleasure going off wild
>
> on the light-headed train   "will write
> & write what there is beyond anything"
>
> it is the "spirit" burns in &
> through "sex" which we know about
>
> saying It's true, I won't place or
> describe it It *is* & refuses the law[56]

It is impossible to excerpt a text which arcs so relentlessly from that slow, delicate, palpably erotic start, through the discursive, self-consciously linguistic account of desire at its (formal) centre, into its implacable, somehow buoyant ending. The affirming conjunction of 'spirit' and 'sex' resists fixity, positioning, even utterance. Here, expressive (in its ancient lyric form, the love song) and antiexpressive (the physical and metalinguistic deconstruction of a desire reliant on a language which can only embody it by taking it apart) collide and interpenetrate.

Such tensions explain why, elsewhere, dialogue underpins a fastidious deconstruction of lyric. In a sequence of poems giving voice to various ambitions, 'Two ambitions to remember' is framed as a duet, its voices independent but harmonising rather than conversing. Ambition 'A' speaks in graceful, end-stopped sentences which discourse on their own subversive powers. As the opening couplet explains, 'A' fails ('The shapes of faces stiff with joy/stir in my mind but do not speak') where 'B' succeeds, although the latter's sensuously visual, impressionistic contributions are never completed:

> A. I see my deafened future come
>   while those true words that have no mouth
>   and leap and dazzle silently
>   go streaming down the fiery air.
>
> B. The crush of trees' thin
>   limbs inward and inward
>
> A. Some words you may use only once.
>   Repeat them to some newer heart
>   and all your accuracy is gone.
>
> B. To sail into the lit tunnel
>   a rush of orange, quietly

It is left to 'A' to conclude, much as the solitary, lovelorn, disembodied presence of Echo (would-be lover of Narcissus) might:

> Insane with loneliness I wring
> the tissues of the air to force
> the full words that would answer me.[57]

Both 'such face bones' and 'two ambitions' prefigure and illumine the argument of Riley's self-reflexive critical essay, 'Is There Linguistic Guilt?'[58] In the former poem, what the essay terms the 'characteristic excess in working with lyric, that buzz of ramifications' conspires in the text's lawlessness.[59] Summoning Wittgenstein, Derrida, Heidegger and eventually Althusser, 'Linguistic Guilt' starts with the unreliable voice. Riley argues that '"I" lies':

Any *I* seems to speak for herself; her utterance comes from her own mouth, and the first person pronoun is hers . . . Yet . . . the *I* which speaks from only one place is simultaneously everyone's everywhere; it's the linguistic marker of rarity but is always democratic . . . my narrating *I* is really anybody's promiscuously . . .[60]

This is difficult enough for the self-aware writer ('when I write *I* and follow up the pronoun with a self-description, feelings of fraud grip me').[61] For the lyric poet, the sense of disempowerment is compounded by formality, the 'Law' refuted in 'such bones'. (This partly explains the regularity with which the lyrics of popular songs appear in her writing.) Riley argues that this disempowerment reverses the very process of composition, let alone the notion of poetic authority:

the lyric 'I' offers a simulacrum of control under the guise of form; a profound artifice, ... held by form I work backwards, chipping away at words, until maybe something gets uncovered which I can acknowledge as what I might have had to say ...[62]

As 'two ambitions' reiterates, the poet's effort to use lyric to utter or construct selfhood, therefore, seems doomed: the dialogic mode reifies the seductive partiality of language while underlining its own duplicity. In the unending, hopeless struggle 'to force/the full words that would answer me', the lying lyric 'I' is trapped in its own viciously isolating circle. Its very loneliness calls the poem's dialogue into question; no wonder the 'answer' eludes. Yet it is also in such complexities that Riley underlines lyric's representative powers. Her essay makes sense of the poem's invocation of Echo (her appropriated voice rendering her forever incapable of dialogue), rescuing in this pointedly female character 'a trope for lyric's troubled nature, in that both are condemned to hapless repetition'.[63] Riley tells Huk:

Narcissism is a condition of being fragmented, but it's *through* that fragmentation and *lack* of a boundary that you become aware of and respond to other people's differences: you're constantly struggling with those differences, and you don't suffer from illusions about your own finished quality. That gives you ... the grounds for some notion of exchange among or between people, which is the grounds for any political understanding. So ... I would read narcissism as a *prerequisite for* politics, and not as something which can be aggressively opposed to a realm of politics.[64]

Riley's self-scrutinising study of how externality invades and subverts even the most intimate forms of self-expression pivots on Althusser's 'interpellation', in which the subject guiltily resists an identification it acknowledges ('naming as threat'). Her book-length study of feminism *Am I That Name?* (1988) suggests that 'Given that the anatomically female person far outstrips the ranges of the limiting label woman, then she can always say in all good faith, "here I am not a woman", meaning "in this contracting description I cannot recognize myself."'[65] Poems such as 'Ah, so' ('Speaking apart, I hear my voice run on') and 'No' ('That body's mine but I am it') extend this, implying that self-recognition depends on a kind of physical self-segmentation, where an apparently unself-conscious sensory 'body' is somehow objectified by the self-awarely subject*ive* 'I' which fully expects self-representation to elude it. As in the epigraph, such examples quietly subvert the gendering effect of the gaze.

The title of 'Wherever you are, be somewhere else' converses with Seamus Heaney's ambivalently political lyric 'Whatever you say, say nothing', but sidelines the duplicitous neutralising coherence that Heaney foregrounds. Riley's language, like the 'I' that wields it, is both fractured and fracturing ('A body shot through, perforated'); this allows it to enact the paradoxical manoeuvre signalled in its title while reiterating the dangers of this. Although the poem licenses the liberating fragmentation of the subject, this involves surrendering the splintered 'I' ('whichever piece is glimpsed') to the risks of the fixing, presumably literary, gaze ('held/in a look'). Thus this self-fragmenting, self-exploring poem reprises but also answers Mulford's warning sense of language as 'indiscriminate copula, concealment, persuasion, yoking'. It is perhaps because it has been authored by a woman that Riley's thoughtfully narcissistic, un/representative poetics, identified by and with a subjectivity it relentlessly dismantles, in language ineluctably subjective but hostage to a proliferating external life, is predicated on ambiguity.

Overview

INTRODUCTION

'As a result of the new wave feminism which took root in the late 60s, I happen to be living at a moment during which, for the first time in history, it's been acceptable – even positive – to be a woman poet!'[1] This claim by Sarah Maguire in 1998 warrants both consolidation and sifting. The burgeoning number of women poets in the last two decades of the twentieth century is certainly remarkable. By the year 2000, we see women penetrate the glass ceiling of literary authority. They not only win compe-titions but also judge them and are endowed with literary fellowships. They are in demand at literary festivals, appointed as writers-in-residence, employed as tutors on creative writing workshops and take on more teaching for the prestigious Arvon poetry courses. Into the next century, they are beginning to achieve the highest honours, such as the T. S. Eliot Prize, although not as yet Poet Laureate or Oxford University Chair of Poetry. Nevertheless, the grip of Oxford and Cambridge old-boy networks is loosened by the number of women carrying Oxbridge credentials which were unavailable sixty years before.[2] They begin to collaborate, pay tribute to each other and cite female poets as literary influences, most noticeably Carol Ann Duffy and Eavan Boland. While many are editors or critics, a few exercise influence as artistic directors. The tendency to rate the visibility of women as a 'false democracy', attributable to successful marketing and fashionably positive discrimination, still means that their poems remain glaringly short of literary validation based on aesthetic considerations.

In a climate of pluralistic democracy which witnesses the decline of imperial power and political devolution of the United Kingdom with a Welsh assembly and Scottish parliament, the meaning of 'English' poetry is increasingly unstable, complex and fragmented. Bloodaxe Books in Northumberland is an outstanding contributor towards a new canon which prioritises men and women newcomers from Britain, Ireland and overseas. Other regional presses which advance women are Carcanet (Manchester), Harry Chambers/Peterloo in Cornwall, Seren (*Poetry Wales*) and Blackstaff, Gallery and Salmon in Ireland. London-based Faber, Anvil and Enitharmon publishers promote some women, while Oxford University Press gives its stamp of approval to a few before controversially closing its list in 1999. Women are well represented in the magisterial *Poetry Review* and *PN Review,* a large number of poetry journals and the Poetry Book Society quarterly choices. The full flavour of the period's poetry has also to be drawn from the small presses such as: Hearing Eye, the organ for an eclectic community in North London; Reality Street along with other experimental outlets; the less prominent institutions such as *Stand, Outposts, Aquarius* and *Acumen;*[3] and the regional journals. Although Virago Press opens its list to poetry in the 1980s, we do not have a women's poetry press nor a women's poetry journal, although there are special 'women poet' numbers of *Poetry Wales* (1987), *Aquarius* (1987), *Women: a cultural review* (1990), *Poetry Review* (1996) and *Feminist Review* (1999). A handful of academic conferences and critical books scrutinise and stimulate women's interventions into literary representations.

Under Thatcherism consumer-targeted politics extends to artists' dependence upon marketing, so that the poet's role as cultural critic is in tension with populist demands for personality and entertainment. The New Generation initiative in 1994 is a successful promotion for page poets who are white and under forty. Other initiatives which take poetry into public places include Poetry on the Underground (1986), National Poetry Day (1994) and Poetry on the Buses (1998). Appointments of writers-in-residence stretch from universities, schools and business corporations to hospitals and prisons. Poetry in the broadsheet newspapers draws attention both to its function as political commentary and to its crucial distinction from journalism. Carol Ann Duffy seizes and deflates reductive tabloidese in her parodic 'Poet for our Times' (1990) – 'Cheers. Thing is, you've got to grab attention/with just one phrase as punters rush on by.' Implicitly, she opposes the market pressures upon artists to crowd-please: 'The poems of the decade . . . *Stuff 'em! Gotcha!/* The instant tits and bottom line of art.'[4] In 'Pep-Talk to Poets from their Sales Manager', the American-Irish Julie O'Callaghan wittily mimics artistic compromises to commodifying seductions:

> Hey – Where's the blarney?
> Quit looking like you were just included
> in a 'Contemporary British Poetry' anthology
> or something; we got books to sell![5]

These self-consciously exaggerated colloquial imitations of the media's proverbial 'dumbing down' are typical of women's success in maintaining the dialogue between so-called popular and literary cultures, vocabularies and forms.

The most striking features of poetry in these decades are urban realism or pastoral, making the ordinary strange and the prevalence of diverse dialects which run across a breathtaking range of forms and themes. We find women noticeably confident with idiomatic speech, in the seemingly personal expression required by the lyric as well as their previously pre-ferred dramatic monologue and dialogue where they now take more risks in playing the literary off against the vernacular. As Carol Rumens states in her introduction to *New Women Poets* (1990), 'Poetry's vital energies derive from the way we speak and it perhaps takes special courage for women poets to write in a way that stresses this relationship, rather than seek approval by flaunting their more academic literary credentials'.[6] Confidence is also manifest in more visible social commentary and crossing boundaries of genre through the visual media of theatre, film and televi-sion. Poets with a strong oral tradition, notably Caribbean and Scottish, boost the status of poetry in performance; their respective pioneers in this period, Grace Nichols and Liz Lochhead, supremely demonstrate that an 'oral' tradition is not necessarily an unliterary one. Their cross-fertilisations of standard English and native dialects open up new territory for Jackie Kay and Kathleen Jamie whose dramatisations and linguistic diversity are best experienced at live readings. The distinctness of poetry which is primarily for stage becomes vitalised by Jean 'Binta' Breeze, Valerie Bloom and Patience Agbabi. The extent to which women have overcome their reti-cence in the most street-level performance poetry, the stand-up 'open mike' community events, is difficult to gauge.

Between 1980 and 2000, anthologies are especially accountable for negotiating between the marketplace and the academy but the representa-tion of women is still erratic. Out of 271 poets in *The School Bag* (1997), twenty-three are women but Neil Astley favours women by twenty-nine to nine in *New Blood* (1999). *The New British Poetry 1968–1988*, whose editors include Gillian Allnutt, is even-handed in its promotion of emerging black and feminist writers. Michael Horovitz's *Grandchildren of Albion: an illus-trated anthology of voices and visions of younger poets in Britain* (1992) privileges antiestablishment protest and performance poetry; its exciting cocktail of black and white men and women enhances cultural differences within cross-cultural community. Unlike the *Penguin Modern Poets* of the

1960s, which featured three women in the total of forty-eight, the revived series from 1994 is egalitarian. Currently, *Anvil New Poets*, Bloodaxe Books' audiotapes *Poetry Quartets* and the CDs by 57 Productions integrate men and women across diverse racial alliances.

A spate of retrospective period-based volumes of poetry by women are directed at redressing their underrepresentation in the past: *Scars upon my Heart: Women's Poetry and Verse of the First World War* (1981), *Chaos of the Night: Women's Poetry and Verse of the Second World War* (1984), *Poetry by English Women: Elizabethan to Victorian* (1990), *English Women Romantic Poets* (1992) and *Victorian Women Poets* (1994). Diana Scott's *Bread and Roses: Women's Poetry of the 19th and 20th Centuries* (1982) is produced in the wake of 1970s feminist criticism which often essentialises female experience as restraint and repression. Anthologies organised by trans-historical themes include Veronica Green's *Rhythm of Our Days* (1991) and Rosemary Parmeira's *In the Gold of the Flesh: Poems of Birth and Motherhood* (1990). Culturally specific collations include *The Heinemann Book of African Women's Poetry* (1995) and *Bittersweet: Contemporary Black Women's Poetry* (1998).

Nonthemed volumes chart an evolution from the more comprehensive recoveries of lost work to the more discriminating, and finally attend to how the specificity of female creativity can be identified and evaluated. Jeni Couzyn's selection in *The Bloodaxe Book of Contemporary Women Poets* (1985) partly signals a 'senior generation' who continue beyond the millennium. In addition to Fleur Adcock, Ruth Fainlight, Elaine Feinstein, Denise Levertov, Elizabeth Jennings, Jenny Joseph, Kathleen Raine, Anne Stevenson and herself, she includes Sylvia Plath and Stevie Smith whose posthumous publications brought overdue recognition. The profiles by or about each poet propose an aesthetic in the interface of their writing and lives: 'First and foremost, I wanted poems that were genuinely trying to make sense of experience' (Feinstein) – 'A specifically female anger has been the impetus for many of my poems' (Fainlight).[7] Couzyn's preference is for poets who are writing 'as *women*, poems that no man could possibly have written, and challenging the way we have defined ourselves in relation to men – as lovers, mothers, wives' (p. 18). Antithetically, in *The Faber Book of 20th-Century Women's Poetry* (1987), Fleur Adcock solidifies a predominantly Anglo-American canon which stops at poets born in 1945. She prizes 'wit' and, referring to Plath, 'the technical ability to transform her emotions and experiences into literature and not just "self-expression"' (p. 5). Similarly, Rumens excluded the 'merely self-expressive' from *Making for the Open: The Chatto Book of Post-Feminist Poetry* (1985). By the time of

New Women Poets (1990), however, Rumens welcomes the increase of published women's poetry: 'I believe that we have a process of democratisation on our hands, with women taking a major role in it, and that "more" has not in fact meant "worse", as the bleak old men of the right always assumed, but simply "various"' (p. 12). Half the names in Rumens's anthology have enjoyed subsequent attention. Linda France's *Sixty Women Poets* (1993) is a rich collection of 'three generations'. Their work is strikingly diverse but united by female-specific features such as 'experience within patriarchy', 'paradox and the concept of duality and non-linearity', 'the pleasure principle' and 'much laughter, at many pitches ... irony, parody as well as the big joke' (pp. 16–17).

FOUR GENERATIONS

Generational divides, immediately the most definable, are largely inappropriate when women's publishing ages so markedly vary, but they provide a point of departure for examining the period-specific treatment of cultural politics, female identities and stylistic trends later on. Some of the oldest writers had their most productive periods at the end of their careers but publicity packaging tends towards ageism. As Rumens observed, 'Our senior women poets are dismally unhonoured, and many of the most accomplished writers of the older generations, from Sheila Wingfield to Anne Stevenson, have never had the recognition they deserve.'[8] Jennings (b. 1926) is one of those short of due recognition, particularly by women. Martin Booth's summation is salutary:

Elizabeth Jennings is a quiet poet, one who writes very much from the innermost corners of her privacies. She is not a 'great' poet because she shuns publicity: a cruel statement up to a point but one that is valid. Unless poets these days seek out audiences, they reduce their chances of greatness, but what sort of greatness it is is questionable. Our world demands that the great stand in the spotlight otherwise they are lesser. Elizabeth Jennings is nevertheless great as a poet, but she doesn't look it. Few critical books contain much on her, the public at large do not know of her (to their considerable loss) and she keeps clear of the reading circuit and the poetry machine. Her greatness lies in her work, not her abilities to shout about it.[9]

Between 1980 and 2000, the thirteen volumes by Jennings, whose CBE (1992) should not go unnoticed, doubled her list.

Born before 1920, Laura Riding, Ruth Pitter, Kathleen Raine, Anne Ridler, and E. J. Scovell were still publishing and enjoyed moments of revived attention. Along with the particularly late starters Jean Earle, Pamela Gillilan and Sheila Wingfield, and the late publications of Olive

Fraser, these respected figures softened the ground for the next generation, born between 1920 and 1945, by loosening the bonds of conflict between women's duties and desires. Although not denying their gender as poets, they resisted the concept of gendered creativity: 'honesty of perception and exact observation remain defences against sentimentality – a sense of things rather than ideas'.[10] The most acclaimed – Adcock, Stevenson and Rumens – tended towards an impersonal poetic persona. For Adcock, publishing since 1964 in New Zealand, the last two decades of the century were particularly fruitful. Freed from the clutter of congenital English class-consciousness, her metrical precision produces a seemingly neutral, if occasionally standoffish, standard English speech and her pronouns are usually ungendered: 'It took me a long time to realise I wasn't just a man in some basic sense. The poets I modelled myself on were men and I earned my living and I got a mortgage and I did the things men do. And then it leaked through almost by accident.'[11] The lengthy *Hotspur* ballad (1986) is sung by Henry Percy's wife, Elizabeth Mortimer, but specifically female characters are rare, especially in her early books. Stevenson is notoriously hostile to gendered, along with all, classifications and the variousness of her work successfully evades them. However, in the preface to her *Collected Poems 1955–1995*, she distances herself from an early 'affected and impressionistic style' and in 'The Fiction Makers (i.m. Frances Horovitz)' implies that this necessitated detachment from the prescriptions of 'sanctified Pound':

> squeezing the goddamn iamb
> out of our verse,
> making it new in his
> archaeological plot – [12]

As above, many of Stevenson's poems pay tribute to literary figures. She wrote two long elegiac sequences after Horovitz's death in 1983. Other notable women with whom she connects are Elizabeth Bishop ('Waving to Elizabeth') and Sylvia Plath, whom she famously configured in the biography *Bitter Fame* (1989). Stevenson is most unashamedly lyrical in poems about her children: 'Certainly I've never had you/As you still have me, Caroline.'[13]

Rumens, too, confesses to being stifled by trying to be 'literary' at the start of her career: 'as a younger woman I wrote too many poems in a would-be polite, fit-to-be-in-literary-company sort of accent'.[14] Although unsure about separatist aesthetics, she became more able to embrace the arrival of the 'woman poet'.[15] She often examines the cost of women's unprecedented opportunities. 'Two Women' captures the silent strain of the many who attempt all available options about marriage, motherhood, education and employment:

> Daily to a profession – paid thinking
> and clean hands – she rises,
> unquestioning. It's second nature now.
> The hours, though they're all of daylight, suit her.
> The desk, typewriter, carpets, pleasantries
> are a kind of civilisation – built on money
> of course, but money, now she sees, is human.
> She has learned giving from her first chequebook,
> intimacy from absence. Coming home
> long after dark to the jugular torrent
> of family life, her smile
> cool as the skin of supermarket apples,
> she's half the story. There's another woman
> who bears her name, a silent, background face
> that's always flushed with effort.
> The true wife, she picks up scattered laundry,
> and sets the table with warmed plates to feed
> the clean-handed women. They've not met.
> If they were made to touch, they'd scald each other.[16]

According to Rumens, it 'is a poem that shines a fairly bright "political" light on an area of personal experience. I see late twentieth-century England as an increasingly harsh and ungenerous society. I doubt that poetry by itself can effect big political changes, but I think it helps in its gently subversive way to increase the power of opposition.'[17] Here we see Rumens's predilection for duality, especially private and public bifocals. 'Ballad of the Morning After' homes in on the misleading liberation of extra-marital affairs where a mistress is as prey to the duplicity of male desire as ever: 'He sat down at my table./He finished all the wine./ "You're nothing, dear, to me," he said,/But his body covered mine'.[18] Poets of this generation, from the more visible Ruth Padel to the modest Jane Duran, are increasingly comfortable with a distinct but individual feminist impetus.

Most periodising centres on the group born between 1945 and 1960 who grew up during the sexual revolution of the 1960s and 1970s. In achieving the accolade of 'representative poet of our times', yet also paving a path for other women, Duffy is rightly revered. Kate Clanchy testifies that 'My road to Damascus was reading Carol Ann Duffy's *The Other Country* ... I transformed my thinking – here was a woman writing about desire, anger, loss, and not in disguise, through the mirrors and refractions that I had been taught to look for, but directly, in full colour, with music, with smells. I thought – perhaps I can do that.'[19] Duffy's ten collections model the dominant themes and strategies which are distributed more thinly among other poets. Her work assembles the bricks and mortar of period-icity where the 'unpoetic' jostles with the 'literary', largely by imitating contemporary speech rhythms and idioms. As we discuss in Chapter 10, Duffy's trademark is her ventriloquising through dramatic monologue and dialogic dramatisations of human interaction, frequently in the present tense. Her love poems appropriate the traditional lyric to a candidly contemporary and female location.

Individuals born after 1960 form a dynamic and diverse network who are hard to rank because mostly in their noviciate. The consistently expert Jackie Kay is invigorated by the creative tension involved in unstitching essentialising versions of gender and race and reworking the concept of a subject in order to empower minorities. She is accompanied by those whose off-beat poetry refreshes and redefines notions of gender, Englishness, the literary canon and poetic language. We thus see women forging and manipulating the pluralistic concept of 'postmodernism', which, along with its siblings 'postcolonialism' and 'postfeminism', keeps check on the hegemonic reductionism of 'grand narratives'. They walk a tightrope between poststructuralist disregard for artistic representation and the urge to articulate authentically sensed experience.

RACE AND REGION

At the end of the century, heightened awareness of cultural diversity means that cultural distinctiveness becomes an acute imperative. Although race or region may seem no more desirable or possible as an aesthetic than gender or sexuality, its negotiations with language and tradition are the stuff of contemporary poetic imaginations. So much so that Susan Wicks, a white poet from Kent, or the well-spoken Oxford-based Alice Oswald, remain unlabelled. Nevertheless, we have to record the tendency to classify poets by their race or region while attending to the limits and reductionism of these demarcations. The biggest challenge has been how to situate the poets who are published as 'Irish'. With the cooperation of their chiefs, Eavan Boland and Medbh McGuckian, they are included here since the principal reading position is gender not nation. Like them, we want their work to be promoted but want to avoid the pit of assimilation. While acknowledging that mobility is a feature of the times and national identity is rarely monochrome, we are sensitive to the insecurities of decolonisation. All the groupings here are complex and come under the umbrella of 'British' insofar as they influence its literary consciousness by the work being published or known in Britain.

The Irish present a case study of how female solidarity now offers the greatest freedom for individual creativity. The indigenous presses championed much of their poetry but it is instructive to see Irish poets increasingly published in England or the United States, either simultaneously or later, and that these presses also publish English poets. A number of anthologies have aided the work's availability while book-length critical works establish them in new literary canons. The distinct profile of Irish women poets has been produced and recorded by a substantial number of publications which should guarantee their durability. The smallness of the island and a shared Gaelic heritage fosters interreliance between poets. Translations of Nuala ní Dhomhnaill by both men and women indicate how younger poets often unite against the currents and countercurrents of nationalism. The solidarity across political barriers has paradoxically sharpened the productivity and reputed distinction of each individual and released her into an international span of markets.

Women's shared oppression within the multiple patriarchies which constitute the complexity of Irish politics surrounding the church, nationalism and class sharpens their collective potency. Irish poetry is expected to negotiate with an antithetical construction of Britain, most obviously by putting Catholicism and the rural agricultural landscapes centre stage. The attendant sentiments of belonging or exile are particularly hospitable to women's impulses towards and away from nationalism, which offers security but imprisons them in the past. Although on the level of quotidian routine women may identify with their local version of Irish culture, they are alienated from the religious hegemony which regulates their bodies, from the warfare which takes its toll on their families and neighbourhoods, and from patriotic traditions which gag or confine them. Their stark omission from Irish literary histories which resounded in the three *Field Day* anthologies inflamed the vigour to add two women-only volumes and other collaborations.[20] As the esteemed critic Edna Longley observes, 'Of course there is ultimately no iron border between poetry written by Northerners and Southerners. Not least of the overlaps is the poets' fruitful awareness of one another, the cross-border influences now at work.'[21] Furthermore, they move about not only within Ireland, for education, employment, family or other imperatives, but also between Ireland and the United States, England and the rest of Europe.

The dominance of women originating in the south of Ireland is partly due to their struggle against Catholic controls on their sexual freedom and the misogyny of 'Ulster' poets, but McGuckian paved the way for followers like Sinéad Morrissey and Colette Bryce in the North.[22] We find few poems on The Troubles except for depictions of their victims, where elegies such as Paula Meehan's 'Child Burial' are among the most haunting. The Bible and the folk traditions offer appealingly democratic resources, although women show less enthusiasm for traditional storytelling. We find allegory and symbolism often employed in 'making strange', a self-conscious mediation between realism and the absurd; this element of the fantastic offers a way out of binary representations which perpetuate patriotic and patriarchal fervour. As Peggy O'Brien observes in her enthusiastic introduction to *The Wake Forest Book of Irish Women's Poetry 1967–2000*: 'Just as the inevitable but gradual attainment of pluralism in Ireland has begun to defeat the ambition, ironically pursued by diverse lobbyists, to put a single name on Irishness, so these poems subvert every preconception about what it means to be at once a woman and Irish, or even occasionally what it means to be a poem.'[23]

Eavan Boland is a guiding star whose poetry and critical writing address the competing allegiances of marriage, motherhood, poetry and Irish roots. She spells out a specifically female negotiation with poetic traditions in her seminal *Object Lessons: The Life of the Woman and the Poet in Our Time* (1995), a collection of her essays of the calibre of *A Room of One's Own*. Born in Dublin but brought up in London and New York, she broke from traditions which offered her 'War poetry. Nature poetry. Love poetry. Pastoral poetry. The comic epic. The tragic lyric', but not 'the name of my experience, of what I felt and saw' (p. 23). Both the more self-reflexive lyrics like 'Nightfeed' and the more palpably public treatises such as the *In A Time of Violence* sequence interrogate history past and in the making as it is experienced through the commonplace. She is accompanied by Eiléan ní Chuilleanáin, Nuala ní Dhomhnaill, Nuala Archer and Mary O'Donnell. Meehan had an itinerant upbringing and career in England, Dublin, Europe and the United States. Battling with traditionalist Northern Irish culture, McGuckian's language confounds conventions of literary representation and interpretation. A number of younger women benefit from the experiments of these pioneers. Katie Donovan, Mary O'Malley, Vona Groarke, Siobhán Campbell and Moya Cannon exhibit confident individuality, diminishing but not extinguishing the flame of Irish place, culture and shared consciousness. Their blending of lyricism and satire and their capacity to write touchingly or playfully about their bodies mark their emancipation. The fiercely contemporary Rita Ann Higgins is as concerned about class oppression as nationalism and, along with Morrissey, goes off limits about sex, death, religion and politics.

Defining a 'Scottish' poet other than by birthplace is slippery when poets are subject to huge disparities of location, religious denomination and class, and when they cross the national border temporarily or permanently. *An Anthology of Scottish Women Poets* (1991) slots women into existing linguistic traditions such as Gaelic, Aristocratic verse, vernacular ballads and the expansive Anglo-Scots.[24] Corresponding to Boland in Ireland, Liz Lochhead opened doors with a specifically female treatment of her heritage. True to the democratic traditions of Scottish verse, there is a strong element of entertainment through humour, storytelling, dramatic characterisation and dialogue which are enhanced by readings and performances. Her bilingual 'Kidspoem/Bairnsang' is the epitome of women's conjunctive impulses to preserve and subvert Scottish traditionalism.[25] As Helen Kidd perceives, 'It is more noticeable among women poets that the urge to express and encompass the whole is predominantly absent. The recognition that differences are not to be elided but celebrated is what distinguishes the range of women poets in Scotland and hence a synthesis of Scottish tongues is not on the agenda as it is simply too universalising.'[26]

Lochhead's *The Grimm Sisters* (1981) was a landmark revision of national and gender mythologies by dramatising the characters and roles of archetypal men and women. Their situations investigate the legacy of the past as enmeshed in the macrocosm of education or the closer confines of the family and marriage. In *Dreaming Frankenstein and Other Poems* (1984) she interweaves the actual and the fanciful while *Bagpipe Muzak* (1991) is a collection of more public and communal works which are highly entertaining and musical; some are prose pieces and 'Five Berlin Poems' are affectionately ironic about Scottish places and ritual. Lochhead graduated towards playwriting, which Glasgow-born Jackie Kay has always enjoyed. Kay reads in a Scottish accent, interweaves Scottish vocabulary and makes urban Scotland the backdrop in many poems. Carol Ann Duffy, born in Scotland (to Irish parents) but educated in Staffordshire, is not unduly concerned with Scottish identity. It is Kathleen Jamie who takes up Lochhead's baton, nimbly orchestrating Standard English and Scots dialects to interrogate the condition of Scotland. The dramatic dialogism of her work is highly performable but has a sharper political edge and often a darker note than Lochhead's. Core to this is the dilemma over discarding tradition: 'Do we save this toolbox, these old-fashioned views/addressed, after all, to Mr and Mrs Scotland?'[27] The title poem of *The Queen of Sheba*

(1994) buoyantly spotlights the complexity of female allegiances and alienation within a man's world:

> she wants to strip the willow
> she desires the keys
>   to the National Library
> she is beckoning
>   the lasses
>   in the awestruck crowd ...

'Mother-May-I' is a poignant study of physical and mental suppression. The first person pronoun of 'May-I' wrestles with the objectifying third person 'she'.[28] Typically, the individual implicitly speaks for the collective. Also born in Scotland, Elma Mitchell published two collections at the end of her career while Alison Fell was starting out. Fell's earlier work is threaded with Scottish place and language but her later poems centre on gender or shared experience of contemporary life. Exciting newer poets include Eleanor Brown and Tracey Herd. Katrina Porteus, who was born in Aberdeen then settled in the north-east of England, is sensitive to borderline terrains. She articulates the period's recurring preoccupation with revising global narratives through the personal and immediate: 'What I love about poetry is that it is at once bigger than national identity and smaller; concerned with universal issues which it locates in the minutely local ... While Britain is continually redefined, internally and within Europe, local identity becomes ever more important.'[29]

It is difficult to define a literary Welshness but class and gender seem less urgent than connecting with, or probing, what 'country' means. The tenacious remnants of a bardic culture maintain the public role of the poet to critically nurture nationalist sensibilities. *Poetry Wales*, which spawned its own press (now Seren Books), was not intended to foster a closed circuit of 'Welsh' poets but to provide a space for sustaining and traversing Anglo-Welsh borders. Gillian Clarke edited *Anglo-Welsh Review* between 1976 and 1984 and was an ambassador for poetry based in the Welsh landscape and history. Her poetry often obliquely protests against abuses of power, which extend from women to the environment. Sheenagh Pugh also explores the worlds of and beyond both urban and rural spaces. 'Earth Studies' (1982), a sequence of nineteen poems on the environment, is an accumulation of her modern pastorals. Deryn Rees-Jones confesses an 'anxiety' about her Welsh ancestry and is driven more by feminist and carnivalesque politics.[30] Gwyneth Lewis, one of Astley's *New Blood*, writes in both Welsh, her first language, and English. Menna Elfyn's first six collections were solely in Welsh. Since 1995 she has published three books of dual texts which were translated by Clarke and others. She is co-editor of *The Bloodaxe Book of Modern Welsh Poetry: 20th-Century Welsh Language Poetry in Translation.*

Black women inheriting Caribbean traditions brought music and theatre to their hugely popular performances. Grace Nichols can be grouped with the more page-orientated Olive Senior, Lorna Goodison, Merle Collins and Amryl Johnson. They self-consciously assert their gender and race without essentialising their struggles for recognition and equality:

> maybe this poem is to say
> that I like to see
> we black women
> full-of-we-selves walking
>
> Crushing out
> with each dancing step
> the twisted self-negating
> history
> we've inherited
> Crushing out
> with each dancing step.[31]

Continuing the influences of Una Marson and Louise Bennett, Grace Nichols juggles Standard English, nation language and Creole: 'As someone from the Caribbean, I feel very multicultural and have been affected by all the different strands in that culture – African, Amerindian, Asian, European.'[32] Jamaica-born Jean 'Binta' Breeze and Valerie Bloom are dynamic entertainers who move between Dub traditions, political satires and more universalising lyrics and elegies. Black and Scottish, Maud Sulter frequently critiques cultural stereotypes while Patience Agbabi is the newest highly visual performer who dazzles with postmodern cultural eclecticism.

Sujata Bhatt, Moniza Alvi and Imtiaz Dharker can be fashioned into a trio who treat their Indian ancestry and languages in distinct ways. Given the permeation of upbeat British-Asian art in fiction and the popular media, their acclaim has been oddly tardy although they have featured on the National Curriculum for schools. All these draw heavily upon fantasy to investigate and bypass their multicultural spaces: 'If I stare at the country long enough/I can prise it off the paper/Like a flap of skin' (Alvi, 'Map of India'). In concentrated images Alvi repeatedly addresses the mutual ignorance of colonised and Western peoples: 'My

English grandmother/took a telescope/and gazed across continents' ('The Sari').[33] With a light touch, these cameos evoke the gut-wrenching conflict between denying or celebrating her ancestry. For Alvi, cultural duality seesaws between the negative experiences of inbetweenness and split loyalties – 'Uncle Aqbar drives down the mountain/to arrange his daughter's marriage./She's studying Christina Rossetti' – and the more positive opportunities of bothness: 'I live in one city/but then it becomes another/The point where they mesh – /I call it mine.'[34]

Bhatt was born in India then lived in the United States before settling in Germany but her work is published in Britain. It maintains a dialogue between old and new worlds as well as between continents. Her experiments with Gujarati phrases and Sanskrit in 'Search for my Tongue' and 'Udaylee' are gestures towards racial assimilation which resist any hybrid flattening of linguistic distinctiveness. Dharker was born in Pakistan, raised in Glasgow and then moved to Bombay where she resides. Her first collection, *Purdah* (1988), is an act of rebellion against the literal and figurative veiling of the female body. The poems uncover the disadvantages of Indian women within both Indian and British cultures. A controversial motif in *Postcards from god* (1997) is how writing in English brings solace and release:

> call this freedom now,
> > Watch the word cavort luxuriously strut
> > My independence across whole continents of
> Sheets.

Drawn from the sacred space of the bedroom, the sheets work as a deliberately suggestive metaphor. In asserting the independence of her body, which is ritually the property of her husband, she symbolises the freedom of uncensored writing in a forbidden tongue. Dharker's provocative drawings, which accompany the poetry, accentuate how self-expression is an antidote to the psychological fragmentation produced by alienation and silencing. Insistently, the torment of exile from two cultures is partially eased by inscribing it:

> And so I scratch, scratch, scratch
> through the night, at this growing scab of black on white.
> Everyone has a right to infiltrate a piece of paper
> A page doesn't fight back.[35]

Similarly, in 'To the English Language', Debjani Chatterjee speaks of transforming the initial 'whiplash' of a foreign tongue into a source of consolation. It ends: 'It is now my turn to call you at my homecoming,/I have learnt to love you/ – the hard way.'[36] Chatterjee concentrated on community initiatives and publicity, especially with Bengali and Bangladeshi women, in North-East England. Her *Redbeck Anthology of British South Asian Poetry* (2000) places many names on the table but they are short of due critical responses. In *Nine Indian Women Poets* (1997), Eunice de Souza stimulatingly appraises two generations of post-1947 poets who include Dharker and Bhatt while drawing attention to overlooked others such as herself and Melanie Silgardo.

Grouping by racial identity beckons and challenges feminist postcolonial readings by heightening the complexity of gendered cultural specificity. Kay is the self-confessed paradigm of multiplicity: a black daughter born to a Nigerian father and white mother, she was adopted by white Glaswegian parents. Kay's speakers interact externally and inwardly with other voices. Where she does articulate the personal, it is fluid and fragmented: 'But actually I am somebody else/I have been somebody else all my life.'[37] Throughout *The Adoption Papers, Other Lovers* and *Off Colour*, her multivocal dramas reinvent the traditionally unitary lyric persona to assert the struggles of self-realisation. Other poets with multiple origins include Mimi Khalvati, who emigrated from Tehran to Switzerland and then London, and Jeni Couzyn, who was born in South Africa, became a Canadian citizen and settled in London. Pascale Petit was born in Paris and grew up in France and Wales before coming to England where she is an editor of *Poetry London*. Leland Bardwell emigrated from India to Ireland. The dynamic of American-Englishness in the work of Denise Levertov, Anne Stevenson, Anne Rouse and Eva Salzman tends to be overlooked.

Poetry in translation, which has trickled into the newly opened canons, offers cross-cultural solidarity. In the Preface to her *Collected Poems*, Feinstein records that 'It was translation, however, that helped me to find my own voice'; she connected with Marina Tsvetayeva's sense of exile and 'domestic impracticality [which] mean the usual tensions of wife, mother and poet were written horrifyingly large. She taught me to be unafraid of exposing my least dignified emotions, as well as the technical discipline of a rhythm flowing down a page even when held in stanzas. After that, I rarely used completely open forms.'[38] Fainlight, Adcock, Rumens, Levertov, Pugh, Riley and Shapcott are among the other women who have notably contributed to making European work available in translation.

POSTMODERNISM POLITICS AND/OF THE PERSONAL

In 'The Woman Poet: her dilemma', Boland evokes an ideal of 'humanising femininity' but collectively poetry by women achieves a more radical feminising of humanity.[39] Confident as social observers, they no longer assume male uniforms but direct a female democratic eye towards war victims, the underclasses, the environment and abuse of children. Against the backdrop of wars and terrorism in the Falklands (1982), the Gulf (1990), and former Yugoslavia (1991–93), poetry challenges the reductive but powerful spins of television and journalism; attendantly it defies a conceptual schism between politics and art. Boland usefully redefined the political poem as 'a balancing of the perceived relation of power between an inner and outer world: a realigning of them so that one can comment on the other, and not crush it'.[40] In her best-known second volume, *Phrase Book* (1992), Shapcott demonstrates how the individual's engagement with the external world is mediated by numerous information systems; television newsflashes of the Gulf War are interpolated by extracts from an old-fashioned book of English idioms for foreigners: 'what's love in all this debris?/Just one person pounding another into dust,/into dust. I do not know the word for it yet.'[41] Judith Kazantzis's long and compassionate *A Poem for Guatemala* (1988) assumes a public idiom which does not compromise her striking imagery and colloquial ease. In 'Siege', Clarke recounts the attack on the Iranian embassy in London alongside hearing the radio news in the safety of her Welsh home. Anna Adams's 'For the six children of Dr Goebbels' is a 'woman's poem' on the Holocaust: 'Mother is sobbing, longing to die:/six more dead children in History Pie.'[42]

Rumens's 'Outside Oswiecim' is a lengthy multivoiced meditation on the Holocaust which indicates her sympathy with Jewish people. She frequently pitches human rights against the terrors of totalitarianism, a tension gleaned from her residences in Britain, Prague and Northern Ireland. She draws no line between 'looking inwards at emotional reality, or outwards at the world': 'instead of the metaphor being the public thing of my personal experience it turns out that my personal experience seems to have been the metaphor for some public thing'.[43] Her distaste for a certain kind of Englishness in 'A Lawn for the English Family' indirectly comments on how the market-driven competitiveness of the 1980s permeates every layer of social experience. The sequence 'A Geometry-Lesson for the Children of England' is also 'anti-Thatcher, anti-right, a mid-eighties poem. That's the one I would feel I was most objective about and yet, even with that one, I was looking back to schooldays and being oppressed in the classroom – so even that one is personal.'[44] 'An Easter Garland' indicates disdain for Thatcherite individualism as it became manifest in clingfilm-covered suburban privacy: 'The misted lights of front lounges' are off-set with 'the frills on bruised babies'.[45] Few poets tackle Thatcherism as head-on as Carol Ann Duffy in her superbly satirical pamphlet *William and the ex-Prime Minister* (1992):

> William stood upon a soapbox,
> said *She is a norful sort.*
> *Half the country reckons hope's lost.*
> *Jolly well resign, she ought.*[46]

We find Duffy's empathy for the unemployed here – '*But there's thousands jobless! Millions!/Thanks to that narsy ole witch*' – replicated in 'Education for Leisure' and 'Like Earning a Living'.

Rumens's Introduction to *New Women Poets* (1990) is a useful benchmark of women's brave new freedom to be colloquial: 'There may be no startling formal discoveries: what is new, I think, is the emergence of a kind of late twentieth-century urban dialect, a montage that reverberates with the noise, colour, slanginess, jargonising and information-glut of daily life' (p. 15). Several poets specialise in unsentimental clips of marginality which contradict political euphemisms about classlessness. U. A. Fanthorpe, Carole Satyamurti, Ruth Silcock and Elizabeth Bartlett (who, apart from Duffy, is rare in her working-class origin) mine their experiences within the health and social services to produce a literary and social middleground of shared languages and perceptions. For them, women are among several casualties of British conventionality and right-wing legislation. The consequences of 'Care in the Community', which turned out the mentally ill from sheltered institutions, is registered in snapshots of borderline existence such as 'Epistle to the Man who Sleeps in Sherwood Street' by Adams. Her 'Intensive Care: In the Cardiac Unit' meddles with her misleading label as a nature poet, although there are fine painterly poems on the environment in *Green Resistance: New and Selected Poems* (1996). *The Accumulation of Small Acts of Kindness* (1989) by the deceptively playful Selima Hill is a polyphonic sequence of poems in the form of a journal kept by a woman who cannot speak. Mingling imaginary voices, associated with schizophrenia, with the words of doctors, visitors and family members, it displays the estranging yet social and narrative focus which characterises her nine books. Wendy Cope is a clever satirist who ventures from the light-hearted rhymes of *Making Cocoa for Kingsley Amis* (1986) into the dark corners of loneliness, depression and psychotherapy in *Serious Concerns* (1992). Shaking off the tag of a mere 'parodist', her social anecdotes empower women by tackling the literary establishment embodied in the 'typically useless male poet' 'Tump'.[47] Throughout the 1990s, the rhetoric of democracy in tension with capitalist individualism continues to be a zeitgeist. Kay's 'Teeth' presents the compelling drama of an underhand assault on asylum seekers:

> They came wearing her number
> on their arms. *Did you know*, her mother says,
>
> *they taped my daughter's mouth to choke her*
> *screams. They covered her mouth in white tape.*
>
> The small boy pulled at the sharp trousers.
> He was soundless. The big men flung him
>
> into that grey corner. His voice burst.
> He will stand there, that height, forever, see

The device of speaking through the victim's mother and son challenges sweeping tabloid indictments of refugees. In 'Crown and Country', the extended symbolism of dentistry exposes economic imbalances: 'We do not talk much, we say/cheese; pints of creamy gleaming teeth,/pouring out our white grins, our gold caps; smirks.' Kay's 'Where it Hurts' and others in the bitingly contemporary *Off Colour* (1998) confront the fine line between emotional health and sickness: 'The weary wabbit world of the worried unwell.'[48]

Longley's observation that 'A post-religious sense of loss gives modern poetry its persistent metaphysical dimension' applies most aptly to work by Pauline Stainer, Alice Oswald, Sally Purcell and Annemarie Austin.[49] Patricia Beer's refusal of the certainties of her Plymouth Brethren upbringing results in some agnostic investigations of self-help culture and newspaper wisdom.   Anglo-Asian or Irish poets tend to unpick the historically patriarchal assumptions of religion but occasionally reclaim their mystical inheritances. Fainlight's sense of Jewish identity seems somewhat dispassionate, while Levertov evokes greater spiritual engagement; both are rooted in a feminised exactness of the everyday. Duffy's anthology sonnet 'Prayer' is a monument to cross-faith epiphanies which occur outside orthodox institutions:

> Some days, although we cannot pray, a prayer
> utters itself. So, a woman will lift

> her head from the sieve of her hands and stare
> at the minims sung by a tree, a sudden gift.[50]

Here we have the renovated lyric. Woman is the universal signifier, depicted through alternating first and third person pronouns as both the object, with bowed head, and the speaking subject. The sonnet's final line borrows from the shipping forecast; a conspicuous example of how non-literary but shared language is set in dialogue with the canonical. Just as praying is taken out of its religious rituals to the unexpected moments of the mundane, so poetry implicitly bursts through literary edifices.

The vast corpus of women's lyrics declare a rippling but nonessentialising shared female interiority. They are often cross-dressed with narrative or dialogue to produce the emphatically socialised, mobile and fragmentary processes of identity – 'a fluid/uncertain edged someone that could be anything', writes Austin in 'She':

> I need this figure that strides half obscured
> as if by smoke: there's nothing for me in the
> shopwork either-or of saint or whore,
> hands tight or open; instead she must escape,
> sliding where those others cannot go: underwater[51]

'Woman' cannot be pinned down by archaic binary oppositions but becomes an interactive process to do with her multiple roles, as daughter, mother, sister, lover, and the variables of race, region, religion, sexuality, employment and education, all of which are heterogeneous and context-ually framed. As here, we see women no longer anxious about form or rhyme and using metaphor as their principal tool for avoiding fixity. The vision of slipping off to uncharted territory dispels language's rigid arbitra-tion between realism and fantasy. Many poets, especially in their older years, confront their heritage of femaleness by exploring their family histories. In *Close Relatives* (1981), Vicki Feaver spotlights the tragedy of alienation between mothers and daughters, characteristically dramatising their twin placatory and savage urges. The treatment of mothering ranges from Elizabeth Garrett's gleeful 'Mother, Baby, Lover'[52] or Jamie's buoy-ant sequence in *Jizzen* (1999) to Helen Dunmore's unsentimental lyrics: 'The child's a boy and will not share/One day these obstinate, exhausted mornings.'[53] In 'Prampushers', Adams details the 'married loneliness' of women with babies who feel shunted into 'a quiet siding'.[54] Most strik-ingly, women write about their bodies as never before. In 'Vanity', Penelope Shuttle documents concern about her sagging middle-aged breasts and in 'Ultra Sound' the trauma surrounding breast examination;

white spaces around the typing elicit what cannot be spoken.[55] The unspeakable torture of mastectomy is skilfully visualised through symbol by ní Chuilleanáin, Bartlett and Boland.[56] Boland's 'Anorexic' and Rumens's tragicomic *The Miracle Diet* disclose women's difficult relationship with food.[57] The fat black woman in Nichols's poetry pokes fun at the fashion and slimming industries. She celebrates her 'bleed': 'Month after month/it tells me who I am/reclaiming me.'[58] Donovan's 'Underneath Our Skirts' connects the secrecy of menstruation with concealed emotional pain and in 'Udaylee' Bhatt exposes its religious uncleanness: 'Only paper and wood are safe from a menstruating woman's touch/So they built this room/for us, next to the cowshed.'[59] Agbabi builds female solidarity with her amusingly performative 'It's Better Post- than Pre-'.[60] Lochhead's 'An Abortion' is not the only one to confront another female experience previously rare in literature.[61]

By exploring their desires unashamedly and critically, women at the end of the twentieth century ultimately dispense with sentimentalised idealisations of the feminine. Fuelled by editing the *Literary Companion to Sex* (1992) and the *Literary Companion To Low Life* (1995), Fiona Pitt-Kethley opens herself to charges of populist vulgarity. She plunders The Spice Girls' antifeminine autonomy – 'I lead a freelance life in everything' ('Independent Means') – and reviles the male-dependent narcissism of *Bridget Jones's Diary*. Like both phenomena, she may have a short shelf-life but at her best she tackles the female-targeted mass marketing of beauty and romance. In the vein of Aphra Behn, she satirises commercialised sexual arrangements and sentimental ideals: 'He offered me the sun and moon – as men/will do when they have little else to give' ('Long-stemmed Rose').[62] In *Dogs* (1993), various deprecations of machismo include the book trade, the Arts Council and the outfields of condoms and oral sex. More firmly a 'Nineties' poet, Sophie Hannah is almost wearisomely sceptical about the thoroughly modern world of cars and karaokes. More self-reflexive, Hill refuses predictability in her bizarre rescripting of unfulfilled desires, famously in 'I Want to be a Cow' or such lines as, 'I said *I want a lover*. It's not true./I'm happy as I am being happy/pretending I'm a large kangaroo.'[63]

A reductive accusation of 'a rather monotonous empiricism'[64] in contemporary women's poems scapegoats them for a more general zeitgeist where 'confessionalism' is marketable. Some of the bedroom confidences may seem overly hermetic but the frequently dialogic dramatisations of disintegrating partnerships rework the unitary stability of the traditional lyric. Julia Copus's 'The Back Seat of my Mother's Car', 'The Marriage' and 'Don't Talk to me about Fate' are conversations of the age, as are the highly metaphorical 'This Dead Relationship' by the emerging Katherine Pierpoint and Duffy's 'Disgrace'.[65] Agbabi's haunting 'Sentences' manipulates prose vernacular into a disturbing narrative of domestic violence.[66] Clanchy's 'The Personals'[67] and Connie Bensley's 'Personal Column' and 'Single Parent', from *Choosing to be a Swan* (1994), are refreshingly witty. Bensley excels at dramatising the complexity of threesomes located in a shared classless existence of newspaper reports, supermarkets and multi-storeys. As if in therapy, her speakers cut through defence mechanisms to unspoken desires and 'that hinterland/which borders love and emptiness'.[68] Dunmore brings her storyteller skills to snaps of patchwork families in 'Second Marriages' – 'his former wife and her child-swapping/ remnants of weekday companionship' – and 'The Deserted Table': 'Four children, product of two marriages,/two wives, countless slighter relations/ and friends all come to the table.'[69] Duffy's 'Adultery', 'Advice on Adultery' by Lewis and Copus's ironic 'In Defence of Adultery' refuse to take infidelity lying down. Poems which transform woman from the victim to the investigator of broken relationships include Lochhead's 'The Other Woman', France's 'New York Spring' and 'The End of Love' by Hannah. The interface between fantasy and realism in these subversions or appropriations of the lyric allows some aesthetic consolation for the pains of loss, sadness or frustration.

Sylvia Kantaris's title sequence of *Dirty Washing* (1989) makes intimacy collective and public by synthesising household chores with interior monologue: 'My mother used to spit twice on her iron/Then wipe the coal-dust off before she wielded it./Mine weeps and sizzles like a heart and spits out rust' (p. 103). The coherence of symbolism and internal rhymes jars with the psychological fragmentation. Although the allegory is rather prolonged, the upfrontness of domestic metaphor validates both 'women's work' and its place in literature. Upturning the motif of emotional 'drowning', Lomax points to a rarely articulated yearning 'for something beyond/ the love of men' through the image of swimming freely out to sea.[70] Duffy's 'Warming Her Pearls' is the epitome of coded and repressed same-sex passion and Kay's love lyrics are often sexually ambivalent, among women and erotic. Overtly lesbian love poetry tends to be confined to specialist publications but is helped in gaining literary credibility by the Americans Marilyn Hacker and Adrienne Rich.

The mid 1980s 'New Man', arguably another consumer ideal sold to women, is noticeably absent as a central figure. Recurringly and cumulatively, however, we find overweening masculinity redefined by the paradoxical demands of feminist autonomy and a new female self-identification through mutual partnership. Anne Rouse's highly conversational *Timing* (1997) has feisty caricatures of masculine prowess such as 'Spunk Talking', 'The Bluff', 'The Anaesthetist', 'Play On' or 'Cigarettes'. These debunkings belong, however, in a wider context of the struggle for individual vitality in the face of deadening cultural controls. France's 'Acts of Love' is an antilyrical sequence of a girl's emotional damage from a lifetime of sexual assaults, while 'Samantha' investigates the alleged false memory of child abuse.[71] In her first collection, *The Brief History of a Disreputable Woman,* Jane Holland exploits her career as a snooker player; 'Baize Queens' or 'Invention' occupy a traditionally male domain. Lavinia Greenlaw shows an 'unfeminine' interest in science inventions and technology. These poems support Ian Gregson's conclusion that 'Women poets have been concerned to show the extent to which the "unitary language of culture and truth" actually imposes a masculinist vision on those, both men and women, who use it. In opposing this, their poetry has evoked a subtle, dialogue of genders, which while chary of essentialist simplifications, has explored the boundaries of the feminine and the masculine, and exposed the way that the "true word" is a masculine monologue, a gendered monolith.'[72]

The armoury of largely female-centred writing finally blasts reductive and essentialising stereotypes of femininity by exploring the varieties of female experience. As signalled in Judith Kazantzis's *The Wicked Queen* (1980), the rewriting of classical myths and fairy stories which liberate female identity from the stranglehold of nationalism, cultural elitism and chauvinism are frequent. Duffy's witty sequence of dramatic monologues in *The World's Wife* simultaneously models and parodies blatant feminist revisionism. Published in 1999, it stands as a lighthouse for the recovery of silenced women and questions whether the sex war is over or inexorable. Feaver's prize-winning 'Judith' and other dramatic monologues are Duffyesque in depicting women's capacity for both tenderness and violence: 'I was brought up in a girls' school to be a nice girl, and then a nice woman. In life I continue to try to be a fairly nice woman. In poetry I fight it. I try to keep in mind Virginia Woolf's image of the Angel in the House who strangles the writer.'[73] Feaver's 'The Handless Maiden', based on a fairytale in which a father cuts off his daughter's hand, symbolises history's treatment of women writers. Poets connecting with and breaking from black, Indian, Irish or Scottish traditionalism draw upon their respective mythologies.

Some of the most lively poems investigate the formative aspects of female education, exemplified by Lochhead's reverberating sequence 'In the Dreamschool'[74] and Duffy's well-known 'Head of English', 'Mrs Tilscher's Class' and 'The Good Teachers'.[75] Her 'The Laughter of Stafford Girls' High' is a vehement end-of-century dystopian satire. Not in a collection until *Feminine Gospels* (2002), it was composed before the millennium.[76] Set in the 1960s, its surreal narrative of a giggling epidemic which ultimately closes the school is a sharply humorous denouncement of deadening female education, especially its patriarchal curriculum:

> the chalky words rubbed away to dance as dust
> on the air, the dates, the battles, the kings and queens,
> the rivers and tributaries, poets, painters, playwrights,
> politicos, popes ...
>
> (p. 39).

The poem's length, the far-reaching lines and the light-footed assonance imitate the girls' uncontrollable laughter which overturns the rigid and endless routine of the women teachers trapped in a repressive system.

While female-centred perspectives and subject matter indicate women's emancipation from limiting stereotypes, we have both to challenge and to defend the verdict that women are tenacious about 'realism' and thus irrelevant to postmodernism's shifting sands of narrative unreliability. In an essay on the appropriation of Baudrillard's hyperreality by contemporary poets, Stan Smith concludes that 'Significantly, it's the women writers among these poets who reveal the strongest urge to hold on to the referent.'[77] Citing 'Away and See', he distinguishes Duffy's deference to the processes of signification from the more representational dialogics through 'substitutions of metaphor'. [78] Here, she is explicit about the gap between the thing and the word, urging us to seize, extend and go beyond language:

> Away and see the things that words give a name to, the flight
> of syllables, wingspan stretching a noun. Test words
> wherever they live; listen and touch, smell, believe.
> Spell them with love.[79]

We glimpse here some of Duffy's favourite antics with metre, line lengths, assonance and internal rhyme. To some extent, Smith rightly observes that women value their long-fought-for prerogative for imaginative but authentic self-expression. Sarah Maguire is one who explicitly resists the tide of antirealism:

But frolicking in the boundless ocean of contingency is not an activity open to the (increasing numbers) of poor, homeless and exploited. The unbridled relativism of certain aspects of postmodernism strikes me as being deeply reactionary, the freeplay of signifiers having more in common with so-called 'free' trade and the freeplay of money markets than its promulgators would have us believe ... I worry about the (apparent) lack of politics in some postmodernism – which is itself a mask for a reactionary agenda and, in fact, a very political stance.[80]

Most of the poets discussed here are acutely aware of the politics of language and happily play in the waters which bridge the material and hyperreal. They rarely let go of a female-specific vantage point or concern with democracy. All thirty poets in Maura Dooley's *Making for Planet Alice: new women poets*, who published their first collection in the 1990s, 'pay no attention to the restrictions of this universe'.[81] Rees-Jones's lyric, 'Making for Planet Alice', supremely teases the reader with self-signifying metaphor and hidden dialogue. Shapcott and Hill model self-conscious 'ex/centricity', an exaggerated and creative manufacturing of rootlessness and alienation. They often transcend the limits of human interaction, especially the confines of a recognisable dialogue of genders, through the personae of vegetables, animals or cartoon characters. *Her Book* (2000), a compilation of Shapcott's three earlier collections, provoked surveys of her development and individuality. As John Kinsella duly acclaimed: 'Jo Shapcott is doing no less than rewriting the English poetic canon – challenging sources, verse structure, and the primacy of the patriarchal voice. Her "class" or social milieu is female in a world of mass media, where all language is negotiated through male power structures; her verse undoes this and creates an alternative. It is critical and self-aware, amusing and cutting.'[82] Greenlaw self-confessedly progressed from 'too much narrative' in her first collection, *Night Photograph* (1993), to 'the mechanics of perception', inspired by Elizabeth Bishop. 'Gods, miracles and a lot of faith crop up' in her next book, *A World Where News Travelled Slowly* (1997) which indicates a rejection of the known and knowable in favour of the unexplained or unpresentable: 'Maybe I got tired of being rational and provisional, and wanted to risk absolute faith in what can never be proved.'[83]

Radically innovative syntax and forms arguably reposition every reader in the same unfamiliar linguistic territory. Untethered signifiers allow for the depiction of provisionality and are open to multiple reading positions. McGuckian harnesses postmodern release from orthodox referentiality to untie the triple bind of the Irish woman poet. Her mystifying metaphors and other disruptions frustrate our familiar meaning-making apparatus. Similarly, the most linguistically risk-taking, who point to a new signifying logic, deal insistently with female subjectivity. Caroline Bergvall, Maggie O'Sullivan, Wendy Mulford, Paula Claire and Denise Riley continue to break ground with cross-media performance pieces, choral texts and sound poems. O'Sullivan set up the Magenta Press and other initiatives included the International Concrete Poetry Archive set up by Claire, who also established ICPA publications. Collectively, these poets provide linguistic freedom and potency to thwart Freud's theory of the repressive Oedipal condition which has unobtrusively clouded women's writing throughout the twentieth century.

SUMMARY

The task of recording recent and living history is peculiarly exciting and risky. We have tried to tread a line between reproducing the most prominent names while suggesting others which are in danger of being undervalued. As the past teaches, significant poets can be lost if they do not invite publicity, wear fashion labels or have the right connections. The following monuments of 1980 – 2000 are intended to draw some highwater marks.[84] The posthumous influence of Smith was partly yielded by *Me Again: The Uncollected Writings of Stevie Smith* (1981) and *Stevie Smith: A Selection* by Hermione Lee (1983). The death of Horovitz in 1983 took her poems into the limelight. We had *Collected Poems* by the women flourishing at the end of their careers – Riding (1980), Raine (1981), Wingfield (1983), Jennings (1986), Scovell (1988) and Beer (1988) – and these were often not their last publications. Fainlight consistently produced books and a *Selected Poems* (1987), while Boland's *Outside History: Selected Poems 1980–1990* signals the 1980s as a productive decade for her. *Selected Poems*, which provide a niche for poets whom publishers sense have a readership, also came from Levertov and ní Chuilleanáin (1986). In terms of output and reputation it was an important decade for Fanthorpe, Feinstein, Rumens, Lochhead and Kazantzis, with several books each. With five books, Kantaris is perhaps one of the most 'Eighties' poets but she is insufficiently talked about. Poets who started to make their mark and strode confidently into the next decade included Duffy, Hill, Shuttle and McGuckian. Positive responses to their first collections launched Feaver and Shapcott into more adventurous works. As for individual poems, Satyamurti's 'Behind the lines', which won the National Poetry Competition in 1986, is an exponent of the period's psychodynamic preoccupation with the coexistence of childhood in the adult.

Highlights of the 1990s have to be Linda France's *Sixty Women Poets* (1993) and the 1994 New Generation promotion of Alvi, Stainer, Wicks, Duffy, Garrett, Greenlaw, Jamie and Maguire on the radio and television and in public centres around the country. Among the best collections were Kay's *The Adoption Papers* (1991) and *Off Colour* (1998). Adcock's *Looking Back* (1997) is arguably her warmest and most personal. *Two Women Dancing: New and Selected Poems* (1995) exhibits Bartlett at her best. Other *Selected Poems* which refine the poets' image came from Duffy, Adams and Satyamurti. *Collected Poems* gave due gravitas to Boland, Clarke, Pitter, Ridler and posthumously Downie. Of the older generation, Pugh and Jennings had formidably productive decades, while after a late start Gillilan developed momentum. Shapcott, Bhatt, Bensley, 'Binta' Breeze, Jamie, Meehan, Feaver and Higgins, who had made a splash in the 1980s, stirred more waves. Just beginning to resonate were Dharker, Clanchy and Donovan who are highly colloquial, incisive and immediate. Notable first collections came from Hannan, Holland, Sansom, Morrissey and Herd. In 'The Outlands', the promising Rouse distils the newly flexible female lyric: 'I've been walking the outlands of the self,/recording its cold impasses and its wounds,/its mudflats and fervent suns and thrashing water.'[85]

Some excellent collections coincided with the millennium: *Collected Poems* by Adcock; Duffy's *Salmon* and *Selected Poems* by Riley. Feinstein's *Gold*, Agbabi's *Transformatrix* and *Carrying My Wife* by Alvi exhibit the elasticity of women's language and imaginations. Fanthorpe's *Consequences* marked a new direction away from the local to more global matters, history and the landscape. Anticipating Bartlett's *Appetites of Love* (2001), Bensley's *The Back and the Front of It* (2000) captures the period's preoccupation with complicated relationships: 'Across the table he is watching his ex-wife./She is laughing and murmuring with her new husband.'[86] Other emerging writers to watch are Julia Copus, Polly Clark, Janet Fisher, Jane Griffiths, Frieda Hughes and Katherine Gallagher, while, judging by their predecessors, many of the previously mentioned have yet to enter their most fruitful periods.

Whereas in the past women have been starved of the critical attention which would shore up a literary reputation, now there are promising vocabularies for reading their work other than in detrimental comparison with men. Additionally, reactionary critics and institutions are divested of absolute power, as Astley intended: 'Bloodaxe has challenged the literary establishment. I don't accept that tastes and reputations should be dictated by out of touch professors with literary critical hang-ups or reviewers more concerned with fashion than excellence.' Books by women have largely constituted, not just benefited from, a poetry revolution which 'has enabled poetry to touch the people it never reached in the past. It's no longer the case that "most people ignore poetry because most poetry ignores people". Today's poets are much more tuned in to how people think about the world and feel about themselves. Poets used to be regarded as a separate species. The difference now is what the best poets write is relevant to people's lives and to their experiences of the world, on an everyday as well as on a more spiritual level.'[87]

Duffy's 'Little Red-Cap', which opens her bestselling *The World's Wife* (1999), is an allegory of escape from the lair of the Male Poet. When the heroine conquers this beast, she finds, as if for the first time, what a weeping willow tree or a jumping salmon are like if not mediated via dead language. The ten years of captivity to the wolf represent Duffy's writing career and the grandmother stands for the ancestry of woman poets who are liberated by his demise: 'I stitched him up.' The displacement of a cliché is typical of Duffy. Also typically, we cannot tidily translate her reworking of the fairytale myth into realist terms; the female empowerment occurs in a space between the recognisable and the fantastic. The final line, 'Out of the forest I come with my flowers, singing, all alone', leads distinctly female creativity into the next millennium but its direction is left open.[88]

Duffy's casually streetwise manner and idiom and her exploitation of popular tastes signal her disrespect for canonical norms and traditions. Since she attracts more critical comment, and a wider readership, than any other poet of her gender and generation, her work appears in almost all of the following chapters. Differently, but as stridently, Boland's revisions of representation and subjectivity also run through this period. Recognising that any category or boundary can be overlaid and complicated by another, Chapter 9 explores the textured treatment of place by a range of poets of whom Kay, Nichols, Khalvati and Lochhead are the best known. Continuing on from the dramatic monologues of early twentieth-century poets and the radically colloquial Smith, Chapter 10 further undercuts hierarchical distinctions between page and oral poetry or between social differences which are demarcated by dialects and traditions. Postmodernism's antibinary disregard for *either* essentialist *or* materialist assumptions allows women to constitute a new kind of human subject which is self-in-relation. They manipulate intonation to direct readers' responses to various experiences of suppression or celebration. In Chapter 11 we look at how poets rework ancient and new stories, through the borrowed voices of mythic creatures. Shapcott and Greenlaw are among the women who find the parallel but vertiginous world of the scientist compelling. Just as we began, so we end with the lyric. We find an unprecedented ease and adventurousness with transforming female experience. Where a poet handles the old but still universal themes of loss and longing, she reconstitutes the lyric's consoling function.

CHAPTER 9

"These parts":
identity and place

Where do you come from?
'Here,' I said. 'Here. These parts.'[1]

Robert Crawford argues that 'Where do you come from? is one of the most important questions in contemporary poetry – where's home?'[2] Yet, as Helen Dunmore points out, 'Is home where you were born, is it where you live, is it where you speak the language, or is it simply where you feel at home? . . . To ask "Where do I come from?" invites, for many poets, many possible answers.'[3] She goes on, 'To be British is, on the whole, to be a mixture, played upon by diverse cultural, social and linguistic influences.' Towards the end of the century, a heterogeneous community of women poets, many 'British' more by association than nationality, identify themselves with an often productively uncertain sense of 'home'. For the black, white and Asian-British writers whose colonised past animates their cultural present, those who unpiece the linguistic and literary complex of the British Isles, and, of course, for a large company of expatriate poets, the impulse to use place as a cultural identifier is complicated but enriched by their experience of territorial, social and linguistic alienation. Thus the migrant Sujata Bhatt writes, coolly, from 'my home which does not fit/ with any geography'.[4] For Debjani Chatterjee, the systematic socio-cultural disenfranchisement of immigrant Asian women in Britain begins linguistically: 'Sister, may your understanding grow/Of your alien status/ And deepen with the years.'[5]

While gender invariably deepens the three versions of cultural disloca-tion, it also underwrites the creative opportunities inherent in them. As New Zealander Adcock notes, 'I have always some residual feeling of being an outsider: a fruitful position for a writer, perhaps . . . But now I wonder: has being a woman contributed to this? Are women natural outsiders?'[6] This sense of estrangement is compounded by the need to negotiate with a literary tradition historically colonised by men. If, as Crawford observes (but, Joanne Winning notes, fails to pursue), 'The poetic celebrants of home at the moment tend not to be women' it is probably because such poets prefer to identify themselves, in varying ways, with the ambivalent separatism to which Imtiaz Dharker (speaking to a more universal alienation) resorts: [7]

> ... I'll be happy to say,
> 'I never learned your customs.
> I don't remember your language
> or know your ways.
> I must be
> from another country.'[8]

Born to a Nigerian father and white Scottish mother, but adopted as a baby by white working-class communist parents, Jackie Kay's unusual background has sensitised her to the effects of cultural alterity on identity and imagination. 'Kail and Callaloo' declares 'there's nowhere to write/Celtic-Afro-Caribbean/in answer to the "origin" question;/they think that's a contradiction//how kin ye be both?'[9] A more mature and confident interrogation of this fertile 'contradiction', 'In My Country' both exposes and collapses the idea of cultural difference in imagery which implies that the speaker is accustomed to being made to feel alien:

> ... when she finally spoke
> her words spliced into bars
> of an old wheel. A segment of air.
> *Where do you come from?*
> 'Here,' I said, 'Here. These parts.'

Weighing the idioms of Kay and Grace Nichols, Paraskevi Papaleonida finds the idea of 'syncretism' (used by postcolonial theorists to signify 'the process by which previously distinct categories, and by extension, cultural formations, merge into a single new form') inadequate to their poetic language. She favours the term 'synthesis' instead: as ' "putting together" ... it creates the idea of a mosaic, in which each "bead" can keep its concrete and separate individual identity.'[10] Its closing words assertive but not confining, 'In My Country' extends the particular cultural 'synthesis' which 'Kail and Callaloo' defends to the notion of (female) identity itself. Kay's complex origins underpin both her confident claim on her immediate environs – the carefully vague 'these parts' which are her home and birthright – and, conversely, on the cultural 'otherness' which her questioner pursues. The political and creative opportunities which her experiences of alterity license in her poetics are replayed, on several levels, in her remarkable first work, *The Adoption Papers* (1991).

This semi-autobiographical, play-like poem is more about what can be gained – socially, politically and poetically – from cultural undecidability than about what is lost.[11] Relayed in three distinct female voices (of child, birth-mother and adoptive mother), the narrative searches from their interleaved – synthesised – perspectives the way that parentage anchors the identity in place. In another poetics of dislocation, Carol Rumens renders the securing potential of this relationship: 'I watch a ewe fold round her lamb,/Her brownish, and its snowy, fleece/Making in soft, unbroken form/The oldest word for *native place*.'[12] Poignantly, the boisterous, acutely sensitive daughter of *The Adoption Papers* lacks the 'soft, unbroken form' of the ancient security Rumens notices: 'after mammy telt me she wisnae my real mammy/I was scared to death she was gonnie melt/or something or mibbe disappear ... /... How could I tell if my mammy/was a dummy with a voice spoken by someone else?'[13] By extension, she is denied the historical and familial details which might secure her sense of cultural belonging: 'I want to know my blood ... who were my grandmothers/what were the days like/passed in Scotland/the land I come from.' While without these details she has no way of explaining how she has come to be where she is, on the other hand, their absence informs her increasingly self-possessed awareness of her individuality. Despite the sometimes painful discovery of her difference from other people, not least her 'mammy', the daughter always seems less lost than a birth mother whom the poem imagines with increasing compassion (their only troubled 'meeting' is apparently dreamed). This is obliquely affirmed in a poignant inversion of Rumens's powerful image: as her baby is collected by its new parents, the birth-mother is captured in solitary flight: 'The rhythm of the train carries me/over the frigid earth /... / a rocking cradle ...'[14] These ambivalent lines suggest the narrowed horizons of a life in which fertility, like adulthood, seems to have been tragically self-cancelling yet the adoptive daughter's existence, and complex sense of identity, belies this. On the whole, both adoptive mother and daughter find the many tensions and contradictions of their intertwining domestic situation stimulating, even empowering.

In its loving deconstruction of one particular version of female displacement, *The Adoption Papers* resists any simplistic linking of selfhood with 'place', geographical and/or social context, by rendering matrilinearity (the roots of such links) unreliable. In her penetrating discussion of Irish women poets, Clair Wills observes, tellingly, that 'the writer who rejects the association of woman and land thereby questions the relationship between poet and community'.[15] Kay's poem inscribes the liberating effect of this interrogation: the daughter's blood ties always seem less important to her cultural identification than the redoubtable quasi-maternal figure whose loving protection has always overwritten them and through whose determined lead the daughter learns to value the freedoms of her divided cultural status. She does and doesn't 'come from' the Scotland she lives in, does and doesn't belong among the white people who constitute her family; it does and doesn't matter. The text itself reflexively argues the significance of Kay's own multicultural background to her creative life, implying that the absence of her birth-parents has been partially compensated for by the 'parts' of her productively divided imagination. This seems to be confirmed by the final poem of *Off Colour* (1998) when her elusive father indirectly prompts a sudden moment of self-validation: a 'stranger on the train/located even the name/of my village in Nigeria/in the lower part of my jaw'.[16] In the ensuing conversation, this man conjures for Kay the vision of a joyous family reunion, representing a creative cultural history she can excitedly embrace:

> I danced a dance I never knew I knew.
> Words and sounds fell out of my mouth like seeds.
> I astonished myself.[17]

Even here, an encounter which renders the self momentarily strange is also self-renewing: 'When I looked up, the black man had gone./Only my own face startled me in the dark train window.' The return to her own reflection, in the very last lines of the collection, acknowledges her father's presence in herself. The incident reinscribes the uncertain sense of 'home' running through a poetics in which historical (biological) accident, although apparently isolating, is transformed into political and aesthetic opportunity.

On one hand, Kay's Nigerian origins admit her into a canon of black British women poets led by Grace Nichols. Nichols's *i is a long-memoried woman* (1983) reaches across time, merging continents and cultures ('the Congo surfaced/so did Sierra Leone and the Gold Coast') in recuperating the subjugating narratives of colonisation and slavery from a hitherto silent female perspective. Mythologising black African women's history, Nichols's lyrical, loose-limbed account is articulated in synthesisingly female – like Kay's, often maternal – terms. A moving testament to cultural loss and suffering, it is also a gendered celebration of a borderless black nation, a postcolonial 'country of strong women':

> We the women who cut
> clear fetch dig sing
>
> We the women making
> something from this
> ache-and-pain-a-me
> back-o-hardness[18]

As Nichols has it, women's experiences of colonisation find them powerful in their disempowerment, vocal in their silent endurance, creative despite the 'hardness' to which they and their children are brutally sacrificed. Here, if 'mother is supreme burden' it is also supreme resistance, unlikely either to betray itself ('I was traded by men/the colour of my own skin'), or to yield to privation.[19]

On the other hand, the more immediate fact of Kay's birthplace connects her with poets whose sense of cultural dislocation has nearer political resonance. Certainly, the synthesising approach Papaleonida discerns in Kay and Nichols reappears in the poetic idioms of other women, whose collective reply to the dilemma of cultural identification is to refuse to allow the binaries they mediate between to dissolve. Instead – as Kay does so effectively in *The Adoption Papers* – they elevate displacement, estrangement and alienation alongside rootedness and security, often through polyphonic linguistic play, to critique and challenge socio-cultural power relations. Under such poets' determined scrutiny, as Dharker puts it, 'Every borderline becomes a battlefield.'[20] Helen Kidd interprets the strategy in a more positive way: 'unlike the male canon, the need to outwrite or out-universalize one another is not manifest. This women's writing is a collective process, a co-operative venture, delighting in the gaps as well as the seams.'[21] Jo Shapcott, for example, has expressed her doubts about a national identity which, since it is predicated upon colonial ambition, remains a painful reminder of how social alienation attends and intersects with territorial displacement. Like Kay, she genders the recognition; she recalls Kristeva, describing 'the theorist as "an impertinent traveller" passing across "whole geographic and discursive continents". It is in this context that Englishness, the meaning of being English – and, yes, an Englishwoman, because gender certainly has something to do with it – has nagged at me.'[22] On the other hand, again like Kay, Shapcott discerns poetic opportunity in her own aporia-laden discomfort. One of her finest poems, 'Motherland', finds the dictionary itself problematising the title-word by refusing to define it. It falls open instead, suggestively, at '*Distance. Degree/of remoteness, interval of space*', forcing the poet to conclude, rather miserably, on a contradiction: 'England .../... This country makes me say/too many things I can't say. Home/of me, myself, my motherland.'[23]

As Wills powerfully shows, for the Irish woman poet in particular, inheriting the many-layered cultural burden of 'Mother Ireland', the concept of 'motherland' is still more loaded.[24] In 'Anna Liffey', Eavan Boland uses Shapcott's troping association of womanhood and territory to reclaim a cultural terrain in which binaries such as historical and contemporary, highland and lowland, political and domestic, are provocatively synthesised. Boland's historic, topographical and imaginative rebalancing act proves literally revitalising:

> Life, the story goes,
> Was the daughter of Cannan,
> And came to the plain of Kildare.
>
> . . .
> The river took its name from the land.
> The land took its name from a woman
>
>   *
>
> . . .
> There, in the hills above my house,
> The river Liffey rises, is a source.
> It rises in rush and ling heather and
> Black peat and bracken and strengthens
> To claim the city it narrated.[25]

Boland answers Shapcott's self-conscious critiquing of language by yoking utterance – the story, the affirmative exchange of names, the narration of the city – with creativity, in the heavily nuanced figure of 'Life'. This mythologising gesture not only proudly genders Boland's poetic practice, but places female cultural identity at the heart of the Irish imagination. In this, she goes instructively further than Mimi Khalvati ('Some idea of a lost home, or lost sense of belonging, informs a lot of what I write'), who insists on a sense of female cultural identity which is time- as well as place-specific.[26] 'Rubaiyat' mourns and dignifies a woman, representative of more than herself, whose traditions, language and wisdom seem unlikely to survive her ('I have inherited her tools: her anvil,/her axe, her old scrolled mat, but not her skill;'):

> My grandmother would rise and take my arm,
> then sifting through the petals in her palm
> would place in mine the whitest of them all:
> "Salaam, dokhtaré-mahé-man, salaam!"

"Salaam, my daughter-lovely-as-the-moon!"
Would that the world could see me, Telajune,
through your eyes! Or that I could see a world
that takes such care to tend what fades so soon.[27]

To some extent, Khalvati writes about Iran to cherish and protect her links with a familiar world as it recedes with time. Its title drawn from the writings of Hélène Cixous, *In White Ink* overtly genders the divided identity it examines; it is chiefly as woman, partly friend and mother, that this poet feels custodial responsibility to the two cultures she bridges.

Born in Pakistan but raised in England in the 1950s and 1960s, Moniza Alvi, who was influenced by Khalvati into writing about her own cultural dualism, betrays no such sense of duty. Alvi explains that her first collection *The Country at My Shoulder* (1993) summons Pakistan primarily as imaginative resource, as 'a fantasy, nourished by vivid family stories, extraordinary gifts, letters, news items and anecdotes'.[28] Her Pakistani father's native culture is magnetisingly distant, a place which seems otherworldly even in its actuality. Reconstructing it in poetry helps both to demystify and to heighten the enriching sense of difference with which Alvi, not unlike Kay, grew up.

In this, Alvi's chief responsibility is to herself: she sees writing as 'an act of discovery on the border where inner and outer worlds meet'; exploring her own cultural complexity creates 'something positive about what was, in childhood and adolescence, rather unsettling and difficult to think about'.[29] In 'The Laughing Moon', an apparently youthful voice savours dual identity: 'I had two pillows and one was England,/two cheeks and one was England.' The poem closes with the speaker balanced, thrillingly, on a threshold where past, present and future meet: 'The continents were very old,/but I was new and breathing in/midnight . . .'.[30] The breathless tone conveys the pleasure of 'chanc[ing] upon an area of writing that was my own – unexplored territory'.[31] The changing carpet of 'O Maharani' ('at first India/which melted into England/and then became//England mixed with India.//A knotted carpet') not only signifies how this territory knots together – synthesises – two cultural poles, but also represents the elision of social and topographical in an identity divided evenhandedly between two homes.[32] Like Kay, Boland, Shapcott and Khalvati, Alvi is struck by the social ramifications of a cultural paradox which problematises geography. She repeatedly uses tropes of the body to explore a self-image which is, as 'Blood' says, fundamentally 'blurred'.[33] In part, this reflects the segregating traditions of Asian society. Both Bhatt ('Udaylee') and Khalvati

('The Waiting House') pursue the ambiguities of such social organisation in treating the conventional seclusion of menstruating women, for example. Taking her lead from the story retold in her epigraph, Khalvati imagines the interchange between the bleeding woman and 'Earth Mother' as a spiritual and sensual experience of female mutuality: 'dreaming still/your blood/will live, as mine in yours, in mine'.[34] For Bhatt, sequestration 'next to the cow-shed' stimulates a burst of imaginative activity both inscribed in, and offering release from, the female cycle.[35] Both recognise in their culture's essentialising of womanhood a social practice which both threatens and enhances female creative life.

The same kind of equivocation colours Alvi's interest in the traditional clothing which – extending the trope of the female body – makes 'the invisible visible'.[36] In 'The Sari', the new baby is greeted with a garment which metaphorically reunites India with Pakistan, East with West, both marking and eliding the divisions which, since they comprise only part of her cultural heritage, feed into but also (proscriptively) gender the new postcolonial order she represents: 'they wrapped and wrapped me in it/ whispering *Your body is your country*'.[37] The gift, like the wrapping action, is both affirming and circumscribing.

The layered social, political and aesthetic intercourse between Alvi's two native continents is rehearsed in the 'dialogue' (in the last two words of its title) which 'Hindi Urdu Bol Chaal' stages between the two major languages of the Indian subcontinent. The poem's triads utter the linguistic subtleties of a cultural interaction which no political moves can fully disentangle. The multiplicity that Alvi problematises ('I introduce myself to two languages,/but there are so many – of costume,/of conduct and courtesy') complicates a palimpsest-like 'dialogue' in which ancient is overlaid by and synthesised in modern:

> I imagine the meetings and greetings
> in Urdu borrowed from Sanskrit,
> Arabic and Persian.
>
> I shall be borrowed from England.
> Pakistan, assalaam alaikum –
> Peace be with you – Helloji.[38]

In one of the few scholarly discussions of Asian-British women poets, C. L. Innes notes that whereas for 'British poets of Caribbean descent there is a choice of Englishes . . . those of Asian descent [must choose] between English and another language'.[39] For Alvi – as for Dharker, Bhatt, Khalvati and Chatterjee, all drawing suggestively on their 'native' non-English languages, the first two sometimes calling on native scripts – this proves little hindrance. Bhatt's long meditation 'Search for my Tongue' depicts the generative nature of the linguistic synthesis her idiom rests on literally, in the fabric of a poem woven through with her native Gujarati script, each interpolation followed by its transliteration. The dialogic mode stages the inherent complexity of utterance: 'I ask you, what would you do/if you had two tongues in your mouth,/and lost the first one, the mother tongue,/and could not really know the other,/the foreign tongue.'[40]

To some extent, the linguistic distances these writers find themselves negotiating are liberating. However, Khalvati openly envies 'the lucky West Indian/ . . . a language that can be/ . . . at least read/by oppressors'.[41] Caribbean-British poets such as the Guyanese Nichols, Valerie Bloom and Jean 'Binta' Breeze (both Jamaican), Merle Collins (Grenadian), Amryl Johnson (Trinidadian), and latterly Londoner Patience Agbabi do not waste their advantage. These writers deliberately position themselves in a poetic tradition which can be retraced to Una Marson, sometimes called the first Caribbean woman poet. Marson's highly political discussions of race and gender issues, published in three collections through the 1930s, were gathered into a *Collected Poems* (*Towards the Stars*) in 1945, just as her countrywoman 'Miss Lou' Bennett, already a household name in Jamaica for her 'dialect poetry', arrived in London to study at RADA. Bennett's legendary status was secured in the 1960s with the appearance of *Jamaica Labrish* (1966). Drawing freely on the expressions, oral forms and materials of Caribbean folklore, her acutely political faux-naïve example continues to animate a black British women's poetics which reworks the rhythmic oral forms of Creole. Bloom's 'Show Dem', 'dedicated to all black children in British schools', ('Wi parents come from cross de wata') speaks, ironically, to difference:

> Show dem sey yuh language different,
> Different like yuh skin and hair,
> Different like de place yuh spring from,
> An de clothes yuh sometimes wear.[42]

Introducing *News from Babylon* (1984), the first comprehensive anthology of 'Westindian-British' poetry, James Berry describes how the Creole language that Bloom and her peers wield so effectively originated in slavery: 'to reduce the risks of plotting, and force the use of plantation speech, it was common practice for two Africans who spoke different languages to be chained together at work'. Their native language forbidden, 'the people picked up seventeenth – and eighteenth – century English on their plantations, changing its stresses and rhythms, dropping words, chopping them, changing their usual arrangement and order, keeping elements of their own words, creating a new language to be called dialect, patois, Bad Talk . . . or Creole.' Less the hybrid conjunction of two languages than a syncretic – or rather, synthesised – third, as Berry says, 'Caribbean Creole has developed into a mother tongue . . . yet in no way can standard English not be part of the Caribbean language heritage.'[43] Nichols remarks, 'I like working in both Standard English and Creole. I tend to want to fuse the two tongues because I come from a background where the two worlds were constantly interacting.'[44] Accordingly, 'Epilogue' reconfigures as gain what seems linguistic loss:

> I have crossed an ocean
> I have lost my tongue
> from the root of the old
> one
> a new one has sprung[45]

For the many poets working within the conflicted borders of the British Isles, the issue of language loss is a live one, signifying a history of cultural dislocation and occlusion. Gillian Clarke's 'Border' ('It crumbles/where the land forgets its name') blames English immigrants for this: 'They came for the beauty/but could not hear it speak.'[46] Welsh poets Menna Elfyn and Einir Jones, and the Scottish Gael Mary Montgomery, like a strong cell of Irish poets led by Nuala ní Dhomhnaill, find in 'nation-language' poetry a final means of resisting this process. Such work serves a double purpose: it honours and preserves native, threatened cultures while temporarily reversing the colonising influence of so-called 'Standard English', which is also the essentially masculine voice of canonical English Poetry. Elfyn's 'Song of the voiceless to British Telecom' is not only resentful – 'I sentence myself to a lifetime/of sentences that make no sense' – she also genders the menacing of Welsh culture: 'The usurper's language pierces/to the very centre of our being.'[47] Yet paradoxically, her very phrasing concedes the centrality of English – widely spoken in Wales for over a century – to 'a distinctive poetic tradition, united by a shared experience of migration, industrialisation, war, language loss and a post-colonial identity crisis [born of] the same context of encroachment upon and erosion of that native tongue'.[48] Gwyneth Lewis's 'Two Rivers' ('I was given two languages/to speak, or, rather, they have spoken me') makes overtly postcolonial use of the linguistic synthesis that Elfyn herself refracts:

> Lord of the Meeting Rivers
> be there when our stories run into the sea,

the multilingual estuary
which speaks sky and Sahara, watered silk and neap,
sweet water and salty. This Babel tide
will not be translated . . .[49]

Such linguistic cross-fertilisation is no more peculiar to Wales than it is
to Creole; similar tensions are replayed in both Scottish and Irish poetry.
Kathleen Jamie's 'Arraheids', mischievously exposed as belonging to 'gran-
nies/aa deid and gaun /. . . /but for thur sherp/chert tongues, that lee/fur
generations in the land/like wicked cherms', uses that unapologetically
female commentary to lampoon masculine (mis)readings of Scottish history which bury women's experience in intellectual, standardising language.[50] Likewise, the offensively patriarchal, capitalist attitudes of
the 'oil-men (fuck/this fuck that fuck/everything) bound for Aberdeen
and/North Sea Crude' on Lochhead's 'Inter-City' crowd her, as woman,
linguistically and culturally out of her 'small dark country'.[51] Both poems
counter the intrusion of a male-identified colonising Englishness on female
political and aesthetic life, combining in a process of linguistic reappro-
priation not unlike that celebrated by the Irish poet Mary O'Malley:

It was hard and slippery as pebbles
. . .
no softness, no sorrow, no sweet lullabies
until we took it by the neck and shook it.

We sheared it, carded it, fleeced it
and finally wove it
into something of our own . . .[52]

Katie Gramich implies that, in the poetries of Wales, language tensions
have displaced gender issues because, with a body of women poets stretching back to the fifteenth century, Welsh poetic tradition 'is not, and never
has been, exclusively male', despite, as Linden Peach points out, the
mythology of a country whose 'national images are essentially male'.[53]
Elsewhere, though, the overshadowed and sidelined figure of the woman
poet remains a common theme. One of the originators and few female
practitioners of 'Dub' poetry, Jean 'Binta' Breeze prompted controversy
when she began to query its implicitly sexist traditions. In a 1990 article
entitled 'Can A Dub Poet Be A Woman?', Breeze recounts how she
belatedly realised 'what a difference it actually made being a woman in
the field'. After 'Riddym Ravings (The Mad Woman's Poem)' 'broke form
so completely that it was impossible to return to the shape of my previous

work', she found publication difficult 'on the grounds that my new work was becoming too personal'.[54] Eventually, she moved to London 'to develop her art in an atmosphere unhampered by the patriarchal mentality which still dominates her native ... country'.[55] Breeze's story haunts the hard-edged, vigorously woman-centred work of Agbabi, who attacks patronising attitudes to the political-radical woman poet in 'Rappin' it Up', who rounds on the oppressive male presences dogging her progress:

> ... I am alive
> and you are dead
> An when you try to speak
> your words are obsolete
> while I communicate ...[56]

Both Lochhead and the spikey, subtle Jamie attack the English and Scottish literary traditions which exclude them. Lochhead's self-translating 'Kidspoem/Bairnsang' wittily proves itself against and contests the polite 'improvement' it performs.[57] Jamie's wonderful 'Meadowsweet' glances critically at Seamus Heaney's much-anthologised 'Bog Queen' in elegising the Gaelic women poets who 'Tradition suggests ... were buried face down'. Her normal sang-froid flecked with pity, Jamie revives the poet, who confronts her buriers on her own, literally earthy and apparently angry, terms: 'mouth young, and full again/of dirt, and spit, and poetry'.[58] In some senses, it is in rounding like this on their shared poetic past, more collectively than other female poetic communities, that Irish women poets have succeeded in changing the terrain of twentieth-century Irish poetry, despite the particular exigencies of their own cultural dilemmas. As Peggy O'Brien warns, 'Each of these voices is distinct and yet together they constitute a burgeoning of poetry that is distinctly Irish and female. This is not, however, to claim a separatist or essentialist endeavor ... Each ... inherits Ireland's history of serial invasion, plantation, and rebellion; [however] no two ... register these contingencies in the same way.'[59]

One luminary of this productive community, Medbh McGuckian, has earned respect in part for a poetics which remains strenuously alert to the divisive effects of such contingencies. For McGuckian, the poem represents an undecidable space in which historical, cultural and political tensions and oppositions can be resolved and dissolved, if temporarily: 'poetry is the place where attitudes are teased out into solutions ... I write poetry to ease the pain of other kinds of language[,] journalism or advertisement.'[60] McGuckian's contemporary Boland uses the poem in a more combative way. Boland's self-aware scrutiny of Ireland's overlapping literary and political history delivers a sustained rebuke to the exclusion of women from native poetic traditions. In essays and interviews, Boland traces the emergence of her own idiom out of the realisation that, as a woman, she had no literary ancestry: 'I could not record the life I lived in the poem I wrote, unless I could find my name in the poetic past. And I could not find it.'[61] Almost everything this poet writes addresses the gendered absence embedded in the Irish canon, seeking to narrow the gap which it reveals, to women at least, between 'the place that happened and the place that happens to you'.[62]

Boland imbibed a dual sense of place as a child in London, her home the Irish Embassy, trapped in the confusing linguistic and cultural alterity explored in poems such as 'An Irish Childhood in England, 1951' and 'Fond Memory'. Her early, uncomprehending sense of exile informs her awareness that Ireland's self-exiling history of colonisation is replayed in its poetry, at women's expense. Her own work explores a historical pattern it can never fully redress. In postcolonial terms, her self-insertion into literary history finds her reconfiguring the female subject-positioning on which its disempowering effects depend. 'A Woman Painted on a Leaf' complains 'I want a poem/I can grow old in. I want a poem I can die in.'[63] Telling Dun Laoghaire, 'I am/part of your story and its outcome', this poet is ready to 'record' her entry into both.[64]

For Boland, politically and practically, 'the poem is a place . . . where all kinds of certainties stop'.[65] Reclaiming her place in – recolonising – poetic history, taking responsibility 'for my own innovations and my own failures', she loosens the grip of a male poetic imagination habituated to representing (gazing at), rather than interrogating or reifying, womanhood.[66] She rescues the realities of women's domestic circumstance down the centuries, recovering the immediate, emotional demands made on those who – like her – are wives and mothers; the daily imperatives of sustenance and shelter, the protective husbanding of family and possessions. The following plea concludes one of the poems in a sequence entitled 'The Domestic Interior':

> If I could only decline her –
> lost noun
> out of context,
> stray figure of speech –
> from this rainy street
>
> again to her roots,
> she might teach me
> a new language:

> to be a sibyl
> able to sing the past
> in pure syllables,
> limning hymns sung
> to belly wheat or a woman –
>
> able to speak at last
> my mother's tongue . . .[67]

In the unfamiliar 'new language' of this authentic female experience – the 'mother's tongue' which is her own as well as her parent's – this self-deprecating poem registers Boland's place among both the colonised ('the lost noun/out of context'), and the postcolonial survivors who can critique the past. As she is aware, her own poetic existence ironically depends on the experience of that colonisation, partly in nudging her towards the 'language' in which she can begin to repair its effects.

The enigmatic female figure of the sibyl mentioned in 'The Muse Mother' takes on a more central role in 'The Journey', in guiding Boland through a Virgilian underworld populated exclusively by women.[68] The resonances are complex: the poet herself provides the imaginative space (she dreams the poem's narrative) in which her mythic guide – to whom, like Dante, she gives a real literary identity ('misshapen, musical –/Sappho – the scholiast's nightingale') – and the female souls she sees, all as mute and abandoned as Dido ('only not beyond love'), coalesce. Claiming Boland as her daughter, the sibylline Sappho formally confers on her a duty to 'the silences in which are our beginnings'.[69] Thus the poem reflexively figures how, lifting herself free of silence, Boland self-consciously reinvents herself, in conversation with and clear reproach to the male predecessors she mimics, as 'not just the author of the poem but the author . . . of myself as a poet'.[70] The same drive towards poetic self-assertion animates 'Anna Liffey', the poem in which the historically, politically and culturally gendered 'lie(s)' of Boland's troubled 'land' are deconstructed and dissolved in the reempowering act, and synthesising, postcolonial challenge, of *female* articulation:

> And I make this mark:
>   A woman in the doorway of her house.
>   A river in the city of her birth.
> The truth of a suffered life.
>   The mouth of it.
>
> . . .
>
> Everything that burdened and distinguished me
> Will be lost in this:
> I was a voice.[71]

It is for statements like this that Boland's 'voice' stands as both beacon and tribute to the other women whose synthesising prosodies inscribe an often provisional, double-jointed sense of linguistic and cultural 'home' on the contested space of their literary landscape.

CHAPTER 10

Dialogic politics in Carol Ann Duffy and others

Women's dramatic monologues and dialogues participate in a perceived mainstream of contemporary British poetry which is characterised by post-modern dialogic. According to Valentin Voloshinov, all utterance is dialogic, in that it assumes an addressee, and thus the entire poetic tradition can be understood as conversational.[1] More applicable is Mikhail Bakhtin's definition of texts with a dynamic of more than one voice.[2] As earlier exemplified by Charlotte Mew and Anna Wickham, dialogic indeterminacy operates as a critique of mythical or idealised female representations and, following on from Stevie Smith, draws attention to the limits of familiar verbalisation. Multivocality particularly suits women poets because it emphasises the social origins and contexts of language. While appearing to avoid female poetic authority, a specifically female aesthetic or the privileging of female identity, they scrutinise the language of power play through dramatised personal and social interactions. These are often between men and women but also between women (notably mothers and daughters) or individuals and institutions. Textually, voices may seem to have equal status but the author can stage-manage their dramatic effects; she may challenge readers' preconceptions, direct their sympathies or collude with an implicitly female audience. Whereas the senior generation, poets such as Anne Stevenson and Fleur Adcock, sometimes synthesise male and female identities, newer contemporary poets retain the concept of sexual difference, albeit unfixed, by placing voices in parallel or opposition. Through 'heteroglossia' poets expose and rearrange stratified social differences. They are integral to the widespread dominance of the vernacular which problematises the lines between literary and popular cultures. Straddling the threshold of page and stage, the poems which mine Scottish and Caribbean oral traditions are often the most vibrant. Carol Ann Duffy is the obvious paradigm of protean dialogic politics; her poems are full of animated voices telling their stories with a colloquialism which cuts across the demands of the verse form.

Although dialogic criticism has become one cover-all methodology, it is particularly relevant to end-of-century poetry practice which is characterised by colloquial vividness and diversity. The impetus arises from a sensitivity towards cultural plurality and the influence of polyphonic post-modern narratives on poetry. In *Contemporary Poetry and Postmodernism: Dialogue and Estrangement* (1996), as the title suggests, Ian Gregson argues that there are two kinds of contemporary poets, 'mainstream' and 'retro-modernist'. The former group appropriate Bakhtin's dialogics for a stylistic 'mélange' while the retro-modernists are characterised by the 'estrangement' techniques described by Viktor Shlovsky. In distinguishing the movements, however, Gregson recognises that 'estrangement and the dialogic are not mutually exclusive'.[3] Much poetry can be located in the cross-currents of these developments. It can be self-consciously fictive and point to the instability of language, experience and representation without forgoing socio-literary politics. Duffy's frequently anthologised 'Standing Female Nude' destabilises the dramatic monologue's inherent assumptions by undermining art's mimetic function. In finally pointing to an unrepresented or unrepresentable self – 'It does not look like me ' – the subject arguably discards the male artist's distortion of her.

Similarly, Maggie Hannan draws on her experiences as a life model to contrast the masculine mediations of Schiel, Matisse and Freud with the photography of Cindy Sherman: *'she's crawling, you're crawling, the floor is dirt/where you're digging. You're naked. I am wearing that dream'.*[4] The italics, common in contemporary dialogic texts, position the reader sympathetically in relation to the subject's desperation. The alternating pronouns foreground the interactive process between 'I', 'she' and 'you' in a tenuous subjectivity. Just as 'Life Model' scrutinises the construction of femininity, Hannan 'explores the idea that we are all, in some fundamental way, created by language' throughout her collection *Liar, Jones* (1995). In her words, Hannan aims 'to capture the restlessness and unreliability of the different narratives. I try to give the subject-matter space to inhabit the different perspectives while compressing the language to the point where the unexpected is allowed to happen . . . a surprise association, a misleading echo, a reassessment of meaning. I want the poems to sound unsettling; I want them to hang like mobiles on the page.'[5] Cumulatively, women's poems negotiate between the subject as she is constituted within existing dialogic matrices and the projection beyond that to an altered state. In other words, while laying bare the fictiveness and therefore the provision-ality of ready-made identity, they can construct a range of women hitherto either erased, or misunderstood, or subordinated to other voices.

Bakhtin's dialogic principles may have been depoliticised and appro-priated for a utopian notion of polyphonic democracy, but they are crucial to examining the linguistic and cultural struggles inherent in the processes of self-realisation. Different voices, and their implied chronotopes, that is, 'time-spaces', may have equal status textually, but, as he points out, the modifications of representation are always evaluative:

Someone else's words introduced into our own speech inevitably assume a new (our own) interpretation and become subject to our evaluation of them; that is, they become double-voiced. All that can vary is the interrelationship between these two voices . . . Our practical everyday speech is full of other people's words; with some of them we completely merge our own voice, forgetting whose they are; others, which we take as authoritative, we use to reinforce our own words; still others, finally, we populate with our own aspirations, alien or hostile to them.[6]

We find poets wielding the monologue and 'hidden dialogic', double-voiced or multivocal lyrics and narrative to scrutinise social assumptions about class, race or gender discrimination as filtered through mythologies, idioms and dialects. The form's demands for freely colloquial speech evade the strictures of traditional literary language and can reverse or equalise social hierarchies through the democratic medium of the page.

Duffy frequently employs heteroglossia, that is, the war of social differ-ences maintained by language, to legitimise the speech of the underclasses or any individual who is positioned as the underdog. In her dramatic monologue 'Dummy', a ventriloquist's stooge speaks back to its manipu-lator, personifying the socially marginalised who are silenced to keep them in their place – 'Just teach me/the right words.' At the same time, the dummy draws attention to the imprisonment of the poet's language:

> Why do you
> keep me in that black box? I can ask questions too,
> you know. I can see that worries you. Tough.[7]

The implicit inclusion of the reader in the interrogative is unsettling. In 'Yes, Officer', Duffy dramatises the police conviction of a man unable to defend himself: 'Without my own language, I am a blind man/in the wrong house.'[8] As for 'Translating the English, 1989', the collage of voices cleverly indicate the anachronisms and contradictions in so-called British culture. The polyphonic 'Comprehensive' interrogates the ideal of racial harmonisation in the face of monolithic nationalism. The parallel narra-tives of Jewish, African, Moslem, Indian and working-class white children present the reader with insoluble yet shared states of alienation. Glancing at her treatment of gender, Gregson is alert to the disguised polemic in Duffy's arrangement of voices:

Because she has urgent political motives [Carol Ann Duffy] has felt it necessary to place a limit on postmodern free play; in this her motives are analogous to those of James Fenton. The power of her work arises from the persuasiveness both of her depiction of the distortive ways in which women are represented (the subtle, apparently 'natural' means of representation, the complex ramifications of the ends of representation) and of her condemnation of these distortions. Moreover, she manages to do both, to depict and to condemn, through the deployment of the dialogic tactics which are available to novelised poets.[9]

Many poets are Duffyesque in traversing the line between postmodern defamiliarisation and poetry's expressive function to give voice to Britain's socially deprived, foreigners and women. *On the Game,* the third section of Linda France's richly textured third collection *Storyville* (1997), is a sequence of dramatic lyrics about the social and emotional politics of prostitution. The first is a dramatic monologue which rejects the predatory logic sold to a vulnerable girl: 'Don't think I'm the only one snagged in the loop/of those big black lies: *easy money/just a job; don't worry, you're in control.*'[10] U. A. Fanthorpe presents characters in socially marginal situations compassionately. She avoids detached voyeurism with universal access points, like railway buffets, illnesses, mothers-in-law and job applications. Italics and parentheses often denote the depths of unspoken feeling. In *Strange Territory* (1983), Elizabeth Bartlett draws upon her working-class environment for urban backcloths of pubs, factories, alleyways and off-licences but seldom introduces class diction into her pertinently conversational poems, often based on her experiences within the health and social services. *Look, No Face* (1991) largely consists of monologues by people who are on the edge – battling with love, marriage breakdown, mental illness or rejection. 'Appointment' is the internalised dialogue between a suicidal woman and a Freudian doctor to whom she recounts her dreams:

> Why do you think this is? he said, and she
> cleverly side-stepped the trap of mythology,
> explaining about not being able to cope with
> children, husband, love, and that other myth
> of women who could sew and garden, bake
> and remember the sequence of pills to take.[11]

As Carol Rumens usefully observes, 'A dialogue with tradition is going on in much of Bartlett's work. The poems often enact interesting negotiations between the formal "big stanza" with its regular metre and rhyme, and vernacular looseness. Her line-formation never breaks faith with the rhythms of modern English speech. Yet the metrical "ghost" is a vital presence and reference. It not only satisfies the reader's often neglected need for melody, but allows the work to subvert, play with and ironically comment on English traditions and at the same time draw strength from them. Generations of love poems and elegies underwrite some of her grittiest settings."[12]

The poetry of Sylvia Kantaris is often formally conventional but packed with voices. The *Lad's Love* sequence, set in the Britain of the 1980s and 1990s, is rooted in a statistic cited in the explanation prefacing the poem that 'Men now outnumber women in the 16–35 age group by 212,000. The toy boy phenomenon could make sense (*Observer*).' The dramatisation of a partnership between a middle-aged woman and her younger lover is initially light-hearted but the narrative darkens as the relationship deteriorates. In 'Domestic', a conversation with the police produces compassion for both parties:

> 'We see dozens of domestics every week,'
> one of the cops said, reassuringly.
> Seems I was lucky that I hadn't snuffed it
> totally – just throttled and my head and face bashed up.
> Oh, we were growing more domestic by the minute
> since grants and housing benefit were cut
> and my lover had nowhere else but here to live
> so he said I had to die 'because of poll tax'.
>
> 'Is this man your son?' they'd asked.
> Final irony. Pity I couldn't laugh.
> He used to joke: 'If anybody ever asks you that,
> say I'm your dad.' I saw him out in handcuffs.
> If it's true that each man kills the thing he loves
> it was himself he really meant to finish off.[13]

The sonnet's connotations of lyrical sentiment are raided by the politically charged interchange. The link between family violence and poverty takes the personal on to a more national scale. Although principally a monologue, we see here the widespread 'hidden dialogicality', where 'the second speaker is present invisibly, his [*sic*] words are not there, but deep traces left by these words have a determining influence on all the present and visible words of the first speaker'.[14] In this way Jackie Kay's 'Condemned Property' is a harrowing monologue of violence to a mother by her adolescent son. The mother's secret misery reaches out to the reader:

> There is something the matter with my eyes.
> They are weeping like drains and changing colour.
> *What could you have done, what could you?*
> I talk to myself in this baby-voice
> I used to use for my son, *tell Mum.*[15]

Exploiting the grimness of drains, Kay works the metaphor to set the scene, confide emotion and point to the lack of available words for it.

In the fantasy realism of the dramatic monologue, the woman poet can wield authority over personal relations, social taboos and the reader's sympathies. Many of these poems satirise or undermine the constricting voices of education and the family on the developing female. Duffy's enjoyable 'Head of English' was an early jibe at the conflict between 'a real live poet' and a traditionalist English school curriculum: 'We don't/ want winds of change about the place.'[16] 'Litany' dramatises the young girl's negotiation between the sanitised vocabulary preserved by her mother's coterie of cellophane-wrapped women and the uncensored slang of a boy in the playground. Significantly, she thrills with power at reciting his forbidden swear words in their face: 'Language embarrassed them'. Such female-centred monologues most palpably emphasise the power dynamics of language in social interchanges. Duffy's popular collection *The World's Wife* (1999) supremely resurrects the silenced or marginalised while investigating available representation. As indicated in the title, her thirty 'heroines', from Mrs Midas and Frau Freud to Queen Kong, are everywoman types. Conflating the worlds of history, literature, myth and the contemporary reader has become something of a classic device for women, but Duffy's potent irony and parody are distinguished by 'in-your-face' vernacular and sexuality. Enhanced by live reading, the monologues appeal to a female community although at their crudest the power-balance is simply reversed. They may seem ingenuous because of their entertainment value but Duffy confronts the formulaic influences of myth in the variety of personalities and their stories. For some, troublesome partnerships are unresolved; others come out victorious. Here is Eurydice, deflating the entire literary tradition and its hegemonic institutions:

> And given my time all over again,
> rest assured that I'd rather speak for myself
> than be Dearest, Beloved, Dark Lady, White Goddess, etc., etc.
>
> In fact, girls, I'd rather be dead.
>
> But the Gods are like publishers,
> usually male,

> and what you doubtless know of my tale
> is the deal.
>
> Orpheus strutted his stuff.[17]

In colluding with the speaker and the direct address to the 'girls', she excludes and alienates the male reader. Likewise, Vicki Feaver combines the fanciful with realism in her Forward Prize-winning 'Judith' and 'The Handless Maiden'. In the latter, as Feaver's footnote explains, according to Grimms' fairytale, the maiden's hands are restored for good conduct after seven years while in a Russian version they return when she saves her drowning baby: 'And I cried for my hands that sprouted/in the red-orange mud – the hands/that write this, grasping/her curled fists.'[18] Since to write with sprouting hands is too far-fetched, the moral closure of fairytale is undermined.

In their male-centred dramatic monologues, women particularly exploit the relationship between the poet as dramatist and the reader. In its kinship with the soliloquy of tragic drama, the medium assumes sympathy for the protagonist, but Lavinia Greenlaw's haunting 'Hurting Small Animals' only *appears* to allow the reader's complicity with the swanker who has assaulted a girl on a party 'pick up'. His cocky intonation is antagonising: 'We went outside and fucked her in the car park/but it was no good, she got a bit loud.'[19] This 'internal polemic', that is 'a sideways glance at someone else's hostile word', propels us towards the absent eighteen-year old victim.[20] The information that her brother taught her to destroy helpless creatures questions whether it is a biological or social imperative for men to vanquish women and whether or not gendered attributes are transferable. In Duffy's 'Psychopath', the form invites sympathy for, but we are repelled by, the blatant boasts of a man who has abducted a girl from a fairground, sexually violated her and thrown her into the canal:

> You can woo them
> with goldfish and coconuts, whispers in the Tunnel of Love.
> When I zip up the leather, I'm in a new skin, I touch it
> and love myself, sighing Some little lady's going to get lucky
> tonight. My breath wipes me from the looking glass.[21]

In also allowing the criminal to disclose his own social and emotional deprivation, Duffy may challenge the social forces behind archetypal masculinity but she does not diminish the 'hero's' moral void. This is the 'hidden polemic', where, as Bakhtin puts it, 'Every struggle between two voices within a single discourse for possession or dominance in that discourse is decided in advance, it only appears to be a struggle.'[22] In Duffy's disturbing evocation of child abuse, 'Lizzie, Six', the adult voice dominates with three-quarters of the lines but the reader recoils from it. The disconcerting effect is produced by this structural tension and the absence of overt moral judgement:

> What are you thinking?
> *I'm thinking of love.*
> I'll give you love
> when I've climbed this stair[23]

Again, the poet's concealed polemic is asserted via the intonation. Sympathy is directed towards the italicised childlike innocence in conflict with the menacing adult. Similarly, Selima Hill's 'A Voice in the Garden' depicts the imprints of an elderly neighbour's secret pursuit of a young girl on the adult woman's memory.[24]

In addition to dramatised voices which imply an audience, many poems consist of reported dialogue between two speakers or the 'hidden dialogue' of two voices constructed in the consciousness of a single speaker. These voices in conflicting, consensual or competitive dialogue particularly expose the power dynamics of self-in-relation. The voices in Carol Rumens's sestina 'Rules for Beginners' belong to distinct characters who are both external to and internalised by the *Educating Rita* type of mature women who grasped at newly available education but met with opposition at home: 'Her husband grumbled – "Where's the dinner, mother?"/"I'm going down the night-school for an O level."'[25] Although temporarily escaping from stifling domestic demands, this woman still fulfils her traditional womanly duties. In Duffy's 'A Clear Note', the voices of three generations construct and contest the continuum of women's suppression within the family unit. The youngest urges the implicitly female reader to fracture the cycle:

> Listen. The hopes of your thousand mothers
> sing with a clear note inside you.
> *Away, while you can, and travel the world.*
>
> I can almost hear her saying it now.
> *Who will remember me?* Bleak decades of silence
> and lovelessness placing her years away
> from the things that seem natural to us.[26]

Here, there is a consensual sympathy between the grandmother, mother and daughter. In 'Big Girls', by the up-and-coming Tracey Herd, they are in conflict:

> *Granny's here.* Her mother's voice was bright
> with pleasure. She turned away in spite.
> *Hello,* she mumbled and dropped her eyes back
> to the book she was reading. It was a book
> for Big Girls. The knowledge stuffed her
> with pride. Granny could go to Hell.[27]

We are asked to side with each generation, strapped in their particular version of womanhood. Although the youngest rebels, she is implicitly prey to the marketing and commodification of contemporary femininity. U. A. Fanthorpe's 'Washing Up' interjects a mother's phrases into her daughter's wistful attempts to connect with her memory, whereas Feaver's dramatic 'Woman's Blood' links menstruation, the initiation into womanhood, with inherently murderous mother/daughter relations.[28] Hill's twenty-page sequence on a lifelong tricky affiliation between sisters also investigates the implications of gender determinacy. The highly dialogic narrative surrounds the death of their mother but through reminiscence the schisms connect with the girls' formative childhood: 'she thinks *she thinks she loves me but she doesn't,/she doesn't understand a word I say* '.[29]

The largest group of poems features the dialogue of genders where, as before, the significant other's voice is reworked into the identity created through internal monologue. Contemporary women poets are not, however, simply reflecting a self/other dependency; by simulating dialogues they fictionalise relationships and manufacture female identities which blur the boundaries of 'lived experience' and the imaginary. By dissolving the binary opposition between private and public, they release women to politicise their personal experiences. As Gregson comments, 'It is not a question of the bland tolerance of difference but of a profound sense that the self has no meaning except in interrelation with others, and that the lived experience of the self can only be expressed through determined efforts to evoke the otherness with which the self continuously interacts.'[30] Since the 'other' is absent, the female speaker manipulates the reported dialogue to create her own identikit. In poems about the end of a relationship, such as Ann Sansom's 'Voice' or 'And Please Do Not Presume' by Deryn Rees-Jones, female power is often reasserted directly – 'don't use the *broken heart again* voice'.[31] Control can be reclaimed by humour and by stretching the limits of the plausible. Where pain and loss are central, the speaker can find restitution by possessing the discourse, as in Rees-Jones's 'It Will Not Do': 'It will not do that I don't shout or cry or rant or plead/ show you the door marked exit that I ought.'[32] Mimi Khalvati's 'Stone of Patience' has a mythical realism in its narrative framework: '"In the old days," she explained to a grandchild bred in England,/"in the old days in Persia'". The speech marks are dropped and the first person voice fuses with the poet's to relate the pain of sexual domination and the shame of illegitimate children:

> a voice that says
> *oh come on darling, it'll be all right, oh do let's.*
> How many children were born from words such as these?
> I know my own were; now learning to repeat them, to outgrow
> a mother's awe of consequences her body bears.[33]

Internalised dialogue constitutes the fractured consciousness of individual female subjectivity. As Sarah Maguire comments on her collection *Spilt Milk* (1991): 'Above all, what I've tried to do in these poems is to push out of the lyric tradition, with its connotations of hermetic intimacy, into the broader contexts of the historical and the social, without employing the exhortations of the polemic, without losing sensuality or richness of language. A small attempt at transgressing yet another boundary.'[34]

The 'time-space' is frequently an amalgam of the recognisable and the remote which exposes and also transcends cultural politics. Moniza Alvi's *Carrying My Wife* (2000) consists of a husband's addresses to an imaginary wife: 'My wife was a rare occurrence/and a common occurrence.' The self-contained metaphor, 'She created a hiding place/in the empty supermarkets of the moon', is the central mediator between the familiar and the strange.[35] Alvi states that 'In a sense the poems are autobiographical, and writing from a male or "husband" viewpoint has been a way of distancing myself from the sensations and difficulties portrayed, and then zooming in closely. I found surreal aspects of relationships emerged ... I suppose I am attracted by fantasy and the strange-seeming and find there some essence of experience.'[36] In Rees-Jones's 'Service Wash', the line between external and imaginary perceptions, and between masculinity and femininity, becomes hard to define. A lonely impoverished laundry-man creates a woman's identity from the clothes he handles. Sympathy is invited for the tragic figure of this attendant, along with his wife and the bellboy, who are all social inferiors to the rich owner of the dress which he tries on: 'I could have cried./My breasts hung empty.' In a turnaround of Freudian prescriptions, does he latently desire to *be* a woman? Towards the end, however, the narrative seems to go beyond the land of unspoken desires with the incantatory repetition of 'sometimes':

> Sometimes I think an afternoon will last for ever.
> Sometimes I think the world is flat. Go on. Convince me.
> Sometimes I think I'll fall in love again.[37]

The speaker's sexuality, the woman's identity, and even her existence, remain uncertain since they are contiguous with the dreamstate of the male narrator. The direct address to the reader – 'Go on. Convince me' – sends the chronotope to the fictive page and the first person pronoun could be the poet's. The strangeness but liberation of altered consciousness is not new but characterises much end-of-century poetry. In 'Superman Sounds Depressed', Jo Shapcott seizes the masculinity emblematised by the cartoon hero, to feed and examine women's fantasies of being desired:

> And I want us to eat scallops,
> and I want to lick the juice from her chin
>
> as though I could save the world that way,
> and I won't even ask what passion is for.[38]

The chronotope is more vividly a 'borderzone' between levels of consciousness.

Kay often suffuses quotidian familiarity with the surreal to deny definitive signification: 'I think I will always be interested in identity, how fluid it is, how people can invent themselves, how it can never be fixed or frozen ... I like mixing fact with fiction and trying to illuminate the border country that exists between them.'[39] As in her collection *Other Lovers* (1993), same-sex relations and passions can especially be coded through unspecified dialogic interchange. The central sequence charts the making and breaking of a love relationship which is vividly intimate yet universal. In 'Mouth', displaced images evoke the unpresentable pain of love turning to hate: 'Words like dead gulls thrown out the sea;/your mouth froths like a drowning man' (p. 58). Fact and fiction share the same territory in memory and Feaver's 'The Singing Teacher' is a retrospective tragedy of a disabled woman's passion for a young girl: 'Oh, Miss Cree, forgive me/for what twisted through you/like a corkscrew.'[40] Feaver typically moves between particularised and imaginary chronotopes in her love poems, such as 'Lacrimae Hominis', a meditation on the male partner's inability to cry, or 'French Lesson', where the speaker tries on a new identity via a foreign language.[41]

Although dialogism does not substitute the universalising authority of masculine discourse with an identifiable female poetic voice, it avoids the linguistic difficulties for women encased between the expressive or the antirepresentational, the personal or the public. Kay's bestselling *The Adoption Papers* (1991), originally a radio drama, exemplifies how multivocality articulates and maintains difference but bypasses the binary opposites of conventional versions of gender and race. The parallel narratives construct the actual and psychological interplay between a birth mother, the adopting mother and the adopted child. Also in *The Adoption Papers*, topical poems introduce debates about environmental and economic abuses and nonheterosexual arrangements. 'Photo in the Locket' explores the alliance between a black and a white girl through intermingling the girls' and their parents' voices. The hidden dialogic in 'Dance of the Cherry Blossom' invites sympathy for two men dying of Aids: 'Both of us are getting worse/Neither knows who had it first' (p. 50). Similarly, the dramatis personae in 'Mummy and Donor and Deirdre' compel emotional understanding: 'Tunde said Do you know who your daddy is?/I said yes he's a friend of a friend of mummy's' (pp. 54–55). 'Sign', from *Other Lovers*, sums up how these occluded individual testimonies can seem like pebbles thrown at an overwhelming giant of dominant rhetoric:

> All this
>
> *distance*
>
> between one language and another, one
> culture and another; one religion
> and another. The *little languages*
> squashed, stamped upon, cleared out
> to make way
> for the big one, better tongue.   (p. 21)

Dialogic representation of Anglo-Asian duality is aimed as much against Western homogenising of Indian culture as it is against inscribing it:

> The multicultural poem does not expect
> The reader to 'understand' anything,
> After all, it is used to being misunderstood.
>
> It speaks of a refraction
> It wants more dialogue
> between the retina of the light
> It says, 'get rid of your squint'
>
> It lives the chapter in history
> They can't teach you in school.[42]

Sujata Bhatt's multilingual creativity is a weapon against the invisibility of hybridity since it maintains differences and holds them alongside each other.

In contrast, Irish poets have tended to operate within their dominant lyric tradition but to some extent the younger women define themselves antithetically to stereotyped Irish sentiment by starkly vernacular English. Rita Ann Higgins's 'The Deserter' is the unsentimental dramatic monologue of a woman whose man has died: 'But in his favour/I will say this for him,/he made a lovely corpse.'[43] In 'Federal Case', Julie O'Callaghan mimics both the addiction for a 'Big Mac' and the disapproval of it: 'Maybe it's a mortal sin cuz/I've got a yen for some junk food.'[44] Knowingly, she pitches slang at literary correctness. Such universalising colloquialisms appear anarchic, not least because they discard the nationalist ideal of unification.

Scottish poets plunder the rich resources of their English heritage, Scottish dialects and Gaelic languages. Liz Lochhead was among the first to exploit the range of native dialects and exhibit a knotty relationship with her repressive heritage. Similarly, Kathleen Jamie recognises that nationalistic pulls to a unified Scottish identity are not advantageous to women:

> Scotland, you have invoked her name
> just once too often
> in your Presbyterian living rooms.
> She's heard, yea
> even unto heathenish Arabia
> your vixen's bark of poverty, come down
> the family like a lang neb, a thrawn streak,
> a wally dug you never liked
> but can't get shot of.[45]

As Helen Kidd explains, 'Scots English is recognisable by certain tropes, whereas women do not have a language that is specifically female, nor a specific set of dialects which are identifiable by women from other cultural contexts. What we do have, however, is a sense of the subversive qualities of language: ironies, digressions, musicalities, as well as a sense of the dangers of certain male discourses which place the female subject in a subordinate position.'[46] At the same time, the national mother tongue disadvantages the English reader. Scots dialects and phonetics both expose and refresh its traditions. Jamie's 'Forget It' asks whose history is preserved and questions whether the poem's function is to reclaim it:

> *Who wants to know?* Stories
> spoken through the mouths
> of closes: who cares
> who trudged those worn stairs,
> or played in now rubbled back greens?
> *What happened about my granddad? Why*

> *did Agnes go? How come*
> *you don't know*
>
> that stories are balm,
> ease their own pain, contain
> a beginning, a middle –
> and ours is a long driech
> now-demolished street. *Forget it!*[47]

Just as the pronunciation of 'Forget It' is up for grabs, so is the resolve to maintain or discard memory. As for other colonised peoples, there is a fine line between holding on to past racial suppression and being stuck there. In other poems in this newest collection, *Jizzen* (1999), Jamie shifts further between realism and the yet-to-be.

With African rhythms, Dub poems and Creole dialects, Caribbean poets investigate and keep alive their histories. Colloquial multivocality retains women's role as custodians of the oral tradition. In 'Language Barrier', Valerie Bloom imbues traditional English quatrains with the nonstandard-ness of nation language:

> But sayin' dis an dat yuh know
> Sometime wi cyan understan one anodda
> Even doah wi all lib yah
> An chat de same patwa[48]

The necessity of pronouncing the words phonetically comments upon the flatness of page text while the sense dispels any ideal of a homogenous Caribbean experience. Bloom is committed to the social inclusiveness of orality and her performances are often participatory. Grace Nichols tends more to disempower the colonising assumptions of English by cross-fertilising oral and literary traditions. In *i is a long-memoried woman*, she switches from the first person singular Creole voice – 'from dih pout/of mih mouth' to the choric standard English: 'Yet we the women/whose praises go unsung/whose voices go unheard' (p. 12). Jean 'Binta' Breeze creates character types who speak for, and potentially to, a community who are united by their marginality and sense of African as well as Caribbean pasts. Whether in 'The First Dance' or 'Dis Lang Time Girl', their politics centralise her experiences as a Jamaican emigrant in England.[49] For Breeze, Dub poetry '"is a public voice, a political voice of social commentary that works to a rhythm ... there's a strong sense of rhythm which is the rhythm of reggae. It's poetry which combines a love of language with a sense of rhythm and music while at the same time recording our stories and oral observations."' Through evoking powerful emotions with the physicality of her theatre and her vocal range, she raises awareness about history, war or the stereotyping of Third World poverty, penetrating 'into the lives of ordinary people'. For her, colonialism '"is an academic term. Let's call it what it is – international theft of resources and robbery of people's land. Colonialism doesn't say that."'[50] Breeze's dialogicality, from the dramatic monologue to the multivocal performance piece, stretch and thus question the perimeters of 'poetry'. Frequently woman-centred, they produce complex female identities which are always in motion: 'I have a really strong sense of my own voice, as a woman, because I write a lot of voices.'[51] As C. Innes puts it, in differing ways these poets 'challenge, often with subversive wit and humour, essentialist concepts of women and race, or monolithic views of culture and insist upon the interplay of multiple heritages and voices in a Britain where they "have arrived".'[52] Patience Agbabi's 'UFO WOMAN (PRONOUNCED OOFOE)' is the monologue of an African-Caribbean finding herself perceived as an alien in England:

> my two-tone hand with its translucent palm,
> life line, heart line, head line, children, journeys,
> prompting the '*Why's it white on the inside*
> *of your hand?''Do you wash? Does it wash off?'*
> Or my core names, Trochaic, Dactylic,
> Galactic beats from ancient poetry,
> names they make me repeat, make them call me
> those sticks-and-stones-may-break-my-bones-but names.
>
> In times of need I ask the oracle.
> Withdrawing to my work station I press
> HELP. I have just two options. HISTORY:
> The screen flashes subliminal visuals
> from the old days which I quickly translate:
> *Slave ship: space ship, racism: spacism.*
>
> Resignedly I select HERSTORY:[53]

Significantly, Agbabi has discarded Creole to play with the possibilities of manipulating more eclectic cultural discourses. The scene ends with a positive future vision of 'not aloneness but oneness', thus picking up the gauntlet from her 'Transformatrix', a rhythmic celebration of female linguistic freedom:

> Give me a stage and I'll cut form on it
> give me a page and I'll perform on it.
>
> Give me a word.
> any word.[54]

CHAPTER 11

Postmodern transformations: science and myth

To some extent, the conversation between modern and postmodern in late twentieth-century culture and aesthetics is reprised in the woman poet's appropriation of the transforming metanarratives of science and myth. For contemporary poets, the overlapping of authority and uncertainty across both discourses says too much about her own position, as both woman and poet, to overlook; the stories which each discourse tells about the female self furnish her with both the justification for and the means of transforming an embedded legacy of female incapacitation and silence. The poem itself plays a central role in this often political refashioning. As Sr. Berenetta Quinn observes, 'The poetic act utilizes metamorphosis – indeed consists of it.'[1]

This chapter considers the restive poetry in which women poets subject the transforming languages of both science and myth to gender-sensitive scrutiny. In doing so, they destabilise the institutionally masculine provinces of authority and 'truth' in a strategy which is illuminated by Heisenberg's 'Principle of Uncertainty' (1926): 'the conditions in which observation occurs alter what is observed'. As Paul Mills astutely clarifies, 'in Heisenberg's theory, the position of reliable narrator remains vacant'.[2] Poets such as Lavinia Greenlaw and Jo Shapcott prove that for women, gender not only colours 'the conditions in which observation occurs [to] alter what is observed', but also, just as pertinently, the way in which the observer is herself perceived.[3] In all the texts discussed here, some degree of narrative unreliability opens an enabling space between speaker and spoken. The habit finds its most provocatively 'postmodern' expression in a further strand of poetic texts that Mills might classify as 'post-scientific'. Like – but not the same as – 'magic realism', this poetry 'follows the drive of defamiliarising reality, but not that of explaining it in any grand complete unified theory ... preferring partial narratives, wide perspectives, a sense of harshness, astonishment, amusement, and ... of uncompleteableness'.[4] As Pauline Stainer's 'Quanta' asserts, '*Things happen/simultaneously/and in every direction/*

at once.[5] The buoyantly 'uncompleteable' 'post-scientific' poem, where myth and science converge and interrogate each other, constitutes a vibrantly subversive aspect of late twentieth-century women's poetry.

SCIENTIFIC TRANSFORMATION(S)

Anthologising later twentieth-century poetry, Jo Shapcott and Matthew Sweeney observe:

> We live in an age when scientists can see inside every cell in the body and are learning more and more through space exploration and the advances of astrophysics . . . about the outer reaches of the universe and the distant history of life itself . . . TV, tabloids, movies, virtual reality, the Internet – all these have encouraged us to take the extraordinary for granted. We have watched men walk on the moon, we talk to each other across space and time, we conduct our business and our courtships on the "net". Isn't it inevitable, then, that these days poetry should be written which makes free with the boundaries of realism, crossing this way and that at will?[6]

Many of the poets 'making fruitful explorations of science as both subject and method' in the last decades of the century have been women.[7] Frequently, they query the socially and politically disempowering gap between female experience and desire which scientific discourse takes for granted. Protesting this from a position which is arguably not dissimilar from the scientist's, the poets invariably seek to close it.

There are parallels betweeen scientific and poetic activity. Helen Dunmore explains that 'A scientist needs intuition, luck and creative boldness in order to discover . . . as well as a solid groundwork of technique and experimentation. It's a way of experiencing the world with which many poets would feel an affinity.'[8] These affinities are examined in Greenlaw's 'Science for Poets', as the poet watches her scientist companion

> measuring deep into decimal places to record
> each molecular shift, in search of an answer
>
> or an answer that fits,
> or else in hope of some wild enlightenment
> that without your eye for detail, I'd surely miss.[9]

The insight into a contrasting (in her view disappointingly ordinary) world finds the poet sympathising with a compulsion which seems familiar: 'an answer that fits,/ . . . some wild enlightenment'. At the same time, however, the poem remains implicitly sceptical of the scientist's precision. Thus it recognises the dialectic David Kennedy describes: 'Science promises and delivers greater understanding of and control over life, the universe and everything; [yet] the expertise involved in it and the technologies derived from it distance us from the reality of that understanding and control.'[10] This paradox charges the medical procedure depicted in Maggie Hannan's 'Tap', resulting in the auditory proliferation the poem stages linguistically. As hearing returns, colloquial and clinical idioms converge ('Cauliflower, jug or shell-like/conjoin with the mechanical synapse') in an intensely felt cacophony: 'Tones dust/the inner drum like a moth glass-trapped./ Hearsay. Static. Molecules become//alphabets ... /... /... unleashing a thesaurus.'[11] The linguistic mélange foregrounds the difficulty of making empirical knowledge fully available in words, with or without the imagination. Self-referentially, it is through verbal and aural rather than visual imagery that Hannan conjures the literally resonant amplitude ('*Babel 61 n. confusion.*') she examines.

Noting the (mostly male) modernist poets' interest in science and technology, Deryn Rees-Jones has argued that Greenlaw's strategic engagement with scientific discourse 'gives her, as a woman poet, a special and uncompromised sense of authority and detachment not usually associated – even in the 1990s – with a female poetic voice'.[12] However, as Rees-Jones also notices, Greenlaw (like Hannan) avails herself of these (transforming) powers mostly to interrogate them. In 'Natural History', Anne Cluysenaar ponders the 'dirty transformation' of the (female) skull of 'Swanscombe Man'. Here, the speaker's empirical expertise ('I feel for the supra-iniac fossa,/sign of otherness, of being Neanderthal') is emptied of significance by a resonantly 'empty' bone, marker of the extent (therefore the limits) of human knowledge of the 'real':

> I raise my hand to my head, seeming
> to feel what's impossible, the hollow sign
> of different being.
> > This labelled cave
> is alien. Empty, like her three curved bones,
> of the real existence of consciousness.
> > . . .
> > So hard, even now,
> To imagine ourselves what we really are.[13]

This lightly gendered text reiterates how little notice scientific history has taken of women, empirically or imaginatively. Yet while silently reproaching the misclassification of the skull, Cluysenaar uses the error to dramatise the porousness of the boundary between verifiable and imagined which (perhaps identifying with the skull's female owner), she seems determined to respect. Meanwhile, the poem uses its deconstruction of gender to insist that the interchange between known and guessed-at reflects the congruence of otherness and selfhood in all human experience, not only women's. As Kennedy says, 'Science ... carries all our most ambivalent feelings about ourselves, our capabilities and our destiny.'[14]

Women poets use science to query masculine authority. The teaching text in Maura Dooley's 'Fundoscopy' underlines the limited powers of clinical diagnosis since, for all his academic expertise, the book's author lacks perception: 'It's like a moment in that film, perhaps,/when he thinks he sees her clearly through/the two-way mirror, but she can't see him at all.'[15] Greenlaw's 'The Gift of Life' and Shapcott's 'Electroplating the Baby' are deeply sceptical of the male scientists they depict. Greenlaw's Dr Pancoast's dispassionately technical account of the insemination procedure, which reduces the nameless 'wife/of a Quaker merchant' to the commodifying status of 'livestock', seems cruelly complacent. The impression is perhaps deepened because the baby is a boy.[16] Pancoast's field of expertise is inverted by Shapcott's more preposterously hubristic Dr Variot, inventor of the 'electro-metallurgy' he sells, in a grotesquely God-like effort to hold mortality at bay, as '*the* way/to obtain indestructible mummies'. This certainty is deflated by the speaker's dry refusal to predict 'the future in store/for this process ... /It would be impossible to say'.[17] The hard-edged patriarchal order these poems question is contested by others which vest scientific authority in women, although their empowerment is never categoric. While Bhatt honours the work of the female scientist ('Marie Curie to Her Husband' and 'Counting Sheep White Blood Cells'), like Greenlaw in 'Galileo's Wife', she registers the difficulties of female entry into the masculine value systems and tensions of a recondite world.[18] Lacking Galileo's obsessive enthusiasm for science, the sensitive and resourceful woman of Greenlaw's poem is prompted into assisting him by the loss of the children he seems never to have mourned. If tragedy has sharpened the dispassionate objectivity which makes her the better scientist, it leaves her without her husband's appetite for public status. Thus while globetrotting temporarily ventilates her world, her contribution to science and history goes unrecorded. Bereft of her children, posterity holds no attraction for her, even if domestic life would have precluded it anyway.

For women poets, then, the mobilising of scientific precepts, practice and terminology hardly seems, as Kennedy suspects, a 'cheap way of "buying in" truth' for the poem.[19] They consistently render 'authority' unreliable, instead viewing science, like Stainer, as 'Simply a way of looking'.[20] The phrase implicitly registers the transforming powers of scientific discourse, while lending these unsettlingly voyeuristic overtones.[21] Thus, when Greenlaw's 'Millefiori' blandly reports the logical but fantastic effect of an operatic aria on a prosthetic eye ('wave upon wave of sound/higher and closer till it struck/the resonant frequency//of blue glass'), the final image seems sharply ironic: 'the molecules of his eye/oscillated into a thousand flowers'.[22] The imaginative and metaphoric possibilities radiating from this deconstruction of (male) sight slyly gender the means by which the apparently opposing domains of science and art, reality and imagination, rationality and emotion, are meshed and elided. The coalescence is refracted in the lustre which refreshes technically precise words like 'molecule' and 'oscillate' when their context is altered.

Stainer's words illuminate the discreetly political nature of Greenlaw's poem. John Berger's analysis of the disenfranchising effect of the (historically, prevailingly male) 'gaze' famously explains: 'Men look at women. Women watch themselves being looked at ... The surveyor of woman in herself is male: the surveyed female. Thus she turns herself into an object of vision; a sight.'[23] In the shattering of vision staged in 'Millefiori', Greenlaw resolutely and not untenderly turns the objectifying male 'gaze' (a parallel for the scientific 'way of looking') back on itself.[24] As well as troubling the – valorising – masculinity assigned to scientific utterance, the poem neatly inverts the lyric paradigm to which the aria belongs (and, presumably sung by a woman, itself inverts). This reverses the conventional dynamic in which the power of the remote, idealised female object of male desire is predicated, self-defeatingly, upon powerlessness and silence.

As Greenlaw suggests in poems like 'Millefiori', science can be used to call the socio-poetic construction of identity, liberatingly, into question. As Hannan remarks; 'what interests me about science is its *power*; it is presented to us as a way of escaping the limits of the Self, and thereby the limits of the perceived world'.[25] In a typically rich variant on the love lyric, Medbh McGuckian's 'Marconi's Cottage' offers the science the cottage embodies (the transmission of radio waves across the Atlantic) as an analogy for the inherently paradoxical nature of human relationship: 'you are all I have gathered/To me of otherness'.[26] Where Greenlaw shatters, and McGuckian evades, the classifying gaze, Stainer subverts it. 'Woman Holding a Balance' addresses the inscrutable subject of Vermeer's painting. In this portrait of a portrait which cleverly conflates modern technology (the ultrasound imaging used both to monitor foetal development and in the maintenance and restoration of painted canvases) with high art, for Stainer the anonymous woman figures a distinctively female ability to counter the intrusive power of science: 'Inclining your cool head,/you weigh/what we have found/questionable:/woman as diviner.'[27] In response, the poet – who, in the act of reading the painting coincidentally assumes the role of 'woman as diviner' – respectfully replays the almost spiritual 'equipoise' which makes the figure in the painting (perhaps pregnant, perhaps not) so resistantly and compellingly ambiguous.[28]

The essentialist emphases of Stainer's treatment are directed at the authority of the poem itself by Moniza Alvi, sanguinely equating poetic composition with the evolutionary, transforming and plainly gendered process of gestation ('You hope something will blossom inside you,/taking shape like a fresh thought'), in which imagination and reality somehow fuse:[29]

> ... life makes for you on the up-escalator,
> whirrs above like a helicopter.
> beckons like a cinema complex.
> And this is because the world
> has a passion for making faces,
> elliptical new faces.
>
> It sings and sighs
> over the faces it creates.[30]

Alvi describes writing as 'an attempt to extend myself and transform that which [is] constantly being taken in'.[31] However, the 'elliptical new faces' made by the self-transforming contemporary woman poet look as often to the mythological past as to the technological future.

MYTH AND METAMORPHOSIS

Various twentieth-century thinkers have suggested some contingency between myth and science. Freud asked Einstein, 'does not every science come in the end to be a kind of mythology ... [cannot] the same be said today of your own Physics?'[32] Conversely, Roland Barthes locates myth, which he defines as 'a system of communication ... a mode of signification, a form', in 'the province of a general science, coextensive with linguistics, which is *semiology*'.[33] The power to transform is one of the characteristics which science, in interpreting empirical data, and myth, organising the imagination, share. As Marina Warner pertinently declares, 'metamorphosis is the principle of organic vitality as well as the pulse in the body of art'.[34] This crucial intersection is rehearsed in the mythic compulsion to explain how 'metamorphosis begins and ends the history of man ... affecting the world within him and the world without'.[35]

In making sense of the pattern of human existence, myth instructs us about our own expectations and anxieties, hence the apparently timeless popularity of Ovid's *Metamorphoses* which Ted Hughes describes: 'by now, many of the stories seem inseparable from our unconscious imaginative life'.[36] This is partly why Barthes, warning that mythologies 'immobilize the world', contends that their universalising force is 'nothing but an Usage . . . that [all men] must take in hand and transform'.[37] However, Barthes perhaps underestimates the peculiar fluidity of mythological narratives: arguably, to retell myth is by definition to alter it. Hughes notes of Ovid that 'His attitude to his material is like that of the many later poets who have adapted what he presents. He too is an adaptor.'[38] When Quinn observes that 'the poets of today go on alchemising the old names and legends, Grecian or Teutonic or Celtic', her choice of verb neatly captures the process of reconfiguration which modern mythmaking entails.[39]

In their different ways, Warner, Hughes and Barthes all detect in metamorphosis the residue of frustrated desire which, they agree, makes it potentially subversive. Implicitly, so does feminism. The relation of desire to transformation is of particular interest to feminist critics such as Hélène Cixous and Luce Irigaray, who performatively contest patriarchy's overwriting of female experience in both theoretical and linguistic terms. As Cixous explains, 'each story, each myth says to her: "There is no place for your desire in our affairs of State."'[40] Cixous concludes that female desire (born of 'a mixture of difference and *inequality*') is best satisfied in the imaginative and political strategy of self-transformation: 'If there is a self proper to woman, paradoxically it is her capacity to depropriate herself.'[41] Having elaborated on the opportunities for self-transformation latent in the feminine 'gift of changeability', Cixous adds, 'This power to be errant is strength . . . No matter how submissive and docile she may be in relation to the masculine order, she still remains the threatening possibility of savagery.'[42]

Stevie Smith crams the somehow menacing cultural, political and aesthetic potential of metamorphosis into the poetic construct:

Poetry is like the goddess Thetis who turned herself into a crab with silver feet, that Peleus sought for and held. Then in his hands she became first a fire, then a serpent, then a suffocating stench. But Peleus put sand on his hands and wrapped his body in sodden sacking and so held her through all her changes, till she became Thetis again, and so he married her, and an unhappy marriage it was. Poetry is very strong and never has any kindness at all.'[43]

In the analogy with shape-shifting Thetis, Smith conjures and confirms the enablingly transformative effect of poetic utterance. Kathleen Jamie agrees:

'To write a poem is to work with change, to deal with a shape-shifter.'[44] Smith's summoning of Thetis also, interestingly, genders the possibilities of self-transformation which are inherent in poetry. If the forced union with Peleus, the product of which is the warrior Achilles, hero of the *Iliad*, signals the genre's productively conflicted disposition, Achilles himself embodies the danger his shape-shifting mother represents to those who threaten her desires.

Thus Smith's comparison utters the attraction of metamorphosis for the woman poet: self-transformation offers a creative, unpredictable and self-empowering route out of the confines of poetic tradition as well as the paradigmatic expectations of cultural history. As Sheenagh Pugh declares, 'it's such *fun*, and so liberating, to get into someone else's skin'.[45] Staged against a suggestively dark backdrop, Annemarie Austin's 'Shape-Shifting' uses stanza and line endings to figure the confluence of past and present in female experience, before 'shifting' into a deconstruction of that experience which emphasises its variousness:

> You see the same face across the generations –
> her there, half a shadow and half concrete
> in a real coat with mud-flecked facings,
> a fraying hem, and lugging a leather suitcase
> tied with string. She sings the same thread song
>
> that her mother whispered above her cradle
> in the winter dark about a thousand years ago;
> . . .
>
> For she rises up wherever you might be watching
> in a different costume, with various coloured hair
> or lion's pelt, bird feathers – your glance catches
> her even in the fireside cat that licks its paws
> then turns its flexing gaze towards your face
>
> before stalking out to the dusk and its dissolving.[46]

Austin's semi-realised questioning of the relationship between self and other also shows how transformation permits, in Sarah Maguire's words, 'a postcolonial and feminist stress on difference and otherness which, whilst emphasizing the deconstruction of meta-narratives (such as notions of gender or race), can retain a materialist and political analysis of inequality and injustice'.[47] Rees-Jones echoes both Austin's poem and Maguire's comments in confiding that 'the postmodern me loves the fragmentation, the multiple levels on which I can experience myself in the urban world or even disappear . . .'[48]

As Rees-Jones implies, the poet who transforms herself often does so for political as well as aesthetic reasons. The four poems of U. A. Fanthorpe's 'Only Here for the Bier' sequence consider 'how the masculine world of Shakespeare's tragedies would look from the woman's angle', while in 'Adventures with my Horse' (1988) Penelope Shuttle argues that the human perspective is sharpened by metamorphosis: 'by looking at, guessing at the animal's oblique yet relevant viewpoint, things move on, out of the dark- ness'.[49] Shapcott, who adopts a range of guises in *Phrase Book* (1992) and *My Life Asleep* (1998), remarks, 'I like ... tales that are both moral and animal. Tales that deal with shape-shifting and the poet as that kind of shape-shifter – which is why the myth of Thetis is so appealing.'[50] Shapcott's 'Thetis' begins by declaring not just sensual delight but joyous confidence in her own gift of proliferation: 'No man can frighten me ... / ... I'm laughing/to feel the surge of other shapes beneath my skin.'[51] The brutal rape which cuts her off mid-flow (the page turn injects a crucial hiatus in a present-tense narrative), grimly ironises the exuberant build-up; if nothing excuses her violation, was this Thetis guilty of vanity or naïveté, or both, in placing such faith in her powers? Carol Ann Duffy's version casts Thetis in a more constructively adaptable light, while preserving a palpable air of resentment: 'I changed, I learned,/turned inside out – or that's/how it felt when the child burst out.'[52] Both poems replay Smith's sense that the transforming process of poetry compounds Thetis's mani- fold, intensely desiring nature, itself differently nuanced by each new treatment. A changed perspective contextualises the unnerving shape- shifting routine on which Thetis embarks in the original myth; in the light of her eventual violation, her behaviour seems less self-indulgent or belligerent than self-protective.

Duffy's 'Thetis' contributes to the semi-sequential monologues of *The World's Wife*. This important collection testifies to the revisionary powers of the self-transforming poet. Duffy's sisterly intervention enables a variety of female personae to cast doubt on the stories which mythologise and poten- tially 'immobilise' them. Eurydice, Penelope and Mrs Midas, for example, all bring their own (putatively unmediated) perspective to the accounts which normally silence them. These women expose their respective partners as arrogant, selfish and foolhardy; god, hero and monarch alike are much diminished by their wives' scrutiny. Two other treatments in the same important collection vary and deepen Thetis's self-transforming model. Inverting the power-balance of Ovid's story, 'Pygmalion's Bride' radically changes the implications of the original.[53] Able to appear inanimate or come to life when she chooses, Duffy's Galatea is nothing like her submissive, silent Ovidian other. Instead, this wily operator stoically endures the advances of her unappealing suitor ('He spoke –/blunt endearments, what he'd do and how./His words were terrible'; 'He ran his clammy hands along my limbs'; 'He let his fingers sink into my flesh') with a passivity intended to repel him. When this fails,

> I changed tack,
> grew warm, . . .
> . . .
> began to moan,
> got hot, got wild,
> arched, coiled, writhed,
> begged for his child,

The intensity of what is, of course, a performance (and therefore a carefully unreliable guide to female desire) not only outmanoeuvres Pygmalion; his rapid disappearance – it is unclear whether this is due more to the manifestation of female sexuality or the mention of a child – confirmingly indicts the male vanity which Duffy relentlessly exposes, and deplores, in patriarchy.

In Ovid's version of the Pygmalion story, metamorphosis displaces frigidity with life, heterosexuality and happiness. By contrast, Duffy interprets Galatea's original animation as expressing a fetishising male desire which simply transfers her from one state of voiceless impotence to another. Duffy's own intervention sympathetically reinvests autonomy in the statue. Different ramifications emerge with figures such as Circe and Medusa, both (unlike Thetis) possessed of the power to transform others. These characters offer Duffy the chance to reiterate the dangerous nature of female desire, challenging a literary history which, if it concedes the existence of such a force, pays it no attention. The erotic recipe which 'Circe' offers ('which uses the cheek – and the tongue in cheek/at that'), not only turns pig into a dismissive analogue for man but takes gluttonous interest in the connection between sexual climax and death.[54] Similarly, when provoked, as lyric convention dictates, by 'A suspicion, a doubt, a jealousy', Medusa solemnly plays by the rules of courtly love, weighing the petrifying power of her own sceptical gaze with the disempowering, idealising effect of that of her (male) literary antecedents. The sexual anxiety she professes has a familiar ring: 'I know you'll go, betray me, stray/from home./So better by far for me if you were stone.' Her parting words taunt an implicitly male voyeur with her own subversive potency: 'Look at me now.'[55]

'THIS IS THE WAY TO GO': WOMEN AND THE
'POST-SCIENTIFIC' POEM

David Kennedy argues that 'Science continues to engage the poetic imagination because poets, like physicists . . . seek to expand our perception of the
world and of ourselves in it.'[56] Shapcott's 'Pavlova's Physics' genders this
compulsion in a playfully expansive conceit of empowerment and desire:
'Everything in my body/has been processed/through at least one star/. . . //
I want to speak to you about it;/I want you to know how much/
I understand – and more and more/reveals itself in waves.'[57] A literally
irrepressible speaker, apparently embodying rather than inhabiting the
solar system ('I need//more dimensions than geography allows') is impossible to position precisely. Her cosmic perspective undermines the deduc-
tive logic of science, exposing the enlightenment which the consciousness
('outdated barn of a thing') pursues as ironically depending on the ana-
chronising imagination ('the light of stars is ancient/history when it gets
here'). She takes the proposition that 'the conditions in which observation
occurs alter what is observed' to a suggestive extreme.

Shapcott's speaker breezily confirms Mills's contention that the concept
of space, in which science and myth arguably converge, 'defers the position
of reliable narrator.'[58] She also echoes Kennedy's conviction that expanding
knowledge of the universe frames 'our perception of the world and of
ourselves in it', with radical consequences for all human discourse.
However, poised between empirical (scientific) fact and the imagination,
'Pavlova's Physics' reveals how what Mills terms the 'post-scientific' poem
proffers the woman poet creative opportunity: the poem does not so much
transgress gender boundaries as outimagine them. Similarly, Linda France's
'Dreaming True' is mostly gendered ('For years she's dreamed/of holding
science like a globe in her hand,/of slipping on space like a leather glove,/of
a singular woman, naked as an eye, far-sighted, herself'); however, a change
of pronoun marks how all such binaries are destabilised by the recognition
that truth and dreams alike 'pin you//to the centre of where you are,/
transformed by space,/naked,/singular'.[59] The conclusion arrives at a curiously postmodern locus, in which here ('the centre') and there ('space'),
dreaming and truth, transformation and nakedness, speaker and addressee
blur. Again, Mills is illuminating: '[T]he sense of glimpsing something . . .
that this something is reality, of being inside it rather than outside, which is
where science has returned us . . . all this feeds the capacity for wonder, . . .
no other versions of reality are waiting out there to tell us how the story will
end or even why it happened.'[60] If so expansive a sense of reality compels,

so (paradoxically) does its power to cause the 'wonder' which calls it into doubt.

Although poets like Stainer (in 'Quanta' and 'The Ice Pilot Speaks'), Greenlaw, France and Dooley (see especially 'More than Twice the Speed of Sound') all explore this fertile territory, the unreliability of the self-transforming contemporary woman poet is at its edgiest in Shapcott's wittily 'post-scientific' alter ego, 'The Mad Cow'.[61] Appearing in a fragmented sequence of poems spanning two collections, the Cow introduces herself with characteristic chutzpah: 'I'm not mad. It just seems that way/ because I stagger and get a bit irritable.'[62] Created amid growing panic about the spread of bovine spongiform encephalopathy (BSE), or 'mad cow disease', in the UK in the early 1990s, this endearing character is sanguine about her affliction:

> There are wonderful holes in my brain
> through which ideas from outside can travel
> at top speed and through which voices,
> sometimes whole people, speak to me
> about the universe. Most brains are too
> compressed. You need this spongy
> generosity to let the others in.

In the upside-down order of the 'idiot savant' (or Wise Fool), where the mute (cow) can talk and lunacy is rational, affliction becomes opportunity and decline, growth. This carnivalesque process renders the powerless suddenly,' if temporarily, powerful. The Cow's political subversiveness is compounded by her gender and the poetic medium. Shapcott explains: 'She's . . . rather a feisty character, rather a terrific sort of animal, and I think I made her that way in order to redeem the idea of a "mad cow", which is something I get called a lot.'[63] The poet's metamorphosis deliberately conflates one form of female disenfranchisement – madness: the conventionally female malady linked with hysteria as well as lunacy – with a more literary one, the woman poet. The Mad Cow represents the disarming apotheosis of Shapcott's own Thetis-like capacity for self-invention.

Shapcott has remarked of her shape-shifting tendencies, 'It may be that I feel the self is enclosing, and I like the idea that you can pass out of it, and get into other places, other imaginations, other skins.'[64] Her transformation into the Cow, an ironic mirror-image of herself, has some distinctly political consequences. The riotous physicality of the 'Mad Cow Dance' ('I like to dance. Bang. I love to dance. Push.//It makes me savage and brilliant. Stomp') takes the 'jouissance' of *écriture féminine* to a new extreme: 'just watch me//become/pure product, pure//use,/pure perfume,/jasmine and fucked'.[65] In that final ambiguous word, the vaporising climax of this orgiastic dance celebrates female sexual energy while protesting the Cow's unjust lot and patriarchy's demeaning commodification of women. The critique extends to the poetic establishment: 'The Mad Cow Tries to Write the Good Poem' performatively and pointedly makes poetry of the lowly materials of her world: 'in the streaky emulsion on the walls,/in my own messing on the floor, in the nation's smeary dailies'.[66] This is perhaps partly why 'The Mad Cow in Love' dreams of translating not only herself on to another plane ('I want to be an angel') but her lover, too ('I fancy for you/the government of the stars and all the elements').[67]

It is in this joyously post-scientific, unquestionably female creature that Shapcott retails the undecidable, and politically and aesthetically productive, interrelation of the transforming discourses of science and myth. If 'The Mad Cow in Space' affirms the power of the woman poet's 'post-scientific' perspective, 'The Mad Cow Believes She is the Spirit of the Weather' finds her somehow translated empoweringly beyond time ('It's harder now, here/in the future'), to a place where mythological ('I was a junior cloud goddess') and scientific (global warming) authority collapse into each other.[68] This has disturbingly real consequences for everyone: 'I'm dangerous to the earth./I spat and a blanket of algae four miles long/ bloomed on the Cornish coast.' In her many post-scientific resonances, the Mad Cow becomes a fertile self-interrogating trope of the woman poet's transgressive literary and political potential. She is endlessly, casually instructive, just as the conclusion of her first poem, drawing on an ironically ancient analogy for rationality and order, promises: 'My brain's like/ the hive: constant little murmurs from its cells/saying this is the way, this is the way to go.'

CHAPTER 12

The renovated lyric:
from Eavan Boland and Carol Rumens to Jackie Kay and the next generation[1]

> you with your smocked mouth
> are what your songs left out.
>
> . . .
>
> We have been sisters
> in the crime.
> Let us be sisters
> in the physic:[2]

Eavan Boland's 'Tirade for the Lyric Muse' speaks to the age-old tradition of lyric healing and consolation, what Sarah Maguire describes as 'poetry's labour: to bring together, carry, transfer pieces of language that have been torn apart . . . through the figure of the intimate self (the invisible mender)'.[3] The 'labour' has consequences for poet and audience alike: Anne Stevenson confides that 'when a poem feels finished I myself feel changed. I have a pleasurable sense of having worked through an ordeal, of having climbed to a new plateau of understanding'.[4] Boland's self-involvement underpins the healing process her 'tirade' urges: avowing the sisterliness of speaker (and poet), addressee (and reader), she begins unpicking women's collectively 'smocked mouth', challenging and changing the literary record. Her 'physic' derives from exposing and repairing the damage of the poetic past, and from the freedoms and power this brings. Whether like Boland they openly contest a status quo which excludes them, or like Stevenson prefer to work from within it, contemporary women use the lyric mode to announce, consolidate and deepen their relationship with poetic tradition. They renovate it in resentful formal and thematic negotiations with a male-dominated canon, and the concerted reversing of the fetishising male gaze. Their redirection of its restorative powers also interestingly transforms the confidently unitary lyric voice, the cohering 'I' of 'the intimate self', into the looser, nonunitary compass of the third person, by which leading end-of-century poets such as Medbh McGuckian emphasise the liberatingly dispersed, fragmented and pluralistic nature of the female self.

Since, in writing lyric poetry, by definition the woman poet unsettles and alters literary convention, her mobilising of the genre cannot but be political. Grace Nichols's 'A Poem for Us' reclaims the dynamic of the love lyric self-affirmingly; the poem makes the act of its own composition (which it parallels with baking) singlehandedly procreative. The resulting poem becomes both an emotional contract and a self-referential assertion of women's artistic independence: 'Now I'm a dealer in mud and water/ Giving shape to our unborn/The child who watches us from some place./ Who is both happy and sad. Watching us.'[5] The equivocation signals the difficulties of inverting an all-too-familiar (literary) hierarchy, problems which are contextualised by Carol Rumens. Her 'Stealing The Genre' self-referentially depicts the poet as 'a woman, English, not young' attempting to seduce, as Rumens herself explains in an interview, 'the Irish Genre, the Aisling poem, traditionally used by men', a kind of Muse of nationhood and poetry.[6] In many senses, the encounter, nuanced by the lesbian love lyric, is anticlimactic; the aisling falls asleep and has vanished by morning. However, the powerful impression her presence leaves ('so condensed, so weighty!') suggests not that the union of speaker and 'genre' is impossible, only that it will differ from foregoing versions; as Rumens says, 'I'm not saying it couldn't be lovely but I'm saying it might not be.'[7] She implies that there is as much consolation ('physic', or perhaps 'inspiration') to be found in conceding the existence and nature of the complexities as in attempting to resolve them.

If it is unclear whether Boland's 'Tirade' is uttered for, or to, the goddess it invokes, the poem dramatises the Muse's centrality to women's reconceiving of the lyric poem. The force Stevie Smith called 'a strong way out' is for Ruth Fainlight defining: 'To be a poet ... means ... never to set barriers against the Muse.'[8] Women's altering of the concentrated, formally self-sufficient, expressive lyric utterance is inherent in their unsettling of the typically male poet's relationship with his female Muse. Whether they conceive this archaic influence as female or male, deity or intimate, mentor or rival, inspiration or irritant, contemporary poets consistently affirm the Muse's power. Elaine Feinstein finds a plainly female force 'strengthening/our fierce and obstinate centres'.[9] Although Linda France's 'The Nine Muses' celebrates a deeply intimate relationship ('Know this/is flesh, the gift of your muse – the map of//your body'), in the final poem of her *On the Game* sequence (about prostitution), 'My Muse, the Whore', the intimacy is problematised: 'my right hand woman, my best friend. I know/I can only trust her as much as

I trust myself.'[10] Rumens's 'The Muse of Argument' finds the intrusion of the female voice altering the Muse's very disposition. This poem conjures a nervy but devastatingly eloquent presence: 'she embodies all/Silence that steels itself/ Under a woman's heartbeat/And stammers to take aim.'[11] As poet offers Muse assistance, rather than the other way round, the 'plaudits, abasements' of courtly love which 'die/At her feet' are held responsible for a self-effacement as shaming – among the gendered resonances of the final image – as it seems dangerous: 'her face has taken on/The colour of a wound,/Its deep, historic rose.' Thus Rumens uses the Muse to unfix the formulaic gender relations of the traditional love lyric and explore her own – as a woman poet, uniquely refreshing – claim upon it. Rumens's discursive piece 'In the Bedroom of the Page', argues through the complexities of gendering this claim:

When a Muse star[t]s to speak she's puzzled at how well she knows her master's tongue, how easy it is in her mouth. When other women tell her that, though she's speaking it, it isn't speaking her, she wants to laugh ... She says:

> . . .
> I have heard this language spoken perfectly by many women.
> Language is not fixed in form as the human body is.

Then she realises that in making these rebuttals she is already doing something new to language – or, at least, *with* language.[12]

These dilemmas notwithstanding, the fact of female authorship seriously disrupts the traditional dynamic of the lyric poem. The woman poet who summons a female Muse can parody or attack the example of her male counterparts by assuming a man's voice; by reconfiguring the sexual tensions of the Muse/Poet relationship or revisiting them from an unexpected angle, such as the lesbian love poem. France's Muse is 'the best// lover I've ever had, the only one to deserve all/the attention she demands'.[13] The Muse need not be female. Remarking that a Muse 'is a shifting thing for everyone', Jo Shapcott comments that 'Those of us who are stuck with a male muse have someone much more stubborn, uncooperative and unwilling – maybe even competitive.'[14] Sylvia Kantaris's 'The Tenth Muse' 'has no aura./The things he grunts are things/I'd rather not hear.'[15] Rumens confides that 'Whenever I had a male muse I thought him utterly beautiful and wanted to get his look onto the page ... [but] I usually found myself writing about a mythological character, a foreign country or myself. Myself, mostly.'[16] Shapcott's poem 'Muse' adopts an ambiguous subject position. In one way, it literally ravishes a male Muse; after much intimate 'fore-play', language finally 'come[s]' – in the double-entendre of the last line – in a kind of climactic burst which the speaker apparently teases out of him.[17] Yet the speaker could easily be the Muse herself, *in flagrante delicto*, so distracted by her lover that her trademark eloquence falters. Both rendering the passive lover mute, the two readings converge in the closing line, confirming the female speaker's dominance of both the sex act itself and its (lyric) representation. Denise Levertov's 'She and the Muse' takes a different route to a similar end; 'the hour's delightful hero' having departed 'in the dustcloud of his own/story', his lover 'eagerly' resumes her creative existence: 'She picks a quill,/dips it, begins to write. But not of him.'[18] Again, the poem inverts the typical love lyric; it is the self-indulgent man who – too vain to notice – is objectified, trivialised and silenced: he is the poem's Muse only by default, by prompting the heroine towards more satisfying inspiration.

The woman who petitions the Muse signals not just her determination to restore 'what your songs left out' but her enjoyment of the resulting (aesthetic and political) complexities. To begin with, her relationship with a prevailingly masculine canon is awkward. Wendy Cope provides a cattily Prufrockian explanation:

> The poets talk. They talk a lot.
> They talk of T S Eliot.
> One is anti. One is pro.
> How hard they think! How much they know!
> They're happy. A cicada sings.
> We women talk of other things.[19]

It is the noise of this self-regarding 'talk' which vexes Shapcott, trailing Byron, Wordsworth and Goethe across Europe: 'so many men's voices shouting/all the names they know, at the dark'.[20] A brilliantly versatile technician, Cope, meanwhile, mercilessly sends up her favourite targets – Wordsworth and Eliot – to imply that what they say is as alienating as the talking itself.[21] U. A. Fanthorpe's 'Seminar: Felicity and Mr Frost' finds Frost sourly determined to obstruct a female student's efforts to learn from him.[22] Nichols's double-edged 'Spring' ('with all the courage of an unemerged butterfly/I unbolted the door and stepped outside//only to have that daffodil baby/kick me in the eye') figures the antagonism more forcefully; as Vicki Bertram points out, 'Spring' is constructed as a cultural, female and creative reawakening which takes a side-swipe at a defensively entrenched male poetic order.[23] Gillian Clarke ('Overheard in County Sligo') and Selima Hill ('Down by the Salley Gardens') argue how dangerously little Yeats knows about the emotional terrain his lyrics romanticise.[24] Both find his naïve idealisations deceiving women into sacrificing themselves for a shallow male fantasy which robs them of their potential. Others avenge themselves poetically; in 'The Whitsun Trainspotters', Kantaris sends up Larkin and male sexuality ('Who hasn't noticed with what verve and dash/the trains come thundering, and with/what creaks and groans they chunter out'), while Cope's self-important creation Strugnell makes poetic hubris a distinctively male failing.[25]

By comparison, perhaps thanks to what Lyn Pykett calls the 'enabling and liberating' effects of feminism, women's conversations with female poetic models seem supportive, constructive and empathetic.[26] Swapping her world for Emily Brontë's parallel but more romantic world, Fleur Adcock's conclusion ('It may not come out as I intend') is as protective of Brontë's poetry as her own.[27] Feinstein pays tribute to the Victorian Amy Levy ('Precocious, gifted girl') partly, it seems, to help to preserve her name and art for posterity.[28] Shapcott's 'Elizabeth and Robert' sequence (conflating the literary partnerships of the Brownings, and Robert Lowell and Elizabeth Hardwick) underlines the self-absorbed male poet's failure to understand his female counterpart. Since, as 'Robert' belatedly concludes, 'The meaning is all in the gaps', 'Elizabeth' herself remains potently elusive; in a female-authored if not overtly female-centred poetic sequence, it is Robert who is overwritten and disempowered.[29] Meanwhile, poets address their female contemporaries with equal respect although, interestingly, these are not necessarily British. Tributes to the Americans Plath, Anne Sexton, Adrienne Rich and Elizabeth Bishop, along with Russians Anna Akmahtova, Marina Tsvetayeva and Irina Ratushinskaya are frequent. Nearer to home, Kathleen Raine, Elizabeth Jennings, Carol Ann Duffy, Stevenson, Clarke and Boland are widely honoured.[30] Rumens's 'The Fuchsia Knight' marks widespread respect for Medbh McGuckian.[31]

If such woman-centred conversations suggest the woman poet's strengthening hold on lyric tradition, this impression is confirmed by the confidence with which she directs the lyric's formal and thematic conventions to suit her own ends. For as long as they have soothed children and mourned the dead with rhyme and song, women have contributed to the flexible, inherently musical, traditions of lyric, 'one of the richest forms in the canon'.[32] The extent of their informal influence over a genre partly defined by orality, albeit difficult to evaluate, has been widely recognised. Catherine Kerrigan observes that ballad, for example, is 'one of the most readily identifiable areas of literary performance by women'.[33] However, if 'Anon ... was often a woman', the ancient lays and lullabies construct a form of female subjectivity which, being predicated upon absence, projects its own self-silencing.[34] Many contemporary poets – Pauline Stainer and

Alice Oswald among them – answer by using ballad to undo female silence.[35] Although her self-consciously lyrical idiom also calls on Steve Winwood ('A Shortened Set'), The Everly Brothers ('*Lure*, 1963') and Neil Sedaka ('Rayon'), Denise Riley's relish for 'the intense and very harsh musicality of border ballads of the thirteenth to fifteenth centuries', explains the moments of 'piercing violence' in texts such as the four-line 'True North':[36]

> My body's frame arched to a drum houses a needle. A splinter of this world has stuck in me, snapped-off, afloat down syrupy blood. It points me on. This thick body can't dim its brilliance though it vexes the car of my flesh. Sliver of outside that I cradle inside and which guarantees me my life also.[37]

Liz Lochhead also plunders 'the blood and guts ballads, the vernacular narratives, the rude and unrespectable rhymes' she loves, for political reasons, as in 'Mirror's Song': 'Smash me looking-glass glass/coffin, the one/that keeps your best black self on ice./Smash me, she'll smash back –/ without you she can't lift a finger ...'[38] Alongside ballad (see especially 'Weighing the Heart'), France makes suggestive use of jazz's subversive aesthetic potential in her powerful lyric sequence *Storyville*, and earlier works.[39] For her part, Jackie Kay pays particular homage to black blues singer Bessie Smith. In 'The Same Note', Smith becomes a channel of cultural affirmation, political consolation and creative self-restitution ('Every note she sang, she bent her voice to her will'):

> She could get it right back like some kind of boomerang.
> She could use it as a shelter, the roof of her mouth,
> stopping the rain, stopping the rain soon as she sang.
> Or she could fly out of Alabama, or float the mouth
> of the Mississippi Delta. Or walk the solid flat plain.
> She could tell every story she wanted to tell;
> . . .
> ... And then again,
> if she wanted, she could rock herself to sleep, to dream.
> Her own cradle swinging the same note, again and again.[40]

Although not all recover oral traditions so self-consciously, music remains central to contemporary women's poetry. In part for dense formality and 'lush' phrasing, Elizabeth Garrett has been called 'as near to a lyric poet as we'll get in our times'. Garrett herself confides that the '*sensual* in words – whatever the language – fascinates me: the way they feel on the tongue; how they strike the ear ... their weight and density. Word-play is one of the ante-chambers of poetry.'[41] The musical properties of language find emotional depth in a cluster of love lyrics forming the core of Garrett's impressive second collection *A Two-Part Invention*, including 'Anatomy of Departure', 'Alliance Française', and 'Love's Parallel'. In the first, the lovers' reluctant uncoupling is echoed in the pared-down doubling economy of the poem's five couplets and agile lineation. The mood of restraint is answered by the gently erotic word-play of the second, the labial image of the tulips worked into a tantalising linguistic sex act. Poised between the universal and the intensely private, the Donne-like 'Love's Parallel' is perhaps the most satisfyingly dualistic utterance of how mind and body converge in an emotional interest which is timeless and timebound, vertiginous and grounded, self-enclosing and self-duplicating:

> For distance is our love's cool parallel,
> And ours the chaste harmony of this hill's
> Contours – that neither break, nor touch, but hold
> The heart's sheer gradient, encircled.[42]

It is partly for her sense of measure (in all the word's implications) that Garrett often seems a natural successor to Stevenson, for whom 'the musical component controls the pace, pitch, tone, even the meaning of a poem[;] I often work months or years to get the noises right.'[43] To illustrate this process, Stevenson, whose latter years have been ironically and sadly marked by a struggle with worsening deafness, offers 'Arioso Dolente', 'titled after the slow movement of Beethoven's Piano Sonata Opus 110'. In this highly wrought elegy, music literally resolves the reverberating tensions of the child/parent relationships it mourns: 'Mother, who read and thought and poured herself into me', and 'Father, who ... /... shouted "G!/D-natural, C-flat!, *Dolente, arioso* –/ Put all the griefs of the world in that change of key."' The strains are gathered up harmoniously together in the last stanza:

> As if our recording selves, our mortal identities,
> could be cupped in a concave universe or lens,
> ageless at all ages, cleansed of memories,
> not minding that meaningful genealogy extends
>   no further than mind's flash images reach back.
>   As for what happens next,
> let all the griefs of the world find keys
>   for that.[44]

Stevenson's metaphoric 'change of key' is more stricken but also more comforting for the sense of inadequacy on which she closes; the key to understanding death is that there is no key or understanding. Like the photograph and the musical phrase it summons, the poem points up the

poignancy which hindsight brings to history. Yet while Stevenson regret-
fully underlines her own lack of foreknowledge, her dedication ('For my
grandchildren when they become grandparents') explains why, in the
penultimate stanza, 'ours is the breath on which the past depends'.

Stevenson's shift of focus from first person singular to third person
plural is significant partly for reiterating that in being more discursive
than art or music, lyric poetry is also more consolingly connective than
either, and especially so (arguably for psychological as well as biological
reasons) when the 'recording sel[f]' is female. This perhaps explains the
frequency with which contemporary women like Stevenson herself, and the
ever-exemplary Boland, mine the family for thematic material. In 'Cofiant'
(meaning 'biography'), Clarke recuperates a once-patriarchal Welsh poetic
tradition, defiantly positioning herself and her own experiences at the head
of an ancestry which, piecing together fragments of personal history, she
can retrace to the eleventh century.[45] Here, the lyric is used to patch
the gaps in personal and literary history, its connective disposition – linking
without closing down creative possibility – rehearsed in the elasticity of
the sequence form.[46] Elsewhere, the number of poems about mothers,
or mother figures, dramatises how the tensions of a complex relationship
dissipate in the comprehending recognition of shared emotional
dilemmas.[47] For example, Jean Earle's 'Jugged Hare' compassionately
portrays 'A tender lady', who, though a wife and mother, remains tormented
by the virgin/whore dichotomy she somehow, perhaps unknowingly,
reconciles: 'She lay now/Outside her frame, in the hare's dark//Hating her
marital skills/And her lady-hands, that could flense a hare/Because she
wooed a man . . .'[48]

The 'physic' to be gained from this sense of solidarity invariably has
wider resonance, as Maura Dooley's 'Mirror', framing the speaker's image
of herself with her baby daughter, refracted by 'the only/glass in which I
look/and smile', suggests:

> Just as this baby smiles
> at the baby who always
> smiles at her, the one in
> her mother's arms, the mother
> who looks like me, who
> smiles at herself in her
> mother's mirror, the friendly
> mirror in her mother's house.[49]

Unabashedly feminising 'the gaze' for three generations of women, Dooley
redirects the traditionally gendered and gendering 'gaze' of love lyrics,

rooted in the courtly romance poem, where female 'power' is predicated, paradoxically, on subjection and objectification.

The contemporary female lyric tends to answer the male gaze either by appropriating it to inspect female selfhood (often, like Dooley, in the form of daughters or mothers) on the poets' own terms or, in Christina Dunhill's words, by 'turn[ing] on men the gaze we've been gazed by'.[50] Although they tend to be kindly about their fathers, especially as strength diminishes with age, illness or death, many poets relish the latter opportunity.[51] As satirists, Fanthorpe, Sophie Hannah, Connie Bensley (who also frequently adopts a male voice), Cope and Kantaris find men easy targets. On the other hand, Moniza Alvi's *Carrying My Wife* (2000) and Deborah Randall's portrayal of John Ruskin from various female perspectives argue that compassion can be just as satisfying as invective.[52] In Sheenagh Pugh's stunning poem 'Envying Owen Beattie', the (masculine) romance of Arctic exploration flows suggestively into fairytale with the discovery of the frozen body of 'five foot four of authentic/Victorian adventurer ... /... John Torrington':

> To have him
> like that; the frail, diseased
> little time-traveller;
>
> to feel the lashes prickle
> your cheek; to be that close
> to the parted lips:
>
> you would know all the fairy-tales
> spoke true: how could you not try
> to wake him with a kiss?[53]

Here, Pugh takes for granted (and stages, in the questioning note on which she ends) the centrality of desire which Deryn Rees-Jones spells out: 'poetry is as much loss as it is a resistance to loss. The mouth's own elegy, as Adam Philips beautifully describes the kiss. For if the kiss is something we desire it is also something we can never give our own lips: we are, in a sense, the kiss but we can never experience it except through another.'[54] Pugh's Platonic remodelling of Sleeping Beauty confidently adjusts lyric's formal and thematic subjection and objectification of women; like it or not, her gender enriches this process.[55] Women's lyrics therefore repair poetic tradition by insisting on their common right to desire, physically as well as poetically, rebutting the sterile convention that they may only be desired. The lasciviousness of Pugh's 'Toast' ('young builders lay/golden and melting on hot pavements', their jeans 'fuzz stretched tight//over unripe peaches') makes the female gaze unapologetically sexual. Nichols is earthier: 'Poems rise to marry good old Consciousness./Poems hug Visionary-Third-Eye./ Kiss Intellect./Before hurrying on down/to burst their way through the crotch.'[56] In 'The Eater of Wives', France adopts the voice of male sexuality: 'all I want is the best, some/girl who'll eat me back'.[57] The poem by Sujata Bhatt which transliterates as 'Shérdi' ('sugar cane'), claims sexual power with an analogy tinged with violence ('I use my teeth/to tear the outer hard *chaal*/then, bite off strips . . .'); the eroticism of Helen Dunmore's 'Wild Strawberries' is more delicately textured: 'I lipped at your palm – /the little salt edge there,/the tang of money you/handled.'[58] Maggie Hannan resonantly inverts the language of love into the Riley-like conclusion to her 'You Sign' sequence, a spare, reflexive account of its own linguistic redundancy: 'my tongue/gently/feathers/her skin//with words/ my tongue/her ear/no lies.'[59]

Although such poems provide dramatic proof of women's determination to open the lyric frame up to female sexual desire, they threaten to distract attention from a less obvious, less ubiquitous but perhaps more daring aspect of the renovated lyric: the reengineering of the lyric voice, the moments of slippage from the voice of the first person to the consolingly inclusive but firmly nonuniversalising third person which Stevenson's 'Arioso Dolente' quietly executes. The shift subtly underpins the healing impulse played on in Feinstein's 'Urban Lyric', in which orality protests a desire of a soberingly different order:

> Last month they cut a cancer out of her throat.
> This morning she tastes sunshine in the dusty air.
>
> And she is made alert to the day's beauty,
> As if her terror had wakened poetry.[60]

A poem which is poised between mind and body uses the third person singular to ventilate the I/you dynamic of the lyric experience. As both subject and object of this renovated healing lyric, 'she' embodies her suffering while herself enshrining the healing solution to that suffering. Invited to identify with her, while remaining at a respectful distance from the sphere of the private experience which the poem skirts, we simultaneously bear witness to and experience the poem-like 'day's beauty', and the 'terror' which it answers and dissipates. The gesture protects the unnamed woman while demonstrably declaring the lyric poem's connective, consoling potential. In paralleling speaker and reader in this cautionary, remote way, Feinstein implicitly deconstructs what begins to seem like the lyric tradition's complacent presumption of a singular, coherent and representable voice. She offers a hopeful but also scrupulous response to Levertov's 'Wondering', which asks whether poetry can 'bridge the gulf/between our sense of being – /node, synapse, locus of hidden counsels/ – and the multitudinous force of/world'.[61]

Arguably, the Belfast-born McGuckian offers the strongest evidence that the end-of-century (woman) poet who calls this 'gulf' into question can do much to 'bridge' it. One of the preeminent poets of her generation, this remarkable writer has earned international respect for an elliptical, melodious, self-investigating and affirmingly self-sufficient poetic idiom which restores to lyric tradition 'what your songs left out', for both aesthetic and political reasons. The originality McGuckian brings to the lyric mode is well illustrated by the shifts of focus in 'Black Note Study' in which love and music, interwoven and mingling, turn into resonant tropes of each other:

> I hear two voices without either
> disturbing the other – four harmonies
> where there was only one.
> One voice spells out the same notes
> as the other in reverse order.
> One violinist starts at the end,
> the other at the beginning,
> the backward version fits perfectly
> against the forward.[62]

The fullness of a poetics which is continually looking both ways, which recognises honesty in duality and inversion, is its trademark. For McGuckian, who has described her poetry as 'a weaving of patterns of ins and outs and contradictions, one thing playing off against another', lyric's healing force lies precisely in the harmonising interrelation of form and content (voice and utterance, player and music, line and sense), mirrored everywhere in experience, which the poetic construct reifies.[63] On one level, the uniquely expressive obliquity of her idiom seems intended to reify the impossibility of making sense of language and linguistic structures. On the other, each highly crafted, polysemous text remains acutely conscious of its self-referential power to make meaning of apparent meaninglessness, and of the risks attending this.

Typically, McGuckian's poems avoid divisive cultural positions; they might best be described as compassionately neutralising. She is circumspect about identifying herself with 'Northern Ireland' : 'I dislike . . . the use of the term in contexts where people are made to feel inferior or left out by it.'[64] This confirms why 'Elegy for an Irish Speaker', in marking human loss, uses the idea of language to play off the cultural history which her father represented, and in which her own cultural identity is rooted, against the future which is already distancing both: 'I cannot live without/your trans-sense of language, the living furrow of your spoken words/that plough up time.' As McGuckian has commented, 'What I tend to do is gloss over . . ., or use poetry to control horror and evil, to make them, not less important, but to put them into their overall context . . . not trying to cover it up, but trying to understand it.'[65] In the elastic timeframe of 'Elegy for an Irish Speaker', the 'no-road-back' of death is contextualised by the instinctively self-critical transgendered resource of language, sometimes Irish and sometimes poetic, both linking and separating father and daughter: 'he speaks so with my consciousness/and not with words, he's in danger/of becoming a poetess'. Personifying Death as female, vanquished rather than vanquisher, the poem depicts the transition from life to death as a faintly illicit consummation:

> The knitting together of your two spines
> is another woman
> reminding of a wife, his life
> surrounds you as a sun
> consumes your light.
>
> Are you waiting to be fertilized,
> dynamic death, by his dark company?[66]

The 'knitting together' hints at the metonymic slippages by which McGuckian 'keeps fluid the oppositions between male and female, logic and emotion, constraint and freedom, waking and dream' in order to interrogate them.[67] Her self-referential privileging of the undecidable over the determinate not only bears provocatively on her forms and language; as critics like Clair Wills show, her troubling of such boundaries has particular consequences for her handling of subjectivity.[68] Among her best-known poems, 'Venus and the Rain' ('my gibbous voice/. . . retelling the story/Of its own provocative fractures') makes self-deconstruction a conspicuous concern. The poet admits that 'I'm usually trying to talk about myself and . . . the mutiny of one self against another, the clash of one life against another.'[69] Perhaps inevitably, this 'mutiny' extends into McGuckian's suggestive fracturing of Maguire's 'invisible mender'. In texts such as 'The Flower Master', and perhaps most powerfully and explicitly 'A Different Same', the cohering disposition of the lyric 'I' is displaced in the dismantling of female selfhood; as its title implies, 'A Different Same' consoles and heals the injustices of poetic tradition in a lyric voice which assures us of its multiplicity. Like so many of McGuckian's poems, this locates the affirming 'same'ness of the female perception in its incontestible, ironically and reassuringly potent 'different'ness.[70] Continually testing her own nonunitary subjectivity, with all the implications this has for her purchase on semantic and sensual experience, McGuckian offers a persuasive, if productively opaque, argument for the 'physic' that late twentieth-century women poets collectively offer their twenty-first-century successors.

Afterword

'The best women's poetry may be still unrecognised if, as I suspect, we have not yet understood how to read it.'

(Germaine Greer, 2001)[1]

In her Introduction to *Making for Planet Alice: new women poets* (1997), Maura Dooley recognises that 'Women are published, read and heard, but their work is not discussed. Until their work is considered and written about consistently, seriously and undifferentiatingly by the major literary journals of the day, their poetry will not have a future as part of the main canon of English Literature.'[2] 'Undifferentiatingly' is a debatable goal. Reviewing *Making for Planet Alice*, Carol Rumens provocatively observes that 'the question of whether there is a "womanly aesthetic", however deliberately constructed, remains unanswered'.[3] And so it must. Since women commonly resist homogenising versions of femininity, criticism has to investigate but not confine their attempts to masquerade in, transform or discard the available uniforms of language. In 'Base Linguistics', Ann Sansom dramatises the contingency of women's alienation from language and their uncertain social identity:

> Together we discover
> that there are no synonyms, no common tongue
> to cover every case and gender
> but there is safety of a kind in numbers.[4]

If their poetry can and should be read in relation to and in conjunction with their male contemporaries and predecessors, women poets also preserve a distinct literary position which allows them to be creators and commentators who employ language subversively. As we have seen in the course of the century, where they enjoy safety in numbers, women are more free to take the risks.

Reviewing the century's diverse poets collectively throws up some striking continuities between their works. In the many poems about being a woman, the common themes are desire, the search for identity and the right to write. However, whether they petition or reject an association with female literary predecessors or contemporaries, few of the poets are at ease with received poetic utterance. Frequently, they shift provocatively between expressive and self-concealing voices and registers, and excel at the dramatic monologue. They are not afraid of experiment: their linguistically innovative poems inscribe a political and aesthetic dynamism which has been unjustly neglected. However, perhaps the greatest shift has been in the treatment of the lyric, where we find them disrupting literary conventions with an irreverence perhaps explained by lack of nostalgia for a tradition which has ignored them. Whether self-evadingly androgynous, or reflecting an assertive female speaker, women's lyrics characteristically refuse or unsettle essentialising gender oppositions. At the start of the century, they avoid centralising a unitary female subject; by the end, they are complicating and repositioning her with adventurous pronouns, syntax, metaphors and rhythms. Contemporary poets also frequently exploit the imaginative possibilities of the lyric to depict the defeat of patriarchal law through the interface of fantasy and realism. Myths are rewritten and history revised in a variety of ways, further liberating female identity from the stranglehold of nationalism, cultural elitism and chauvinism.

Overall, these strategies warn against engineering the kinds of reductive critical connections, through simplistic categories and labels, which circumscribe or overwrite female, let alone poetic, individuality. In answer, we have tried to demonstrate the variety of ways in which poets liberate women from deadening representations. It is instructive to note Kathleen Jamie journeying, in 1999, towards rather than away from distinctly female self-identification, as she reflects on the difficulties of

working with experiences which are wholly female – in an art form which still, at times, likes to imagine that real, proper poetry cannot have women's experiences at its centre. Being in the thick of it rather prevents one from wandering lonely as a cloud. I'm still puzzling about these things – What is authority? What is tradition? What does lie at the heart of woman's experience? I'm surprised at myself, but I think it is an act of choice. As women we still find ourselves in a tangle of briars. We are told what to write, and then told that real art can't be made from those experiences anyway. We have to spend energy clearing space. Having cleared the space to do otherwise, I seem to have chosen, for the time being, to write from women's experience.[5]

Implicitly, Jamie's remarks confirm Germaine Greer's sense that the future of the woman poet depends on the extent to which, and how, her work is made critically available. In answer, however, it seems important to note that at last we do have the beginnings of a critical vocabulary for reading women's dynamic negotiation between language, gender and the literary poetic tradition. Alice Ostriker's *Stealing the Language: The Emergence of Women's Poetry in America* (1986) attempted to open up vocabularies for relating poetry to writers' sense of being women in their worlds. She tended to privilege the more avant-garde American poets and thus reinforced a conceptual link between radical form and feminist politics. Jan Montefiore's irreplaceable *Feminism and Poetry: Language, Experience, Identity in Women's Writing* (1987) set some agendas for a more theoretical approach which could encompass different orbits of writing. Sally Minogue's extensive essay, 'Prescriptions and Proscriptions: Feminist Criticism and Contemporary Poetry' (1990), surveys and evaluates the debates surrounding the desirability and viability of discerning a womanly aesthetic. She opposes essentialising readings which position women negatively in relation to so-called male traditions and which imply that their relationship to conventional forms is inevitably one of subjection.[6] Continuing Minogue's stand against defeatist critical frameworks, Vicki Bertram's *Kicking Daffodils: Twentieth-Century Women Poets* (1997) considers how the 'kicks' at tradition, if occasionally antagonistic, are often skilful manoeuvres with language and form in the context of a shared, albeit unlevel, playing field. The contributors solidify an emerging canon of names and literary groupings which accommodate poets' interventions with historical movements. Some harness various feminist, postmodern or postcolonial theories to explore poets' diverse treatment of the intersections between gender, sexuality and race. In *Contemporary Women's Poetry: Reading/Writing/Practice* (2000), edited by Alison Mark and Deryn Rees-Jones, poets converse about their own and each other's writing. In addition to explaining the principles which inform their individual practices, they experiment with less formal and restricting models of critical writing.

Eavan Boland's *Object Lessons: The Life of the Woman and the Poet in Our Time* (1995) crucially crosses strict demarcations between poetry, experience and criticism. Unabashedly making the personal historical, she develops a flexible terminology which links women across chronological and cultural boundaries. In conclusion, she reiterates how poets, while resisting simplistic definitions for themselves, nevertheless write out of a sense of common history:

The personal witness of a woman poet is still a necessary part of the evolving criteria by which women and their poetry must be evaluated ... What I wished most ardently for myself at a certain stage of my work was that I might find my voice where I had found my vision. I still think this is what matters most and is threatened most for the woman poet.

I am neither a separatist nor a postfeminist. I believe that the past matters . . .
Artistic forms are not static. Nor are they radicalised by aesthetes and intellectuals.
They are changed, shifted, detonated into deeper patterns only by the suffer-
ings and self-deceptions of those who use them. By this equation, women should
break down barriers in poetry in the same way that poetry will break the
silence of women. In the process, it is important not to mistake the easy answer
for the long haul.[7]

Notes

INTRODUCTION

1 Jo Shapcott, 'About Language And How It Works', interview with John Stammers, *Poetry London* 36 (Summer 2000), p. 36.

2 Louise Bernikow, *The World Split Open: Women's Poetry 1552–1950* (London: The Women's Press, 1979), p. 8.

3 Margaret Sackville, Introduction, *A Book of Verse by Living Women* (London: Herbert and Daniel, 1910), pp. xii-xxi.

4 'Woman and Artist', *The Writings of Anna Wickham: Free Woman and Poet*, ed. R. D. Smith (London: Virago, 1984), p. 331.

5 Edith Sitwell, 'Some Observations on Women's Poetry', *Vogue* 65.5 (March 1925), pp. 117–18. Elizabeth Salter and Allanah Harper, eds., *Edith Sitwell: Fire of the Mind* (London: Michael Joseph, 1976), pp. 187–92.

6 Carol Rumens, from 'A Bookshop Revisited', *Poetry Review* 86.4 (1996/97), pp. 36–37.

7 'As Radical as Reality', interview with Marion Lomax, *Poetry Review* 88.4 (Winter 1998/99), pp. 77–82.

8 'Jackie Kay', *Sleeping with Monsters: Conversations with Scottish and Irish Women Poets*, ed. Gillean Somerville-Arjat and Rebecca E. Wilson, (Edinburgh: Polygon, 1991), p. 124.

9 Although this book has not set out to examine the particular cultural complexities affecting the poetry of women writing out of Ireland, we have been unable to ignore the part the poets themselves play in twentieth-century 'British' poetic culture as a whole. Implicitly respected throughout Part III, this is discussed in the Overview and revisited, primarily through the work of Boland and Medbh McGuckian, in Chapters 9 and 12.

10 Stevie Smith, 'Miss Snooks, Poetess', *Me Again: The Uncollected Writings of Stevie Smith* (London: Virago, 1981), p. 226. First printed in *Poetry* (November 1964).

11 We are especially conscious of not having paused on some of the overlooked verse dramas (by Margaret Sackville, 'Lettice Cooper' and Carol Ann Duffy, for example) and translations such as H. D.'s recuperation of Sappho's Greek fragments, Spanish poems on the civil war by Sylvia Townsend Warner and

Nancy Cunard, Frances Cornford's commended *Poems from the Russian* and later multilinguists such as Ruth Fainlight and Elaine Feinstein.

PART I OVERVIEW

1 Camilla Doyle, *The General Shop and Other Poems* (London: St Catherine's Press, 1937).
2 See, for example, Herbert Read, 'Psycho-analysis and the critic', *Criterion* 3 (10 Jan. 1925), pp. 214–30. Sigmund Freud's (1856–1939) *Interpretation of Dreams* (1900) was translated into English in 1913. Carl Jung (1875–1961) influenced literary practice with his theories of the collective unconscious, myth and the role of the artist. Key works included *The Theory of Psychoanalysis* (1912), *Psychology of the Unconscious* (1916) and *Psychological Types* (1923).
3 W. B. Yeats, Introduction to *The Oxford Book of Modern Verse* (Oxford University Press, 1936).
4 See, for example, a review of *The New Criterion*, *TLS* (10 Feb. 1927), p. 94.
5 See correspondence about the sexual needs of women in *The Egoist* 1 (2, 16 March, 1914), pp. 98–99, 120.
6 Examples are 'Women Who Did and Who do Yet' by 'G. W.', *The Egoist* 1 (1 Jan. 1914), p. 16, and a response from R. S. Kerr, 'Women, Education, Marriage', *The Egoist* 1 (15 Jan. 1914), p. 39.
7 Editorial, *The Egoist* 2 (1 Jan. 1915).
8 'Women-Poets', *Poetry Review* (May 1912), pp. 199–200.
9 See Joy Grant, *Harold Monro and the Poetry Bookshop* (London: Routledge and Kegan Paul, 1967) for an account of Monro's initial dealings with the Poetry Society in 1912 and the inauguration of *Poetry and Drama* in 1913. He had been invited to edit *Poetry Review* but gave up after a year because he did not have enough autonomy and was prohibited from encouraging new writing.
10 Margaret Sackville, *A Book of Verse by Living Women* (London: Herbert and Daniel, 1910).
11 For further discussion of Alice Meynell, see Angela Leighton, *Victorian Women Poets: Writing Against the Heart* (Hemel Hempstead: Harvester Wheatsheaf, 1992).
12 M. Jourdain, 'Alice Meynell', *Poetry Review* (May 1912), pp. 211–13.
13 Alfred Noyes, 'Alice Meynell', *Bookman* (Jan. 1923), pp. 191–93.
14 S. Gertrude Ford, 'Alice Meynell', *Bookman* (Oct. 1915).
15 *Poetry: a Magazine of Verse* 3 (Oct.–March 1912/13), pp. 207, 181. Meynell's poem 'Maternity' was printed in this edition.
16 Harold Monro, *Some Contemporary Poets* (London: Leonard Parsons, 1920), p. 43.
17 J. C. Squire, ed., *An Anthology of Women's Verse* (Oxford: Clarendon, 1921). Squire was literary editor of the *New Statesman*, chief literary critic of the *Observer* and founded the *London Mercury* in 1919, which he edited until 1934. Edith Sitwell coined the term 'Squirearchy' to represent the artistic complacency which he was purported to represent. Consequently, 'Squirearchy' became polarised to Bloomsbury. See John Pearson, *Facades: Edith, Osbert and Sacheverell Sitwell* (Basingstoke: Macmillan, 1978), pp. 146–50.

18 Pearson, *Facades*, p. 149.
19 'The Poetry of Women', review of *The House* by Gladys Mary Hazel, *Poems of Motherhood* by Dorothea Still and *The Verse Book of a Homely Woman* by Fay Inchfawn, *TLS* (9 Dec. 1920), p. 810.
20 Ibid. (Emphasis added.)
21 T. S. Eliot, 'Verse Pleasant and Unpleasant', review of *Georgian Poetry 1916–17* and *Wheels. A Second Cycle, The Egoist* 5 (March 1918), pp. 43–44.
22 Vera Brittain, *Testament of Experience: An Autobiographical Story of the Years 1925–1950* (London: Virago, 1979), p. 64.
23 'Women in the Press', advertisement in *Time and Tide* (16 March, 1928).
24 Frank Mott, *A History of American Magazines: Vol. v: sketches of twenty-one magazines 1905–1930* (Cambridge, Massachusetts: Harvard University Press, 1968), p. x.
25 For more discussion of *Time and Tide*, see Lady Margaret Rhondda, *This Was My World* (Basingstoke: Macmillan, 1933) and Jane Dowson, ed., *Women's Poetry of the 1930s*, (London: Routledge, 1996), pp. 181–82.
26 T. S. Eliot, letter to John Rodker, 1919, *The Letters of T. S. Eliot: Vol. 1. 1898–1922*, ed. Valerie Eliot (London: Faber, 1988), p. 348. See also Jane Lidderdale and Mary Nicholson, *Dear Miss Weaver: Harriet Shaw Weaver 1876–1961* (London: Faber, 1970).
27 Sylvia Beach, *Shakespeare and Company*, 1956 (London: Faber, 1960), Harriet Monroe, *A Poet's Life: seventy years in a changing world* (New York: The Macmillan Company, 1938) and Marianne Moore, '*The Dial*: A Retrospect' in *Predilections*, 1931 (New York: Viking, 1955), pp. 103–14.
28 Alida Monro took over the Poetry Bookshop when Harold Monro was called for war service. He then became too unwell to run it and died in 1932. See Grant, *Harold Monro*.
29 For more discussion of Winifred Bryher, see Gillian Hanscombe and Virginia Smyers, *Writing for their Lives: The Modernist Women 1910–1940* (London: The Women's Press, 1987), pp. 33–46. Contact Publishing Company published Bryher, H. D., Mina Loy, Mary Butts, Djuna Barnes, Gertrude Stein and an influential anthology, *A Contact Collection of Contemporary Writers* in 1925.
30 See Charlotte Fyfe, ed., *The Tears of War: The Love Story of a Young Poet and a War Hero* (Upavon: Cavalier, 2000).
31 Frederick Brereton, ed., *An Anthology of War Poems* (London: Collins, 1930).
32 Eleanor Farjeon, *Sonnets and Poems* (Oxford: Blackwell 1918), p. 10.
33 Alice Bensen, *Rose Macaulay* (New York: Twayne, 1969), pp. 62–63.
34 'Georgian Poetry New Style', review of *Georgian Poetry 1918–1919*, *TLS* (11 Dec. 1919), p. 738. Fredegonde Shove, née Maitland, is discussed by Monro in *Some Contemporary Poets*.
35 See, for example, Fleur Adcock's Introduction to *The Faber Book of Twentieth-Century Women's Poetry* (London: Faber, 1987).
36 'Susan Miles', *Lettice Delmer* (London: Persephone Books, 2002).
37 'Susan Miles', *Annotations* (London: Humphrey Milford, 1922).
38 'Susan Miles', *Dunch* (Oxford: Basil Blackwell, 1916–20), pp. 15, 21.

39 Monro, *Some Contemporary Poets*, p. 107.

40 See Virginia Woolf, 'The Leaning Tower', *A Woman's Essays* (Harmondsworth, Penguin, 1992), pp. 159–78, 173.

41 Pearson, *Facades*, p. 149.

42 John Lucas, ed., *Poems of Nancy Cunard* (Nottingham: Trent Editions) was due in 2003 but at the time of writing is still unpublished.

43 Hugh Ford, ed., *Nancy Cunard: Brave Poet, Indomitable Rebel 1896–1965* (Philadelphia: Chilton Book Company, 1968).

44 Iris Tree's long narrative poem *The Marsh Picnic* (Cambridge: Rampant Lions Press, 1966) caused a small stir.

45 Monro, *Some Contemporary Poets*, p. 212.

46 Viola Meynell published *The Frozen Ocean* (London: Martin Secker, 1930), which includes the intriguing verse tribute 'A Daughter to her Mother in Illness'.

47 Anne Ridler, letter to Jane Dowson (1 Sept. 1992).

48 For individual accounts of prejudice from male poets and critics, see Introduction and sections on Raine, Mitchison, Riding, Ridler and Scovell in Dowson, *Women's Poetry of the 1930s*.

49 Stevie Smith, 'Souvenir de Monsieur Poop', *Collected Poems* (London: Allen Lane, 1975), pp. 137–38.

50 W. B. Yeats, *The Oxford Book of English Verse* (1936), p. xxxii.

51 Adrian Caesar, *Dividing Lines: Poetry, Class and Ideology in the 1930s* (Manchester University Press, 1991), p. 37.

52 See 'Stella Far Off', which begins 'It may well be time for a Stella Gibbons revival', in Naomi Mitchison, *You May Well Ask: A Memoir 1920–1940* (London: Victor Gollancz, 1979), pp. 127–37.

53 Vera Brittain, 'Married Love', *Poems of the War and After* (London: Victor Gollancz, 1934), p. 80.

54 Alice Coats, 'The "Monstrous Regiment"', *Women's War Poetry and Verse*, ed. Catherine Reilly (London: Virago, 1997), pp. 159–60.

55 This information on Ada Jackson is taken from a biographical note at the end of *Behold The Jew* (London: The Poetry Society, 1943).

56 'Women-Poets', *Poetry Review* (May 1912), p. 201.

PART II

1 'Women-Poets', *Poetry Review* (May 1912), pp. 199–200.

2 Virginia Woolf, *A Room of One's Own*, 1929 (London: Grafton, 1977), pp. 112, 106.

3 Harold Monro, *Some Contemporary Poets* (London: Leonard Parsons, 1920; Simpkins and Marshall, 1928). Alice Meynell is classified under 'A Glance Backwards' whereas Charlotte Mew, Edith Sitwell, Fredegonde Shove, Rose Macaulay, Anna Wickham, Helen Parry Eden and Frances Cornford are classified as 'Poets and Poetasters of our time'.

4 Woolf, *A Room*, p. 82.

5 Theresa Whistler, Introduction, *The Collected Poems of Mary Coleridge* (London: Rupert Hart-Davis, 1954), p. 50.

6 Katherine Bradley to Robert Browning, 1884, Angela Leighton, *Victorian Women Poets: Writing against the Heart* (Hemel Hempstead: Harvester Wheatsheaf, 1992), p. 202.

7 'The English Metres' (*Last Poems*, 1923), *The Poems of Alice Meynell* (Oxford University Press, 1940), p. 177.

8 'Georgian Poetry', review of *Georgian Poetry 1916–17*, *TLS* (27 Dec. 1917), p. 646.

9 Ian Hamilton, ed., *The Oxford Companion to Twentieth-Century Poetry* (Oxford University Press, 1994), p. 429.

10 Editorial Board, *Poetry Review* 15.4 (Oct.–Dec. 1960), p. 197.

11 Donald Davie, *Elizabeth Daryush: Collected Poems* (Manchester: Carcanet, 1976), p. 13.

12 Vita Sackville-West, Alice Meynell, *Alice Meynell: Prose and Poetry*, eds. F. P., V. M., O. S., and F. M., (London: Jonathan Cape), p. 22.

13 Sackville-West, Meynell, ibid., pp. 22–23.

14 M. Jourdain, 'Alice Meynell', *Poetry Review* (May 1912), pp. 211–13.

15 See June Badeni, *The Slender Tree: A Life of Alice Meynell* (Cornwall: Tabb House, 1981), pp. 150–51; 224–25.

16 Leighton, *Victorian Women Poets*, p. 246.

17 Meynell, 'The Laws of Verse' (*Last Poems*, 1923), *Poems*, p. 173.

18 Meynell in Badeni, *Slender Tree*, pp. 37, 243.

19 Sackville-West, Meynell, *Alice Meynell: Prose and Poetry*, p. 16.

20 Meynell, 'A General Communion' (*Ten Poems*, 1915), *Poems*, p. 113.

21 Meynell, 'In Sleep' (*Ten Poems*, 1915), *Poems*, p. 140.

22 Sackville-West, Meynell, *Alice Meynell: Poetry and Prose*, p. 21.

23 Meynell, 'Maternity' (*Collected Poems*, 1913), *Poems*, p. 119.

24 Meynell, 'A Father of Women' (*A Father of Women*, 1917), *Poems*, pp. 147–48.

25 Meynell, 'The Modern Mother' (*Later Poems*, 1902), *Poems*, p. 91.

26 Leighton, *Victorian Women Poets*, pp. 261–62.

27 Frances Cornford, 'Views and Recollections of a Sunday Poet' (27 March 1956), Mss. 58387, *Literary Papers of Frances Cornford* (London: British Library).

28 Letter from Frances Cornford to Virginia Woolf (1 Feb. 1926). Letters from Frances Cornford to Virginia Woolf 1923–26 Sx.Ms.18. MHL, (VW), (Brighton: University of Sussex Library).

29 Cornford, 'Views and Recollections of A Sunday Poet'.

30 Alison Light defines 'middlebrow' culture as 'one whose apparent artlessness and insistence on its own ordinariness has made it peculiarly resistant to change' in *Forever England: Femininity, Literature and Conservatism between the Wars* (London: Routledge, 1991), pp. 11–12. See also Woolf, 'Middlebrow', *Collected Essays Vol. 2* (London: Hogarth Press, 1966), pp. 196–203.

31 Cornford, 'Lunchtime Talk at Foyle's', Mss. 58386, Literary Papers.

32 'Women as Writers', in Sylvia Townsend Warner, *Collected Poems*, ed. Claire Harman (Manchester: Carcanet, 1982), p. 269.

33 Woolf, *A Room*, p. 10.

34 Frances Cornford, 'The Scholar' (*Collected Poems*, 1960), *Selected Poems*, ed. Jane Dowson (London: Enitharmon, 1996), p. 40.
35 Cornford, Journal, Mss. 58390, Literary Papers.
36 Frances Cornford, 'Ode on the Whole Duty of Parents' (*Mountains and Molehills*, 1934), *Selected Poems*, p. 19.
37 Cornford, 'She Warns Him' (*Different Days*, 1928), *Selected Poems*, p. 15.
38 Cornford, 'The Sick Queen' (*Different Days*, 1928), ibid., p. 15.
39 Letter from Woolf to Cornford, Mss. 58422, *Literary Papers*.
40 Harold Monro, ed., *Twentieth-Century Poetry* (London: Chatto & Windus, 1929). Revised and enlarged by Alida Monro (London: Chatto & Windus, 1933).
41 Cornford, 'A Peasant Woman' (*Mountains and Molehills*, 1934), *Selected Poems*, p. 23.
42 Vita Sackville-West, *Portrait of a Marriage*, ed. Nigel Nicolson (Basingstoke: Macmillan, 1980), p. 102.
43 Virginia Woolf, letter to Sackville-West (31 Jan. 1927), *The Letters of Virginia Woolf and Vita Sackville-West*, eds. Louise De Salvo and Mitchell A. Leaska (London: Hutchinson, 1984), p. 187.
44 Sackville-West, letters to Woolf (8 April 1926 and 3 Dec. 1928), ibid., pp. 131, 315.
45 Sackville-West, letter to Woolf (15 March 1926), ibid., p. 129.
46 Sackville-West, letter to Woolf (3 Dec. 1928), ibid., p. 315.
47 Sackville-West, letters to Woolf (24 June 1933 and 21 July 1933), ibid., pp. 403–4.
48 Fleur Adcock, ed., *The Faber Book of Twentieth-Century Women's Poetry* (London: Faber, 1987), p. 8.
49 Sackville-West, Nicolson, *Portrait*, pp. 17, 42.
50 Victoria Glendinning, *Vita: The Life of Vita Sackville-West* (London: Weidenfeld & Nicolson, 1983), p. 119.
51 Vita Sackville-West, *King's Daughter XI, Collected Poems* (London: Hogarth, 1933), p. 320.
52 Vita Sackville-West, *Solitude* (London: Hogarth, 1938), pp. 27–28.
53 Glendinning, *Vita*, p. 197.
54 Vita Sackville-West, letter to Harold (20 Nov. 1926), Nigel Nicolson, ed., *Vita and Harold: The Letters of Vita Sackville-West and Harold Nicolson 1910–1962* (London: Weidenfeld & Nicolson, 1992), pp. 173–74.
55 Yvor Winters, 'Robert Bridges and Elizabeth Daryush', *American Review* 8.3 (1936–37), pp. 353–67. Reprinted in Francis Murphy, ed. *Uncollected Essays and Reviews of Yvor Winters* (London: Allen and Lane, 1974), pp. 271–83.
56 Daryush, Appendix, *Selected Poems: Verses I–VI* (Manchester: Carcanet, 1972), p. 93.
57 'Mrs Daryush's Poems', review of *Verses: Fourth Book* (London: Oxford University Press, 1934), *TLS* (28 Feb. 1935).
58 Daryush, 'Still Life' (*Selected Poems*, p. 30), *Women's Poetry of the 1930s*, ed. Jane Dowson (London: Routledge, 1996), p. 58.

59 Daryush, 'Children of Wealth' (*Selected Poems*, p. 28), Dowson, *Women's Poetry of the 1930s*, p. 58.
60 Daryush, 'If your love prove', *Selected Poems*, p. 49.
61 Daryush, *Selected Poems*, p. 25.
62 Daryush, 'Off Duty' (*Verses: Sixth Book*, 1938), Dowson, *Women's Poetry of the 1930s*, p. 60.
63 Daryush, 'The woman I'd revere', 'Woman, dweller in the heart', *Selected Poems* (New York: Swallow Press 1948), pp. 46–47.
64 Daryush, *Selected Poems* (1972), p. 70.
65 Ibid., p. 75.
66 See Lord David Cecil, Introduction to *Ruth Pitter: Homage to a Poet*, ed. Arthur Russell (London: n.p., 1969).
67 Elaine Showalter, *A Literature of Their Own: British Women Novelists from Bronte to Lessing* (New Jersey: Princeton University Press, 1977), p. 34.
68 Ibid., pp. 275–89.
69 Woolf, *A Room*, p. 116.
70 Woolf, ibid., p. 111.

PART I 2

1 Virginia Woolf, 'The Leaning Tower', *A Woman's Essays* (London: Penguin 1992), pp. 175–76.
2 Stevie Smith is looked at in more detail in Chapter 5.
3 See works by Barbara Brothers (1989), Gill Plain (1995), Claire Tylee (1990), Noshee Khan (1988), Elizabeth Marsland (1991), Jane Dowson in Mary Joannou (1999) and John Lucas (1997).
4 Thomas Moult, review of *Shepherd of Eternity and Other Poems* by Eva Gore-Booth, *Time and Tide* (10 July 1925), p. 673.
5 Esther Roper, Introduction to *Selected Poems of Eva Gore-Booth* (London: Longman, 1933), p 14. For more discussion of Gore-Booth, see Elizabeth Crawford, *The Women's Suffrage Movement: A Reference Guide 1866–1928* (London: Routledge, 2000), pp. 249–51.
6 See G. D. H. Cole, *The Fabian Society: Past and Present* (London: Fabian Society, 1942).
7 The Left Book Club, a centre for political artists, was founded by Victor Gollancz and its publications reached a wide readership. See Noreen Branson and Margot Heinemann, *Britain in the Nineteen Thirties* (St Albans: Panther, 1973), p. 299.
8 Declaration of the Association of Writers in Defence of Culture, *Left Review* I.11 (Aug. 1935), p. 462.
9 Hugh Ford, ed., *Nancy Cunard: Brave Poet, Indomitable Rebel 1896–1965* (Philadelphia: Chilton Book Company, 1968), p. 37.
10 Nancy Cunard, 'Black Man and White Ladyship', Ford, *Nancy Cunard*, pp. 103–9.
11 Nancy Cunard, Introduction to *Negro: an anthology*, ed. Cunard, 1934 (New York: Frederick Ungar Publishing Co., 1970).

12 Biographical Note, Nancy Cunard, *Poems for France* (London: La France Libre, 1944).

13 Stephen Spender, review of *The Year's Poetry*, 1940, *Horizon* 3.14 (Feb. 1941), p. 139.

14 Cyril Connolly, 'Comment', *Horizon* 1.1 (Jan. 1940), p. 5.

15 Vera Brittain, *Testament of Friendship: the Story of Winifred Holtby* (London: Virago 1980), p. 87.

16 Sylvia Townsend Warner, 'The Way By Which I Have Come', *The Countryman*, 19.2 (1939), pp. 472–86.

17 Eleanor Farjeon, 'A Prayer', *Moonshine* (London: The Labour Publishing Co., 1920), pp. 8–9.

18 Catherine Reilly received spontaneous applause for her contribution to cultural history when she identified herself at an international conference, 'Rethinking Women's Poetry 1770–1930' (Birkbeck College, University of London, July 1995).

19 Maud Anna Bell, 'From a Trench'; Sybil Bristowe, 'Over the Top'; Catherine Reilly, ed., *Women's War Poetry and Verse* (London: Virago, 1997), pp. 10, 13.

20 Ruth Comfort Mitchell, 'He went for a soldier', Reilly, *Women's War Poetry*, p. 75.

21 Margaret Sackville, 'Nostra Culpa', *The Pageant of War* (London: Simpkin, Marshall and Brown, 1916), p. 36.

22 Madeleine Ida Bedford, 'Munition Wages', Reilly, *Women's War Poetry*, pp. 7–8.

23 S. Gertrude Ford, 'A Fight to a Finish', Reilly, *Women's War Poetry*, p. 38. (Emphasis added.)

24 Ford, 'The Tenth Armistice Day', ibid., pp. 38–39.

25 S. Gertrude Ford, 'The Soldier's Mother', *Poems of War and Peace* (London: Erskine Macdonald, 1915), p. 22.

26 Helen Hamilton, 'The Romancing Poet', 'Jingo-Woman', Reilly, *Women's War Poetry*, pp. 47–50.

27 Muriel Stuart, 'The Father', *Selected Poems* (London: Jonathan Cape, 1927), pp. 21–22.

28 May Sinclair, 'Field Ambulance in Retreat'; Charlotte Mew, 'The Cenotaph'; Ursula Roberts, 'The Cenotaph'; Reilly, *Women's War Poetry*, pp. 98, 71, 93. 'Susan Miles' (Ursula Roberts), *Lettice Delmer* (London: The Linden Press, 1958; Persephone Books, 2002).

29 Sylvia Townsend Warner, 'Road 1940', *Collected Poems*, ed. Claire Harman (Manchester: Carcanet, 1982), p. 45.

30 Sylvia Townsend Warner (27 Dec. 1929), *The Diaries of Sylvia Townsend Warner*, ed. Claire Harman (London: Chatto & Windus, 1994), p. 50.

31 Warner, 'Women as Writers', *Collected Poems*, pp. 265–70.

32 Naomi Mitchison, 'The Farm Woman 1942', Reilly, *Women's War Poetry*, p. 219.

33 Dorothy Wellesley, 'Milk Boy', *Selections from the Poems of Dorothy Wellesley* (London: Williams and Norgate, 1949), Reilly, *Women's War Poetry*, p. 254.

34 E. J. Scovell, 'A Wartime Story', Reilly, *Women's War Poetry*, p. 242.

35 Karen Gershon, 'A Jew's Calendar', ibid., pp. 177–78.

36 Ada Jackson, 'Hitler Youth', *World in Labour* (Birmingham: Cornish Bros., 1942), p. 3.

37 Nancy Cunard, 'To Eat Today', *Women's Poetry of the 1930s: a critical anthology*, ed. Jane Dowson (London: Routledge, 1996), p. 53.

38 See Valentine Cunningham, Introduction, *The Penguin Book of Spanish Civil War Verse* (Harmondsworth: Penguin, 1980), p. 50.

39 See 'The Refugees at Perpignan, Miss Cunard's Appeal', Ford, *Nancy Cunard*, p. 196.

40 Sylvia Townsend Warner, 'Benicasim', *Left Review* 3 (March 1938), p. 841; *Penguin Book of Spanish Civil War Verse*, p. 150.

41 Hugh Lyon, Foreword, *Poems by Contemporary Women*, eds. Theodora Roscoe and Mary Winter Were (London: Hutchens, 1944).

42 Margaret Sackville, 'The Pageant of War', *Collected Poems* (London: Richards Press, 1939), pp. 266–72.

43 Mary Borden, 'The Song of the Mud', *The Forbidden Zone* (London: Heinemann, 1929), p. 181.

44 G. S. Fraser, Preface, Sheila Wingfield, *Collected Poems 1938–1983* (London: Enitharmon, 1983), p. xv.

45 Woolf, 'The Leaning Tower', pp. 159–78.

46 Naomi Mitchison, letter to the editor, *Time and Tide* (29 Feb. 1936), p. 292.

47 Naomi Mitchison, 'Breaking up the Home', *Twentieth Century*, Promethean Society 3 (17 July 1932), p. 3. See Jill Benton, *Naomi Mitchison: a biography* (London: Pandora, 1990), p. 76.

48 Mitchison, 'To Some Young Communists from an Older Socialist', Dowson, *Women's Poetry of the 1930s*, pp. 76–77.

49 Mitchison, undated poem from the 1930s, Benton, *Naomi Mitchison*, p. 90.

50 Warner, 'The Way By Which I Have Come', p. 480.

51 Warner, *Opus 7, Collected Poems*, p. 200.

52 Stevie Smith, 'Lord Barrenstock', 'The Bishops of the Church of England', 'Lord Mope', 'Major Macroo', *Collected Poems* (London: Allen Lane, 1975), pp. 69–70, 96, 58, 72–3.

53 Smith, 'Voices against England in the Night', ibid., p. 216.

54 Anna Wickham, 'Notes for a Lecture', *The Writings of Anna Wickham: Free Woman and Poet*, ed. R. D. Smith (London: Virago, 1984), pp. 374–76.

55 Wickham, 'Laura Grey', ibid., p. 335.

56 Wickham, 'School for Mothers', ibid., pp. 372–73.

57 Wickham, 'The Town Dirge', ibid., pp. 167–68.

58 Richard Aldington, 'New Poetry', review of *The Contemplative Quarry* by Anna Wickham (London: The Poetry Bookshop, 1915) *The Egoist* 2 (1 June 1915), pp. 89–90.

59 S. Gertrude Ford, 'Houseless by Night', *Lyric Leaves* (London: C. W. Daniel Co., 1912), pp. 28–29.

60 Cora Kaplan, 'Language and Gender', *Feminist Critique of Language*, ed. Deborah Cameron (London: Routledge, 1990), p. 58.

61 Sylvia Pankhurst, *Writ on Cold Slate* (London: Dreadnought Publishers, 1922), p. 5.

62 Warner, 'Women as Writers', p. 274.

63 Ethel Carnie, 'Why?', *Voices of Womanhood* (London: Headley Brothers, 1914), p. 12.

64 Carnie, 'A Vision', *Voices of Womanhood*, p. 15. The poem was printed in the *Daily Herald*.

PART I 3

1 Michael Roberts, *The Faber Book of Modern Verse*, 1936 (London: Faber, 1970), pp. 13–14.

2 Ibid., pp. 18–19.

3 H. D., *Tribute to Freud*, 1956 (Oxford: Carcanet, 1971), p. 19.

4 H. D., 'Notes on Thought and Vision', *The Gender of Modernism*, ed. Bonnie Kime Scott (Indianapolis: Indiana University Press, 1990), pp. 93–109.

5 H. D., *Tribute to Freud*, p. 98.

6 See H. D., *Notes on Thought and Vision and the Wise Sappho* (London: Peter Owen, 1988), p. 12.

7 H. D., 'Eurydice', H. D. *Collected Poems 1912–1944*, ed. Louis L. Martz (New York: New Directions, 1983), p. 51.

8 Roberts, *Faber Book of Modern Verse*, p. 21.

9 John Pearson, *Facades: Edith, Osbert and Sacheverell Sitwell* (Basingstoke: Macmillan, 1978), p. 79.

10 Edith Sitwell, letter to Robert Nichols (26 Dec. 1918), Pearson, *Facades*, p. 132.

11 Edith Sitwell, 'Some Observations on Women's Poetry', *Vogue* (1925), *Edith Sitwell: Fire of the Mind*, eds. Elizabeth Salter and Allanah Harper, 1956 (London: Michael Joseph, 1976), p. 189.

12 Edith Sitwell, *Collected Poems* (London: Macmillan, 1957), p. xv.

13 Edith Sitwell, letter to John Lehmann (1951), *Edith Sitwell: A Unicorn Among Lions*, Victoria Glendinning (London: Weidenfeld & Nicolson, 1981), p. 24.

14 Sitwell, 'Colonel Fantock', *Collected Poems*, p. 176.

15 Cora Kaplan, 'The Indefinite Disclosed: Christina Rossetti and Emily Dickinson', *Women Writing and Writing about Women*, ed. Mary Jacobus (Beckenham: Croom Helm, 1984), pp. 61–79.

16 Sitwell, 'The Sleeping Beauty', *Collected Poems*, p. 88.

17 H. D., *Tribute to Freud*, p. 77.

18 Edith Sitwell, *Taken Care of: an autobiography* (London: Hutchinson, 1965), p. 61.

19 Sitwell, 'The Sleeping Beauty', *Collected Poems*, p. 85.

20 Sitwell, *Collected Poems*, p. xxii.

21 'The defeat of youth', Review of 'The Sleeping Beauty', *TLS* (3 April 1924), p. 204.

22 Roberts, *Faber Book of Modern Verse*, pp. 19–20.

23 Sitwell, 'The Sleeping Beauty', *Collected Poems*, pp. 64–65.

24 Ibid., pp. 86–87.

25 Ibid., p. 86.

26 Ibid., p. 74.

27 Edith Sitwell, 'Modern Poetry', *Time and Tide* (30 March 1928), pp. 308–9.

28 Edith Sitwell, *A Poet's Notebook* (London: Macmillan, 1943), p. 18.

29 Ibid., p. 23.

30 Sitwell, 'Some Notes on my Own Poetry', *Collected Poems*, p. xxxi.

31 Sitwell, 'Three Rustic Elegies', ibid., pp. 178–89.

32 Roger Conover, ed., *Mina Loy: The Lost Lunar Baedeker*, 1982 (Manchester: Carcanet, 1997), p. xiv.

33 Virginia M. Kouidis, *Mina Loy: American Modernist Poet* (Louisiana State University Press and London: Baton Rouge, 1980), p. 1.

34 Mina Loy, 'Nancy Cunard', Hugh Ford, *Nancy Cunard: Brave Poet, Indomitable Rebel 1896–1965* (Philadelphia: Chilton Book Company, 1968), p. 103.

35 Loy, 'Modern Poetry', *Lost Lunar Baedeker*, pp. 157–61. First published in *Charm* 3.3 (April 1925), pp. 16–17). According to Conover, *Charm* was an 'eclectic magazine published in the 1920s, devoted to women's fashion and clothing' (p. 217).

36 Loy, 'Modern Poetry', *Lost Lunar Baedeker*, pp. 157–61.

37 Loy, Kouidis, *Mina Loy*, p. 108.

38 Loy, *The Last Lunar Baedeker*, ed. Roger Conover (Manchester: Carcanet, 1985), p. 139.

39 Futurism, which originated in Italy, repudiated the literary past and celebrated industrialisation, violence and war. It violated familiar syntax and, at its extreme, words and symbols were used interchangeably. Filippo Marinetti came to England in 1913 and the *Book of Futurists* sold 35,000 copies. Vorticism was associated with the magazine *Blast* edited by Wyndham Lewis. It was similarly antirepresentational in order to destroy received dogmas through destroying their discourses. The First World War interrupted the Vorticists' activities.

40 Kouidis, *Mina Loy*, p. 56.

41 Loy, 'Aphorisms of Futurism', *Lost Lunar Baedeker*, p. 152.

42 Loy, 'The Love Songs or Songs of Joannes', Parts 3 and 12, *Lost Lunar Baedeker*, pp. 53–68.

43 Loy, 'The Effectual Marriage', *Lost Lunar Baedeker*, pp. 36–39.

44 Loy, ibid., p. 38.

45 Loy, 'Parturition', 'Aphorisms on Futurism', ibid., pp. 4–8, 149–52.

46 Loy, 'Gertrude Stein', ibid., p. 94.

47 Mina Loy, review of *The Making of Americans* by Gertrude Stein, *Transatlantic Review* 2 (Sept. and Oct. 1924). See partial reprint, 'Gertrude Stein' in Scott, *Gender of Modernism*, pp. 238–45. See also extracts in Gillian Hanscombe and Virginia Smyers, *Writing for their Lives: The Modernist 'Women' 1910–1940* (London: The Women's Press, 1987), pp. 227–28.

48 Laura Riding, 'Memories of Mortalities', *The Poems of Laura Riding* (new edition of *Collected Poems*, 1938, Manchester: Carcanet, 1980), p. 263.

49 Laura Riding and Schuyler B. Jackson, *The Word 'Woman' and Other Related Writings*, eds. Elizabeth Friedman and Alan J. Clark (New York: Persea, 1993), p. 13.

50 Riding, *Poems*, 1980, p. 1.

51 Laura Riding and Schuyler B. Jackson, *Rational Meaning: A New Foundation for the Definition of Words and Supplementary Essays*, ed. William Harmon (Charlottesville and London: University Press of Virginia, 1997), pp. 23–24.

PART I 4

1 Isobel Armstrong, *Victorian Poetry: Poetry, Poetics and Politics* (London: Routledge, 1993), p. 367.
2 Charlotte Mew, 'At The Convent Gate', first printed 1929, *Charlotte Mew: Collected Poems & Selected Prose*, ed. Val Warner (Manchester: Carcanet, 1997), p. 58. (*CPSP* hereafter.)
3 Mew, 'Ken', *CPSP*, pp. 16–19.
4 Mew, 'The Quiet House', ibid, pp. 20–22.
5 Mew, Penelope Fitzgerald, *Charlotte Mew and Her Friends* (London: Collins, 1984), p. 88.
6 Armstrong, *Victorian Poetry*, p. 367.
7 Ibid, p. 342.
8 Fitzgerald, citing a letter from Charlotte Mew to Mrs Hill (4 Jan. 1917), where she explains that good poetry depends upon 'the emotion given one', *Charlotte Mew and Her Friends*, p. 104.
9 Mew, 'Madeleine in Church', *CPSP*, p. 29.
10 Mew, 'On the Road to the Sea', ibid, pp. 32–34.
11 Armstrong, *Victorian Poetry*, p. 359.
12 For further discussion of 'The Farmer's Bride' and other poems in relation to contemporary legislation, see Kathleen Bell, 'Mew, T. S. Eliot and modernism', *Kicking Daffodils: Twentieth-Century Women Poets*, ed. Vicki Bertram (Edinburgh University Press, 1997), pp. 13–24.
13 Mew, 'The Farmer's Bride', *CPSP*, pp. 1–2.
14 Fitzgerald, *Charlotte Mew and Her Friends*, p. 139.
15 Mew, 'Saturday Market', CPSP, pp. 37–38.
16 Harold Monro, *Some Contemporary Poets* (London: Simpkins and Marshall, 1928), pp. 76, 80, 79.
17 Sylvia Townsend Warner, 'The Absence', *Collected Poems* (Manchester: Carcanet, 1982), p. 12.
18 Warner, 'The Rival', ibid., p. 162.
19 Naomi Boyd Smith, review of *Time Importuned* by Sylvia Townsend Warner (London: Chatto & Windus, 1928), *Time and Tide* (3 Aug. 1928), p. 29.
20 J. G. Fletcher, review of *Time Importuned*, *The Criterion* 8 (30 Sept. 1928), p. 128.
21 Sylvia Townsend Warner with Valentine Ackland, *Whether a Dove or a Seagull* (New York: Viking, 1933) is out of print. Some poems are reproduced in Warner's *Collected Poems* and in Jane Dowson, ed., *Women's Poetry of the 1930s: a critical anthology* (London: Routledge, 1996).
22 Warner, 'Drawing You Heavy with Sleep' (*Whether a Dove or a Seagull*, 1933), Dowson, *Women's Poetry of the 1930s*, p. 157. See also Jan Montefiore, *Feminism and Poetry* (London, Pandora, 1987), p. 158.

23 For more discussion of Warner as a modernist, see Jane Marcus in Bonnie Kime Scott, ed., *The Gender of Modernism* (Indianapolis: Indiana University Press, 1990), pp. 531–38.

24 Wickham was a good friend of Nancy Cunard and they were neighbours on Parliament Hill, London, for a while. She was also friends with Frieda and D. H. Lawrence. Alida Monro was apparently jealous of her because Harold was in love with her, as was David Garnett. For these and other details we are grateful to George (her son) and Margaret (her daughter-in-law, wife of James) Hepburn.

25 Anna Wickham, 'Return of Pleasure', *The Writings of Anna Wickham: Free Woman and Poet*, ed. R. D. Smith (London: Virago, 1984), p. 194.

26 David Garnett relates the gruesome incident in 1915 when Wickham put her hand through a glass door during a quarrel with her husband when he discovered that her poems were to be published by The Poetry Bookshop; apparently, he 'thought anything she wrote worthless and in any case had no intention of allowing his wife to be a poet: she was not to do it again. Anna exploded with rage and found herself certified as insane.' See David Garnett, Introduction, Anna Wickham, *Selected Poems* (London: Chatto & Windus, 1971), p. 8.

27 Wickham, 'Examination' (*The Man With a Hammer*, 1916), *Writings*, p. 193.

28 Wickham, 'Definition', 'The Wife', *Writings*, pp. 199–202.

29 Richard Aldington, 'New Poetry', review of *The Contemplative Quarry* by Wickham (London: The Poetry Bookshop, 1915), *The Egoist* 2 (1 June 1915), pp. 89–90.

30 Wickham, 'Divorce', *Writings*, p. 166.

31 Wickham, 'The Revolt of Wives', ibid., pp. 180–81.

32 Wickham, 'Marriage' (*The Contemplative Quarry* 1915), ibid., p. 178.

33 Wickham, 'The Sick Assailant', *Writings*, p. 286; Dowson, *Women's Poetry of the 1930s*, p. 168.

34 Wickham, 'The Angry Woman', *Writings*, pp. 202–4.

35 Wickham, 'Suppression', 'Woman and Artist', ibid., pp. 327, 331.

36 Wickham, *Fragment of an Autobiography*, ibid., p. 52.

37 See the article by her son James Hepburn, 'Anna Wickham' (*Women's Review* 7, 1986), which includes a suicide note in the form of a poem.

38 Naomi Mitchison, 'Woman Alone', *Time and Tide* (7 Dec. 1935); 'Dick and Colin at the Salmon Nets', *Time and Tide* (25 Feb. 1933); Dowson, *Women's Poetry of the 1930s*, pp. 81–82.

39 Naomi Mitchison, *All Change Here: Girlhood and Marriage* (London: Bodley Head, 1975), p. 52. See Jill Benton, *Naomi Mitchison: a biography* (London: Pandora, 1990), p. 72.

40 Winifred Holtby, 'Beauty the Lovers Gift', *Time and Tide* (8 July 1933); 'Boats in the Bay', *Time and Tide* (18 Feb. 1933); Dowson, *Women's Poetry of the 1930s*, pp. 66–67.

41 Stella Gibbons, 'Artemis Married', *Twentieth-Century Poetry*, ed. Harold Monro (London: Chatto & Windus, 1933), pp. 253–54.

42 Letter from Stella Gibbons, Naomi Mitchison, *You May Well Ask: A Memoir 1920–1940* (London: Victor Gollancz, 1979), p. 132.

43 Ada Jackson, 'The Widow', 'Anne Shakespeare', *The Widow and Other Poems* (London: Methuen Gateway Poets, 1933), pp. 7–8, 17–19.

44 Naomi Mitchison, 'Woman Alone'; Sylvia Lynd, 'The Solitary'; Dowson, *Women's Poetry of the 1930s*, pp. 81, 60; the latter was included in Maurice Wollman, ed., *Modern Poetry 1922–34* (London: Macmillan, 1934).

45 See for example, Valentine Ackland, 'The Lonely Woman' and Ruth Pitter, 'Old Childless, Husbandless', Dowson, *Women's Poetry of the 1930s*, pp. 36, 88–89.

46 Muriel Stuart, 'Mrs Effingham's Swan Song', *In the Orchard: Selected Poems* (Kettilonia: Kingskettle, 2000), pp. 11–14.

47 Muriel Stuart, 'The Bastard', *Selected Poems* (London: Jonathan Cape, 1927), pp. 17–19.

48 Stuart, 'Gay Girl to Good Girl', ibid., p. 25.

49 Luce Irigaray, *This sex which is not one* (Ithaca: Cornell University Press, 1985), pp. 132–34. See also Sandra Gilbert and Susan Gubar, *No Man's Land: The Place of the Woman Writer in the Twentieth-Century vol. 3, Letters to the Front* (New Haven: Yale University Press, 1994), p. 59.

PART II OVERVIEW

1 Robert Hewison, *Under Siege: Literary Life in London 1939–45* (London: Weidenfeld & Nicolson, 1977), p. 63.

2 Cora Kaplan, *Salt and Bitter and Good: Three Centuries of English and American Women Poets* (New York and London: Paddington Press, 1975), p. 19.

3 Geoffrey Summerfield, ed., *Worlds: Seven Modern Poets* (Harmondsworth: Penguin, 1974), p. 12.

4 Blake Morrison and Andrew Motion, eds., *The Penguin Book of Contemporary British Poetry* (Harmondsworth: Penguin, 1975), p. 11.

5 *The Chatto Book of Modern Poetry 1915–55* (London: Chatto & Windus, 1959); *The Penguin Book of Contemporary Verse* (Harmondsworth: Penguin, 1962); *British Poetry since 1945* (Harmondsworth: Penguin, 1970); *The Oxford Book of Twentieth-Century English Verse* (Oxford University Press, 1973); *The Oxford Book of Contemporary Verse, 1945–1980* (Oxford University Press, 1980); Edward Lucie-Smith and Philip Hobsbaum, eds., *A Group Anthology* (Oxford University Press, 1963); Michael Horovitz, ed., *Children of Albion: Poetry of the Underground in Britain,* (Harmondsworth: Penguin, 1969); Calvin Bedient, ed., *Eight Contemporary Poets* (Oxford University Press, 1974); *The New Poetry* (Harmondsworth: Penguin, 1962) respectively.

6 Alvarez eventually includes just two women – Sylvia Plath and Anne Sexton, both American – in his second edition.

7 Clifford Bax and Meum Stewart, eds., 'Prefatory Note', *The Distaff Muse: An Anthology of Poetry written by Women* (London: Hollis & Carter, 1949), p. [i].

8 Kenneth Rexroth, *The New British Poets* (New York: New Directions, 1949), pp. xxviii–xxix.

9 Hermann Peschmann, *The Voice of Poetry 1930–1950* (London: Evans, 1950), p. xxxiv.

10 Bax and Stewart, *The Distaff Muse*, pp. 202, 116.

11 Sylvia Townsend Warner, 'Women As Writers,' *The Journal of the Royal Society of Arts* (May 1959), p. 385.

12 Elizabeth Wilson, *Only Halfway To Paradise: Women in Post War Britain 1945–1968* (London: Tavistock, 1980), p. 22.

13 Howard Sergeant, 'British Poetry 1952–77', *Contemporary Review* 231 (October 1977), p. 196; Eric Mottram, 'The British poetry revival, 1960–1975', Robert Hampson and Peter Barry, eds., *The New British Poetries: The Scope of the Possible* (Manchester University Press, 1993), pp. 15–50.

14 Bax and Stewart note 'a marked use of the severe sonnet-form', *The Distaff Muse*, p. 116.

15 Rexroth, *The New British Poets*, p. xxix.

16 In 1950 Sackville-West was excluded from a poetry reading for the Queen organised by the Society of Authors. The snub went deep: she wrote no more poetry.

17 Vita Sackville-West, 'Winter', *The Garden* (London: Michael Joseph, 1946), p. 14; lines 25–31.

18 Nigel Nicolson, ed., *Portrait of a Marriage* (London: Weidenfeld & Nicolson, 1973), p. 205.

19 Peschmann, *The Voice of Poetry*, p. xxxiv–xxxv.

20 Edith Sitwell, 'Some Notes on my own Poetry', *Collected Poems* (London: Sinclair Stevenson, 1993), p. xlii.

21 Edith Sitwell, 'The Shadow of Cain' (*Three Poems of the Atomic Age*, in *The Shadow of Cain*, 1947), *Collected Poems*, p. 373.

22 Georgina Taylor cites as 'H. D. to Gretchen Wolle Baker, Dec. 20 [1944]', *H. D. And The Public Sphere of Modernist Women Writers, 1913–1946: Talking Women* (Oxford University Press, 2001), p. 174.

23 Taylor, *H. D. And The Public Sphere*, p. 175.

24 Sheila Wingfield, *Beat Drum, Beat Heart, A Kite's Dinner: Poems 1938–1954* (London: Cresset Press, 1954), pp. 31–106.

25 Wingfield, 'Women in Love', (*Beat Drum*) *A Kite's Dinner*, pp. 72–73.

26 Peschmann, Introduction, *The Voice of Poetry*, p. xxxv.

27 Ruth Pitter, 'The Ermine' (*The Ermine* 1953), *Collected Poems* (Petersfield: Enitharmon, 1990), p. 209.

28 Joanne Shattock, 'Pitter, Ruth', *The Oxford Guide to British Women Writers* (Oxford University Press, 1994), pp. 339–40.

29 Elizabeth Jennings, Introduction, Pitter, *Collected Poems*, p. 15.

30 Isobel Armstrong, *The Radical Aesthetic* (Oxford: Blackwell, 2000), p. 123.

31 Kathleen Raine, 'Love, Cambridge, Poetry: Extracts from an unpublished essay', 'Kathleen Raine: The Tenth Decade', ed. Grevel Lindop, *PN Review* 27.2 (November/December 2000), p. 38.

32 Raine, *The Inner Journey Of The Poet* (London: Allen and Unwin, 1982), p. 5.

33 Kathleen Raine, 'Word Made Flesh' (*The Pythoness* 1948), *Selected Poems* (Ipswich: Golgonooza Press, 1988), pp. 24–25.

34 See in particular Kathleen Raine, *Blake and Tradition* (Princeton University Press, 1968); *Blake and the New Age* (1979); *Yeats the Initiate* (1986).

35 Peter Scupham, 'Shelf Lives 9: E. J. Scovell', *PN Review* 26.3 (January/February 2000), p. 27.

36 Anne Ridler, 'Bathing in the Windrush' (*The Golden Bird* 1951), *Collected Poems* (Manchester: Carcanet, 1994), p. 68.

37 John Williams, *Twentieth-Century Poetry: A Critical Introduction* (London: Edward Arnold, 1987), p. 71.

38 Elizabeth Jennings, *Poetry Today* (London: Longman, Green & Co., 1961), pp. 20–21.

39 Elizabeth Jennings, 'The Island' (*Poems* 1953), *New Collected Poems*, ed. Michael Schmidt (Manchester: Carcanet, 2002), p. 6.

40 Jennings, 'The Climbers', 'The Fishermen' (*Poems* 1953), ibid., p. 5.

41 Jonathon Green, *Days In The Life: Voices from the English Underground 1961–1971* (London: Heinemann, 1988), p. vii.

42 Green, *Days*, pp. 122, 119.

43 Mary Stott, 'Women in Newspapers', *On Gender and Writing*, ed. Michelene Wandor (London: Pandora, 1983), p. 129.

44 Patricia Waugh, *Harvest of the Sixties: English Literature and its Background 1960–1990* (Oxford University Press, 1995), p. 222.

45 Denise Riley, 'Waiting', *Truth, Dare, Promise: Girls growing up in Fifties Britain*, ed. Liz Heron (London: Virago, 1985), p. 248.

46 Juliet Mitchell, *Women: The Longest Revolution; Essays on feminism, literature and psychoanalysis* (London: Virago, 1984), p. 17.

47 Libby Houston, 'On Being a Woman Poet', *On Gender and Writing*, pp. 45–46.

48 Joan Murray Simpson, ed., *Without Adam: The Femina Anthology of Poetry* (London: Femina Press, 1968), p. 18; Stevie Smith, 'Poems in Petticoats' (*Observer*, 19 May 1968), *Me Again: The Uncollected Writings of Stevie Smith* (London: Virago, 1981), pp. 180–81.

49 Jennings, *Poetry Today*, p. 51.

50 Anthony Thwaite, *Poetry Today: A Critical Guide to British Poetry 1960–1973* (Harlow: Longman, 1973).

51 Margaret Byers, 'Cautious Vision: Recent poetry by women', *British Poetry since 1960: A Critical Survey*, eds. Michael Schmidt and Grevel Lindop (Manchester: Carcanet, 1972), p. 83.

52 Michael Woods, 'We All Hate Home', *Contemporary Literature* 18.3 (Summer 1977), p. 313.

53 Patricia Beer, 'Vampire', 'Witch', 'Beatrice-Joanna', (*The Survivors* 1963); 'Four Years After', 'In A Country Museum' (*Just Like the Resurrection* 1967), *Collected Poems* (Manchester: Carcanet, 1988) pp. 26, 28, 31; 42, 54.

54 Patricia Beer, 'Finding a Voice', *Poetry Dimension 6: The Best of the Poetry Year*, ed. Dannie Abse (London: Robson Books, 1979), p. 192.

55 Jenny Joseph, 'Jenny Joseph', *Contemporary Poets*, ed. Thomas Riggs (New York, Toronto and London: St James Press, 1996), (6th edition), p. 607.

56 Jenny Joseph, 'The lost continent' (*The Unlooked-for Season* 1960), *Selected Poems* (Newcastle upon Tyne: Bloodaxe Books, 1992), pp. 14, 33.

57 Elizabeth Jennings, *Every Changing Shape: Mystical experience and the making of poems* (1961), (Manchester: Carcanet, 1996).

58 Jennings, quoted Lucie-Smith, *British Poetry Since 1945*, p. 129.

59 Jennings, *Poetry Today*, p. 20.

60 Jennings, 'World I Have Not Made' (*Song for a Birth or a Death* 1961), *New Collected Poems*, p. 37.

61 Jennings, 'At Noon' (*A Sense of the World* 1958), ibid., p. 18.

62 Jennings, 'The Clown', 'About These Things' (*Song for a Birth or a Death* 1961), ibid., pp. 45, 53.

63 Sylvia Plath, 1 April 1956, *The Journals of Sylvia Plath*, ed. Frances McCullough; consulting ed. Ted Hughes (New York: Dial Press, 1982), pp. 137–38.

64 Suzanne Juhasz, *Naked and Fiery Forms: Modern American Poetry By Women: A New Tradition* (New York: Harper Colophon, 1976), p. 3.

65 John Brannigan, *Orwell To The Present: Literature in England 1945–2000* (London: Palgrave, 2003), p. 124.

66 Elizabeth Jennings, ed., *An Anthology of Modern Verse 1940–1960* (London: Methuen, 1961), p. 7.

67 Elizabeth Jennings, 'Still Life and Observer', *Recoveries* (London: Andre Deutsch, 1964), p. 19.

68 Patricia Beer, 'In Memory of Stevie Smith' (*The Estuary* 1971), *Collected Poems* (Manchester: Carcanet, 1988), p. 114.

69 Jeni Couzyn, 'But At Heart You Are Frightened', *Harpers & Queen*, 1972; repr. *Poetry Dimension 1: A Living Record of the Poetry Year*, (London: Robson Books, 1973), pp. 83–86.

70 Claire Buck, 'Poetry and the Women's Movement in Postwar Britain', *Contemporary British Poetry: Essays in Theory and Criticism*, eds. James Acheson and Romana Huk (State University of New York Press, 1996), p. 83.

71 Pat Arrowsmith, 'Escape', *Nine Lives* (St Albans: Brentham Press, 1990), p. 2.

72 'Table 6b.', *The State of Poetry Today: A New Poetry Survey*, compiled by Norman Hidden (London: The Workshop Press, 1978), n. p.

73 C. L. Innes, 'Women Poets Of Many Parts', *Contemporary British Poetry*, pp. 323.

74 Trevor Kneale, ed., *Contemporary Women Poets* (Liverpool: Rondo, 1975); Lilian Mohin, ed. *One Foot on the Mountain: An anthology of British feminist poetry 1969–1979* (London: Onlywomen Press, 1979).

75 Kneale, Introduction, *Contemporary Women Poets*, p. 10.

76 Fleur Adcock, 'Women as Poets,' *Poetry Dimension 2: The Best of the Poetry Year*, ed. Dannie Abse (London: Robson Books, 1974), pp. 231–33.

77 Lilian Mohin, Introduction, *One Foot on the Mountain*, p. 5.

78 Alan Brownjohn and Maureen Duffy, eds., Introduction, *New Poetry 3* (London: The Arts Council of Great Britain, 1977), p. xvii.

79 Wes Magee, 'Patricia Beer', *Contemporary Poets*, ed. Thomas Riggs (New York, Toronto and London: St James Press, 1991) (5th edition), p. 56.

80 Patricia Beer, ed., *New Poems 1975: A P.E.N Anthology of Contemporary Poetry* (London: Hutchinson, 1975); Beer and Kevin Crossley-Holland, eds., *New Poetry 2* (London: The Arts Council of Great Britain, 1976).

81 Gillian Allnutt, 'East Anglian Progenitor'; Medbh McGuckian, 'Aunts', in *New Poetry 5*, ed. Peter Redgrove and Jon Silkin (London: Arts Council of Great Britain, 1979), pp. 9, 105.

82 Elaine Feinstein, 'New Sadness/Old City', 'A Quiet War in Leicester' (*The Magic Apple Tree* 1971), *Collected Poems and Translations* (Manchester: Carcanet, 2002), pp. 51, 52.

83 Feinstein, 'Anniversary' (*The Magic Apple Tree*), *Collected Poems and Translations*, p. 27.

84 Fleur Adcock, 'Rural Blitz', *Poetry Review* 74.2 (1984), p. 12.

85 Fleur Adcock, 'Paths' (*Below Loughrigg* 1979), *Poems: 1960–2000* (Newcastle upon Tyne: Bloodaxe Books, 2000), p. 120.

86 'Elizabeth Bartlett', *Contemporary Women Poets*, ed. Tracy Chevalier (New York, Toronto and London: St James Press, 1991) (5th edition), p. 43.

87 Elma Mitchell, 'The Knitter in Bed 14', 'Census Return', *The Human Cage* (Liskeard: Peterloo Poets, 1979), pp. 13, 35.

88 Jeni Couzyn, 'House Of Changes', *House of Changes* (London: Heinemann, 1978), pp. 1–3.

89 Some of Shuttle's work, including the prose account *The Wise Wound: Menstruation and Everywoman*, is written with her husband, the poet Peter Redgrove.

90 'Penelope Shuttle', *Contemporary Women Poets* (5th edition). p. 892.

91 Jeni Couzyn, 'The Spell', 'The Dance', *House of Changes*, pp. 31–44, 47–61; Jean Earle, 'The Healing Woman – Of Her Gift', *A Trial of Strength* (1980), *Selected Poems* (Bridgend: Seren, 1990), pp. 95–96.

92 Liz Lochhead, *The Grimm Sisters* (London: Next Editions, 1981); Judith Kazantzis, *The Wicked Queen* (London: Sidgwick & Jackson, 1980); Nicki Jackowska, *Incubus* (London: The Menard Press, 1981).

93 Liz Lochhead, Introduction, 'Writers in Brief, 1' (Edinburgh: The Scottish Arts Council, 1978).

94 Anne Stevenson, *Correspondences* (Oxford University Press, 1974); Ruth Fainlight, *Sibyls and Others* (London: Hutchinson, 1980).

95 See also Stevenson's illuminating 'Writing As A Woman,' *Women Writing and Writing About Women*, ed. Mary Jacobus (London: Croom Helm, 1979), pp. 168–76.

96 Ruth Fainlight, 'A Sibyl' (*Sibyls and Others* 1980), *Selected Poems* (London: Sinclair Stevenson, 1995), p. 73.

97 Fainlight, 'Disguise' (*The Region's Violence* 1973); 'Vertical' (*Another Full Moon* 1976), *Selected Poems*, pp. 34; 45.

PART II 5

1 Although it is customary to use 'Stevie', her preferred professional title and one of her many unorthodoxies, 'Smith' is used here for standardisation.

2 Stevie Smith, *Selected Poems of Stevie Smith* (York: Maxwell Press, 1966).

3 'A Turn Outside', BBC Radio Play (23 May 1929), *Me Again: The Uncollected Writings of Stevie Smith*, eds. Jack Barbara and William McBrien (London: Virago, 1988), p. 353.

4 Martin Pumphrey, 'Play, fantasy and strange laughter: Stevie Smith's uncomfortable poetry', *Critical Quarterly* 28.3 (Autumn 1986), pp. 85–96; 86.

5 'Valuable', *CP*, pp. 474–78. *CP* refers to *Stevie Smith: Collected Poems* (London, Allen Lane, 1975).

6 Smith, letter to Kay Dick (25 April, 1953), *Me Again*, p. 294.

7 'Full Well I Know', *CP*, p. 294.

8 Smith, *Over the Frontier*, 1938 (London: Virago, 1989), p. 18.

9 'Freddy', *CP*, p. 65.

10 Stevie Smith, *Novel on Yellow Paper*, 1936 (London: Virago, 1980), p. 162.

11 'So to Fatness Comes', *CP*, p. 538.

12 Smith, Kay Dick, *Ivy and Stevie* (London: Allison and Busby, 1983), p. 12.

13 M. M. Bakhtin, 'Discourse in the Novel', *The Dialogic Imagination: Four Essays by M. M. Bakhtin*, ed. Michael Holquist; trans. Caryl Emerson and Michael Holquist (Austin: University of Texas Press, 1981), pp. 259–442: 262, 294.

14 We are following Bakhtin's definition of texts with a dynamic of more than one voice in 'Discourse in the Novel' (see previous note), particularly the section 'Discourse in Poetry and Discourse in the Novel', pp. 275–300. Bakhtin was writing in the Soviet Union during the 1920s and 1930s and was translated into English in the 1970s.

15 'Childe Rolandine', *CP*, p. 331.

16 Bakhtin, 'Discourse in the Novel', pp. 295, 280.

17 Stevie Smith, *Novel on Yellow Paper*, 1936 (London: Virago, 1986), p. 9.

18 Ibid., p. 39.

19 'The Word', *CP*, p. 542.

20 Smith, '"Books, Plays, Poems", Poems by Living Poets', BBC Home Service, 15 June 1966, in Frances Spalding, *Stevie Smith: A Critical Biography* (London: Faber, 1988), p. 198.

21 See, for example, Dick, *Ivy and Stevie*.

22 'A House of Mercy', *CP*, pp. 410–11.

23 'I Rode with My Darling', ibid. p. 260.

24 'To Carry the Child', ibid., p. 436.

25 'Deeply Morbid', ibid., pp. 296–98.

26 Bakhtin, 'Discourse in the Novel', p. 293.

27 Smith, 'Miss Snooks, Poetess', *Me Again*, p. 226. Printed in *Poetry* (November 1964).

28 'Pretty', *CP*, pp. 469–70.

29 'Cool as a Cucumber', ibid., p. 240.

30 'Votaries of Both Sexes Cry First to Venus', ibid., pp. 399–400.

31 'Drugs Made Pauline Vague', ibid., p. 264.

32 Smith, 'A London Suburb', printed in *Flowers of Cities*, 1949, in *Me Again*, p. 104.

33 'The Wedding Photograph', *CP*, p. 425.

34 'How cruel is the story of Eve', ibid., p. 481.
35 'Girls', ibid., p. 167.
36 Hélène Cixous, 'Sorties', Toril Moi, *Sexual Textual Politics: Feminist Literary Theory* (London: Routledge, 1988), p. 104
37 Smith, *Over the Frontier*, p. 149.
38 'A Dream of Comparison', *CP*, p. 314.
39 'A Mother's Hearse', ibid., p. 234.
40 'The Small Lady', ibid., p. 471.
41 Seven Wade, 'Stevie Smith: the Untruth of Myth', *Agenda* 15.2/3 (Summer/Autumn, 1977), pp. 102–6.
42 'Fafnir and the Knights', *CP*, pp. 322–23.
43 'The After-thought', ibid., p. 256.
44 'I had a dream . . .', ibid., pp. 421–23.
45 'How do You See?', ibid., pp. 516–21.
46 T. S. Eliot, *Four Quartets* 1943, (London: Faber, 1959), p. 14.
47 Philip Larkin, 'Stevie Goodbye', *Observer* (23 Jan. 1972), p. 28.
48 'Behind the Knight', *CP*, p. 231.
49 'Childhood and Interruption', *Stevie Smith: A Selection*, ed. Hermione Lee (London: Faber, 1983), p. 101.
50 'Silence', *Me Again*, p. 236.
51 'The Passing Cloud', *CP*, pp. 351–52.
52 Mark Storey, 'Why Stevie Smith Matters', *Critical Quarterly* 21.2 (Summer 1979), pp. 41–56.
53 Pumphrey, 'Play, fantasy and strange laughter', p. 87.
54 Patricia Beer, 'In Memory of Stevie Smith', *Sixty Women Poets*, ed. Linda France (Newcastle upon Tyne: Bloodaxe Books, 1993), p. 50.

PART II 6

1 Anne Stevenson, 'The Price' (*Enough of Green* 1977), *Collected Poems 1955–1995* (Newcastle upon Tyne: Bloodaxe Books, 2000), p. 72.
2 Maura Dooley, Introduction, *Making for Planet Alice*, ed. Dooley (Newcastle upon Tyne: Bloodaxe Books, 1997), p. 13.
3 Kathleen Raine, Foreword, *Selected Poems* (Ipswich: Golgonooza Press, 1988), p. 5.
4 Diana Wallace, 'Postwar Women's Poetry', *Introduction to Women's Writing*, ed. Marion Shaw (Edinburgh University Press, 1999), p. 143.
5 Adrienne Rich, 'When We Dead Awaken: Writing as Re-Vision', *Feminist Literary Theory: A Reader*, ed. Mary Eagleton (Oxford: Blackwell, 1996), p. 87.
6 See Hannah Gavron's *The Captive Wife: Conflicts of Housebound Mothers* (Harmondsworth: Penguin, 1966), p. 78.
7 Juliet Mitchell, '"Femininity, Narrative and Psychoanalysis": The Longest Revolution', *Feminist Literary Theory*, p. 155.
8 Germaine Greer, *Slipshod Sibyls: Recognition, rejection and the woman poet* (Harmondsworth: Penguin, 1996), p. xv.

9 Jennifer Breen, ed., *Women Romantic Poets 1785–1832: An Anthology* (London: Everyman, 1992), p. 81.

10 Ibid., p. xxv–xxvii.

11 Angela Leighton and Margaret Reynolds, eds., *Victorian Women Poets: An Anthology* (Oxford: Blackwell, 1995), p. xxxv–xxxix.

12 Phyllis Lassner, 'The Quiet Revolution: World War II and the English Domestic Novel', *Mosaic* 23.3 (Summer 1990), p. 89.

13 Sheila Wingfield, Women At Peace, *Beat Drum, Beat Heart IV, A Kite's Dinner: Poems 1938–54* (London: Cresset Press, 1954), p. 97.

14 Lassner, 'The Quiet Revolution', p. 89.

15 Gavron, *The Captive Wife*, p. 144. See also Ann Oakley, *Housewife* (London: Allen Lane, 1974).

16 Lassner, 'The Quiet Revolution', 89.

17 Betty Friedan, *The Feminine Mystique* (Harmondsworth: Penguin, 1965), pp. 14–16.

18 Eavan Boland, 'The Wrong Way', *Strong Words: Modern Poets on Modern Poetry*, eds., W. N. Herbert and Matthew Hollis (Newcastle upon Tyne: Bloodaxe Books, 2000), pp. 215–16.

19 E. J. Scovell, 'A Wife', *Collected Poems* (Manchester: Carcanet, 1988), pp. 57–58.

20 Denise Levertov, 'Marriage II' (*Here and Now* 1957), *Selected Poems* (Newcastle upon Tyne: Bloodaxe Books, 1986), p. 15.

21 6 March 1956, *The Journals of Sylvia Plath*, ed. Frances McCullough (New York: Dial Press, 1982) p. 122.

22 Jeni Couzyn, 'Sylvia Plath', *The Bloodaxe Book of Contemporary Women Poets: Eleven British Writers* (Newcastle upon Tyne: Bloodaxe Books, 1985), p. 146.

23 A. Alvarez, *A Savage God* (London: Weidenfeld & Nicolson, 1971), p. 22.

24 Sylvia Plath, 'Point Shirley', *The Collected Poems of Sylvia Plath*, ed. Ted Hughes (London: Faber, 1981), p. 110.

25 Plath, 'Lesbos', 'Kindness', ibid., pp. 227, 269.

26 Janice Markey, *A Journey into the Red Eye: The Poetry of Sylvia Plath* (London: The Women's Press, 1993), p. 117.

27 Plath, 'The Bee Meeting', 'The Arrival of the Bee Box', *Collected Poems*, pp. 211; 212–13.

28 Christina Britzolakis, *Sylvia Plath and the Theatre of Mourning* (New York: Oxford University Press, 1999) p. 96.

29 Plath, 'Stings', *Collected Poems*, p. 214.

30 Geoffrey Thurley, *The American Moment: American poetry in the mid-century* (London: Edward Arnold, 1977), p. 121.

31 Denise Levertov, 'The Five-Day Rain', *With Eyes at the Back of Our Heads* (Norfolk, Connecticut: James Laughlin, 1960), p. 13.

32 Thurley, *The American Moment*, p. 121.

33 Eavan Boland, Preface, *Collected Poems* (Manchester: Carcanet, 1995), pp. xi–xii.

34 Eavan Boland, 'Ode to Suburbia', 'Suburban Woman' (*The War Horse* 1975), *Collected Poems*, pp. 40; 50–52: 52.

35 Levertov, 'Abel's Bride' (*The Sorrow Dance* 1967), *Selected Poems*, p. 61.

36 Elma Mitchell, 'Recreation', *People Etcetera: Poems New and Selected* (Calstock: Peterloo Poets, 1987), p. 42.

37 Couzyn, Introduction, *Contemporary Women Poets*, p. 15.

38 Patricia Beer, 'Summer Song for me and my Aunts' (*Just Like the Resurrection* 1967), *Collected Poems* (Manchester: Carcanet, 1988), p. 55; Clive Wilmer, 'In conversation with Patricia Beer', *PN Review* 19.5 (May/June 1993), p. 45.

39 Carol Rumens, 'Houses by Day' (*A Strange Girl in Bright Colours* 1973), *Selected Poems* (London: Chatto & Windus, 1987) p. 17; see Lyn Pykett's interesting discussion, 'Women Poets and "Women's Poetry": Fleur Adcock, Gillian Clarke and Carol Rumens', *British Poetry from the 1950s to the 1990s: Politics and Art*, ed. Gary Day and Brian Docherty (London: Macmillan, 1997), pp. 253–67.

40 Ruth Fainlight, 'Domestical', *Sibyls and Others* (London: Hutchinson, 1980), pp. 74–75: 75.

41 'Gillian Clarke', *Six Women Poets*, ed. Judith Kinsman (Oxford University Press: 1992), p. 1.

42 Joseph, 'Jenny Joseph', *Contemporary Women Poets*, p. 169.

43 Simone de Beauvoir, *The Second Sex* (London: Jonathan Cape, 1963), pp. 469–72.

44 Plath, 'Wintering', *Collected Poems*, pp. 217–19.

45 Stevenson, 'Writing as a woman', *Women Writing and Writing About Women*, ed. Mary Jacobus (Beckenham: Croom Helm, 1979), p. 164.

46 Joseph, *Contemporary Women Poets*, p. 169.

47 De Beauvoir, *The Second Sex*, pp. 472–73.

48 Stevenson, *Women Writing*, pp. 164–65.

49 Denise Levertov, 'Zest' (*Here and Now* 1957), *Selected Poems* (Newcastle upon Tyne: Bloodaxe Books, 1986), p. 13.

50 James Breslin, 'Denise Levertov', *Denise Levertov: Selected Criticism*, ed. Albert Gelpi (University of Michigan Press, 1993), p. 79.

51 Denise Levertov, 'Matins', *The Jacob's Ladder* (New York: New Directions, 1961), pp. 57–60: 60.

52 Geoffrey Grigson, ed., *Poetry of the Present: An Anthology of the Thirties and After* (London: Phoenix House, 1949), p. 19; Kenneth Allott, ed., *The Penguin Book of Contemporary Verse* (London: Penguin, 1962), p. 210.

53 Peter Scupham, 'Shelf Lives 9: E. J. Scovell', *PN Review* 26.3 (January/February 2000), 28.

54 E. J. Scovell, 'In a Flat', *Collected Poems* (Manchester: Carcanet, 1988), p. 85.

55 Scovell, 'Domestic', ibid., pp. 207–8.

56 Scovell, 'A Short Night', ibid., p. 118.

57 Elizabeth Jennings, 'Her Garden' (*A Sense of the World* 1958), *Selected Poems* (Manchester: Carcanet, 1979), p. 36.

58 Levertov, 'From the Roof' (*The Jacob's Ladder* 1961), *Selected Poems*, pp. 41–42.

59 Ruth Pitter, 'The New House' (*Still By Choice* 1966), *Collected Poems* (Petersfield: Enitharmon, 1990), p. 238.

60 Tess Cosslett, *Women Writing About Childbirth: Modern discourses of motherhood* (Manchester University Press, 1994), p. 118. See also Oakley, *Housewife*, especially pp. 186–221.

61 See also Karin Voth Harman, 'Delivering the Mother: Three anthologies of birth poetry', *Kicking Daffodils: Twentieth-Century Women Poets*, ed. Vicki Bertram (Edinburgh University Press, 1997), pp. 178–88.

62 Adrienne Rich, *Of Woman Born: Motherhood as experience and institution* (London: Virago, 1977), pp. 100–1. (Emphases original.)

63 Ibid., p. 167.

64 Plath's 'Metaphors' and 'The Manor Garden' (*Collected Poems*, pp. 116, 125) were written in the United States, at the artists' colony Yaddo.

65 De Beauvoir, *The Second Sex*, pp. 512–13.

66 Nina Baym, 'The Madwoman and her Languages', *Feminisms: An anthology of literary theory and criticism*, eds. Robyn R. Warhol and Diane Price Herndl (Basingstoke: Macmillan, 1997. Revised edition), p. 289.

67 Rich, *Of Woman Born*, p. 167.

68 Elaine Feinstein, 'Calliope in the Labour Ward' (*In a Green Eye* 1966), *Collected Poems and Translations* (Manchester: Carcanet, 2002), p. 3.

69 Mitchell, 'At First, My Daughter', *People Etcetera*, p. 35.

70 Plath, 'Morning Song', *Collected Poems*, p. 156.

71 Anne Ridler, 'A Matter of Life and Death' (*A Matter of Life and Death* 1959), *Collected Poems* (Manchester: Carcanet, 1994), p. 115.

72 Stevenson, 'The Spirit is too Blunt an Instrument' (*Travelling Behind Glass* 1974) *Collected Poems*, p. 24; Scovell, 'The First Year', *Collected Poems*, p. 63.

73 Levertov, 'The Earthwoman and the Waterwoman' (*Here and Now* 1957), *Selected Poems*, p. 12.

74 Tillie Olsen, *Silences* (London: Virago, 1980), p. 33.

75 Plath, 'Stillborn', *Collected Poems*, p. 142.

76 Stevenson, 'The Victory' (*Travelling Behind Glass* 1974), *Collected Poems*, p. 25.

77 Feinstein, 'Mother Love' (*In a Green Eye* 1966), *Collected Poems*, p. 4.

78 Quoted by Jane Tompkins, 'Me and My Shadow', Warhol and Price Herndl, *Feminisms*, p. 1107.

79 Alvarez, 'Sylvia Plath', *The Modern Poet: Essays from 'The Review'*, ed. Ian Hamilton (London: Macdonald, 1968), pp. 75–82: p. 77.

80 Nancy Chodorow, 'The Psychodynamics of the Family', *Psychoanalysis and Woman: A Reader*, ed. Shelley Saguaro (Basingstoke and London: Macmillan, 2000), p. 119.

81 Anne Ridler, 'Anne Ridler in conversation with Grevel Lindop', *PN Review* 21.3 (January/February 1995), p. 17.

82 Ridler, 'The Gaze' (*A Matter of Life and Death* 1959), *Collected Poems*, p. 123.

83 Stevenson, *Women Writing*, p. 175.

PART II 7

1 Judith Kazantzis, 'the long-haired woman', *One Foot on the Mountain: An Anthology of British Feminist Poetry 1969–1979*, ed. Lilian Mohin (London: Onlywomen Press, 1979), p. 122.

2 Louise Bernikow, *The World Split Open: Four Centuries of Women Poets in England and America, 1552–1950* (London: The Women's Press, 1979), p. 7.

3 Jan Williams, Hazel Twort and Ann Bachelli, 'Women and the Family,' *The Body Politic: Women's Liberation in Britain*, ed. Michelene Wandor (London: Stage One, 1979), p. 31.

4 Michelene Wandor, 'Masks and Options: An Introduction,' *On Gender and Writing*, ed. Wandor (London: Pandora, 1983), p. 5.

5 For evidence, see 'Liz Lochhead', *Sleeping with Monsters: Conversations with Scottish and Irish Women Poets*, eds. Gillean Somerville-Arjat and Rebecca E. Wilson (Edinburgh: Polygon, 1991), pp. 8–17; Carol Rumens, 'As Radical as Reality', interview with Marion Lomax, *Poetry Review* 88.4 (Winter 1998/99), pp. 77–82 .

6 Sally Minogue, 'Prescriptions and Proscriptions: Feminist Criticism and Contemporary Poetry', *Some Problems for Feminist Criticism*, ed. Minogue (London: Routledge, 1990), pp. 179–236; Claire Buck, 'Poetry and the Women's Movement in Postwar Britain', *Contemporary British Poetry: Essays in Theory and Criticism*, eds. James Acheson and Romana Huk (State University of New York, 1996), pp. 81–111; Vicki Bertram, 'Postfeminist Poetry?: "one more word for balls"', in *Contemporary British Poetry*, pp. 269–92.

7 Rumens, 'As Radical As Reality', p. 80.

8 Alan Robinson shows how Anne Stevenson, Fleur Adcock, Carol Ann Duffy, Fiona Pitt-Kethley and Medbh McGuckian negotiate with feminist ideas. See Robinson, *Instabilities in Contemporary British Poetry* (Basingstoke: Macmillan, 1988) pp. 161–208. Lyn Pykett finds Stevenson, Adcock, Gillian Clarke and Rumens 'appropriat[ing] feminist perspectives and debates as a means of addressing their own concerns ... with a confidence and authority borrowed from the women's movement'. See 'Women Poets and "Women's Poetry"', *British Poetry from the 1950s to the 1990s: Politics and Art*, eds. Gary Day and Thomas Docherty (Basingstoke: Macmillan, 1997), pp. 253–67. Marilyn Hacker locates U. A. Fanthorpe, Elma Mitchell, Duffy, Rumens, Lochhead and Wendy Cope in 'an undercurrent of feminist poetry in England, outside the women's movement literary circles' definitively concerned with 'the revision of history through the perspective of the historically silenced and powerless'. See 'Unauthorized Voices: U. A. Fanthorpe and Elma Mitchell,' *Grand Street* 8 (1989), p. 150.

9 Some found wider circulation in later women-only anthologies like Diana Scott's *Bread and Roses* (London: Virago, 1982), Rumens's controversial *Making for the Open: The Chatto Book of Post-Feminist Poetry 1964–1984* (London: Chatto & Windus, 1986) and Gillian Allnutt's 'Quote Feminist Unquote Poetry' section of *The New British Poetry*, eds. Fred D'Aguiar, Gillian Allnutt, Ken Edwards and Eric Mottram (London: Paladin, 1988) pp. 75–217.

10 Buck, *Contemporary British Poetry*, p. 83.

11 See the essays in *On Gender and Writing*.

12 Wandor, Afterword, *Touch Papers*, eds. Judith Kazantzis, Michèle Roberts and Michelene Wandor (London: Allison and Busby, 1982), p. 95.

13 Michelene Wandor and Michèle Roberts, eds., *Cutlasses And Earrings* (London: Playbooks, 1977); Alison Fell, Stef Pixner, Tina Reid, Michèle Roberts and Ann

Oosthuizen, eds., *Licking The Bed Clean: Five Feminist Poets* (London: Teeth Imprints, 1978). See also Fell, Pixner, Reid, Roberts and Oosthuizen, eds., *Smile, Smile, Smile, Smile* (London: Sheba Feminist Publishers, 1980).

14 Wandor and Roberts, Introduction, *Cutlasses*, p. 5.

15 Editors' Preface, *Licking*, p. 1.

16 Anna Coote and Beatrix Campbell, eds., *Sweet Freedom: The struggle for Women's Liberation* (London: Picador, 1982), p. 237.

17 Editors' Preface, *Licking*, pp. 1–2.

18 Sheila Rowbotham, 'The Role of Women in the Revolution defined by some Socialist men (1968)', *Cutlasses*, p. 37.

19 Michèle Roberts, 'Klevshaven', *The Mirror of the Mother: Selected Poems 1978–1985* (London: Methuen, 1986), p. 22.

20 'Alison Fell', *Bread and Roses*, p. 198.

21 Fell, 'Women in the Cold War', *Cutlasses*, p. 22–23; *Kisses for Mayakovsky* (London: Virago, 1984), p. 54.

22 Fell, 'Girl's gifts', *Kisses for Mayakovsky*, p. 8.

23 Fell, 'Hysteria 1', *Cutlasses*, p. 19; 'Butterfingers', 'Sail Away', *Kisses for Mayakovsky*, pp. 59, 26.

24 Fell et al., *Smile, Smile . . .*, p. 77.

25 Wandor, 'Lullaby', *Cutlasses*, p. 49.

26 Roberts, 'Questions and Answers', *On Gender and Writing*, p. 64.

27 Ibid.

28 Ibid.

29 Roberts, 'And then I have been wanting to mourn', *The Mirror of the Mother*, p. 32; see *Licking*, p. 48.

30 Roberts, 'Questions and Answers', *On Gender and Writing*, pp. 63–66.

31 Roberts, 'Memories of trees', *Licking*, pp. 49–50: p. 50.

32 Wandor, 'Love Poem', *Cutlasses*, pp. 53–54: p. 54.

33 Kazantzis, 'The Errant Unicorn', *On Gender and Writing*, pp. 26–30.

34 Coote and Campbell cite as *The Redstockings Manifesto* (New York: Redstockings, 1979), *Sweet Freedom*, p. 15.

35 Kazantzis, 'The Errant Unicorn', *On Gender and Writing*, pp. 26–30.

36 Fell, 'For Maria Burke', *Kisses for Mayakovsky*, p. 46.

37 Scott, 'A Love Poem to Myself', *One Foot*, p. 83.

38 Kazantzis, 'the long-haired woman', ibid., p. 122.

39 Mohin, Introduction, ibid., p. 1.

40 Scott, 'Introduction, The Renaming; Poetry Coming from the Women's Liberation Movement 1970–80', *Bread and Roses*, p. 190.

41 Bernikow, *The World Split Open*, p. 7.

42 Fleur Adcock, ed., *The Faber Book of Twentieth-Century Women's Poetry* (London: Faber, 1987) p. 13.

43 Barbara Zanditon's 'The Big Tease Lady Playing Games with Death' (*One Foot*, p. 40) is dedicated to Sexton, while 'for Sylvia Plath' subtitles Roberts's 'Madwoman at Rodmell', *The Mirror of the Mother*, p. 73. (It is missing from the version in *Bread and Roses*).

44 Buck, *Contemporary British Poetry*, p. 91.
45 Stephanie Markman, 'And mother why did you tell me', *One Foot*, p. 226.
46 Gill Hague, 'Uncertainty', ibid., p. 86.
47 Pauline Long, 'If women could speak what language would they use,' ibid., pp. 204–5.
48 Editors' Preface, *Licking*, p. 3.
49 John Wain, ed., *Everyman Book of English Verse* (London: Dent, 1981), p. 26.
50 Carol Rumens, Introduction, *Making for the Open: The Chatto Book of Post-Feminist Poetry 1964–84* (London: Chatto & Windus, 1987), p. xv.
51 See Lorna Mitchell (*One Foot*, p. 155) and Diana Scott, on setting aside 'considerations of "sounding like literature",' *Bread and Roses*, p. 190.
52 Editors' Preface, *Licking*, p. 3.
53 Gillian Allnutt, 'Quote Feminist Unquote Poetry', *The New British Poetry*, pp. 77–78.
54 Buck, *Contemporary British Poetry*, pp. 89–90.
55 Roberts, Afterword, *Touch Papers*, p. 64.
56 Oosthuizen, 'Bulletins from the Front Line', *Licking*, p. 61.

PART II 8

1 Denise Riley explains that '"modernism". . . tends to get used as a pointer to the audience which says expect fragmentation. Expect something which looks bizarre on the page. Expect difficulty. Do not expect narrative. Do not expect confession. But are there any trustworthy rules of thumb for what modernist writing is?' See Romana Huk, 'Denise Riley in conversation with Romana Huk', *PN Review* 21.5 (1995), pp. 17–18.
2 Carlyle Reedy, 'Working Processes of a Woman Poet', *Poets on Writing: Britain, 1970–91*, ed. Denise Riley (London: Macmillan Academic, 1992), p. 261.
3 Maggie O'Sullivan, 'riverrunning (realisations For Charles Bernstein' [*sic*], *Contemporary Women's Poetry: Reading/Writing/Practice*, eds. Alison Mark and Deryn Rees-Jones (Basingstoke: Macmillan, 2000), p. 51.
4 Wendy Mulford, "Curved, Odd . . . Irregular. A Vision of Contemporary Poetry by Women', *Women: A Cultural Review* 1.3 (Winter 1990), p. 263.
5 Mulford, 'Notes on Writing: A Marxist/Feminist Viewpoint', *On Gender and Writing*, ed. Michelene Wandor (London: Pandora, 1983) p. 33. (Mulford's emphases.)
6 Clair Wills, 'Contemporary Women's Poetry: experimentalism and the expressive voice', *Critical Quarterly* 36.3 (1994), pp. 34–52; Linda A. Kinnahan, 'Experimental Poetics and the Lyric in British Women's Poetry: Geraldine Monk, Wendy Mulford, and Denise Riley', *Contemporary Literature* 37.4 (1996), pp. 620–66; Romana Huk, 'Feminist Radicalism', *Kicking Daffodils: Twentieth-Century Women Poets*, ed. Vicki Bertram (Edinburgh University Press, 1997), pp. 227–49.
7 As young writers, both Mulford and Riley were actively involved in the Women's Movement. For the other view, see Caroline Bergvall, 'No

Margins to this Page: Female Experimental Poets and the Legacy of Modernism', *fragmente* 5 (1993), pp. 30–38.

8 Wills, 'Experimentalism and the expressive voice', pp. 38–42; 44.

9 Huk, *Kicking Daffodils*, p. 229.

10 Kinnahan, 'Experimental Poetics', p. 626.

11 Maggie O'Sullivan, ed., *Out of everywhere: linguistically innovative poetry by women in North America and the UK* (London: Reality Street Editions, 1996).

12 Simon Jarvis, 'Rosemary Tonks', *British Women Writers: A Critical Reference Guide*, ed. Janet Todd (New York: Continuum, 1989), p. 669.

13 Rosemary Tonks, 'The Sofas, Fogs and Cinemas', *Notes on Cafes and Bedrooms* (London: Putnam, 1963).

14 Ibid. (all ellipses Tonks's).

15 Alison Bielski, 'General Statement', *New Poetry* 50 (Autumn 1980), p. 45.

16 Veronica Forrest-Thomson, 'The Further-Off-From', *Collected Poems and Translations*, ed. Anthony Barnett (London: Allardyce, 1990), p. 44.

17 Letter to Alice Entwistle (11 Oct. 2003).

18 Alison Mark, 'Hysteria and Poetic Language: A reading of the work of Veronica Forrest-Thomson', *Women: A Cultural Review* 5.3 (1994), pp. 264–77; Mark, 'Reading Between the Lines: Identity in the early poems of Veronica Forrest-Thomson', *Kicking Daffodils*, pp. 210–26.

19 Veronica Forrest-Thomson, *Poetic Artifice: A theory of twentieth-century poetry* (Manchester University Press, 1978). See also her articles, including 'Irrationality And Artifice: A problem in modern poetics', *The British Journal of Aesthetics* 2.2 (1971), pp. 123–33; 'Dada, Unrealism and Contemporary Poetry', *Twentieth Century Studies* 12 (1974), pp. 77–93; 'Rational Artifice: Some remarks on the poetry of William Empson', *Yearbook of English Studies* 4 (1974), pp. 225–38.

20 G. S. Fraser, 'Veronica: A Tribute', *Adam International Review* 39 (1975), p. 43.

21 Mark, *Kicking Daffodils*, p. 211.

22 Ibid., p. 214.

23 Forrest-Thomson, *Poetic Artifice*, p. xii.

24 Forrest-Thomson, 'Rational Artifice', p. 232.

25 See Mark's helpful discussion of 'The Hyphen', *Kicking Daffodils*, pp. 215–18.

26 Forrest-Thomson, 'Note', *Collected Poems and Translations*, pp. 262–63.

27 Forrest-Thomson, 'Through the Looking Glass', ibid., p. 221.

28 Forrest-Thomson, 'Antiphrasis', 'Antiquities', 'Gemini', 'Identi-Kit', 'Sagittarius', ibid., pp. 29, 31, 206, 208, 227.

29 Suzanne Raitt, 'Veronica Forrest-Thomson, *Collected Poems and Translations*', *Women: A Cultural Review* 1.3 (Winter 1990), pp. 304–8.

30 Forrest-Thomson, 'An Impersonal Statement', *Collected Poems and Translations*, p. 260.

31 Ian Gregson, *Contemporary Poetry and Postmodernism: Dialogue and Estrangement* (London: Macmillan, 1996), p. 196.

32 Raitt, 'Veronica Forrest-Thomson', p. 307.

33 Forrest-Thomson, 'The Lady of Shalott: Ode', *Collected Poems and Translations*, pp. 86–7: 86.

34 Forrest-Thomson, 'The Garden of Proserpine', ibid., pp. 88–90.

35 Forrest-Thomson, 'Cordelia: or, "A Poem Should not Mean but Be"', ibid., pp. 104–8.

36 Wendy Mulford, 'l.', 'The ABC of Writing', *and suddenly, supposing: selected poems* (Buckfastleigh, Devon: Etruscan Books, 2002), p. 64.

37 Mulford, *On Gender and Writing*, p. 31.

38 Ibid., p. 32.

39 Mulford, 'p', *selected poems*, p. 66.

40 Mulford, Afterword, ibid., p. [178].

41 Mulford, '7', ibid., p. 83.

42 Mulford, *On Gender and Writing*, p. 34.

43 Mulford, 'The meaning of blue', *selected poems*, p. 15.

44 Mulford, 'Trawls', ibid., p. 50.

45 Mulford, 'The Ancrene Riwle', ibid., p. 34.

46 Mulford, 'How do you live?', ibid., p. 92.

47 Wendy Mulford, Introduction, *The Virago Book of Love Poetry*, eds. Mulford, Helen Kidd, Julia Mishkin and Sandi Russell (London: Virago, 1991), p. xvi.

48 Wendy Mulford, '"How do you live?"', *Angels of Fire: An Anthology of Radical Poetry in the 80s*, eds. Sylvia Paskin, Jay Ramsay and Jeremy Silver (London: Chatto & Windus 1986), p. 118. (These lines do not appear in Mulford's *selected poems*.)

49 Kinnahan, 'Experimental Poetics and the Lyric in British Women's Poetry', p. 651.

50 Mulford, 's', *selected poems*, p. 67.

51 Denise Riley, 'Wherever you are, be somewhere else', *Mop Mop Georgette: New and Selected Poems 1986–1993* (Saxmundham and London: Reality Street Editions, 1993), p. 27.

52 Riley, 'Letter to the Editor', *PN Review* 20.4 (1994), p. 2.

53 Denise Riley, 'A note on sex and "the reclaiming of language"', *Dry Air* (London, Virago: 1985), p. 7.

54 Denise Riley, 'Waiting', *Truth, Dare, Promise: Girls growing up in Fifties Britain*, ed. Liz Heron (London: Virago, 1985), p. 237.

55 Riley, 'she has ingested her wife . . .', *Dry Air*, p. 11.

56 Riley, 'such face bones honeycombed sockets . . .', ibid., p. 19.

57 Riley, 'two ambitions to remember,' ibid., p. 56.

58 Denise Riley, 'Is There Linguistic Guilt?', *Critical Quarterly* 39.1 (1997), pp. 75–110.

59 Ibid., p. 84.

60 Ibid., p. 76.

61 Ibid., p. 78.

62 Ibid., p. 84.

63 Ibid., p. 98.

64 Riley, 'Denise Riley in conversation', p. 20. (Huk's emphases.)

65 Denise Riley, *Am I That Name? Feminism and the Category of 'Women' in History* (Basingstoke: Macmillan, 1988), p. 111.

PART III OVERVIEW

1 Sarah Maguire and Andy Brown, *Binary Myths: conversations with contemporary poets* (Exeter: Stride Publications, 1998), pp. 23–25.

2 Oxford and Cambridge graduates include: Allnutt, Brackenbury, Cope, Fanthorpe, Feinstein, Garrett, Hill, Jennings, Joseph, Kazantzis, Lewis, Oswald, Padel, Porteus, Purcell, Shapcott and Stainer.

3 From its inception in April 1985, *Acumen* was edited by a woman, Patricia Oxley.

4 Carol Ann Duffy, 'Poet for our Times' (*The Other Country*, 1990), *Selected Poems* (London: Penguin, 1994), pp. 70–71.

5 Julie O'Callaghan, 'Pep-Talk to Poets from their Sales Manager', *What's What?* (Newcastle upon Tyne: Bloodaxe Books, 1991), pp. 24–25.

6 Carol Rumens, Introduction, *New Women Poets* (Newcastle upon Tyne: Bloodaxe Books, 1993), p. 15.

7 Elaine Feinstein, Ruth Fainlight, *The Bloodaxe Book of Contemporary Women Poets*, ed. Jeni Couzyn (Newcastle upon Tyne: Bloodaxe Books, 1985), pp. 114, 130.

8 Carol Rumens, *New Women Poets* (Newcastle upon Tyne: Bloodaxe Books, 1993), p. 13.

9 Martin Booth, *British Poetry 1964–84: Driving Through the Barricades* (London: Routledge and Kegan Paul, 1985), pp. 177–78.

10 Christine Evans, 'Is there a woman's poetry?', *Poetry Wales* 23.1 (1987), p. 44.

11 Fleur Adcock, *Poets Talking*, ed. Clive Wilmer (Manchester: Carcanet, 1994), p. 32.

12 Anne Stevenson, 'The Fiction Makers', *Collected Poems 1955–1995* (Newcastle upon Tyne: Bloodaxe Books, 2000), p. 99.

13 Stevenson, 'Poem for a Daughter', ibid., p. 89.

14 Carol Rumens, *Don't Ask Me What I Mean: Poets in their own words*, eds. Clare Brown and Don Paterson (London: Picador, 2003), p. 252.

15 See Carol Rumens, 'A Bookshop Revisited', *Poetry Review* 86.4 (1996/7), pp. 36–7.

16 Carol Rumens, 'Two Women' (*Selected Poems* 1987), *Thinking of Skins: New and Selected Poems* (Newcastle upon Tyne: Bloodaxe Books, 1993), p. 103.

17 Carol Rumens, *Six Women Poets*, ed. Judith Kinsman (Oxford University Press, 1992), pp. 74–75. The version of 'Two Women' is slighty different in this anthology.

18 Rumens, 'Ballad of the Morning After', *Thinking of Skins*, p. 107.

19 Kate Clanchy, *Poetry Book Society Bulletin* 168 (Spring 1996), p. 8.

20 *Field Day Anthology of Irish Writing Vol. 4: Irish Women's Writing and Tradition* (Part 1), ed. Angela Burke et al. (Cork University Press, 2002).

21 Edna Longley, *The Living Stream: Literature and Revisionism in Ireland* (Newcastle upon Tyne: Bloodaxe Books, 1994), pp. 221–22.

22 See interview with Edna Longley, *Aquarius Women* 19/20 (1992), pp. 122–27.

23 Peggy O'Brien, Introduction, *The Wake Forest Book of Irish Women's Poetry 1967–2000* (Winston-Salem: Wake Forest University Press, 1999), pp. xvi–xvii.

24 Catherine Kerrigan, ed., *An Anthology of Scottish Women Poets* (Edinburgh University Press, 1991).

25 Liz Lochhead, 'Kidspoem/Bairnsang', *Penguin Modern Poets Vol. 4* (Harmondsworth: Penguin, 1995), p. 61.

26 Helen Kidd, 'Writing Near the Fault Line: Scottish Women Poets and the Topography of Tongues', *Kicking Daffodils: Twentieth-Century Women Poets*, ed. Vicki Bertram (Edinburgh University Press, 1997), p. 99.

27 Kathleen Jamie, 'Mr and Mrs Scotland are Dead', *Mr and Mrs Scotland are Dead: Poems 1980–1994* (Tarset: Bloodaxe Books, 2002), p. 134.

28 Jamie, 'The Queen of Sheba', 'Mother-May-I', ibid., pp. 112, 114.

29 Katrina Porteus, *Poetry Society News* (Autumn 2003), p. 3.

30 Rees-Jones, 'Be prepared!', interview with Stephen Troussé, *Poetry News* (Winter 1998), p. 11.

31 Grace Nichols, 'Of course when they ask for poems about the "Realities" of black women', *Lazy Thoughts of a Lazy Woman and other poems* (London: Virago, 1989), pp. 52–54.

32 Nichols, *Six Women Poets*, p. 33.

33 Moniza Alvi, 'The Sari', 'Map of India', *Carrying My Wife* (Tarset: Bloodaxe Books, 2000), pp. 137–38.

34 Moniza Alvi, 'The Country at My Shoulder', *The Country at My Shoulder* (Oxford University Press, 1993), p. 135; 'The Double City', *A Bowl of Warm Air* (Oxford University Press, 1996), pp. 4–5.

35 Imtiaz Dharker, 'Choice', 'Minority', *Postcards from god* (Newcastle upon Tyne: Bloodaxe Books, 1997), pp. 49–50; 157–59.

36 Debjani Chatterjee, 'To the English Language', *The Redbeck Anthology of British South Asian Poetry*, ed. Chatterjee (Bradford: Redbeck Press, 2000), pp. 36–37.

37 Jackie Kay, 'Somebody Else', *Off Colour* (Newcastle upon Tyne: Bloodaxe Books, 1998), p. 27.

38 Elaine Feinstein, Preface, *Collected Poems and Translations* (Manchester: Carcanet, 2002).

39 Eavan Boland, 'The Woman Poet: her dilemma', *The American Poetry Review* 16 (Jan./Feb. 1987), pp. 17–20. Repr. *Object Lessons: The Life of the Woman and the Poet in Our Time* (Manchester: Carcanet, 1995), pp. 239–54.

40 Eavan Boland, *PBS Bulletin* 160 (Spring 1994), pp. 1–2.

41 Jo Shapcott, *Phrase Book* (London: Oxford University Press, 1992), pp. 26–27.

42 Anna Adams, 'For the six children of Dr Goebbels', *Green Resistance: New and Selected Poems* (London: Enitharmon, 1996), pp. 72–73.

43 Rumens, interview with Marion Lomax, *Poetry Review* 88.4 (Winter 1998/9), pp. 77–82.

44 Rumens, ibid.

45 Carol Rumens, 'A Lawn for the English Family' (*From Berlin to Heaven*, 1989), 'An Easter Garland' (*Star Whisper* 1983), *Thinking of Skins*, pp. 147–48; 72.

46 Carol Ann Duffy, *William and the ex-Prime Minister* (London: Anvil Press, 1992), pp. 1–2.

47 Wendy Cope, 'Tumps', *Serious Concerns* (London: Faber, 1992), pp. 34–35.

48 Kay, 'Teeth', 'Crown and Country', 'Where it Hurts', *Off Colour,* pp. 15–16; 12, 9.

49 Edna Longley, Introduction, *The Bloodaxe Book of 20th-Century Poetry from Britain and Ireland* (Tarset: Bloodaxe Books, 2000), p. 24.

50 Carol Ann Duffy, 'Prayer', *Mean Time* (London: Anvil Press, 1993), p. 52.

51 Annemarie Austin, 'She', *The Flaying of Marsyas* (Newcastle upon Tyne: Bloodaxe Books, 1995), p. 52.

52 Elizabeth Garrett, 'Mother, Baby, Lover', *The Rule of Three* (Newcastle upon Tyne: Bloodaxe Books, 1991); *Sixty Women Poets,* ed. Linda France (Newcastle upon Tyne: Bloodaxe Books, 1993), pp. 141–42.

53 Helen Dunmore, 'Patrick I', *Short Days, Long Nights: New and Selected Poems* (Newcastle upon Tyne: Bloodaxe Books, 1991), p. 78.

54 Adams, 'Prampushers', *Green Resistance,* pp. 59–60.

55 Penelope Shuttle, 'Vanity', 'Ultra Sound', *A Leaf Out of His Book* (Manchester: Carcanet, 1999), pp. 18, 68.

56 Eiléan ní Chuilleanáin, 'She Opened the Egg', *Wake Forest Book of Irish Women's Poetry,* p. 74; Elizabeth Bartlett, 'Mixed Infants', *Two Women Dancing: New and Selected Poems* (Newcastle upon Tyne: Bloodaxe Books, 1995), pp. 105–6; Eavan Boland, 'Mastectomy', *Collected Poems* (Manchester: Carcanet, 1995), pp. 60–61.

57 Boland, 'Anorexic', *Collected Poems,* pp. 58–60.

58 Grace Nichols, 'Ode to my Bleed', *Lazy Thoughts of a Lazy Woman,* p. 24.

59 Katie Donovan, 'Underneath Our Skirts', *Watermelon Man* (Newcastle upon Tyne: Bloodaxe Books, 1993), p. 33; Sujata Bhatt, 'Udaylee', (*Brunizem* 1988), *Point No Point : Selected Poems* (Manchester: Carcanet, 1997), p. 18.

60 Agbabi, 'It's Better Post- than Pre-', *R.A.W.* (London: Gecko Press, 1995), pp. 58–63.

61 Liz Lochhead, 'An Abortion', *Dreaming Frankenstein and Collected Poems 1967–84* (Edinburgh: Polygon, 1984), pp. 9–11.

62 Fiona Pitt-Kethley, 'Independent Means', 'Long-stemmed Rose', *Dogs* (London: Sinclair Stevenson, 1993), pp. 14, 12.

63 Selima Hill, 'I want a lover', *Violet* (Newcastle upon Tyne: Bloodaxe Books, 1997), p. 68.

64 Leonie Rushforth, *Aquarius Women* 19/20 (1992), p. 135.

65 Katherine Pierpoint, 'This Dead Relationship', *Truffle Beds* (London: Faber, 1995), pp. 40–41; Duffy, 'Disgrace', *Mean Time,* p. 48.

66 Agbabi, 'Sentences', *R.A.W.,* pp. 28–30.

67 Kate Clanchy, 'The Personals', *Samarkand* (London: Picador, 1999), p. 30.

68 Connie Bensley, 'The Stable Relationship', *Central Reservations: New and Selected Poems* (Newcastle upon Tyne: Bloodaxe Books, 1990), p. 32.

69 Dunmore, 'Second Marriages', 'The Deserted Table', *Short Days/Long Nights,* pp. 97–98.

70 Marion Lomax ,'Beyond Men', *Sixty Women Poets,* p. 197.

71 Linda France, 'Acts of Love', 'Samantha', *Red* (Newcastle upon Tyne: Bloodaxe Books, 1992), pp. 22–8, 46.

72 Ian Gregson, *Contemporary Poetry and Postmodernism: Dialogue and Estrangement* (Basingstoke: Macmillan, 1996), p. 7.

73 Vicci Bentley, 'No More "Mrs Nice"', interview with Vicki Feaver, *Magma* 13 (Winter 1998), pp. 44–51.

74 Lochhead, 'In the Dreamschool', *Dreaming Frankenstein*, pp. 57–60.

75 These three poems are in *Penguin Modern Poets Vol. 2* (1995).

76 An excerpt from 'The Laughter of Stafford Girls' High' appeared in *Poetry Review* 91.1 (Spring 2001), pp. 22–25.

77 Stan Smith, 'The things that words give a name to: The "New Generation" poets and the politics of the hyperreal', *Critical Survey* 8.3 (1996), pp. 306–22, 320.

78 Ibid., p. 321.

79 Duffy, 'Away and See', *Mean Time*, p. 23.

80 Sarah Maguire, *Poetry Review*, New Generation Poets Special, 84.1 (Spring 1994), pp. 68–69.

81 Maura Dooley, Introduction, *Making for Planet Alice: new women poets* (Newcastle upon Tyne: Bloodaxe Books, 1997).

82 John Kinsella, 'Her Life Awake', *Poetry Review* 90.1 (Spring 2000), pp. 81–82.

83 Lavinia Greenlaw, interview with Tim Kendall, *Thumbscrew* 8 (Summer 1997), pp. 2–8.

84 See Paul Hyland's landmarks, *Getting into Poetry: A Readers' and Writers' Guide to the Poetry Scene* (Newcastle upon Tyne: Bloodaxe Books, 1996), pp. 83–101.

85 Anne Rouse, 'The Outlands', *Timing* (Newcastle upon Tyne: Bloodaxe Books, 1997), p. 64.

86 Connie Bensley, 'Politesse', *The Back and the Front of It* (Tarset: Bloodaxe Books, 2000), p. 16.

87 Neil Astley, *Poetry Book Society Bulletin* 179 (Summer 1998), pp. 16–7.

88 Carol Ann Duffy, 'Little Red-Cap', *The World's Wife* (London: Picador, 1999), pp. 3–5. At the time of writing, *The World's Wife* has sold 35,000 copies, which is phenomenal for poetry sales.

PART III 9

1 Jackie Kay, 'In My Country', *Other Lovers* (Newcastle upon Tyne: Bloodaxe Books, 1993), p. 24.

2 Robert Crawford, *Identifying Poets: Self and Territory in Twentieth-Century Poetry* (Edinburgh University Press, 1993), p. 144.

3 Helen Dunmore, 'The Country at my Shoulder', *Poetry Review* 85.2 (Summer 1995), p. 4.

4 Sujata Bhatt, 'The One Who Goes Away' (*The Stinking Rose* 1995), *Point No Point* (Manchester: Carcanet, 1997), pp. 105–7: 107.

5 Debjani Chatterjee, 'Primary Purpose', *I Was That Woman* (Frome: Hippopotamus Press, 1989), pp. 21–22.

6 'Fleur Adcock', *The Bloodaxe Book of Contemporary Women Poets: Eleven British Writers*, ed. Jeni Couzyn (Newcastle upon Tyne: Bloodaxe Books, 1985), p. 202.

7 Crawford, *Identifying Poets*, p. 144; Joanne Winning, 'Curious Rarities? The work of Kathleen Jamie and Jackie Kay', *Contemporary Women's Poetry: Reading/Writing/Practice*, eds. Alison Mark and Deryn Rees-Jones (Basingstoke: Macmillan, 2000), p. 233.

8 Imtiaz Dharker, 'They'll say, "She must be from another country"', *I Speak For The Devil* (Newcastle upon Tyne: Bloodaxe Books, 2001), p. 38.

9 Jackie Kay, 'Kail and Callaloo', *Charting the Journey: Writings by Black and Third World Women*, eds. Shabnam Grewal, Jackie Kay, Liliane Landor, Gail Lewis and Pratibha Parmar (London: Sheba Feminist Publishers, 1988), pp. 195–97.

10 Paraskevi Papaleonida, '"holding my beads in my hand": Dialogue, synthesis and power in the poetry of Jackie Kay and Grace Nichols', *Kicking Daffodils: Twentieth-Century Women Poets*, ed. Vicki Bertram (Edinburgh University Press, 1997), pp. 125–39; 127.

11 The poem was first broadcast on Radio 3's 'Drama Now' series in August 1990.

12 Carol Rumens, 'Clouding the Borders' (*Thinking of Skins* 1993), *Selected poems*, p. 48.

13 Jackie Kay, 'Chapter 6: The Telling Part', *The Adoption Papers* (Newcastle upon Tyne: Bloodaxe, 1991), p. 22.

14 Kay, 'Chapter 4: Baby Lazarus,' ibid., p. 16.

15 Clair Wills, *Improprieties: Politics and Sexuality in Northern Irish Poetry* (Oxford: Clarendon, 1993), p. 57.

16 Jackie Kay, 'Pride', *Off Colour* (Newcastle upon Tyne: Bloodaxe Books, 1998), p. 62.

17 Ibid., p. 64.

18 Grace Nichols, 'We The Women', *i is a long-memoried woman* (London: Karnak House, 1983), p. 12.

19 Nichols, 'Taint'; 'Web of Kin', ibid., pp. 18; 8.

20 Imtiaz Dharker, 'No-Man's Land', *Purdah* (Oxford University Press, 1988), p. 51.

21 Helen Kidd, 'Writing Near The Fault Line: Scottish Women Poets and the Topography of Tongues', *Kicking Daffodils*, p. 107.

22 Jo Shapcott, 'Confounding Geography', *Contemporary Women's Poetry*, p. 42.

23 Jo Shapcott, 'Motherland' (*Phrase Book* 1992), *Her Book: Poems 1988–1998* (London: Faber, 2000), p. 124.

24 Wills, *Improprieties*, pp. 47–77.

25 Eavan Boland, 'Anna Liffey' (*In a Time of Violence* 1994), *Collected Poems* (Manchester: Carcanet, 1995), p. 199.

26 David Mattin, 'English from a different viewpoint', *The Times* (26 October 2002), p. 15.

27 Mimi Khalvati, 'Rubaiyat', *In White Ink* (Manchester: Carcanet, 1991), pp. 50–51.

28 Moniza Alvi, 'The Least International Shop in The World', *Contemporary Women's Poetry*, p. 37.

29 Ibid., pp. 39; 36.

30 Moniza Alvi, 'The Laughing Moon' (*A Bowl of Warm Air* 1996), *Carrying My Wife* (Newcastle upon Tyne: Bloodaxe Books, 2000), p. 94.

31 Alvi, 'The Least International Shop', *Contemporary Women's Poetry*, p. 36.

32 Alvi, 'O Maharani', (*A Bowl of Warm Air*), *Carrying My Wife*, p. 92.

33 Alvi, 'Blood', *Carrying My Wife*, p. 47.

34 Khalvati, 'The Waiting House', *In White Ink*, p. 30. The epigraph is cited as Anne Cameron's *Daughters of Copper Women*.

35 Bhatt, 'Udaylee' (*Brunizem* 1988), *Point No Point*, p. 18.

36 Alvi, 'The Least International Shop', *Contemporary Women's Poetry*, p. 36.

37 Alvi, 'The Sari' (*The Country at My Shoulder* 1993), *Carrying My Wife*, p. 137.

38 Alvi, 'Hindi Urdu Bol Chaal' (*A Bowl of Warm Air* 1996), ibid., p. 71.

39 C. L. Innes, 'Accent and Identity: Women Poets of Many Parts', *Contemporary British Poetry: Essays in Theory and Criticism*, eds. James Acheson and Romana Huk (State University of New York Press, 1996), pp. 330–31. Innes has also published *A History of Black and Asian Writing in Britain: 1700–2000* (Cambridge University Press, 2002).

40 Bhatt, 'Search for my Tongue' (*Brunizem*), *Point No Point*, p. 35.

41 Khalvati, 'Turning the Page', *In White Ink*, p. 41.

42 Valerie Bloom, 'Show Dem', *Touch Mi Tell Mi* (London: Bogle-L'Ouverture, 1983), p. 60.

43 James Berry, Introduction, *News from Babylon* (London: Chatto & Windus, 1984), pp. xii–xxv.

44 'Grace Nichols,' *Six Women Poets*, ed. Judith Kinsman (Oxford University Press, 1992), p. 31.

45 Nichols, 'Epilogue', *i is a long-memoried woman*, p. 87.

46 Gillian Clarke, 'Border' (*Letting in the Rumour* 1989), *Collected Poems* (Manchester: Carcanet, 1997), p. 95.

47 Menna Elfyn, 'Cân y di-lais i British Telecom', *Welsh Women's Poetry 1460–2001: An Anthology*, eds. Katie Gramich and Catherine Brennan (Dinas Powys, South Glamorgan: Honno Classics, 2003), pp. 284–87.

48 Gramich, *Welsh Women's Poetry*, p. xlii.

49 Gwyneth Lewis, 'Two Rivers', *Welsh Women's Poetry*, pp. 327–29.

50 Kathleen Jamie, 'Arraheids', *The Queen of Sheba* (Newcastle upon Tyne: Bloodaxe Books, 1994), pp. 11, 40.

51 Liz Lochhead, 'Inter-City', *Dreaming Frankenstein and Collected Poems* (Edinburgh: Polygon, 1984), p. 33.

52 Mary O'Malley, 'The Shape of Saying', *Where the Rocks Float* (Galway: Salmon, 1993), pp. 12–13.

53 Gramich, *Welsh Women's Poetry*, pp. xli–xlii; Linden Peach, 'Wales and the Cultural Politics of Identity: Gillian Clarke, Robert Minhinnick, and Jeremy Hooker', *Contemporary British Poetry*, p. 374.

54 Jean 'Binta' Breeze, 'Can A Dub Poet Be A Woman?', *Women: a cultural review* 1.1 (April 1990), pp. 47–49.

55 Christian Haberkost, *Verbal Riddim: The Politics and Aesthetics of African-Caribbean Dub Poetry* (Amsterdam: Rodopi, 1993), p. 203.

56 Patience Agbabi, 'Rappin' it Up', *R. A. W.* (London: Gecko Press, 1995), p. 63.

57 Lochhead, 'Kidspoem/Bairnsang', *Penguin Modern Poets Vol. 4* (Harmondsworth: Penguin, 1995), p. 61.

58 Kathleen Jamie, 'Meadowsweet', *Jizzen* (London: Picador, 1999), p. 49.

59 Peggy O'Brien, Editor's Preface, *The Wake Forest Book of Irish Women's Poetry 1967–2000* (Winston Salem: Wake Forest University Press, 1999), p. xvii.

60 Letter to Alice Entwistle (9 March 2004).

61 Eavan Boland, 'Gods Make Their Own Importance: The authority of the poets in our time', *PN Review* 21.4 (1995), p. 11.

62 Eavan Boland, 'The Woman, The Place, The Poet', *PN Review* 17.3 (1991), p. 35.

63 Eavan Boland, 'A Woman Painted on a Leaf', (*In A Time of Violence* 1994), *Collected Poems*, p. 210.

64 Eavan Boland, 'The Harbour', *The Lost Land* (New York: W. W. Norton, 1998), p. 14.

65 Jody Allen-Randolph, 'An Interview with Eavan Boland', *PN Review* 20.1 (1993), p. 55.

66 Ibid., p. 54.

67 Boland, 'The Muse Mother' (*Night Feed* 1982), *Collected Poems*, p. 93.

68 Boland, 'The Journey' (*The Journey* 1986), ibid., pp. 120–22.

69 Ibid., pp. 121–22.

70 Boland, 'Letter to a Young Woman Poet', *PN Review* 24.2 (November/December 1997), p. 19.

71 Boland, 'Anna Liffey', *Collected Poems*, pp. 202, 205.

PART III 10

1 See extract from 'Discourse in life and Discourse in Art', Voloshinov/Bakhtin, *The Bakhtin Reader: Selected Writings of Bakhtin, Medvedev, Voloshinov*, ed. Pam Morris (London: Edward Arnold, 1994), pp. 160–73.

2 See Chapter 5, notes 13 and 14.

3 Ian Gregson, *Contemporary Poetry and Postmodernism: Dialogue and Estrangement* (Basingstoke: Macmillan, 1996), p. 9.

4 Maggie Hannan, 'Life Model', (*Liar, Jones*, 1995), *New Blood*, ed. Neil Astley (Newcastle upon Tyne: Bloodaxe Books, 1999), pp. 141–42.

5 Hannan, *New Blood*, p. 140.

6 M. M. Bakhtin 'Problems of Dostoevsky's Poetics' (1963), *The Bakhtin Reader: Selected Writings of Bakhtin, Medvedev, Voloshinov*, ed. Pam Morris (London: Edward Arnold, 1994), pp. 105–7.

7 Carol Ann Duffy, 'The Dummy', *Selling Manhattan* (London: Anvil Press, 1987), p. 20.

8 Duffy, 'Yes, Officer', ibid., p. 31.

9 Gregson, *Contemporary Poetry*, p. 106.

10 Linda France, 'Selling Yourself Short', *Storyville* (Newcastle upon Tyne: Bloodaxe Books, 1997), p. 62.

11 Elizabeth Bartlett, 'Appointment', *Two Women Dancing: New and Selected Poems* (Newcastle upon Tyne: Bloodaxe Books, 1995), p. 202.

12 Rumens, Introduction to Bartlett, *Two Women Dancing*, p. 15.

13 Sylvia Kantaris, *Lad's Love* (Newcastle upon Tyne: Bloodaxe Books, 1993), p. 58.

14 Bakhtin, 'Problems of Dostoevsky's Poetics', p. 108.

15 Jackie Kay, 'Condemned Property', *Other Lovers* (Newcastle upon Tyne: Bloodaxe Books, 1993), p. 54.

16 Carol Ann Duffy, 'Head of English', *Standing Female Nude* (London: Anvil Press, 1985), p. 12.

17 Carol Ann Duffy, 'Eurydice', *The World's Wife* (London: Picador, 1999), pp. 58–61.

18 Vicki Feaver, 'The Handless Maiden', *The Handless Maiden* (London: Jonathan Cape, 1994), p. 12.

19 Lavinia Greenlaw, 'Hurting Small Animals', *New Women Poets* (1987), ed. Carol Rumens (Newcastle upon Tyne: Bloodaxe Books, 1990), p. 165.

20 Bakhtin, 'Problems of Dostoevsky's Poetics', p. 108.

21 Duffy, 'Psychopath', *Selling Manhattan*, pp. 28–29.

22 Bakhtin, 'Problems of Dostoevsky's Poetics', pp. 107, 112.

23 Duffy, 'Lizzie, Six', *Standing Female Nude*, p. 13.

24 Selima Hill, 'A Voice in the Garden', *Saying Hello at the Station* (London: Chatto & Windus, 1984), p. 29.

25 Carol Rumens, 'Rules for Beginners' (*Unplayed Music*, 1981), *Thinking of Skins: New and Selected Poems* (Newcastle upon Tyne: Bloodaxe Books, 1993), p. 60.

26 Duffy, 'A Clear Note', *Standing Female Nude*, pp. 27–31.

27 Tracey Herd, 'Big Girls', *No Hiding Place* (Newcastle upon Tyne: Bloodaxe Books, 1996), p. 40.

28 U. A. Fanthorpe, 'Washing up', *A Watching Brief* (Calstock: Peterloo Poets, 1987), pp. 30–31; Feaver, 'Women's Blood', *Handless Maiden*, p. 19.

29 Hill, 'My Sister's Sister', *Violet* (Newcastle upon Tyne: Bloodaxe Books: 1997), pp. 11–32.

30 Gregson, *Contemporary Poetry*, p. 7.

31 Ann Sansom, 'Voice', *Romance* (Newcastle upon Tyne: Bloodaxe Books, 1994), Deryn Rees-Jones, 'And Please Do Not Presume', *The Memory Tray* (Bridgend: Seren, 1994); Maura Dooley, ed., *Making for Planet Alice: new women poets* (Newcastle upon Tyne: Bloodaxe Books, 1997), pp. 163, 151.

32 Rees-Jones, 'It Will Not Do', *Making for Planet Alice*, p. 152.

33 Mimi Khalvati, 'Stone of Patience', *In White Ink* (Manchester: Carcanet, 1991); *Making for Planet Alice*, pp. 112–13.

34 Sarah Maguire, 'On *Spilt Milk*', *PBS Bulletin* (1991), repr. in *Don't Ask Me What I Mean: Poets in their own words*, eds. Clare Brown and Don Paterson (London: Picador, 2003), p. 171.

35 Moniza Alvi, 'Missing', *Carrying My Wife* (Newcastle upon Tyne: Bloodaxe Books, 2000), p. 3; Astley, *New Blood*, p. 108.

36 Alvi, *New Blood*, p. 107.
37 Rees-Jones, 'Service Wash', *The Memory Tray*; *Making for Planet Alice*, p. 149.
38 Jo Shapcott, 'Superman Sounds Depressed', *Her Book: Poems 1988–1998* (London: Faber, 2000), pp. 46–47.
39 Kay, *New Blood*, p. 73.
40 Feaver, 'The Singing Teacher', *Handless Maiden*, p. 18.
41 Feaver, 'Lacrimae Hominis', 'French Lesson', ibid., pp. 43, 32.
42 Sujata Bhatt, 'The Multicultural Poem', *Augatora* (Manchester: Carcanet, 2000), pp. 100–3.
43 Rita Ann Higgins, 'The Deserter' (*Philomena's Revenge*, 1992), *Sunnyside Plucked: New and Selected Poems* (Newcastle upon Tyne: Bloodaxe Books, 1996), p. 63.
44 Julie O'Callaghan, 'Federal Case' in 'Opening Lines: *Dramaticules*', *What's What?* (Newcastle upon Tyne: Bloodaxe Books, 1991), p. 34.
45 Kathleen Jamie, 'The Queen of Sheba', *Mr and Mrs Scotland are Dead: Poems 1980–1994* (Tarset: Bloodaxe Books, 2002), p. 114.
46 Helen Kidd, 'Writing Near the Fault Line: Scottish Women Poets and the Topography of Tongues', *Kicking Daffodils: Twentieth-Century Women Poets*, ed. Vicki Bertram (Edinburgh University Press, 1997), p. 100.
47 Kathleen Jamie, 'Forget It', *Jizzen* (London, Picador, 1999), pp. 5–7.
48 Valerie Bloom, 'Language Barrier', *Touch Mi Tell Mi* (London: Bogle-L'Ouverture, 1983), pp. 41–42.
49 Both poems are in 'Poetry in Performance' Vol. 1 (London: 57 Productions, 2002). For an incisive discussion, see Denise de Caires Narain, 'Speaking and performing the Creole Word: the work of Valerie Bloom, Jean "Binta" Breeze, Merle Collins and Amryl Johnson', *Contemporary Caribbean Women's Poetry: Making Style* (London: Routledge, 2001), pp. 89–147.
50 Jean 'Binta' Breeze, interview with Henry Palmer, *new internationalist* 31 (March 1999).
51 'A Round-Table Discussion on Poetry in Performance', *Feminist Review* 62 (Summer 1999), p. 33.
52 C. Innes, 'Accent and Identity: Women Poets of Many Parts', *Contemporary British Poetry: Essays in Theory and Criticism*, eds. James Acheson and Romana Huk (New York: State University of New York Press, 1996), p. 339.
53 Patience Agbabi, 'UFO WOMAN (PRONOUNCED OOFOE)', *Transformatrix* (Edinburgh: Payback Press, 2000), pp. 15–16.
54 Agbabi, 'Transformatrix', ibid., p. 11.

PART III 11

1 Sr. Berenetta Quinn, *The Metamorphic Tradition in Modern Poetry: Essays on the work of Ezra Pound, Wallace Stevens, William Carlos Williams, T. S. Eliot, Hart Crane, Randall Jarrell and W. B. Yeats* (New York: Gordian Press, 1966), p. 1.
2 Paul Mills, 'The Quantum Uncertainty of the Narrator', *Poetry Review* 85.1 (Spring 1995), pp. 40–43.

3 Ibid., p. 40.

4 Ian Gregson notes 'a radically puzzled poetic mode that, in drawing on surrealism, is akin to the use of magic realism in women novelists like Angela Carter'. See *Contemporary Poetry and Postmodernism: Dialogue and Estrangement* (Basingstoke: Macmillan, 1996), p. 239.

5 Pauline Stainer, 'Quanta' (*The Ice Pilot Speaks* 1994), *The Lady and the Hare: New and Selected Poems* (Tarset: Bloodaxe Books, 2003), p. 98. Mills explains that 'Quanta of light used for measuring particles in motion affect their behaviour in ways which are unpredictable.' (p. 40.)

6 Jo Shapcott and Matthew Sweeney, eds., *Emergency Kit: Strange Poems for Strange Times* (London: Faber, 1996), p. xvii.

7 Michael Hulse, David Kennedy and David Morley, eds., *The New Poetry* (Newcastle upon Tyne: Bloodaxe Books, 1993), p. 24.

8 Helen Dunmore, quoted by David Kennedy, 'The Poetry Lab.', *Poetry Review* 83.2 (Summer 1993), p. 26.

9 Lavinia Greenlaw, 'Science for Poets', *Night Photograph* (London: Faber, 1993), p. 48. Greenlaw says, 'For me, the impulse to write a poem often comes from making sense of how things work ... pattern, machinery and design ...' See 'Interior With Extension Cord', *Strong Words: Modern Poets on Modern Poetry*, eds. W. N. Herbert and Matthew Hollis (Tarset: Bloodaxe Books, 2000), p. 275.

10 Kennedy, 'The Poetry Lab.', p. 29.

11 Maggie Hannan, 'Tap', *Liar, Jones* (Newcastle upon Tyne: Bloodaxe Books, 1995), p. 30.

12 Deryn Rees-Jones, 'Objecting to the Subject: Science, Femininity and Poetic Process in the work of Elizabeth Bishop and Lavinia Greenlaw', *Kicking Daffodils: Twentieth-Century Women Poets*, ed. Vicki Bertram (Edinburgh University Press, 1997), p. 268.

13 Anne Cluysenaar, 'Natural History', *Timeslips: New and Selected Poems* (Manchester: Carcanet, 1997), pp. 110–11.

14 Kennedy, 'The Poetry Lab.', p. 29.

15 Maura Dooley, 'Fundoscopy' (*Explaining Magnetism* 1991), *Sound Barrier: Poems 1982–2002* (Tarset: Bloodaxe Books, 2002), p. 54.

16 Greenlaw, 'The Gift of Life', *Night Photograph*, p. 21.

17 Jo Shapcott, 'Electroplating the Baby' (*Electroplating the Baby* 1988), *Her Book: Poems 1988–1998* (London: Faber, 2000), pp. 20–24.

18 Sujata Bhatt, 'Marie Curie to Her Husband' (*Brunizem* 1988), 'Counting Sheep White Blood Cells' (*Monkey Shadows* 1991), *Point No Point: Selected Poems* (Manchester: Carcanet, 1997), p. 41, pp. 84–86; Greenlaw, 'Galileo's Wife', *Night Photograph*, pp. 29–31.

19 Kennedy, 'The Poetry Lab.', p. 27.

20 Stainer, quoted in 'The Poetry Lab.', p. 26.

21 For some implications, see Gillian Beer's illuminating review, 'The Observers Observed', *Women: a cultural review* 1.3 (Winter 1990), pp. 293–303. See also Sandra Harding, 'Feminism and Theories of Scientific Knowledge', *Women: a cultural review* 1.1 (April 1990), pp. 87–97.

22 Greenlaw, 'Millefiori', *A World Where News Travelled Slowly* (London: Faber, 1997), p. 34.

23 John Berger, *Ways of Seeing* (Harmondsworth: Penguin, 1972), p. 47. For an extended discussion, see Laura Mulvey, *Visual and Other Pleasures* (London: Macmillan, 1989).

24 Describing how moving house as a child coincided with growing suddenly short-sighted, Greenlaw suspects that she 'became interested in light and the psychological effects of light because the most profound upheaval of my life was articulated for me through images of fading light'. Review, *Daily Telegraph* (8 November 2003), p. 12.

25 Hannan, quoted in 'The Poetry Lab.', p. 29.

26 Medbh McGuckian, 'Marconi's Cottage', *Marconi's Cottage* (Newcastle upon Tyne: Bloodaxe Books, 1992), p. 103. As Peggy O'Brien explains, this refers to a house McGuckian owns on the north Antrim coast which belonged to 'Guglielmo Marconi, the famous Italian engineer ... The first man to send a wireless message successfully across the span of the Atlantic, he spent his time in 1898 in that house bouncing signals off nearby Rathlin Island rehearsing for the [transmission] of these ... pioneering waves, silent and invisible but audible on impact, dilating across a huge body of water ...' See *The Wake Forest Book of Irish Women's Poetry 1967–2000*, ed. O'Brien (Winston-Salem: Wake Forest University Press, 1999), p. xv.

27 Stainer, 'Woman Holding a Balance' (*Sighting the Slave Ship*, 1992), *The Lady and the Hare*, p. 57.

28 Kennedy says, 'The scientific empiricist in [Stainer] withdraws from substantial avowal: it is this that produces the quirkily unstable frissons in her work and generates her attempts at scientific demonstrations of the sacred and vice versa.' See *The New Poetry*, p. 24.

29 Donna Haraway observes in *Primate Visions: Gender, Race and Nature in the World of Modern Science* (London: Routledge, 1990): 'Evolutionary discourse generally [is] highly narrative; story-telling is central to [its] scientific project. The narratives are complex and protean.' Extracted in 'Women Look at Science', *Women: a cultural review* 1.2 (Autumn 1990), pp. 88–104: 100.

30 Moniza Alvi, 'The World Has A Passion', *Carrying My Wife* (Newcastle upon Tyne: Bloodaxe Books, 2000), p. 56.

31 Moniza Alvi, 'The Least International Shop in the World', *Contemporary Women's Poetry: Reading/Writing/Practice*, eds. Alison Mark and Deryn Rees-Jones (Basingstoke: Macmillan, 2000), p. 39.

32 Sigmund Freud, *Standard Edition*, XXII (London: Hogarth Press and the Institute of Psychoanalysis, 1933) p. 211, cited Juliet Mitchell, 'The Question of Feminity and The Theory of Psychoanalyis', *Psychoanalysis and Woman: A Reader*, ed. Shelley Saguaro (Basingstoke and London: Macmillan, 2000), p. 129.

33 Roland Barthes, *Mythologies*, selected and trans. Annette Lavers (London: Paladin, 1973), pp. 109–11.

34 Marina Warner, *Fantastic Metamorphoses, Other Worlds: Ways of Telling The Self* (Oxford University Press, 2002), p. 2.

35 Quinn, *The Metamorphic Tradition*, p. 1.
36 Ted Hughes, *Tales from Ovid: Twenty-four passages from the metamorphoses* (London: Faber, 1997), p. viii.
37 Barthes, *Mythologies*, pp. 155–56.
38 Hughes, *Tales from Ovid*, p. ix.
39 Quinn, *The Metamorphic Tradition*, p. 11.
40 Hélène Cixous and Catherine Clements, *The Newly Born Woman*, trans. Betsy Wing, *The Theory and History of Literature Vol. 24* (Manchester University Press, 1986), p. 67.
41 Ibid., p. 79.
42 Ibid., pp. 87; 91.
43 Stevie Smith, 'My Muse' (1960), *Stevie Smith: A Selection*, ed. Hermione Lee (London: Faber, 1983), p. 151.
44 Kathleen Jamie, 'Holding Fast – Truth and Change in Poetry', *Strong Words*, p. 279.
45 'Sheenagh Pugh', interview with Richard Poole, *Poetry Wales* 30.3 (January 1995), pp. 39–44.
46 Annemarie Austin, 'Shape-Shifting', *On the Border* (Newcastle upon Tyne: Bloodaxe Books, 1993), p. 35.
47 Sarah Maguire, 'Postmodernism', *Poetry Review* 84.1 (Spring 1994), 69.
48 Deryn Rees-Jones, 'The Nothing That Is Not There and the Nothing That Is', *Contemporary Women's Poetry*, p. 60.
49 U. A. Fanthorpe, 'Only Here for the Bier' (*Standing To* 1982), *Selected Poems* (Harmondsworth, Penguin, 1986), p. 51; 'Penelope Shuttle', *Don't Ask*, p. 263.
50 Janet Philips, 'The Shape-shifter', interview with Jo Shapcott, *Poetry Review* 91.1 (2001), p. 21.
51 Shapcott, 'Thetis' (*My Life Asleep* 1998), *Her Book*, p. 87.
52 Carol Ann Duffy, 'Thetis', *The World's Wife* (London: Picador, 1999), pp. 5–6.
53 Duffy, 'Pygmalion's Bride', ibid., pp. 51–52.
54 Duffy, 'Circe', ibid., pp. 47–48: p. 47.
55 Duffy, 'Medusa', ibid., pp. 40–41: p. 41.
56 Kennedy, 'The Poetry Lab.', p. 29.
57 Shapcott, 'Pavlova's Physics' (*Phrase Book* 1992), *Her Book*, pp. 41–42.
58 Mills, 'The Quantum Uncertainty', p. 41.
59 Linda France, 'Dreaming True', *Red* (Newcastle upon Tyne: Bloodaxe Books, 1992), pp. 16–18.
60 Mills, 'The Quantum Uncertainty', p. 43.
61 Stainer, 'Quanta', 'The Ice Pilot Speaks' (*The Ice Pilot Speaks* 1994), *The Lady and the Hare*, pp. 68, 98; Dooley, 'More than Twice the Speed of Sound' (*Kissing A Bone* 1996), *Sound Barrier*, p. 132.
62 Shapcott, 'The Mad Cow Talks Back' (*Phrase Book* 1992), *Her Book*, p. 69.
63 'Jo Shapcott Reads' (Cassette) *The Poetry Quartets 5: Helen Dunmore, U. A. Fanthorpe, Elizabeth Jennings, Jo Shapcott* (Newcastle upon Tyne: Bloodaxe Books, 1999).
64 Philips, 'The Shape-shifter,' p. 21.

65 Shapcott, 'Mad Cow Dance' (*Phrase Book*), *Her Book*, pp. 73–74.
66 Shapcott, 'The Mad Cow Tries to Write the Good Poem' (*Phrase Book*), ibid., p. 76.
67 Shapcott, 'The Mad Cow in Love' (*Phrase Book*), ibid., pp. 71–72.
68 Shapcott, 'The Mad Cow in Space' (*My Life Asleep*), 'The Mad Cow Believes She is the Spirit of the Weather' (*Phrase Book*), *Her Book*, pp. 108, 79.

PART III 12

1 In between the writing and publishing of this chapter, 'Next Generation Poets' was used as the title for a poetry promotion by the Poetry Book Society in October 2004.
2 Eavan Boland, 'Tirade for the Lyric Muse' (*The Journey* 1986), *Collected Poems* (Manchester: Carcanet, 1995), pp. 130–31.
3 Sarah Maguire, 'Poetry Makes Nothing Happen', *Strong Words: Modern Poets on Modern Poetry*, eds. W. N. Herbert and Matthew Hollis (Tarset: Bloodaxe Books, 2000), p. 251.
4 Anne Stevenson, 'Purifying the Cistern', *PN Review* 26.3 (2000), pp. 34–39.
5 Grace Nichols, 'A Poem for Us', *Lazy Thoughts of a Lazy Woman and other poems* (London: Virago, 1989), p. 48.
6 Carol Rumens, 'Stealing The Genre', *Thinking of Skins: New and Selected Poems* (Newcastle upon Tyne: Bloodaxe Books, 1993), p. 36; 'As Radical as Reality', interview with Marion Lomax, *Poetry Review* 88.4 (Winter 1998/9), p. 79.
7 Rumens, *Thinking of Skins*, p. 36; 'As Radical as Reality', pp. 79–80.
8 Stevie Smith, 'My Muse' (1960), *Stevie Smith: A Selection*, ed. Hermione Lee (London: Faber, 1983), p. 151; 'Ruth Fainlight', *The Bloodaxe Book of Contemporary Women Poets: Eleven British Writers*, ed. Jeni Couzyn (Newcastle upon Tyne: Bloodaxe Books, 1985), p. 130.
9 Elaine Feinstein, 'Muse' (*City Music* 1990), *Collected Poems and Translations* (Manchester: Carcanet, 2002), p. 126.
10 Linda France, 'The Nine Muses', 'My Muse, the Whore', *Storyville* (Newcastle upon Tyne: Bloodaxe Books, 1997), p. 51; pp. 79–80.
11 Rumens, 'The Muse of Argument', *Thinking of Skins*, p. 21.
12 Carol Rumens, 'In the Bedroom of the Page', *Poetry Wales* 30.2 (September 1994), pp. 33–34: 34.
13 France, 'My Muse, the Whore', *Storyville*, p. 79.
14 Jo Shapcott, interview with John Stammers, *Poetry London* 36 (Summer 2000), p. 36.
15 Sylvia Kantaris, 'The Tenth Muse' (*The Tenth Muse* 1983), *Dirty Washing: New and Selected Poems* (Newcastle upon Tyne: Bloodaxe Books, 1989), p. 18.
16 Rumens, 'In the Bedrooom of the Page', p. 33.
17 Jo Shapcott, 'Muse' (*Phrase Book* 1992), *Her Book: Poems 1988–1998* (London: Faber, 2000), p. 58.
18 Denise Levertov, 'She and the Muse' (*Candles in Babylon* 1982), *Selected Poems* (Newcastle upon Tyne: Bloodaxe Books, 1986), p. 164.

19 Wendy Cope, 'Poem Composed in Santa Barbara', *Serious Concerns* (London: Faber, 1992), p. 36.

20 Shapcott, 'On Tour: The Alps' (*Phrase Book*), *Her Book*, p. 64.

21 Wendy Cope, 'A Policeman's Lot', *Making Cocoa for Kingsley Amis* (London: Faber, 1986), p. 15; 'A Nursery Rhyme', *Making Cocoa*, pp. 18, 19; 'Waste Land Limericks', *Making Cocoa*, pp. 20–21.

22 U. A. Fanthorpe, 'Seminar: Felicity and Mr Frost' (*Voices Off* 1984), *Selected Poems* (Harmondsworth: Penguin, 1986), p. 113.

23 Grace Nichols, 'Spring', *The Fat Black Woman's Poems* (London: Virago, 1984), p. 34; Introduction, *Kicking Daffodils: Twentieth-Century Women Poets*, ed. Vicki Bertram (Edinburgh University Press, 1997), p. [1].

24 Gillian Clarke, 'Overheard in County Sligo' (*Letting in the Rumour* 1989), *Collected Poems* (Manchester: Carcanet, 1997), p. 97; Selima Hill, 'Down by the Salley Gardens', *Saying Hello at the Station* (London: Chatto & Windus, 1984), p. 42.

25 Kantaris, 'The Whitsun Trainspotters', *Dirty Washing*, p. 126; Strugnell first featured in *Making Cocoa*, pp. 45–65. He reappears briefly in later volumes.

26 Lyn Pykett, 'Women Poets and "Women's Poetry"': Fleur Adcock, Gillian Clarke and Carol Rumens', *British Poetry from the 1950s to the 1990s: Politics and Art*, eds. Gary Day and Thomas Docherty (Basingstoke: Macmillan, 1997), pp. 253–67: p. 258.

27 Fleur Adcock, 'Roles' (*Time Zones* 1991), *Poems 1960–2000* (Newcastle upon Tyne: Bloodaxe Books, 1993), p. 203.

28 Feinstein, 'Amy Levy' (*Daylight* 1997), *Collected Poems*, p. 156.

29 Shapcott, 'Robert Watches Elizabeth Knitting' (*Electroplating the Baby* 1988), *Her Book*, pp. 31–32.

30 See the numerous tributes in *The Way You Say The World: A celebration for Anne Stevenson*, eds. John Lucas and Matt Simpson (Beeston, Nottingham: Shoestring Press, 2003).

31 Rumens, 'The Fuchsia Knight', *Thinking of Skins*, p. 35.

32 Boland, 'The Serinette Principle', *PN Review* 19.4 (1993), p. 20.

33 Catherine Kerrigan, Introduction, *An Anthology of Scottish Women Poets*, ed. Kerrigan (Edinburgh University Press, 1991), p. 2. See also *Modern Scottish Women Poets*, eds. Dorothy McMillan and Michel Byrne (Edinburgh: Canongate, 2003), p. xxxiv; *Welsh Women's Poetry 1460–2001: An Anthology*, eds. Katie Gramich and Catherine Brennan (Dinas Powys, South Glamorgan: Honno Classics, 2003), p. xxi.

34 See Virginia Woolf: 'I would venture to guess that Anon, who wrote so many poems without signing them, was often a woman.' *A Room of One's Own* (London: Grafton, 1977), pp. 50–51.

35 Pauline Stainer, 'The Ballad of the Lock-Keeper's Daughter', 'The Ballad of the Abbot's Fish Pond' (*The Honeycomb* 1989), *The Lady and the Hare: New and Selected Poems* (Tarset: Bloodaxe Books, 2003), pp. 18, 21; Alice Oswald, 'Ballad of a Shadow', *The Thing in the Gap-Stone Stile* (Oxford University Press, 1996), p. 25.

36 Denise Riley, 'A Shortened Set', '*Lure, 1963*', 'Rayon', *Mop Mop Georgette: New and Selected Poems 1986–1993* (London: Reality Street Editions, 1993) pp. 16–24; 30; 41; Romana Huk, 'Denise Riley in conversation' with Romana Huk, *PN Review* 21.5 (1995), pp. 17–22.

37 Riley, 'True North', *Mop Mop Georgette*, p. 40. See also, among many, 'Knowing in the real world', pp. 33–34; 'Poem beginning with a Line from Proverbs', p. 35; 'Lyric', p. 36.

38 'Liz Lochhead', *Six Women Poets*, ed. Judith Kinsman (Oxford University Press, 1992), p. 119; Liz Lochhead, 'Mirror's Song', *Dreaming Frankenstein and Collected Poems 1967–84* (Edinburgh: Polygon, 1984), pp. 67–68.

39 France, 'Weighing the Heart', *The Gentleness of the Very Tall* (Newcastle upon Tyne: Bloodaxe Books, 1994), pp. 26–28. See also *Storyville*, pp. 10–24.

40 Jackie Kay, 'The Same Note', *Other Lovers* (Newcastle upon Tyne: Bloodaxe Books, 1993), p. 12. See also 'In the Pullman, p. 10; 'The Right Season', p. 11; 'The Red Graveyard', pp. 13–14; 'Twelve Bar Bessie', p. 15.

41 Peter Forbes, 'Elizabeth Garrett', *New Generation Poets: A Poetry Review, Poetry Review* 84.1 (Spring 1994), p. 44.

42 Elizabeth Garrett, 'Love's Parallel', *A Two-Part Invention* (Newcastle upon Tyne: Bloodaxe Books, 1998), p. 36.

43 Stevenson, 'Purifying the Cistern', pp. 34–39. For Stevenson, the inherent musicality of poetic language precisely renders it unusable for political purposes. See 'Defending the Freedom of the Poet/Music Under the Skin', *Contemporary Women's Poetry: Reading/Writing/Practice*, eds. Alison Mark and Deryn Rees-Jones (London: Macmillan, 2000), pp. 1–11.

44 Stevenson, 'Arioso Dolente', *Granny Scarecrow* (Newcastle upon Tyne: Bloodaxe Books, 2000), p. 20.

45 Clarke, 'Cofiant' (*Letting in the Rumour* 1989), *Collected Poems*, pp. 121–36.

46 In 1994 Clarke noted, 'For the past ten years, the poetic sequence, with its freedom to let theme and image play out their lines over deep waters, its need for rapt concentration, has become my habitual way into poetry.' See *A Calendar of Modern Poetry, PN Review* 21.2 (November/December 1994), p. 80.

47 For example, see Pamela Gillilan, 'Semi-detached', *All-Steel Traveller: New and Selected Poems* (Newcastle upon Tyne: Bloodaxe Books, 1994), p. 45; Vicki Feaver, 'Crab-Apple Jelly', *The Handless Maiden* (London: Cape, 1994), pp. 13–14; Carol Ann Duffy, 'The Way My Mother Speaks' (*The Other Country* 1990), *Selected Poems*, p. 88; Selima Hill, 'Chicken Feathers', (*Saying Hello at the Station* 1984), *Trembling Hearts in the Bodies of Dogs: New and Selected Poems* (Newcastle upon Tyne: Bloodaxe Books, 1994), pp. 21–24; Susan Wicks, 'Dispersal', *The Clever Daughter* (London: Faber, 1996), p. 21.

48 Jean Earle, 'Jugged Hare', *Selected Poems* (Bridgend: Seren, 1990), p. 16.

49 Maura Dooley, 'Mirror', *Sound Barrier: 1982–2002* (Tarset: Bloodaxe Books, 2002), p. 149.

50 Christina Dunhill, Introduction, *As Girls Could Boast: New poetry by women*, ed. Dunhill (London: The Oscars Press, 1994), p. 9.

51 Kantaris, 'In Passing', *Dirty Washing*, pp. 119–25; Maura Dooley, 'Mansize' (*Explaining Magnetism* 1991), *Sound Barrier*, p. 64. Wicks's *The Clever Daughter* contains some subtle treatments of this relationship.

52 Deborah Randall, *White Eyes, Dark Ages* (Newcastle upon Tyne: Bloodaxe Books, 1993).

53 Sheenagh Pugh, 'Toast', *The Beautiful Lie* (Bridgend: Seren, 2002), pp. 66–67; 'Envying Owen Beattie', *Stonelight* (Bridgend: Seren, 1999), pp. 21–22.

54 Deryn Rees-Jones, 'The Nothing That Is Not There and the Nothing That Is', *Contemporary Women's Poetry*, p. 58.

55 Pugh is notoriously impatient of critical moves to gender poetry: 'I think there is a simpler name for it than women's poetry, black poetry or whatever … mediocre. I object violently to being shunted into some sub-group of humanity and judged as being anything but an individual.' See 'Symposium: Is there a women's poetry', *Poetry Wales* 23.1 (1987), p. 31.

56 Nichols, 'On Poems and Crotches', *Lazy Thoughts*, p. 16.

57 France, 'The Eater of Wives', *The Gentleness of the Very Tall*, p. 47.

58 Sujata Bhatt, 'Shérdi' (*Brunizem* 1988), *Point No Point: Selected Poems* (Manchester: Carcanet, 1997), p. 20; Helen Dunmore, 'Wild Strawberries' (*The Raw Garden* 1988), *Out of the Blue: Poems 1976–2001* (Newcastle upon Tyne: Bloodaxe Books, 2001).

59 Maggie Hannan, 'You Sign 6', *Liar, Jones* (Newcastle upon Tyne: Bloodaxe Books, 1995), p. 36.

60 Elaine Feinstein, 'Urban Lyric' (*City Music*), *Collected Poems*, p. 115.

61 Denise Levertov, 'Wondering', *Sands of the Well* (Newcastle upon Tyne: Bloodaxe Books, 1998), p. 9.

62 Medbh McGuckian, 'Black Note Study', *Captain Lavender* (Oldcastle: The Gallery Press, 1994), p. 39.

63 'Medbh McGuckian', *Sleeping with Monsters: conversations with Scottish and Irish women poets*, eds. Gillean Somerville-Arjat and Rebecca E. Wilson (Edinburgh: Polygon, 1991), p. 2.

64 Letter to Alice Entwistle (9 March 2004).

65 'Medbh McGuckian', *Sleeping with Monsters*, p. 2.

66 McGuckian, 'Elegy for an Irish Speaker', *Captain Lavender*, pp. 42–43.

67 Elmer Andrews, '"Some Sweet Disorder" – the poetry of subversion: Paul Muldoon, Tom Paulin and Medbh McGuckian', *British Poetry from the 1950s*, pp. 118–42: 139.

68 Clair Wills, *Improprieties: Politics and Sexuality in Northern Irish Poetry* (Oxford: Clarendon, 1993), pp. 158–93.

69 McGuckian, 'Venus and the Rain', *Venus and the Rain* (Oldcastle: The Gallery Press, 1994) p. 32; 'Medbh McGuckian', *Sleeping with Monsters*, p. 5.

70 McGuckian, 'The Flower Master' (*The Flower Master* 1993), *Selected Poems 1978–1994* (Oldcastle: The Gallery Press, 1994), p. 24; 'A Different Same', *Marconi's Cottage* (Newcastle upon Tyne: Bloodaxe Books, 1992), p. 49.

AFTERWORD

1 Germaine Greer, 'To the Reader', *101 Poems by 101 Women* (London: Faber, 2001), p. ix.

2 Maura Dooley, ed., Making for Planet Alice: *new women poets* (Newcastle upon Tyne: Bloodaxe Books, 1997), p. 12.

3 Carol Rumens, 'My Leaky Coracle', *Poetry Review* 86.4 (Winter 1996/97), p. 26.

4 Ann Sansom, 'Base Linguistics', *Romance* (Newcastle upon Tyne: Bloodaxe Books, 1994), p. 9.

5 Kathleen Jamie, *Don't Ask Me What I Mean: Poets in their own words,* eds. Clare Brown and Don Paterson (London: Picador, 2003), pp. 127–28.

6 Sally Minogue, 'Prescriptions and Proscriptions: Feminist Criticism and Contemporary Poetry', *Some Problems for Feminist Criticism,* ed. Minogue (London: Routledge, 1990), pp. 179–236.

7 Eavan Boland, *Object Lessons: The Life of the Woman and the Poet in Our Time* (Manchester: Carcanet, 1995), pp. 253–54.

Bibliography

POETRY WORKS BY BRITISH AND IRISH WOMEN 1900–2000

The following poets are British born, published in Britain and / or judged to have made a significant impact on poetry in Britain.
(The occasional missing date or detail has eluded our enquiries.)

Valentine Ackland 1906–69

1933 *Whether a Dove or a Seagull* (with Sylvia Townsend Warner) New York: Viking; London: Chatto & Windus, 1934

1957 *Twenty Eight Poems* Privately printed, London and Wells: Clare, Son & Co. Ltd

1970 *Later Poems by Valentine Ackland* London and Wells: Clare, Son & Co. Ltd

1973 *The Nature of the Moment* London: Chatto & Windus

1978 *Further Poems of Valentine Ackland* Kent: Welmont Publishing

Anna Adams b. 1926

1969 *A Journey Through Winter and other poems* Manchester: Manchester Institute of Contemporary Art

1975 *Parabola* West Kirby: Headland Publications

1978 *Unchanging Seas* West Kirby: Headland Publications

1979 *A Reply to Intercepted Mail* Liskeard: Peterloo Poets

1983 *An Island Chapter* Hebden Bridge: Littlewood Press

1983 *Brother Fox* Ashington, Northumberland: MIDNAG

1986 *Dear Vincent* Todmorden: Arc Publications

1986 *Trees in Sheep Country* Liskeard: Peterloo Poets

1987 *Six Legs Good* Hitchin: Mandeville

1988 *Angels of Soho* London: Royal Academy

1990 *Nobodies* Calstock: Peterloo Poets

1991 *Island Chapters* Todmorden: Arc Publications

1994 *Life on Limestone* Otley: Smith Settle

1996 *Green Resistance: New and Selected Poems* London: Enitharmon
1996 *A Paper Ark* Calstock: Peterloo Poets

Fleur Adcock b. *1934*

1964 *The Eye of the Hurricane* Wellington, New Zealand: Reed
1967 *Tigers* Oxford University Press
1971 *High Tide in the Garden* Oxford University Press
1974 *The Scenic Route* Oxford University Press
1979 *The Inner Harbour* Oxford University Press
1979 *Below Loughrigg* Newcastle upon Tyne: Bloodaxe Books
1983 *Selected Poems* Oxford University Press
1986 *The Incident Book* Oxford University Press
1986 *Hotspur. A Ballad for Music* Newcastle upon Tyne: Bloodaxe Books
1988 *Meeting the Comet* Newcastle upon Tyne: Bloodaxe Books
1991 *Time Zones* Oxford University Press
1997 *Looking Back* Oxford University Press
2000 *Poems 1960–2000* Newcastle upon Tyne: Bloodaxe Books

Patience Agbabi b. *1965*

1995 *R. A. W.* London: Gecko Press
2000 *Transformatrix* Edinburgh: Payback Press

Gillian Allnutt b. *1949*

1981 *Spitting the Pips Out* London: Sheba Feminist Publishers
1987 *Beginning the Avocado* London: Virago
1994 *Blackthorn* Newcastle upon Tyne: Bloodaxe Books
1997 *Nantucket and the Angel* Newcastle upon Tyne: Bloodaxe Books

Moniza Alvi b. *1954*

1993 *The Country at My Shoulder* Oxford University Press
1996 *A Bowl of Warm Air* Oxford University Press
2000 *Carrying My Wife* Newcastle upon Tyne: Bloodaxe Books

Nuala Archer b. *1955*

1981 *Whale on the Line* Dublin: The Gallery Press
1989 *Two Women, Two Shores* (with Medbh McGuckian) Co. Clare: Salmon
1992 *The Hour of Pan/Amā* Galway: Salmon
1995 *From a Mobile Home* Galway: Salmon

Pat Arrowsmith b. 1930

1975 *Breakout: Poems and Drawings from Prison* Edinburgh: Edinburgh Student Publications Board
1990 *Nine Lives* St Albans: Brentham Press
2000 *Drawing to Extinction* London: Hearing Eye

Annemarie Austin b. 1943

1987 *The Weather Coming* Stamford: Taxus
1993 *On the Border* Newcastle upon Tyne: Bloodaxe Books
1995 *The Flaying of Marsyas* Newcastle upon Tyne: Bloodaxe Books
1999 *Door Upon Door* Newcastle upon Tyne: Bloodaxe Books

Elizabeth Bartlett b. 1924

1979 *A Lifetime of Dying* Liskeard: Peterloo Poets
1983 *Strange Territory* Liskeard: Peterloo Poets
1986 *The Czar is Dead* London: Rivelin Grapheme
1991 *Instead of a Mass* West Kirby: Headland
1991 *Look, No Face* Bradford: Redbeck Press
1995 *Two Women Dancing: New and Selected Poems* Newcastle upon Tyne: Bloodaxe Books

Joan Barton b. 1908

1972 *The Mistress and Other Poems* Yorkshire: Sonus Press
1981 *A House Under Old Sarum: New and Selected Poems* Liskeard: Peterloo Poets
1983 *Night Journey on the Plain: Sixteen New Poems* Salisbury: self-published

Patricia Beer 1924–99

1959 *The Loss of the Magyar and Other Poems* London: Longman
1963 *The Survivors* London: Longman
1967 *Just Like the Resurrection* London: Macmillan
1971 *The Estuary* London: Macmillan
1975 *Driving West* London: Victor Gollancz
1979 *Selected Poems* London: Hutchinson
1983 *The Lie of the Land* London: Hutchinson
1988 *Collected Poems* Manchester: Carcanet
1993 *Friend of Heraclitus* Manchester: Carcanet
1997 *Autumn* Manchester: Carcanet

Frances Bellerby 1889–1975

1946 *Plash Mill and Other Poems* London: Peter Davies
1949 *The Brightening Cloud and Other Poems* London: Peter Davies
1957 *The Stone Angel and the Stone Man* Plymouth, Ted Wilkins
1970 *The Stuttering Water* Kent: ARC 7
1970 *Selected Poems* (ed. Charles Causley) London: Enitharmon
1972 *A Possible Prayer for New Year's Day* (one poem) Privately printed
1975 *The First-Known and Other Poems* London: Enitharmon
1975 *In Memory of Frances Bellerby* (2 poems and photograph), London: Enitharmon
1986 *Selected Poems* (ed. Anne Stevenson, introduced by Robert Gittings) London: Enitharmon

Louise ('Miss Lou') Bennett b. 1919

1942 *Jamaica Dialect Verses* Jamaica: George R. Bowen
1966 *Jamaica Labrish* Jamaica: Sangster's Book Stores
1983 *Selected Poems* Jamaica: Sangster's Book Stores

Connie Bensley b. 1929

1981 *Progress Report* Liskeard: Peterloo Poets
1984 *Moving In* Liskeard: Peterloo Poets
1990 *Central Reservations: New and Selected Poems* Newcastle upon Tyne: Bloodaxe Books
1994 *Choosing to be a Swan* Newcastle upon Tyne: Bloodaxe Books
2000 *The Back and the Front of It* Newcastle upon Tyne: Bloodaxe Books

Stella Benson 1892–1933

1935 *Poems* London: Macmillan

Anne Beresford b. 1929

1967 *Walking Without Moving* London: Turret Books
1968 *The Lair* London: Rapp and Whiting
1972 *Footsteps on Snow* London: Agenda Editions III
1975 *The Curving Shore* London: Agenda Editions
1980 *The Songs of Almut From God's Country* Yoxford: Yoxford Publications
1980 *Love Songs A Thracian Taught Me* London: Marion Boyars
1988 *The Sele Of The Morning* London: Agenda Editions/Turret Books
1994 *Landscape with Figures* London: Agenda Editions
1997 *Selected and New Poems* London: Agenda Editions
1998 *No Place For Cowards* London: Katabasis

Caroline Bergvall b. 1962

1989 *An Oblique View of a Room in Movement* (illustrated by Guri Dahl) London: Monolith
1993 *Strange Passage: a Choral Poem* Cambridge: Equipage
1995 *Alterran Poetry Assemblage* compilation
1996 *Éclat* Lowestoft: Sound and Language
1999 *Goan Atom 1* Rem Press

Sujata Bhatt b. 1956

1988 *Brunizem* Manchester: Carcanet
1991 *Monkey Shadows* Manchester: Carcanet
1995 *The Stinking Rose* Manchester: Carcanet
1997 *Point No Point: Selected Poems* Manchester: Carcanet
2000 *Augatora* Manchester: Carcanet

Alison Bielski b. 1925

1965 *Twentieth-Century Flood and Other Poems* London: Outposts Publications
1970 *Across the Burning Sand* Llandysul: Gomerian Press
1971 *Monogrampoems* London: The Writers' Forum
1973 *Eve* Solihull: Aquila Publications
1973 *Zodiacpoems* Bristol: Xenia Press
1974 *Mermaid Poems* Bristol: Xenia Press
1974 *The Lovetree* Llandybïe: Triskel Poets
1979 *Discovering Islands* Bristol: Xenia Press
1980 *Seth: A poem sequence* Tenby: Hub Publications
1983 *Eagles* Port Talbot: Alun Books
1996 *That Crimson Flame: Selected Poems* University of Salzburg Press/Poetry Salzburg
1997 *The Green-Eyed Pool* University of Salzburg Press

Valerie Bloom b. 1956

1983 *Touch Mi Tell Mi* (introduced by Linton Kwesi Johnson) London: Bogle-L'Ouverture
1992 *Duppy Jamboree and Other Poems* Cambridge University Press
2000 *The World is Sweet* London: Bloomsbury

Robyn Bolam (see Marion Lomax)

Eavan Boland b. 1944

1967 *New Territory* Dublin: Allen Figgis

1975   *The War Horse* London: Gollancz; Dublin: Arlen House
1980   *In Her Own Image* Dublin: Arlen House
1981   *Introducing Eavan Boland* Princeton: Ontario Review Press
1982   *Night Feed* Dublin: Arlen House; London and Boston: Marion Boyars; Manchester: Carcanet, 1994.
1986   *The Journey and Other Poems* Dublin: Arlen House; Manchester: Carcanet 1987
1989   *Selected Poems* Manchester: Carcanet
1990   *Outside History* Manchester: Carcanet
1991   *Outside History: Selected Poems 1980–1990* New York: W. W. Norton
1994   *In A Time of Violence* Manchester: Carcanet; Dublin: Arlen House; New York: W. W. Norton
1995   *Collected Poems* Manchester: Carcanet
1996   *An Origin Like Water: Collected Poems 1967–1987* New York: W. W. Norton
1998   *The Lost Land* Manchester: Carcanet; New York: W. W. Norton

Mary Borden 1887–1968

1929   *The Forbidden Zone* (war sketches and poems) London: Heinemann

Lilian Bowes Lyon 1895–1949

1934   *The White Hare and Other Poems* London: Jonathan Cape
1936   *Bright Feather Fading* London: Jonathan Cape
1941   *Tomorrow is Revealing* London: Jonathan Cape
1943   *Evening in Stepney and Other Poems* London: Jonathan Cape
1946   *A Rough Walk Home and Other Poems* London: Jonathan Cape
1948   *Collected Poems* (introduced by C. Day Lewis) London: Jonathan Cape
1981   *Uncollected Poems* Edinburgh: Tragara

Alison Brackenbury b. 1953

1981   *Dreams of Power and Other Poems* Manchester: Carcanet
1984   *Breaking Ground and Other Poems* Manchester: Carcanet
1988   *Christmas Roses and Other Poems* Manchester: Carcanet
1991   *Selected Poems* Manchester: Carcanet
1995   *1829* Manchester: Carcanet
2000   *After Beethoven* Manchester: Carcanet

Jean 'Binta' Breeze b. 1956

1988   *Riddym Ravings and Other Poems* London: Race Today
1992   *Spring Cleaning* London: Virago

1997   *On the Edge of an Island* Newcastle upon Tyne: Bloodaxe Books
2000   *The Arrival of Brighteye* Newcastle upon Tyne: Bloodaxe Books

Vera Brittain 1896–1970

1918   *Verses of a VAD* London: Macdonald
1934   *Poems of the War and After* London: Victor Gollancz

Heather Buck b. 1926

1982   *At the Window* London: Anvil Press
1987   *The Sign of the Water Bearer* London: Anvil Press
1995   *Psyche Unbound* London: Anvil Press
1998   *Waiting for the Ferry* London: Anvil Press

May Wedderburn Cannan 1893–1973

1917   *In War Time* Oxford: Blackwell
1919   *The Splendid Days* Oxford: Blackwell
1923   *The House of Hope* (woodcuts by Phyllis Gardner) London: Humphrey
       Milford

Ethel Carnie (Holdsworth) 1886–1962

1908   *Rhymes from the Factory* Blackburn: R. Denham & Co.; Southport:
       Shackerley Literary Agency
1911   *Songs of a Factory Girl* London: Headley Brothers
1914   *Voices of Womanhood* London: Headley Brothers

Brenda Chamberlain 1912–71

1958   *The Green Heart* Oxford University Press
1962   *Tide-Race* London: Hodder and Stoughton
1965   *A Rope Of Vines* London: Hodder and Stoughton
1969   *Poems* Petersfield: Enitharmon

Debjani Chatterjee b. 1952

1989   *I Was That Woman* Frome, Somerset: Hippopotamus Press
1997   *The Sun Rises in the North* Huddersfield: Smith/Doorstep Books
1997   *A Little Bridge* (with Simon Fletcher and Basir Sultan Kazami), Hebden
       Bridge: Pennine Press
1998   *Albino Gecko* University of Salzburg Press

Tessa Rose Chester b. 1950

1996 *Provision of Light* Oxford University Press

Kate Clanchy b. 1965

1996 *Slattern* London: Chatto & Windus; Picador
1999 *Samarkand* London: Picador

Gillian Clarke b. 1937

1978 *The Sundial* Dyfed: Gomer Press
1982 *Letter from a Far Country* Manchester: Carcanet
1985 *Selected Poems* Manchester: Carcanet
1989 *Letting in the Rumour* Manchester: Carcanet
1993 *The King of Britain's Daughter* Manchester: Carcanet
1996 *Selected Poems* (new edition) Manchester: Carcanet
1997 *Collected Poems* Manchester: Carcanet
1998 *Five Fields* Manchester: Carcanet
1999 *The Animal Wall and other poems* (illustrated by Karen Pearce) Llandysul: Pônt Books

Anne Cluysenaar b. 1936

1971 *Nodes: Selected Poems 1960–1968* Dublin: Dolmen Press
1985 *Double Helix* Manchester: Carcanet
1997 *Timeslips: New and Selected Poems* Manchester: Carcanet

Margaret Postgate Cole 1893–1980

n.d. *Bits of Things* By five Girton students
1918 *Poems* London: Allen and Unwin.

Mary Elizabeth Coleridge 1861–1907

1896 *Fancy's Following* (as 'Anodos')
1897 *Fancy's Guerdon*
1908 *Poems*
1954 *The Collected Poems of Mary Coleridge* London: Rupert Hart-Davis

Gladys Mary Coles

1975 *The Sounding Circle and Other Poems* Liverpool: Rondo Publications

1977 *Sinerva and Other Poems* West Kirby: Headland
1983 *The Snow Bird Sequence* West Kirby: Headland
1984 *Liverpool Folio* London: Duckworth
1984 *Stoat, in Winter* Berkhamsted: Priapus Poets
1986 *Leafburners: New and Selected Poems* London: Duckworth
1992 *The Glass Island* London: Duckworth

Merle Collins b. 1950

1985 *Because the Dawn Breaks!* London: Karia
1992 *Rotten Pomerack* London: Virago

Wendy Cope b. 1945

1980 *Across the City* (limited edition) London: Priapus Press
1986 *Poem from a Colour Chart of House Paints* (limited edition) London: Priapus Press
1986 *Making Cocoa for Kingsley Amis* London: Faber
1988 *Does She Like Word Games?* London: Anvil Press
1988 *Men and Their Boring Arguments* London: Wykeham
1988 *Twiddling your Thumbs* London: Faber
1991 *The River Girl* London: Faber
1992 *Serious Concerns* London: Faber

Julia Copus b. 1969

1995 *The Shuttered Eye* Newcastle upon Tyne: Bloodaxe Books

Elsa Corbluth

1970 *Stone Country* Walton-on-Thames: Outposts Publications
1976 *Brown Harvest* Weymouth: Word and Action
1983 *From St Patrick's Night* Leamington: Other Branch Readings
1988 *St Patrick's Night* Calstock: Peterloo Poets

Frances Cornford 1886–1960

1910 *Poems* London: The Priory Press
1912 *Death and the Princess: a morality* Cambridge: Bowes and Bowes
1915 *Spring Morning* London: The Poetry Bookshop
1928 *Different Days* London: Hogarth
1934 *Mountains and Molehills* (illustrated by Gwen Raverat) Cambridge University Press

1948 *Travelling Home and Other Poems* (illustrated by Christopher Cornford)
     London: Cresset Press
1954 *Collected Poems* London: Cresset Press
1960 *On A Calm Shore* London: Cresset Press
1996 *Selected Poems of Frances Cornford* (ed. Jane Dowson, foreword by Hugh
     Cornford) London: Enitharmon

Jeni Couzyn b. 1942

1970 *Flying* London: Workshop Press
1972 *Monkey's Wedding* London: Jonathan Cape; London: Heinemann, 1978
1975 *Christmas in Africa* London: Heinemann
1978 *House of Changes* London: Heinemann
1978 *The Happiness Bird* Victoria, British Columbia: Sono Nis
1985 *Life by Drowning: Selected Poems* Newcastle upon Tyne: Bloodaxe Books
1993 *In the Skin House* Newcastle upon Tyne: Bloodaxe Books
2000 *Selections: The Selected Poems of Jeni Couzyn* Toronto: Excle Editions

Nancy Cunard 1896–1965

1921 *Outlaws* London: Elkin Mathews
1923 *Sublunary* London: Hodder and Stoughton
1925 *Parallax* London: Hogarth
1930 *Poems (Two) 1925* London: Aquila Press
1934 *Negro: an anthology* New York: Frederick Ungar Publishing Co.
1944 *Relève into Marquis* Derby: The Grasshopper Press
1944 *Poems for France*, ed. London: La France Libre
1949 *Poèmes à la France*, ed. Paris: Pierre Seghers
1958 *Sonnets on Spain* (unpublished)

Elizabeth Daryush 1887–1977

1917 *Verses* Oxford: Blackwell
1921 *Sonnets from Hafaz and Other Verses* London: Milford
1930 *Verses* Oxford University Press
1932 *Verses: Second Book* Oxford University Press
1933 *Verses: Third Book* Oxford University Press
1934 *Verses: Fourth Book* Oxford University Press
1935 *Selected Poems* London: Macmillan
1936 *The Last Man and Other Verses* Oxford University Press
1938 *Verses: Sixth Book* Oxford University Press
1948 *Selected Poems* (ed. Yvor Winters) New York: Swallow Press
1971 *Verses: Seventh Book* (ed. Roy Fuller) Manchester: Carcanet

1972 *Selected Poems: Verses I–VI* Manchester: Carcanet
1976 *Collected Poems* (ed. Donald Davie) Manchester: Carcanet

Imtiaz Dharker b. 1954

1988 *Purdah* Delhi: Oxford University Press
1997 *Postcards from god* Newcastle upon Tyne: Bloodaxe Books

Eva Dobell

1904 *Songs and Sonnets* London: Elkin Matthews
1919 *A Bunch of Cotswold Grasses* London: A. H. Stockwell
1925 *Snap-shots of Travel* London: Erskine Macdonald
1942 *Youth and the Swallows and Other Verse* London: Favil Press
1949 *A Gloucestershire Year* Bradford: Jongleur Press
1959 *Verses New and Old* London: Favil Press

Katie Donovan b. 1962

1993 *Watermelon Man* Newcastle upon Tyne: Bloodaxe Books
1997 *Entering the Mare* Newcastle upon Tyne: Bloodaxe Books

Maura Dooley b. 1957

1991 *Explaining Magnetism* Newcastle upon Tyne: Bloodaxe Books
1996 *Kissing A Bone* Newcastle upon Tyne: Bloodaxe Books

Hilda Doolittle ('H. D.') 1886–1961

1916 *The Sea Garden* London: St James Press; St Martin's Press, 1975
1921 *Hymen* London: The Egoist Press; New York: Henry Holt & Co.
1924 *Heliodora and Other Poems* London: Jonathan Cape; Boston: Houghton Mifflin
1940 *Collected Poems of H. D. 1925* New York: Boni & Liveright
1972 *Hermetic Definition* New York: New Directions; Manchester: Carcanet
1973 *Trilogy* New York: New Directions; Manchester: Carcanet
1983 *H. D. Collected Poems 1912–1944* (ed. Louis L. Martz) New York: New Directions
1985 *Helen in Egypt* New York: Grove Press, 1961; Manchester: Carcanet

Mary Dorcey

1982 *Kindling* London: Onlywomen Press

1991 *Moving into the Space Cleared by our Mothers* Galway: Salmon
1995 *The River That Carries Me* Galway: Salmon

Freda Downie 1929–93

1977 *A Stranger Here* London: Secker and Warburg
1981 *Plainsong* London: Secker and Warburg
1995 *Collected Poems* Newcastle upon Tyne: Bloodaxe Books

Camilla Doyle

1923 *Poems* Oxford: Blackwell
1927 *Poems* London: Ernest Benn
1937 *The General Shop and Other Poems* London: St Catherine's Press

Ann Drysdale b. 1942

1995 *The Turn of the Cucumber* Calstock : Peterloo Poets
1996 *Gay Science* Calstock : Peterloo Poets

Carol Ann Duffy b. 1955

1985 *Standing Female Nude* London: Anvil Press
1986 *Thrown Voices* (frontispiece by Eileen Cooper) London: Turret Books
1987 *Selling Manhattan* London: Anvil Press
1990 *The Other Country* London: Anvil Press
1992 *William and the ex-Prime Minister* London: Anvil Press
1993 *Mean Time* London: Anvil Press
1994 *Selected Poems* London: Penguin
1998 *The Pamphlet* London: Anvil Press
1999 *The World's Wife* London: Picador
2000 *Salmon: Poems selected and new: 1985–99* Co. Clare: Salmon

Maureen Duffy b. 1933

1968 *Lyrics for the Dog Hour* London: Hutchinson
1971 *The Venus Touch* London: Weidenfeld & Nicolson
1975 *Even Song* London: Sappho Publications
1979 *Memorials for the Quick and the Dead* London: Hamish Hamilton
1985 *Collected Poems 1949–1984* London: Hamish Hamilton

Helen Dunmore b. 1952

1983 *The Apple Fall* Newcastle upon Tyne: Bloodaxe Books

1986 *The Sea Skater* Newcastle upon Tyne: Bloodaxe Books
1988 *The Raw Garden* Newcastle upon Tyne: Bloodaxe Books
1991 *Short Days, Long Nights: New and Selected Poems* Newcastle upon Tyne:
      Bloodaxe Books
1994 *Secrets* Newcastle upon Tyne: Bloodaxe Books
1994 *Recovering a Body* Newcastle upon Tyne: Bloodaxe Books
1997 *Bestiary* Newcastle upon Tyne: Bloodaxe Books

Jane Duran b. *1944*

1991 *Boogie Woogie* London: Hearing Eye
1995 *Breathe Now, Breathe* London: Enitharmon

Jean Earle *1909–2002*

1980 *A Trial of Strength* Manchester: Carcanet
1984 *The Intent Look* Bridgend: Seren
1987 *Visiting Light* Bridgend: Seren
1990 *Selected Poems* Bridgend: Seren
1995 *The Sun in the West* Bridgend: Seren

Menna Elfyn b. *1951*

1976 *Mwyara* Llandysul: Gwasg Gomer
1977 *Stafelloedd Aros* Llandysul: Gwasg Gomer
1982 *Tro'r Haul Arno* Llandysul: Gwasg Gomer
1993 *Dal Clêr* Caerdydd: Hughes a'i Fab
1995 *Eucalyptus* Dyfed: Gomer Press
1996 *Cell Angel* (trans. Gillian Clarke et al.) Newcastle upon Tyne: Bloodaxe
      Books

Christine Evans b. *1943*

1983 *Looking Inland* Bridgend: Poetry Wales Press
1986 *Falling Back* Bridgend: Poetry Wales Press
1989 *Cometary Phases* Bridgend: Seren
1995 *Island of Dark Horses* Bridgend: Seren

Ruth Fainlight b. *1931*

1966 *Cages* London: Macmillan; USA: Dufour, 1967
1967 *Eighteen Poems from 1966* London: Turret Books
1968 *To See the Matter Clearly* London: Macmillan; USA: Dufour, 1969

1971 *Poems* (with Ted Hughes and Alan Sillitoe) London: Rainbow Press
1973 *Twenty-One Poems* London: Turret Books
1973 *The Region's Violence* London: Hutchinson
1976 *Another Full Moon* London: Hutchinson
1980 *Sibyls and Others* London: Hutchinson
1983 *Fifteen to Infinity* London: Hutchinson; Pittsburgh: Carnegie-Mellon
    University Press, 1986
1983 *Climates* Newcastle upon Tyne: Bloodaxe Books.
1987 *Selected Poems* London: Hutchinson
1990 *The Knot* London: Hutchinson
1993 *This Time of Year: a Collection of Poems* London: Sinclair Stevenson
1995 *Selected Poems* (enlarged and revised) London: Sinclair Stevenson
1997 *Sugar-paper Blue* Newcastle upon Tyne: Bloodaxe Books

U. A. Fanthorpe b. *1929*

1978 *Side Effects* Liskeard: Peterloo Poets
1982 *Standing To* Liskeard: Peterloo Poets
1984 *Voices Off* Liskeard: Peterloo Poets
1986 *Selected Poems* Liskeard: Peterloo Poets; Harmondsworth: Penguin
1987 *A Watching Brief* Calstock: Peterloo Poets
1992 *Neck-Verse* Calstock: Peterloo Poets
1995 *Safe As Houses* Calstock: Peterloo Poets
2000 *Consequences* Calstock: Peterloo Poets

Eleanor Farjeon *1881–1965*

1911 *Dream Songs for the Beloved* London: Orpheus Press
1918 *Sonnets and Poems* (Initiates – 'a series of poetry by proved hands' – vol. 2)
    Oxford: Blackwell
1918 *All the Way to Alfriston* (drawings by Robin Guthrie) London: Morland Press
1920 *Tomfooleries* (by 'Tomfool') London: The Labour Publishing Co. and Allen
    and Unwin
1921 *Moonshine* (by 'Tomfool') London: The Labour Publishing Co. and Allen
    and Unwin
1922 *Songs for Music & Lyrical Poems* London: Selwyn & Blount
1947 *First and Second Love* London: Michael Joseph; London: Oxford University
    Press, 1959

Vicki Feaver b. *1943*

1981 *Close Relatives* London: Secker and Warburg
1994 *The Handless Maiden* London: Jonathan Cape

Elaine Feinstein b. 1930

1966 *In a Green Eye* London: Goliard Press
1970 *The Circle* London: New Authors; Harmondsworth: Penguin, 1973
1971 *The Magic Apple Tree* London: Hutchinson
1972 *At the Edge* Rushden, Northants: Sceptre Press
1973 *The Celebrants and Other Poems* London: Hutchinson
1973 *The Glass Alembic* London: Hutchinson
1974 *The Children of the Rose* London: Hutchinson; Harmondsworth: Penguin
1976 *The Crystal Garden* Harmondsworth: Penguin
1977 *Some Unease and Angels: Selected Poems* London: Hutchinson; Michigan: Green River Press
1978 *The Shadow Master* London: Hutchinson
1980 *The Feast of Euridyce* London: Next Editions
1980 *The Silent Areas* London: Hutchinson
1982 *The Survivors* London: Hutchinson
1984 *The Border* London: Hutchinson; London: Methuen, 1985
1986 *Badlands* London: Hutchinson
1990 *City Music* London: Hutchinson
1994 *Selected Poems* Manchester: Carcanet
1997 *Daylight* Manchester: Carcanet
2000 *Gold* Manchester: Carcanet

Alison Fell b. 1944

1984 *Kisses for Mayakovsky* London: Virago
1988 *The Crystal Owl* London: Methuen
1997 *Dreams, like Heretics: New and Selected Poems* London: Serpent's Tail

Michael Field (Katherine Bradley 1846–1914 and Edith Cooper 1862–1913)

1908 *Wild Honey from Various Thyme* London: T. Fisher Unwin
1912 *Poems of Adoration* London and Edinburgh: Sands
1913 *Mystic Trees* London: Evelyn Nash
1914 *Whym Chow: Flame of Love* London: privately printed at the Eregny Press
1914 *Dedicated: An early work of Michael Field* London: G. Bell
1923 *A Selection from the Poems of Michael Field* London: The Poetry Bookshop
1930 *The Wattlefold: Unpublished Poems by Michael Field* (ed. Emily Fortey) Oxford: Blackwell

Janet Fisher b. 1943

1990 *Raw: Poems* Huddersfield: Wide Skirt
1992 *Nobody Move* Nottingham: Slow Dancer

S. Gertrude Ford

1912 *Lyric Leaves* London: C. W. Daniel Co.
1915 *Poems of War and Peace* London: Erskine Macdonald
1917 *'A Fight to a Finish' and other songs of peace sung in war time* London: C. W. Daniel Co.
1928 *The England of My Dream and Other Poems* London: C. W. Daniel Co.

Veronica Forrest-Thomson 1947–75

1967 *Identi-Kit* London: Outposts Publications
1970 *Twelve Academic Questions* Cambridge: The Author, 1970
1971 *Language-Games* Leeds University Press
1976 *On the Periphery* Cambridge: Street Editions
1990 *Collected Poems and Translations of Veronica Forrest-Thomson* (ed. Anthony Barnett) London: Allardyce
1999 *Selected Poems: Language-Games, On the Periphery and Other Writings* (ed. Anthony Barnett; postscript by Alison Mark) London: Invisible Books

Linda France b. 1958

1992 *Red* Newcastle upon Tyne: Bloodaxe Books
1994 *The Gentleness of the Very Tall* Newcastle upon Tyne: Bloodaxe Books
1997 *Storyville* Newcastle upon Tyne: Bloodaxe Books

Olive Fraser 1909–77

1981 *The Pure Account: Poems of Olive Fraser* (ed. Helena M. Shire) Aberdeen: Aberdeen University Press
1989 *The Wrong Music: The Poems of Olive Fraser* (ed. Helena M. Shire) Edinburgh: Canongate

Cynthia Fuller b. 1948

1992 *Moving Towards Light* Jesmond: Flambard
1996 *Instructions for the Desert* Newcastle upon Tyne: Flambard

Elizabeth Garrett b. 1958

1990 *Mortal Light* Hitchin: Mandeville
1991 *The Rule of Three* Newcastle upon Tyne: Bloodaxe Books
1998 *A Two-Part Invention* Newcastle upon Tyne: Bloodaxe Books

Viola Garvin b. 1898

1922 *As You See It* (essays and poems) London: Methuen
1926 *Corn in Egypt* (tales and poems) London: Methuen
1928 *Dedication* London: Victor Gollancz

Glenda George b. 1951

1976 *Slit Here* Hebden Bridge: Pressed Curtains

Karen Gershon b. 1923

1959 *The Relentless Year* London: New Poets
1966 *Selected Poems* London: Victor Gollancz
1972 *Legacies and Encounters: Poems 1966–1971* London: Victor Gollancz
1975 *My Daughters, My Sisters* London: Victor Gollancz
1979 *Coming Back from Babylon: 24 poems* London: Victor Gollancz
1990 *Collected Poems* London: Papermac

Stella Gibbons 1902–89

1930 *The Mountain Beast and Other Poems* London: Longman
1934 *The Priestess and Other Poems* London: Longman
1938 *The Lowland Venus and Other Poems* London: Longman
1950 *Collected Poems* London: Longman

Valerie Gillies b. 1948

1977 *Each Bright Eye: Selected Poems 1971–1976* Edinburgh: Canongate
1984 *Bed Of Stone* Edinburgh: Canongate
1989 *Tweed Journey* Edinburgh: Canongate
1990 *The Chanter's Tune* Edinburgh: Canongate
1995 *The Ringing Rock* Edinburgh: Scottish Cultural Press
2000 *Men and Beasts: Wild Men and Tame Animals of Scotland* Edinburgh: Luath

Pamela Gillilan 1918–2001

1986 *That Winter* Newcastle upon Tyne: Bloodaxe Books
1993 *The Turnspit Dog* (woodcuts by Charlotte Cory) Newcastle upon Tyne:
       Bloodaxe Books
1994 *All-Steel Traveller: New and Selected Poems* Newcastle upon Tyne: Bloodaxe
       Books
1998 *The Rashomon Syndrome* Newcastle upon Tyne: Bloodaxe Books

Eva Gore-Booth 1870–1926

1898 *Poems* London: Longman
1904 *Unseen Kings: and other Poems* London: Longman
1904 *The One and the Many* London: Longman
1905 *The Three Resurrections and the Triumph of Maeve* (Poems and drama in verse)
1907 *The Egyptian Pillar* Dublin: Maunsel
1907 *The Sorrowful Princess* (verse drama) London: Longman
1912 *The Agate Lamp* London: Longman
1918 *Broken Glory* Dublin: Maunsel
1925 *The Shepherd of Eternity and Other Poems* London: Longman
1926 *The House of Three Windows* London: Longman
1929 *Poems of Eva Gore-Booth* (complete edition) London: Longman.
1933 *Selected Poems of Eva Gore-Booth* London: Longman.

Ida Affleck Graves 1902–99

1929 *The China Cupboard and Other Poems* (Ida Graves) London: Hogarth
1936 *Epithalamion* (engravings by Blair Hughes-Stanton) London: Gemini Press
1945 *Mother and Child* London: Fortune Press
1996 *A Kind Husband* Oxford University Press
1999 *The Calf Bearers* Oxford University Press

Lavinia Greenlaw b. 1962

1993 *Night Photograph* London: Faber
1997 *A World Where News Travelled Slowly* London: Faber

Caroline Halliday b. 1947

1983 *Some Truth, Some Change: Poems* London: Onlywomen Press

Helen Hamilton

1917 *The Compleat Schoolmarm: A Story of Promise and Fulfilment* Oxford: Blackwell
1918 *Napoo! A Book of War Bêtes Noires* Oxford : Blackwell
1924 *Hope and Other Poems* Bristol: Horseshoe Publishing
1932 *The Vision of Fra Bartolo: sonnets and lyrics* Aberdeen: D. Wythie

Sophie Hannah b. 1971

1995 *The Hero and the Girl Next Door* Manchester: Carcanet

1996 *Hotels like Houses* Manchester: Carcanet
1999 *Leaving and Leaving You* Manchester: Carcanet

Maggie Hannan b. 1962

1995 *Liar, Jones* Newcastle upon Tyne: Bloodaxe Books

Diana Hendry b. 1941

1995 *Making Blue* Calstock: Peterloo Poets

Kathleen Herbert

1989 *Here and Now: Selected Poems, 1928–1988* Sutton: Hippopotamus Press

Tracey Herd b. 1968

1996 *No Hiding Place* Newcastle upon Tyne: Bloodaxe Books

Phoebe Hesketh b. 1909

1939 *Poems* London: Sherratt and Hughes/St Anne's Press
1948 *Lean Forward, Spring* London: Sidgwick & Jackson
1952 *No Time For Cowards* (introduced by Herbert Palmer) London: Heinemann
1954 *Out of the Dark* London: Heinemann
1956 *Between Wheels And Stars* London: Heinemann
1958 *The Buttercup Children* London: Rupert Hart-Davis
1966 *Prayer for Sun* London: Rupert Hart-Davis
1974 *A Song of Sunlight* London: Chatto & Windus
1977 *Preparing to Leave: Poems* Petersfield: Enitharmon
1980 *The Eighth Day: Selected Poems 1948–1978* (ed. and introduced by John Baron Mays) Petersfield: Enitharmon
1985 *A Ring of Leaves* Hayloft
1986 *Over The Brook* Leicester: Taxus
1989 *Netting The Sun: New and Collected Poems* (introduced by Anne Stevenson) Petersfield: Enitharmon
1992 *Sundowner* Petersfield: Enitharmon
1994 *The Leave Train: New and Selected Poems* Petersfield: Enitharmon

Rita Ann Higgins b. 1955

1986 *Goddess on the Mervue Bus* Galway: Salmon
1988 *Witch in the Bushes* Galway: Salmon

1988 *Goddess & Witch* Galway: Salmon
1992 *Philomena's Revenge* Galway: Salmon
1996 *Sunnyside Plucked: New and Selected Poems* Newcastle upon Tyne: Bloodaxe Books
1996 *Higher Purchase* Knockeven: Salmon

Selima Hill b. 1945

1984 *Saying Hello at the Station* London: Chatto & Windus
1988 *My Darling Camel* London: Chatto & Windus
1989 *The Accumulation of Small Acts of Kindness* London: Chatto & Windus
1993 *A Little Book of Meat* Newcastle upon Tyne: Bloodaxe Books
1994 *Trembling Hearts in the Bodies of Dogs: New and Selected Poems* Newcastle upon Tyne: Bloodaxe Books
1997 *Violet* Newcastle upon Tyne: Bloodaxe Books

Molly Holden 1927–81

1968 *To Make Me Grieve* London: Chatto & Windus
1971 *Air and Chill Earth* London: Chatto & Windus
1975 *The Country Over* London: Chatto & Windus
1987 *Molly Holden: New and Selected Poems* Manchester: Carcanet

Jane Holland b. 1966

1997 *The Brief History of a Disreputable Woman* Newcastle upon Tyne: Bloodaxe Books

Teresa M. Hooley 1888–1973

1913 *Gloom and Gleam* London: A. C. Fifield
1926 *Collected Poems* London: Jonathan Cape
1930 *Eve and Other Poems* London: Jonathan Cape
1933 *New Poems* London: Jonathan Cape
1935 *Orchestra and Other Poems* Oxford: Blackwell
1936 *Nature Poems* London: Nature Lover Publications
1944 *The Singing Heart Poems* London: Frederick Muller
1947 *Selected Poems* (drawings by Freda Nichols) London: Jonathan Cape
1959 *Wintergreen* Stoke-on-Trent: A. J. Chapple

Frances Horovitz 1938–83

1970 *The High Tower: Poems 1967–1969* London: New Departures

1980 *Water Over Stone* London: Enitharmon
1983 *Snow Light, Water Light* Newcastle upon Tyne: Bloodaxe Books
1985 *Collected Poems* Newcastle upon Tyne: Bloodaxe Books

Libby Houston b. *1941*

1967 *A Stained-Glass Raree Show* London: Allison and Busby
1971 *Plain Clothes* London: Allison and Busby
1981 *At The Mercy* London; New York: Allison and Busby
1988 *Necessity* Nottingham: Slow Dancer Press
1993 *All Change: Poems* Oxford University Press
1999 *Cover of Darkness: Selected Poems 1961–1998* London: Slow Dancer Press

Frieda Hughes b. *1960*

1999 *Wooroloo* Newcastle upon Tyne: Bloodaxe Books; USA: Harper Collins,
      1998; Freemantle, Australia: Arts Centre Press, 1999

Nicki Jackowska b. *1942*

1973 *The King Rises* Cardiff: Second Aeon Publications
1974 *The Words That Manda Spoke. A Poem* Bristol: Bridgewest
1981 *The Knot Garden* Berkhamsted: Priapus Press
1981 *Incubus* London: The Menard Press
1981 *The House That Manda Built* London: The Menard Press
1984 *Letters To Superman* London: Rivelin Grapheme
1985 *Gates to the City* Durham: Taxus
1993 *Gates to the City* London: Sinclair Stevenson
1998 *Lighting a Slow Fuse* London: Enitharmon

Ada Jackson

1933 *The Widow and Other Poems* London: Methuen
1938 *Narrow Homes: a collection of epitaphs* Birmingham: Cornish Bros.
1940 *Against the Sun* New York: Macmillan
1942 *World in Labour* Birmingham: Cornish Bros.
1943 *Behold the Jew* (The Greenwood Prize Poem for 1943) London: Poetry Society

Kathleen Jamie b. *1962*

1981 *Black Spiders* Edinburgh: Salamander Press
1986 *A Flame in Your Heart* (with Andrew Greig) Newcastle upon Tyne:
      Bloodaxe Books

1987 *The Way We Live* Newcastle upon Tyne: Bloodaxe Books
1993 *The Autonomous Region* (with Sean Mayne Smith) Newcastle upon Tyne: Bloodaxe Books
1994 *The Queen of Sheba* Newcastle upon Tyne: Bloodaxe Books
1999 *Jizzen* London: Picador

Elizabeth Jennings 1926–2002

1953 *Poems* Oxford: Fantasy Press
1955 *A Way of Looking* London: Andre Deutsch
1958 *A Sense of the World* London: Andre Deutsch
1961 *Song for a Birth or a Death* London: Andre Deutsch
1964 *Recoveries* London: Andre Deutsch
1966 *The Mind Has Mountains* London: Macmillan
1967 *Collected Poems* London: Macmillan
1969 *The Animals' Arrival* London: Macmillan
1970 *Lucidities* London: Macmillan
1972 *Relationships* London: Macmillan
1975 *Growing Points* Cheadle: Carcanet
1977 *Consequently I rejoice* Cheadle: Carcanet
1979 *Selected Poems* Manchester: Carcanet
1980 *Moments of Grace* Manchester: Carcanet
1982 *Celebrations and Elegies* Manchester: Carcanet
1985 *Extending the Territory* Manchester: Carcanet
1986 *Collected Poems: 1953–85* Manchester: Carcanet
1989 *Tributes* Manchester: Carcanet
1992 *Times and Seasons* Manchester: Carcanet
1994 *Familiar Spirits* Manchester: Carcanet
1996 *In the Meantime* Manchester: Carcanet
1998 *Praises* Manchester: Carcanet

Amryl Johnson b. c.1960

1985 *Long Road To Nowhere* London: Virago
1991 *Tread Carefully in Paradise* Coventry: Cofa
1992 *Gorgons* Coventry: Cofa

Einir Jones b. 1950

1972 *Pigo Crachan* Llandybie ac Abertawe: C. Davies
1980 *Gwellt Medi* Caenarfon: Gwasg Gwynedd
1991 *Daeth Awst, Daeth Nos* Cyhoeddiadau Barddas
1991 *Gweld y Garreg Ateb* Caenarfon: Gwasg Gwynedd

Jenny Joseph b. 1932

1960 *The Unlooked-for Season* Northwood: Scorpion
1974 *Rose in the Afternoon* London: Dent
1978 *The Thinking Heart* London: Secker and Warburg
1983 *Beyond Descartes* London: Secker and Warburg
1986 *Persephone* Newcastle upon Tyne: Bloodaxe Books
1989 *The Inland Sea: a selection from the poems of Jenny Joseph* Watsonville,
       California: Papier Mache Press
1991 *Beached Boats* London: Enitharmon
1992 *Selected Poems* Newcastle upon Tyne: Bloodaxe Books
1995 *Ghosts and Other Company* Newcastle upon Tyne: Bloodaxe Books
1997 *Extended Similes* Newcastle upon Tyne: Bloodaxe Books

Sylvia Kantaris b. 1936

1975 *Time and Motion* Prism/Poetry Society of Australia; Helston: Menhir Press,
       1986
1983 *The Tenth Muse* Liskeard: Peterloo Poets; Menhir Press, 1986
1983 *News from the Front* (with D. M Thomas) Todmorden: Arc
1985 *The Sea at the Door* London: Secker and Warburg
1988 *The Air Mines of Mistila* (with Philip Gross) Newcastle upon Tyne: Bloodaxe
       Books
1989 *Dirty Washing: New and Selected Poems* Newcastle upon Tyne: Bloodaxe
       Books
1993 *Lad's Love* Newcastle upon Tyne: Bloodaxe Books

Jackie Kay b. 1961

1991 *The Adoption Papers* Newcastle upon Tyne: Bloodaxe Books
1993 *Other Lovers* Newcastle upon Tyne: Bloodaxe Books
1998 *Off Colour* Newcastle upon Tyne: Bloodaxe Books

Judith Kazantzis b. 1940

1977 *Minefield* London: Sidgwick & Jackson
1980 *The Wicked Queen* London: Sidgwick & Jackson
1984 *Let's Pretend* London: Virago
1988 *A Poem for Guatemala* (pamphlet) Pateley Bridge: Bedlam Press
1988 *Flame Tree* London: Methuen
1992 *The Rabbit Magician Plate* London: Sinclair Stevenson
1995 *Selected Poems 1977–92* London: Sinclair Stevenson
1997 *Swimming Through the Grand Hotel: Poems 1993–96* London: Enitharmon
1999 *The Odysseus Poems: Fictions on the Odyssey of Homer* Cornwall: Cargo Press

Mimi Khalvati b. 1944

1990 *Persian Miniatures* Huddersfield: Smith/Doorstop
1991 *In White Ink* Manchester: Carcanet
1995 *Mirrorwork* Manchester: Carcanet
1997 *Entries on Light* Manchester: Carcanet
2000 *Selected Poems* Manchester: Carcanet

Susanne Knowles

1942 *Arpies & Sirens: Verse*
1945 *Birth of Venus and Other Poems* London: Macmillan
1962 *Mediterranean and Other Poems* London: Heinemann
1974 *The Sea-Bell and Other Poems* London: Dent

Lotte Kramer b. 1923

1980 *Ice Break* Peterborough: Annakinn
1983 *A Lifelong House* Sutton: Hippopotamus Press
1987 *The Shoemaker's Wife and Other Poems* Sutton: Hippopotamus Press
1994 *Earthquake and Other Poems* Ware, Herts: Rockingham Press
1994 *The Desecration of Trees* Sutton: Hippopotamus Press
1997 *Selected and New Poems 1980–1997* Ware, Herts: Rockingham Press

Winifred Letts 1882–1971

1913 *Songs from Leinster* London: Smith Elder & Co.; repr. 1914, 1947
1916 *Hallow-e'en, and Poems of the War* London: Smith Elder & Co.
1917 *The Spires of Oxford and Other Poems* (new edition) New York: E. P. Dutton & Co.
1926 *More Songs from Leinster* London: John Murray

Denise Levertov 1923–97

1946 *The Double Image* London: Cresset Press
1957 *Here and Now* San Francisco: City Lights Bookshop
1960 *With Eyes at the Back of our Heads* Norjock, Connecticut: James Laughlin
1961 *The Jacob's Ladder* New York: New Directions
1964 *O Taste and See* New York: New Directions
1967 *The Sorrow Dance* New York: New Directions; London: Jonathan Cape, 1968
1968 *A Tree Telling of Orpheus* Los Angeles: Black Sparrow Press
1968 *Poems 1960–1967* London: Jonathan Cape
1970 *Relearning the Alphabet* USA: New Directions; London: Jonathan Cape
1971 *To Stay Alive* New York: New Directions

1972 *Footprints* New York: New Directions
1975 *The Freeing of the Dust* New York: New Directions
1978 *Life in the Forest* New York: New Directions
1979 *Collected Earlier Poems 1940–60* New York: New Directions
1981 *Light up the Cave* New York: New Directions
1982 *Candles in Babylon* New York: New Directions
1983 *Poems 1960–67* New York: New Directions
1984 *Oblique Prayers* New York: New Directions; Newcastle upon Tyne:
       Bloodaxe Books, 1986
1985 *Selected Poems* New York: New Directions; Newcastle upon Tyne: Bloodaxe
       Books, 1986
1987 *Breathing the Water* New York: New Directions ; Newcastle upon Tyne:
       Bloodaxe Books, 1988
1989 *A Door in the Hive* New York: New Directions; Newcastle upon Tyne:
       Bloodaxe Books, 1992
1992 *Evening Train* New York: New Directions
1996 *Sands of the Well* New York: New Directions; Newcastle upon Tyne:
       Bloodaxe Books, 1998

Gwyneth Lewis b. 1959

1990 *Sonedau Redsa* Gwasg Gomer
1995 *Parables and Faxes* Newcastle upon Tyne: Bloodaxe Books
1996 *Cyfrif Un ac Un yn Dri* Cyhoeddiadau Barddas
1998 *Zero Gravity* Newcastle upon Tyne: Bloodaxe Books
1999 *y llofrudd Iaith* Cyhoeddiadau Barddas

Liz Lochhead b. 1947

1972 *Memo For Spring* Edinburgh: Reprographia
1981 *The Grimm Sisters* London: Next Editions
1984 *Dreaming Frankenstein and Other Poems 1967–84* Edinburgh: Polygon
1985 *True Confessions and New Cliches* (reprinted 1993) Edinburgh: Polygon
1991 *Bagpipe Muzak* Harmondsworth: Penguin

Marion Lomax (Robyn Bolam) b. 1953

1989 *The Peepshow Girl* Newcastle upon Tyne: Bloodaxe Books
1996 *Raiding the Borders* Newcastle upon Tyne: Bloodaxe Books

Mina Loy 1882–1966

1923 *Lunar Baedecker* [*sic*] Paris: Contact Publishing Co.

1958 *Lunar Baedeker & Timetables* North Carolina: Jonathan Williams Highlands
1982 *The Last Lunar Baedeker* (ed. Roger Conover) North Carolina: Jonathan Williams Highlands; Manchester: Carcanet, 1985
1997 *The Lost Lunar Baedeker* (ed. Roger Conover) Manchester: Carcanet

Sylvia Lynd 1888–1952

1916 *The Thrush and the Jay: Poems and Prose Sketches* London: Constable
1920 *The Goldfinches: Poem* London: R. Cobden-Sanderson
1928 *Selected Poems* London: Ernest Benn
1931 *The Yellow Placard: Poems* London: Victor Gollancz
1934 *The Enemies: Poems* London: Dent
1945 *Collected Poems* London: Macmillan

Rose Macaulay 1881–1958

1919 *Three Days* London: Constable

Sarah Maguire b. 1957

1991 *Spilt Milk* London: Secker and Warburg
1997 *The Invisible Mender* London: Jonathan Cape

Una Marson 1905–65

1930 *Tropic Reveries* Jamaica: Gleaner Co.
1932 *Heights and Depths* Jamaica
1937 *The Moth and The Star* Jamaica: Una Marson
1945 *Towards the Stars* University of London Press

Gerda Mayer b. 1927

1980 *Monkey on the Analyst's Couch* Sunderland: Ceolfrith Press
1985 *March Post Man* Berkhamsted: Priapus Poets
1988 *A Heartache of Grass* Calstock: Peterloo Poets
1999 *Bernini's Cat: New and Selected Poems* North Shields: Iron Press

Medbh McGuckian b. 1950

1980 *Single Ladies: sixteen poems* Budleigh Salterton: Interim
1980 *Portrait of Joanna* Belfast: Ulsterman Publications
1982 *The Flower Master* Oxford University Press; Oldcastle: The Gallery Press 1993

1988 *On Ballycastle Beach* Oxford University Press; Winston-Salem: Wake Forest; Oldcastle: Gallery Press, 1995

1989 *Two Women, Two Shores: Poems by Medbh McGuckian and Nuala Archer* Baltimore: New Poets Series

1991 *Marconi's Cottage* Oldcastle: Gallery Press; Winston-Salem: Wake Forest; Newcastle upon Tyne: Bloodaxe Books, 1992

1993 *The Flower Master and Other Poems* Oldcastle: The Gallery Press

1994 *Captain Lavender* Oldcastle: The Gallery Press

1994 *Venus and the Rain* Oxford University Press; Oldcastle: The Gallery Press, 1994

1997 *Selected Poems 1978–1994* Oldcastle: The Gallery Press

1998 *Shelmalier* Oldcastle: The Gallery Press

Paula Meehan b. 1955

1984 *Return and No Blame* Dublin: Beaver Row

1986 *Reading the Sky* Dublin: Beaver Row

1991 *The Man who was Marked by Winter* Oldcastle: Gallery Press; Spokane, USA: EWU Press, 1994; Washington: Eastern Washington University Press, 1994

1994 *Pillow Talk* Oldcastle: The Gallery Press

1996 *Mysteries of the Home: A Selection of Poems* Manchester: Carcanet

2000 *Dharmakaya* Manchester: Carcanet; Winston-Salem: Wake Forest, 2001

Charlotte Mew 1869–1928

1916 *The Farmer's Bride.* London: The Poetry Bookshop (*Saturday Market*, USA, 1921)

1921 *The Farmer's Bride* (new edition with 11 new poems) London: The Poetry Bookshop

1929 *The Rambling Sailor.* London: The Poetry Bookshop

1953 *Collected Poems.* London: Duckworth

1997 *Charlotte Mew: Collected Poems and Selected Prose* (ed. Val Warner) Manchester: Carcanet

1999 *Charlotte Mew: Selected Poems* (ed. Ian Hamilton) London: Bloomsbury Poetry Classics

Alice Meynell 1847–1922

1902 *Later Poems* London and New York: John Lane

1911 *Poems* London: John Lane

1913 *Collected Poems* London: Burns and Oates

1914 *The Shepherdess and Other Verses* London: Burns Oates

1915 *Poems on the War* Privately printed

1915 *Ten Poems 1913–1915* Privately printed

1917 *A Father of Women and Other Poems* London: Burns and Oates
1921 *Poems London* Burns, Oates and Washbourne
1923 *The Last Poems of Alice Meynell* London: Burns, Oates and Washbourne
1930 *Selected Poems of Alice Meynell* London: Nonesuch
1940 *The Poems of Alice Meynell* (complete edition) 1923. London: Oxford University Press
1947 *Alice Meynell: Prose and Poetry* (eds. F. P., V. M., O. S., and F. M., introduced by Vita Sackville-West) London: Jonathan Cape

Viola Meynell 1886–1956

1919 *Verses* London: Martin Secker
1930 *The Frozen Ocean* London: Martin Secker

'Susan Miles' (Ursula Roberts) 1887–1975

1918 *Dunch* (*Adventurers All*: 'A series of young poets unknown to fame', no. 18) Oxford: Blackwell, 1916–1920
1922 *Annotations* London: Humphrey Milford
1924 *Little Mirrors, and other studies in free-verse* Oxford: Blackwell
1924 *The Hares and Other Verses* London: Elkin Matthews
1958 *Lettice Delmer* London: The Linden Press; Persephone Books, 2002

Elma Mitchell 1919–2000

1976 *The Poor Man in the Flesh* Stockport: Peterloo Poets
1979 *The Human Cage* Liskeard: Peterloo Poets
1983 *Furnished Rooms* Liskeard: Peterloo Poets
1987 *People Et Cetera: Poems New and Selected* Calstock: Peterloo Poets

Naomi Mitchison 1897–1999

1926 *The Laburnum Branch* London: Jonathan Cape
1933 *The Delicate Fire, Short Stories and Poems* London: Jonathan Cape
1939 *The Alban Goes Out* (wood engravings by Gertrude Hermes) Harrow: Raven Press
1978 *The Cleansing of the Knife and Other Poems* Edinburgh: Canongate

Geraldine Monk b. 1952

1979 *Rotations* Staithes: Siren
1979 *Long Wake* London: The Writers' Forum
1980 *Spreading the Cards* Staithes: Siren

1980 *La Quinta del Sordo* London: The Writers' Forum
1982 *Tiger Lilies* Bradford: Rivelin Press
1984 *Banquet* Sheffield: Siren
1985 *Animal Crackers* London: The Writers' Forum
1986 *Sky Scrapers* Newcastle upon Tyne: Galloping Dog
1990 *Quaquaversals* London: The Writers' Forum
1991 *Walks in a Daisy Chain* Hebden Bridge: Magenta Press
1992 *The Sway of Precious Demons: Selected Poems* Twickenham: North & South
1994 *Interregnum* London: Creation Press

Sinéad Morrissey b. *1972*

1996 *There was Fire in Vancouver* Manchester: Carcanet

Wendy Mulford b. *1941*

1977 *Bravo to Girls and Heroes* Cambridge: Street Editions
1979 *No fee: a line or two for free* (with Denise Riley) Cambridge: Street Editions
1980 *The Light Sleepers: Poems 1980* Bath: Mammon Press
1980 *Reactions to Sunsets* London: Ferry Press
1982 *River Whose Eyes* London: AVOCADOTOAVOCADO
1982 *Some Poems* (with Denise Riley) Cambridge: C. M. R. Press
1985 *The ABC of Writing and Other Poems* Southampton: Torque Press
1987 *Late Spring Next Year: Poems 1979–85* Bristol: Loxwood Stoneleigh
1990 *Lusus Naturae* London: Circle Press
1991 *Nevrazumitelny* Cambridge: Poetical Histories
1992 *The Bay of Naples* London: Reality Studios
1998 *The East Anglian Sequence* Peterborough: Spectacular Diseases

Suniti Namjoshi b. *1941*

1967 *Poems* Calcutta: The Writer's Workshop
1970 *More Poems* Calcutta: The Writer's Workshop
1979 *Cyclone in Pakistan* Calcutta: The Writer's Workshop
1980 *The Jackass and the Lady* Calcutta: The Writer's Workshop
1981 *Feminist Fables* London: Virago
1982 *The Authentic Lie* Fredicton: Fiddlehead Poetry
1985 *The Conversations of Cow* London: Women's Press
1986 *Flesh and Paper* (with Gillian Hanscombe) Seaton: Jezebel Tapes and Books
1989 *Because of India: Selected Poems* London: Onlywomen Press
1989 *The Mothers of Maya Dip* London: Women's Press

Grace Nichols b. *1950*

1983 *i is a long-memoried woman* London: Karnak
1984 *The Fat Black Woman's Poems* London: Virago
1985 *A Dangerous Knowing* London: Sheba Feminist Publishers
1988 *Come on into my Tropical Garden* London: Black
1989 *Lazy Thoughts of a Lazy Woman and Other Poems* London: Virago
1996 *SUNRIS* London: Virago

Eiléan ní Chuilleanáin b. *1942*

1972 *Acts and Monuments* Dublin: The Gallery Press
1975 *Site of Ambush* Dublin: The Gallery Press
1977 *The Second Voyage: Selected Poems* Dublin: The Gallery Press; Newcastle
       upon Tyne: Bloodaxe Books, 1986
1981 *The Rose Geranium* Oldcastle: The Gallery Press
1986 *The Second Voyage: Selected Poems* Winston Salem: Wake Forest University
       Press
1989 *The Magdelene Sermon* Oldcastle: The Gallery Press
1991 *The Magdelene Sermon and Earlier Poems* Winston Salem: Wake Forest
       University Press
1994 *The Brazen Serpent* Oldcastle: Gallery Press; Winston Salem: Wake Forest
       University Press, 1995

Nuala ní Dhomhnaill b. *1952*

1981 *An Dealg Droighinn* Cork: The Mercier Press
1984 *Féar Suaithin seach* Ma Nuat Maynooth: An Sagart
1986 *Selected Poems/ Rogha Dánta* (trans. Michael Hartnett) Raven Arts
1990 *Pharaoh's Daughter* (various translators) Oldcastle: The Gallery Press
1992 *The Astrakhan Cloak* (trans. Paul Muldoon) Oldcastle: The Gallery Press;
       Winston Salem: Wake Forest University Press
1998 *Cead Aighuis* An Daingeau: An Sagart
1999 *The Waterhorse* (trans. Medbh McGuckian and Eiléan ní Chuilleanáin)
       Oldcastle: The Gallery Press; Winston Salem: Wake Forest University Press

Kathleen Nott b. *1909*

1947 *Landscapes and Departures* London: Editions Poetry London
1953 *The Emperor's Clothes* London: Heinemann
1956 *Poems from the North* Kent: Hand and Flower Press
1960 *Creatures and Emblems* London: Routledge and Kegan Paul
1981 *Elegies and Other Poems* Surrey: Keepsake Press

Julie O'Callaghan b. *1954*

1983 *Edible Anecdotes and Other Poems* Mountrath: Dolmen Press
1991 *What's What?* Newcastle upon Tyne: Bloodaxe Books
1998 *Two Barks* Newcastle upon Tyne: Bloodaxe Books
2000 *No Can Do* Newcastle upon Tyne: Bloodaxe Books

Mary O'Donnell b. *1954*

1990 *Reading the Sunflowers in September* Co. Clare: Salmon
1993 *Spiderwoman's Third Avenue Rhapsody* Co. Clare: Salmon
1998 *Unlegendary Heroes* Co. Clare: Salmon

Mary O'Malley

1990 *A Consideration of Silk* Galway: Salmon
1993 *Where the Rocks Float* Galway: Salmon
1997 *The Knife in the Wave* Galway: Salmon
2001 *Asylum Road* Galway: Salmon

Maggie O'Sullivan b. *1951*

1982 *Concerning Spheres* Bristol: Broken Ground
1984 *An Incomplete Natural History* London: The Writers' Forum
1985 *A Natural History in 3 Incomplete Parts* Hebden Bridge: Magenta Press
1985 *Unassuming Person* London: The Writers' Forum
1986 *Divisions of Labour* Newcastle upon Tyne: Galloping Dog
1986 *From the Handbook of That and Furriery* London: The Writers' Forum
1987 *States of Emergency* Oxford: International Concrete Poetry Archive
1988 *Unofficial Word* Newcastle upon Tyne: Galloping Dog
1993 *In the House of the Shaman* London and Cambridge: Reality Street Editions
1993 *Ellen's Lament*
1993 *Excla* (with Bruce Andrews) London: The Writers' Forum
1993 *That Bread Should Be Nothing*
2000 *Red Shifts* Buckfastleigh: Etruscan Books

Alice Oswald b. *1966*

1996 *The Thing in the Gap-Stone Stile* Oxford University Press

Ruth Padel b. 1944

1985 *Alibi* London: The Many Press
1990 *Summer Snow* London: Hutchinson
1993 *Angel* Newcastle upon Tyne: Bloodaxe Books
1996 *Fusewire* London: Chatto & Windus
1998 *Rembrandt Would Have Loved You* London: Chatto & Windus
1998 *Touch and Go* London: Chatto & Windus

Sylvia Pankhurst 1882–1960

1922 *Writ on Cold Slate* London: Dreadnought Publications

Helen Parry Eden

1913 *Bread and Circuses* London: John Lane
1918 *Coal and Candlelight and other verses* London: John Lane
1943 *Poems and Other Verses* Milwaukee: The Bruce Publishing Co.

Pascale Petit b. 1953

1998 *Heart of a Deer* London: Enitharmon
2000 *The Zoo Father* Bridgend: Seren

Fiona Pitt-Kethley b. 1954

1986 *Gesta* London: Turrett
1986 *Sky Ray Lolly* London: Chatto & Windus
1987 *Private Parts* London: Chatto & Windus
1988 *Journeys to the Underworld* London: Chatto & Windus
1989 *The Perfect Man* London: Abacus
1993 *Dogs* London: Sinclair Stevenson
1993 *A School for Life: fourteen poems* (woodcuts by Stan Dobbin) Witney,
      Oxford: The Previous Parrot Press
1996 *Double Act* London: Arcadia Books
1997 *Memo from a Muse* (chapbook) Privately printed
2000 *My Schooling* Tamworth: Tamworth Press
2000 *Baker's Dozen* Tamworth: Tamworth Press

Ruth Pitter 1897–1992

1920 *First Poems* London: Cecil Palmer

1927 *First and Second Poems 1912–25* (preface by Hilaire Belloc) London: Sheed and Ward

1931 *Persephone in Hades* Privately printed

1934 *A Mad Lady's Garland* London: Cresset Press; New York: Macmillan

1936 *A Trophy of Arms: Poems 1926–1935* (preface by James Stephens) London: Cresset Press; New York: Macmillan

1939 *The Spirit Watches* London: Cresset Press; New York: Macmillan

1941 *The Rude Potato* (illustrated by Roger Furse) London: Cresset Press

1945 *The Bridge: Poems 1939–1944* London: Cresset Press; New York: Macmillan

1946 *Pitter On Cats* London: Cresset Press

1951 *Urania* London: Cresset Press

1953 *The Ermine: Poems 1942–1952* London: Cresset Press

1966 *Still By Choice* London: Cresset Press

1968 *Poems 1926–1966* London: Barrie and Rockliff

1969 *Ruth Pitter: Collected Poems* New York: Macmillan

1975 *End of Drought* London: Barrie and Jenkins

1987 *A Heaven to Find* London: Enitharmon

1990 *Collected Poems* (introduced by Elizabeth Jennings) Petersfield: Enitharmon

1996 *Collected Poems* (revised edition) London: Enitharmon

Stef Pixner

1985 *Sawdust and White Spirit* London: Virago

Sylvia Plath 1932–63

1960 *The Colossus* London: Heinemann

1962 *The Colossus and Other Poems* New York: Random House

1965 *Ariel* London: Faber

1971 *Crossing the Water* London: Faber

1971 *Crystal Gazer and Other Poems* London: Rainbow Press

1971 *Fiesta Melons* Exeter: Rougemont Press

1971 *Lyonesse: Poems* London: Rainbow Press

1971 *Winter Trees* London: Faber

1976 *The Bed Book* London: Faber

1981 *Collected Poems* London: Faber

1985 *Sylvia Plath: Selected Poems* London: Faber

2000 *Sylvia Plath: Poems* London: Faber

Jessie Pope d. 1941

1915 *Jessie Pope's War Poems* London: Grant Richards Ltd

1915 *More War Poems* London: Grant Richards Ltd

1916 *Simple Rhymes for Stirring Times* London: Pearson
1920 *Hits and Misses* London: Grant Richards Ltd

Katrina Porteus b. 1960

1996 *The Lost Music* Newcastle upon Tyne: Bloodaxe Books
1996 *On Lynmouth Beach* (film poem with Tony Glover)
1996 *Book of the North* (CD)

Sheenagh Pugh b. 1950

1977 *Crowded by Shadows* Swansea: C. Davies
1979 *What a Place to Grow Flowers* Swansea: Treskel
1982 *Earth Studies and Other Voyages* Bridgend: Poetry Wales Press
1987 *Beware Falling Tortoises* Bridgend: Poetry Wales Press
1990 *Selected Poems* Bridgend: Seren
1993 *Sing for the Taxman* Bridgend: Seren
1997 *Id's Hospit* Bridgend: Seren
1999 *Stonelight* Bridgend: Seren

Sally Purcell 1944–98

1971 *Holly Queen* London: Kegan Paul
1977 *Dark of Day* London: Anvil Press
1997 *Fossil Unicorn* London: Anvil Press

Kathleen Raine 1908–2003

1943 *Stone and Flower 1935–1943* London: Nicholas and Watson
1945 *Ecce Homo* London: Enitharmon
1946 *Living in Time* London: Editions Poetry London
1949 *The Pythoness and Other Poems* London: Hamish Hamilton
1952 *The Year One and Other Poems* London: Hamish Hamilton
1956 *Collected Poems* London: Hamish Hamilton
1965 *The Hollow Hill and Other Poems 1960–1964* London: Hamish Hamilton
1968 *Ninfa Revisited* London: Enitharmon
1968 *Six Dreams and Other Poems* London: Enitharmon
1971 *The Lost Country* London: Dolmen Press and Hamish Hamilton
1973 *On a Deserted Shore* London: Hamish Hamilton
1977 *The Oval Portrait and Other Poems* London: Enitharmon
1978 *15 Short Poems* Privately printed

1980 *The Oracle in the Heart and Other Poems 1975–1978* Dublin: Dolmen Press; London: Allen and Unwin
1981 *Collected Poems 1935–1980* London: Allen and Unwin
1987 *The Presence Poems 1984–7* Ipswich: Golgonooza Press
1988 *To the Sun* Dorset: Words
1988 *Selected Poems* Ipswich: Golgonooza Press

Deborah Randall b. 1957

1989 *The Sin Eater* Newcastle Upon Tyne: Bloodaxe Books
1993 *White Eyes, Dark Ages* Newcastle upon Tyne: Bloodaxe Books

Elaine Randell b. 1951

1978 *A Larger Breath of All Things* Spectacular Diseases
1982 *Songs for the Sleepless* Durham: Pig Press
1986 *Beyond All Other* Durham: Pig Press

Carlyle Reedy b. 1938

1979 *Sculpted In This World* London: Lo Bluff Books
1984 *The Orange Notebook* London: Reality Studios
1995 *Obituaries and Celebrations* London: Words Worth Books
1999 *Etruscan Reader IV* (with Bob Cobbing and Maurice Scully)

Deryn Rees-Jones b. 1968

1994 *The Memory Tray* Bridgend: Seren
1998 *Signs Round a Dead Body* Bridgend: Seren

Nicky Rice

1984 *Lazarus Rising* Canterbury: Yorick
1994 *Coming Up to Midnight* London: Enitharmon

Laura (Riding) Jackson 1901–91

1926 *The Close Chaplet* London: Hogarth; New York: Adelphi
1930 *Poems: A Joking Word* London: Jonathan Cape
1930 *Twenty Poems Less* Paris: Hours Press
1931 *Laura and Francisca* Deya: Seizin Press
1933 *Poet: A Lying Word* London: Arthur Barker

1933 *The Life of the Dead* London: Arthur Barker
1938 *Collected Poems* London: Cassell; New York: Random House
1970 *Selected Poems: In Five Sets* London: Faber
1980 *The Poems of Laura Riding* (new edition of *Collected Poems* 1938) Manchester: Carcanet
1992 *First Awakenings: The Early Poems* (eds. Elizabeth Friedmann, Alan J. Clark and Robert Nye) Manchester: Carcanet
1994 *A Selection of the Poems of Laura Riding* (ed. Robert Nye) Manchester: Carcanet

Anne Ridler 1912–2001

1939 *Poems* Oxford University Press
1941 *A Dream Observed* London: Poetry London
1943 *The Nine Bright Shiners* London: Faber
1951 *The Golden Bird and Other Poems* London: Faber
1959 *A Matter of Life and Death* London: Faber
1961 *Selected Poems* New York: Macmillan
1963 *Who is My Neighbour and How Bitter the Bread* London: Faber
1972 *Some Time after and Other Poems* London: Faber
1976 *Italian Prospect: Six Poems* Oxford: Perpetua
1980 *Dies Natalis: Poems of Birth and Infancy* Oxford: Perpetua
1988 *New and Selected Poems* London: Faber
1994 *Collected Poems* Manchester: Carcanet

Denise Riley b. 1948

1977 *Marxism for Infants* Cambridge: Street Editions
1979 *No Fee: a line or two for free* (with Wendy Mulford) Cambridge: Street Editions
1982 *Some Poems 1968–1988* Cambridge: Street Editions
1985 *Dry Air* London: Virago
1992 *Stair Spirit* Cambridge: Equipage
1993 *Mop Mop Georgette: New and Selected Poems 1986–1993* London: Reality Street Editions
1993 *Four Falling* Cambridge: Peter Riley
2000 *Selected Poems* London: Reality Street Editions

Lynette Roberts 1909–95

1944 *Poems* London: Faber
1951 *Gods with Stainless Ears: a heroic poem* London: Faber

Michèle Roberts b. 1949

1986 *The Mirror of the Mother: Selected Poems 1978–1985* London: Methuen
1991 *Psyche and the Hurricane* London: Methuen
1995 *All the Selves I Was: New and Selected Poems* London: Virago

Sally Roberts Jones b. 1935

1969 *Turning Away* Llandysul: Gomerian Press
1976 *Strangers and Brothers* Port Talbot: Alun Books
1977 *Sons and Brothers* Llandysul: Gomerian Press
1977 *The Forgotten Country* Llandysul: Gomerian Press
1985 *Relative Values* Bridgend: Poetry Wales Press

Anne Rouse b. 1954

1993 *Sunset Grill* Newcastle upon Tyne: Bloodaxe Books
1997 *Timing* Newcastle upon Tyne: Bloodaxe Books

Carol Rumens b. 1944

1973 *A Strange Girl in Bright Colours* London: Quartet Books
1979 *A Necklace of Mirrors* Belfast: Ulsterman Publications
1981 *Unplayed Music* London: Secker and Warburg
1982 *Scenes from the Gingerbread House* Newcastle upon Tyne: Bloodaxe Books
1983 *Star Whisper* London: Secker and Warburg
1985 *Direct Dialling* London: Chatto & Windus
1986 *Icons, Waves* The Star Wheel Press
1987 *Selected Poems* London: Chatto & Windus
1987 *Plato Park* London: Chatto & Windus
1988 *The Greening of the Snow Beach* Newcastle upon Tyne: Bloodaxe Books
1989 *From Berlin to Heaven* London: Chatto & Windus
1993 *Thinking of Skins: New and Selected Poems* Newcastle upon Tyne: Bloodaxe Books
1995 *Best China Sky* Newcastle upon Tyne: Bloodaxe Books
1997 *The Miracle Diet* (cartoons by Viv Quillan) Newcastle upon Tyne: Bloodaxe Books
1998 *Holding Pattern* Belfast: Blackstaff Press

Margaret Sackville 1881–1963

1911 *Bertrud and Other Dramatic Poems* Edinburgh: William Brown

1916   *The Pageant of War* London: Simpkin, Marshall and Brown
1939   *Collected Poems* London: Richards Press

Vita Sackville-West 1892–1962

1917   *Poems of West and East* London: Bodley Head
1921   *Orchard and Vineyard* London: Bodley Head
1926   *The Land* London: Heinemann
1929   *The King's Daughter* London: Hogarth
1931   *Sissinghurst* London: Hogarth
1931   *Invitation to Cast out Care* London: Faber
1931   *Rilke* (trans.) London: Hogarth
1933   *Collected Poems* London: Hogarth
1938   *Solitude* London: Hogarth
1941   *Selected Poems* London: Hogarth
1946   *The Garden* London: Michael Joseph
1964   *Sissinghurst* London: Hogarth

Eva Salzman b. 1960

1992   *The English Earthquake* Newcastle upon Tyne: Bloodaxe Books
1997   *Bargain with the Watchman* Oxford University Press

Ann Sansom b. 1951

1994   *Romance* Newcastle upon Tyne: Bloodaxe Books

Carole Satyamurti b. 1939

1987   *Broken Moon* Oxford University Press
1990   *Changing the Subject* Oxford University Press
1994   *Striking Distance* Oxford University Press
1998   *Selected Poems* Oxford University Press
2000   *Love and Variations* Newcastle upon Tyne: Bloodaxe Books

E. J. Scovell 1907–99

1944   *Shadows of Chrysanthemums* London: Routledge
1946   *The Midsummer Meadow* London: Routledge
1956   *The River Steamer* London: Cresset Press
1982   *The Space Between* London: Secker and Warburg
1986   *Listening to Collared Doves* Herts: Mandeville
1988   *Collected Poems* Manchester: Carcanet

1991 *Selected Poems* Manchester: Carcanet

Jo Shapcott b. *1953*

1988 *Electroplating the Baby* Newcastle upon Tyne: Bloodaxe Books
1992 *Phrase Book* Oxford University Press
1998 *My Life Asleep* Oxford University Press
2000 *Her Book: Poems 1988–1998* London: Faber

Fredegonde Shove (née Maitland) d. *1949*

1918 *Dreams and Journeys* Oxford: Blackwell
1922 *Daybreak* London: Hogarth
1956 *Poems* (includes unpublished and uncollected poems) Cambridge University Press

Penelope Shuttle b. *1947*

1980 *The Orchard Upstairs* Oxford University Press
1983 *The Child-Stealer* Oxford University Press
1986 *The Lion from Rio* Oxford University Press
1988 *Adventures with my Horse* Oxford University Press
1992 *Taxing the Rain* Oxford University Press
1997 *Selected Poems 1980–1996* Oxford University Press
1999 *A Leaf Out of His Book* Manchester: Carcanet

Ruth Silcock b. *1926*

1987 *Mrs Carmichael* London: Anvil Press
1996 *A Wonderful View of the Sea* London: Anvil Press

Valerie Sinason b. *1946*

1987 *Inkstains and Stilettos* West Kirby: Headland
1995 *Night Shift: New Poems* London: Karnak

May Sinclair *1865–1946*

1886 *Nakiketa and Other Poems* (pseudonym 'Julian Sinclair') Privately printed
1924 *The Dark Night* London: Jonathan Cape

Edith Sitwell 1887–1964

1915 *The Mother* Oxford: Blackwell
1918 *Clowns' Houses* Oxford: Blackwell
1918 *Mother and Other Poems* Oxford: Blackwell
1920 *The Wooden Pegasus* Oxford: Blackwell
1922 *Façade* London: Favil Press
1923 *Bucolic Comedies* London: Duckworth
1924 *The Sleeping Beauty* London: Duckworth; New York: Alfred Knopf
1925 *Troy Park* London: Duckworth
1927 *Rustic Elegies* London: Duckworth; New York: Alfred Knopf
1929 *Gold Coast Customs* London: Duckworth
1930 *Collected Poems* London: Duckworth
1933 *Five Variations on a Theme* London: Duckworth
1936 *Selected Poems* London: Duckworth
1940 *Poems New and Old* London: Faber
1942 *Street Songs* London: Macmillan
1943 *Collected Poems* (reprint) London: Macmillan
1944 *Green Song and Other Poems* London: Macmillan
1945 *The Song of the Cold* London: Macmillan; New York: Vanguard Press
1947 *The Shadow of Cain* London: John Lehmann
1949 *The Canticle of the Rose: Selected Poems 1920–1947* London: Macmillan
1950 *Façade and Other Poems 1920–1935* London: Duckworth
1952 *Selected Poems* Harmondsworth: Penguin
1953 *Gardens and Astronomers: New Poems* London: Macmillan
1954 *Collected Poems* London: Macmillan; New York: Vanguard Press, 1957
1962 *The Outcasts* London: Macmillan
1965 *Selected Poems* London: Macmillan
1982 *Street Songs* London: Macmillan
1993 *Collected Poems* (new edition) London: Sinclair Stevenson

Stevie Smith 1902–71

1937 *A Good Time Was Had By All* London: Jonathan Cape
1938 *Tender Only to One* London: Jonathan Cape
1942 *Mother, What is Man?* London: Jonathan Cape
1950 *Harold's Leap* London: Jonathan Cape
1957 *Not Waving but Drowning* London: Jonathan Cape
1958 *Some are More Human than Others: A Sketch-book* London:
      Gabberbocchus
1962 *Selected Poems* London: Longman
1966 *The Frog Prince* London: Longman
1971 *Two in One* London: Longman
1972 *Scorpion and Other Poems* London: Longman

1975 *Collected Poems* London: Allen Lane
1978 *Selected Poems* Harmondsworth: Penguin
1981 *Me Again: The Uncollected Writings of Stevie Smith* London: Virago, 1988
1983 *Stevie Smith: A Selection* London: Faber

Muriel Spark b. *1918*

1952 *The Fanfarlo: and Other Verse* Aldington: Hand and Flower Press
1967 *Collected Poems* London: Macmillan

Pauline Stainer b. *1941*

1989 *The Honeycomb* Newcastle upon Tyne: Bloodaxe Books
1992 *Sighting the Slave Ship* Newcastle upon Tyne: Bloodaxe Books
1994 *The Ice Pilot Speaks* Newcastle upon Tyne: Bloodaxe Books
1996 *The Wound-Dresser's Dream* Newcastle upon Tyne: Bloodaxe Books
1999 *Parable Island* Newcastle upon Tyne: Bloodaxe Books

Margaret Stanley-Wrench

1937 *The Man in the Moon* (The Newdigate Prize Poem) Oxford: Basil Blackwell
1938 *Newsreel and Other Poems* London: Macmillan
1959 *A Tale for the Fall of the Year and Other Poems* London: Linden Press

Anne Stevenson b. *1933*

1969 *Reversals* Middletown: Wesleyan University Press
1974 *Correspondences* Oxford University Press
1974 *Travelling behind Glass: Selected Poems 1963–73* Oxford University Press
1977 *Enough of Green* Oxford University Press
1982 *Minute by Glass Minute* Oxford University Press
1985 *The Fiction Makers* Oxford University Press
1987 *Selected Poems 1956–1986* Oxford University Press
1990 *The Other House* Oxford University Press
1993 *Four and A Half Dancing Men* Oxford University Press
1996 *The Collected Poems of Anne Stevenson 1955–1995* Oxford University Press;
       Newcastle upon Tyne: Bloodaxe Books, 2000.
2000 *Granny Scarecrow* Newcastle upon Tyne: Bloodaxe Books

Muriel Stuart *1885–1967*

1916 *Christ at Carnival and other poems* London: Herbert Jenkins
1918 *The Cockpit of Idols* London: Methuen

1922 *Poems* London: Heinemann
1926 *New Poems and Old* USA: Valentine Mitchell
1927 *Selected Poems* London: Jonathan Cape
2000 *In the Orchard: Selected Poems* Kettilonia: Kingskettle

Maud Sulter b. 1960

1985 *As A Black Woman* Hebden Bridge: Urban Fox
1989 *Zabat: Poetics of a Family Tree* Hebden Bridge: Urban Fox

Rosemary Tonks b. 1932

1963 *Notes on Cafés and Bedrooms* London: Putnam
1967 *Iliad of Broken Sentences* London: Bodley Head

Iris Tree 1897–1968

1919 *Lamplight and Starlight* New York: Boni & Liveright
1920 *Poems* (decorated by Curtis Moffat) London and New York: John Lane
1927 *The Traveller and Other Poems* New York: Boni & Liveright
1966 *The Marsh Picnic* (introduced by John Betjeman) Cambridge: Rampant Lions Press

Katherine Tynan 1861–1931

1911 *New Poems* London: Sidgwick & Jackson
1915 *Flower of Youth: Poems in War Time* London: Sidgwick & Jackson
1916 *The Holy War* London: Sidgwick & Jackson
1917 *Late Songs* London: Sidgwick & Jackson
1930 *Collected Poems* London: Macmillan

Catherine Walsh b. 1964

1989 *Short Stories* Twickenham: North & South
1994 *Pitch* Durham: Pig Press
1996 *Idir Eatortha & Making Tents* London: Invisible Books

Michelene Wandor b. 1940

1982 *Upbeat: Poems and Stories* London: Journeyman Press
1984 *Gardens of Eden* London: Journeyman Press/Playbooks

Sylvia Townsend Warner 1893–1978

1925 *The Espalier* London: Chatto & Windus
1928 *Time Importuned* London: Chatto & Windus
1931 *Opus 7* London: Chatto & Windus
1932 *Rainbow* New York: Alfred Knopf
1933 *Whether a Dove or a Seagull* (with Valentine Ackland) New York: Viking; London: Chatto & Windus, 1934
1960 *Boxwood* London: Chatto & Windus
1968 *King Duffus and Other Poems* London and Wells: Clare, Son & Co. Ltd.
1980 *Twelve Poems* London: Chatto & Windus
1982 *Collected Poems* Manchester: Carcanet
1985 *Selected Poems* Manchester: Carcanet

Val Warner b. 1946

1971 *These Yellow Photos* Oxford: Carcanet
1983 *Under The Penthouse* Cheadle: Carcanet
1986 *Before Lunch* Manchester: Carcanet
1997 *Tooting Idyll* Manchester: Carcanet

Dorothy Wellesley 1889–1978

1920 *Poems* London: privately printed
1926 *Genesis: An Impression* London: Heinemann
1930 *Deserted House: A poem sequence* London: Hogarth
1934 *Poems of Ten Years* London: Macmillan
1936 *Selections from the Poems of Dorothy Wellesley* London: Macmillan
1942 *The Last Planet and Other Poems* London: Hogarth
1946 *Desert Wells: New Poems* London: Michael Joseph
1949 *Selections from the Poems of Dorothy Wellesley* London: Williams and Norgate
1954 *Rhymes for Middle Years* London: Barrie
1955 *Early Light: The Collected Poems of Dorothy Wellesley* London: Rupert Hart-Davis

Anna Wickham 1884–1947

1911 *Songs* (pseudonym 'John Oland') London: privately printed
1915 *The Contemplative Quarry* London: The Poetry Bookshop
1916 *The Man with a Hammer* London: Grant Richards
1921 *The Little Old House* London: The Poetry Bookshop
1936 *Anna Wickham* (Richards Shilling Selections) London: Richards Press
1971 *Selected Poems* London: Chatto & Windus

1984 *The Writings of Anna Wickham: Free Woman and Poet* (ed R. D. Smith)
London: Virago

Susan Wicks b. 1947

1992 *Singing Underwater* London: Faber
1994 *Open Diagnosis* London: Faber
1996 *The Clever Daughter* London: Faber
1997 *The Key* London: Faber
1998 *Little Thing* London: Faber

Margaret Willy b. 1919

1946 *The Invisible Sun* London: Chaterson
1951 *Every Star a Tongue* London: Heinemann

Sheila Wingfield 1906–92

1938 *Poems* London: Cresset Press
1946 *Beat Drum, Beat Heart* London: Cresset Press
1949 *A Cloud Across the Sun* London: Cresset Press
1954 *A Kite's Dinner: Poems 1938–1954* London: Cresset Press
1964 *The Leaves Darken* London: Weidenfeld & Nicolson
1977 *Her Storms: Selected Poems 1938–77* Dublin: Dolmen Press; London: John
Calder
1977 *Admissions: Poems 1974–77* Dublin: Dolmen Press and London: John Calder
1983 *Collected Poems 1938–1983* (preface by G. S. Fraser) London: Enitharmon;
New York: Hill and Wang

Margaret Louise Woods 1856–1945

1902 *The Princess of Hanover* (a drama in prose and verse) London: Duckworth &
Co.
1907 *Poems Old and New* London: Macmillan.
1914 *The Collected Poems of Margaret L. Woods* London: John Lane
1923 *A Poet's Youth* London & Sydney: Chapman and Dodd
1921 *The Return and other poems* New York: John Lane: London

ANTHOLOGIES OF WOMEN'S POETRY

Adcock, Fleur, ed. *The Faber Book of Twentieth-Century Women's Poetry*. London:
Faber, 1987.

Balmer, Josephine, trans. *Classical Women Poets*. Newcastle upon Tyne: Bloodaxe Books, 1996.

Bax, Clifford and Meum Stewart, eds. *The Distaff Muse: An Anthology of Poetry written by Women*. London: Hollis & Carter, 1949.

Bernikow, Louise. *The World Split Open: Four Centuries of Women Poets in England and America, 1552–1950*. London: The Women's Press, 1979.

Boland, Eavan. *Three Irish Poets: an anthology*. Manchester: Carcanet, 2003.

Breen, Jennifer, ed., *Women Romantic Poets 1785–1832: An Anthology*. London: Everyman, 1992.

Brereton, Frederick, ed. *An Anthology of Women's Poems*. London: Collins, 1930.

Burford, Barbara, ed. *A Dangerous Knowing: Four Black Woman Poets: Barbara Burford, Gabriella Pearse, Grace Nichols, Jackie Kay*. London: Sheba Feminist Publishers, 1985.

Burford, Barbara, Lindsay MacRae and Sylvia Paskin, eds. *Dancing The Tightrope: New love poems by women*. London: The Women's Press, 1987.

Chipasula, Stella and Frank, eds. *The Heinemann Book of African Women's Poetry*. London: Heinemann, 1995.

Cobham, Rhonda and Merle Collins, eds. *Watchers And Seekers: Creative Writing by Black Women in Britain*. London: The Women's Press, 1987.

Cope, Wendy. *Is that the new moon? Poems by women poets*. 1989. London: Collins, 2002.

Cosman, Carol, Joan Keefe and Kathleen Weaver, eds., *The Penguin Book of Women Poets*. Harmondsworth: Penguin, 1978.

Couzyn, Jeni, ed. *The Bloodaxe Book of Contemporary Women Poets: Eleven British Writers*. Newcastle upon Tyne: Bloodaxe Books, 1985.

Dawson, Jill, ed. *The Virago Book of Wicked Verse*. London: Virago, 1992.

De Souza, Eunice, ed. *Nine Indian Women Poets: an anthology*. Delhi and Oxford: Oxford University Press, 1997.

Deletant, Andrea and Brenda Waler, trans. *Silent Voices: An Anthology of Contemporary Romanian Women Poets*. Introduced by Fleur Adcock. London: Forest Books, 1986.

Dooley, Maura, ed. *Making for Planet Alice: new women poets*. Newcastle upon Tyne: Bloodaxe Books, 1997.

Dowson, Jane, ed. *Women's Poetry of the 1930s: a critical anthology*. London: Routledge, 1996.

Duffy, Carol Ann, ed. *I Wouldn't Thank You For A Valentine: an anthology of women's poetry*. Harmondsworth: Penguin, 1992.

Dunhill, Christina, ed. *As Girls Could Boast: new poetry by women*. London: The Oscars Press, 1994.

Fell, Alison, Stef Pixner, Tina Reid, Michèle Roberts and Ann Oosthuizen, eds. *Licking The Bed Clean: Five Feminist Poets*. London: Teeth Imprints, 1978.

Fell, Alison, Stef Pixner, Tina Reid, Michèle Roberts and Ann Oosthuizen, eds. *Smile, Smile, Smile, Smile*. London: Sheba Feminist Publishers, 1980.

France, Linda, ed. *Sixty Women Poets*. Newcastle upon Tyne: Bloodaxe Books, 1993.

Gramich, Katie and Catherine Brennan, eds. *Welsh Women's Poetry 1460–2001: An Anthology.* Dinas Powys, South Glamorgan. Wales: Honno Classics, 2003.

Green, Veronica, ed. *Rhythm of Our Days.* Cambridge University Press, 1991.

Greer, Germaine, ed. *101 Poems by 101 Women.* London: Faber, 2001.

Hall, Linda, ed. *Tracing the Tradition: an anthology of poetry by women.* London: Cassell, 1994.

Hooley, Ruth, ed. *The Female Line: Northern Irish Women Writers.* Belfast: Northern Ireland Women's Rights Movement, 1985.

John, N. A., ed. *Holloway Jingles.* Glasgow: WSPU, 1912.

Kaplan, Cora. *Salt and Bitter and Good: Three Centuries of English and American Women Poets.* New York and London: Paddington Press, 1975.

Kazantzis, Judith, Michèle Roberts and Michelene Wandor, eds. *Touch Papers.* London: Allison and Busby, 1982.

Kelly, A. A., ed. *Pillars of the House: an anthology of verse by Irish women from 1690 to the present.* Dublin: Wolfhound Press, 1997.

Kerrigan, Catherine, ed. *An Anthology of Scottish Women Poets.* Edinburgh University Press, 1991.

Kinsman, Judith, ed. *Six Women Poets.* Oxford University Press, 1992.

Kneale, Trevor, ed. *Contemporary Women Poets.* Liverpool: Rondo, 1975.

Leighton, Angela and Margaret Reynolds, eds. *Victorian Women Poets: An Anthology.* Oxford: Blackwell, 1995.

McCarthy, Karen, ed. *Bittersweet: Contemporary Black Women's Poetry.* London: The Women's Press, 1998.

McMillan, Dorothy and Michel Byrne, eds. *Modern Scottish Women Poets.* Edinburgh: Canongate, 2003.

Mohin, Lilian, ed. *One Foot on the Mountain: An Anthology of British Feminist Poetry 1969–1979.* London: Onlywomen Press, 1979.

Mohin, Lilian, ed. *Beautiful Barbarians: Lesbian Feminist Poetry.* London: Onlywomen Press, 1986.

Mulford, Wendy, with Helen Kidd, Julia Mishkin, Sandi Russell, eds. *The Virago Book of Love Poetry.* London: Virago, 1991.

Murray Simpson, Joan, ed. *Without Adam: The Femina anthology of Poetry.* London: Femina Press, 1968.

O'Brien, Peggy, ed. *The Wake Forest Book of Irish Women's Poetry 1967–2000.* Winston-Salem: Wake Forest University Press, 1999.

O'Sullivan, Maggie, ed. *Out of everywhere: linguistically innovative poetry by women in North America and the UK.* London and Suffolk: Reality Street Editions, 1996.

Palmeira, Rosemary, ed. *In the Gold of the Flesh: Poems of Birth and Motherhood.* London: The Women's Press, 1990.

Powell, Anne, ed. *Shadows of War: British Women's Poetry of the Second World War.* Stroud, Glos.: Sutton Publishing, 1999.

Pritchard, R. E., ed. *Poetry by English Women: Elizabethan to Victorian.* Manchester: Carcanet, 1990.

Reilly, Catherine, ed. *Scars upon my Heart: Women's Poetry and Verse of the First World War*. London: Virago, 1981.

Reilly, Catherine, ed. *Chaos of the Night: Women's Poetry and Verse of the Second World War*. London: Virago, 1984.

Reilly, Catherine, ed. *Women's War Poetry and Verse*. London : Virago, 1997.

Roscoe, Theodora and Mary Winter Were, eds. *Poems by Contemporary Women*. London: Hutchens, 1944.

Rumens, Carol, ed. *Making for the Open: The Chatto Book of Post-Feminist Poetry 1964–1984*. London: Chatto & Windus, 1987.

Rumens, Carol, ed. *New Women Poets*. Newcastle upon Tyne: Bloodaxe Books, 1990. Repr. 1993.

Sackville, Margaret, ed. *A Book of Verse by Living Women*. London: Herbert and Daniel, 1910.

Sackville-West, Vita, ed. and foreword. *Poems of the Land Army: an anthology of verse by members of the women's land army*. London and Bedford: The Sidney Press, n.d.

Scott, Diana, ed. *Bread and Roses: Women's Poetry of the 19th and 20th Centuries*. London: Virago, 1982.

Sharp, Elizabeth A., ed. *Women Poets of the Victorian Era*. London and New York: Walter Scott, 1887.

Silgardo, Melanie and Janet Beck, eds. *Virago New Poets*. London: Virago, 1993.

Spraggs, Gillian, ed. *Love Shook My Senses: lesbian love poems*. London: The Women's Press, 1998.

Squire, J. C., ed. *An Anthology of Women's Verse*. Oxford: Clarendon Press, 1921.

Viner, Fanny, ed. *In the Pink: The Raving Beauties Choose Poems from the Show*. London: The Women's Press, 1983.

Viner, Fanny, ed. *No Holds Barred*. London: The Women's Press, 1985.

Wandor, Michelene and Michèle Roberts, eds. *Cutlasses and Earrings*. London: Playbooks, 1977.

Penguin Modern Poets Vol. 2, Carol Ann Duffy, Vicki Feaver, Eavan Boland. Harmondsworth: Penguin, 1995.

Penguin Modern Poets Vol. 8, Jackie Kay, Merle Collins, Grace Nichols. Harmondsworth: Penguin, 1996.

Purple and Green: poems by 33 women. London: Rivelin Grapheme Press, 1985.

The Poetry Quartets Vol. 2, Fleur Adcock, Carol Ann Duffy, Selima Hill, Carol Rumens. (Cassette) Newcastle upon Tyne: British Council/Bloodaxe Books, 1998.

The Poetry Quartets Vol. 5, Helen Dunmore, U. A. Fanthorpe, Elizabeth Jennings, Jo Shapcott. (Cassette) Newcastle upon Tyne: British Council/Bloodaxe Books, 1999.

Selected Works on Women Poets

Ackland, Valentine. *For Sylvia: An Honest Account*. London: Chatto & Windus, 1985.

Adcock, Fleur. 'Women as Poets'. *Poetry Dimension 2: The Best of the Poetry Year.* Ed. Dannie Abse. London: Robson Books, 1974, pp. 229–33.

Allen-Randolph, Jody. 'A Backward Look: An Interview with Eavan Boland'. *PN Review* 26.5 (May/June 2000), pp. 43–48.

Allen-Randolph, Jody. 'An Interview with Eavan Boland'. *PN Review* 20.1 (1993), pp. 52–57.

Alma, Roger. 'The Poetry of Molly Holden'. *Poetry Nation 2* (1974), pp. 92–99.

Badeni, June. *The Slender Tree: A Life of Alice Meynell.* Cornwall: Tabb House, 1981.

Bensen, Alice. *Rose Macaulay.* New York: Twayne, 1969.

Benton, Jill. *Naomi Mitchison: a biography.* London: Pandora, 1990.

Bergvall, Caroline. 'No Margins to this Page: Female Experimental Poets and the Legacy of Modernism'. *fragmente* 5 (1993), pp. 30–38.

Bertram, Vicki. 'Postfeminist Poetry?: "one more word for balls"'. *Contemporary British Poetry: Essays in Theory and Criticism.* Eds. James Acheson and Romana Huk. State University of New York Press, 1996, pp. 269–92.

— ed. *Kicking Daffodils: Twentieth-Century Women Poets.* Edinburgh University Press, 1997.

— *Gendering Poetry: Contemporary women and men poets.* London: Rivers Oram Pandora Press, 2004.

Boland, Eavan. 'Gods Make Their Own Importance: The authority of the poet in our time'. *PN Review* 21.4 (1995), pp. 10–14.

— 'Letter to a Young Woman Poet'. *PN Review* 24.2 (November/December 1997), pp. 16–21.

— *Object Lessons: The Life of the Woman and the Poet in Our Time.* Manchester: Carcanet, 1995.

— 'The Serinette Principle: the Lyric in Contemporary Poetry'. *PN Review* 19.4 (March/April 1993), pp. 20–26.

— 'The Woman, The Place, The Poet'. *PN Review* 17.3 (1991), pp. 35–40.

Breeze, Jean 'Binta'. 'Can A Dub Poet Be A Woman?' *Women: A Cultural Review* 1.1 (April 1990), pp. 47–49.

Britzolakis, Christina. *Sylvia Plath and the Theatre of Mourning.* New York: Oxford University Press, 1999.

Brooker, Jewel Spears. *Conversations with Denise Levertov.* Jackson: University Press of Mississippi, 1998.

Brothers, Barbara. 'Against the Grain: Sylvia Townsend Warner and the Spanish Civil War.' *Women's Writing in Exile.* Eds. Mary Lynn Broe and Angela Ingram. Chapel Hill: University of Carolina Press, 1989, pp. 350–66.

Buck, Claire. 'Poetry and the Women's Movement in Postwar Britain'. *Contemporary British Poetry: Essays in Theory and Criticism.* Eds. James Acheson and Romana Huk. State University of New York, 1996, pp. 81–111.

Burke, Carolyn. *Becoming Modern: The Life of Mina Loy.* New York: Farrar, Straus, Giroux, 1996.

Byers, Margaret. 'Cautious vision: recent poetry by women'. *British Poetry since 1960.* Ed. Michael Schmidt. Manchester: Carcanet, 1972, pp. 74–84.

Calder, Jenni. *The Nine Lives of Naomi Mitchison*. London: Virago, 1997.

Collecott, Diana. *H. D. and Sapphic Modernism*. Cambridge University Press, 1999.

De Caires Narain, Denise. *Contemporary Caribbean Women's Poetry: Making Style*. London: Routledge, 2001.

Doolittle, Hilda (H. D.). *Notes on Thought and Vision and the Wise Sappho*. London: Peter Owen, 1988.

Dowson, Jane. *Women, Modernism and British Poetry 1910–39: Resisting Femininity*. Aldershot: Ashgate, 2002.

—— '"For older sisters are very sobering things": contemporary poets and the female affiliation complex'. *Feminist Review* 62 (Summer 1999), pp. 6–20.

Elfyn, Menna, ed. *Trying the Line: a volume of tributes to Gillian Clarke*. Dyfed: Gomer, 1997.

Fielding, Daphne. *The Rainbow Picnic – a portrait of Iris Tree*. London: Methuen, 1974.

Fitzgerald, Penelope. *Charlotte Mew and Her Friends*. 1974. London: Collins, 1984.

Ford, Hugh, ed. *Nancy Cunard: Brave Poet, Indomitable Rebel 1896–1965*. Philadelphia: Chilton Book Company, 1968.

Forrest-Thomson, Veronica. *Poetic Artifice: A theory of twentieth-century poetry*. Manchester University Press, 1978.

Fraser, P. M., ed. *The Waves of Autolycus: selected literary essays of Alice Meynell*. Oxford University Press, 1965.

Gelpi, Albert, ed. *Denise Levertov: Selected Criticism*. Ann Arbor: University of Michigan Press, 1993.

Glendinning, Victoria. *Edith Sitwell: A Unicorn Among Lions*. London: Weidenfeld & Nicolson, 1981.

Glendinning, Victoria. *Vita: The Life of Vita Sackville-West*. London: Weidenfeld & Nicolson, 1983.

Gonzalez, Alexander G., ed. *Contemporary Irish Women Poets: Some Male Perspectives*. London: Greenwood Press, 1999.

Gramang, Gerlinde. *Elizabeth Jennings*. New York: Edwin Mellen, 1995.

Greene, Richard, ed. *Selected Letters of Edith Sitwell*. London: Virago, 1997.

Greer, Germaine. 'A biodegradable art: changing fashions in anthologies of women's poetry'. *Times Literary Supplement* (30 June 1995), pp. 7–8.

Greer, Germaine. *Slipshod Sibyls: Recognition, Rejection and the Woman Poet*. New York: Viking Press, 1995.

Guest, Barbara. *Herself Defined: The Poet and Her World*. London: Collins, 1985.

Haberstroh, Patricia, ed. *Women Creating Women: Contemporary Irish Poets*. New York and Dublin: Syracuse University Press, 1996.

Hacker, Marilyn. 'Unauthorized Voices: U. A. Fanthorpe and Elma Mitchell'. *Grand Street* 8, 1989, pp. 147–64.

Hanscombe, Gillian and Virginia Smyers. *Writing for their Lives: The Modernist Women 1910–1940*. London: The Women's Press, 1987.

Harman, Claire, ed. *The Diaries of Sylvia Townsend Warner*. London: Chatto & Windus, 1994.

Homans, Margaret. *Women Writing and Poetic Identity*. Princeton University Press, 1980.

Hooker, Jeremy.'Frances Bellerby In Place'. *PN Review* 7.6 (1981), pp. 31–34.

Houston, Libby. 'On Being a Woman Poet'. *On Gender and Writing*. Ed. Michelene Wandor. London: Pandora, 1983, pp. 42–50.

Innes, C. L. 'Women Poets Of Many Parts'. *Contemporary British Poetry: Essays in Theory and Criticism*. Ed. James Acheson and Romana Huk. State University of New York Press, 1996, pp. 315–41.

Jones, Jennifer Vaughan. *Anna Wickham: A Poet's Daring Life*. Wisconsin: Madison Brooks, 2005.

Juhasz, Suzanne. *Naked and Fiery Forms. Modern American Poetry By Women: A New Tradition*. New York: Harper Colophon, 1976.

Kaplan, Cora. 'Language and Gender.' *Feminist Critique of Language*. Ed. Deborah Cameron. London: Routledge, 1990, pp. 57–69.

Keller, Lyn and Cristanne Miller, eds. *Feminist Measures: Soundings in Poetry and Theory*. Ann Arbor: Michigan, 1994.

Khan, Nosheen. *Women's Poetry of the First World War*. London: Harvester Wheatsheaf, 1988.

Kinnahan, Linda A. *Poetics of the Feminine: Authority and Literary Tradition in William Carlos Williams, Mina Loy, Denise Levertov and Kathleen Fraser*. Cambridge University Press, 1994.

— 'Experimental Poetics and the Lyric in British Women's Poetry: Geraldine Monk, Wendy Mulford, and Denise Riley'. *Contemporary Literature* 37.4 (1996), pp. 620–66.

Kouidis, Virginia M. *Mina Loy: American Modernist Poet*. Louisiana State University Press and London: Baton Rouge, 1980.

Lehmann, John and Derek Parker, eds. *Edith Sitwell: Selected Letters*. Basingstoke: Macmillan, 1970.

Leighton, Angela. *Victorian Women Poets: Writing Against the Heart*. Hemel Hempstead: Harvester Wheatsheaf, 1992.

Levertov, Denise. *New and Selected Essays*. New York: New Directions, 1992.

Lindop, Grevel.'Kathleen Raine: The Tenth Decade'. *PN Review* 27.2 (November/December 2000), pp. 36–50.

Lochhead, Liz.'Knucklebones of Irony'. Interview. Colin Nicholson, *Poem, Purpose and Place: Shaping Identity in Contemporary Scottish Verse*. Edinburgh: Polygon, 1992, pp. 203–23.

Lucas, John and Matt Simpson, eds. *The Way You Say The World: A celebration for Anne Stevenson*. Beeston, Nottingham: Shoestring Press, 2003.

Maguire, Sarah. 'Dilemmas and Developments: Eavan Boland Re-examined', *Feminist Review* 62 (Summer 1999), pp. 58–66.

Mark, Alison and Deryn Rees-Jones, eds. *Contemporary Women's Poetry: Reading/Writing/Practice*. Basingstoke: Macmillan, 2000.

Markey, Janice. *A Journey into the Red Eye: The Poetry of Sylvia Plath*. London: The Women's Press, 1993.

Maxwell, William, ed. *The Letters of Sylvia Townsend Warner*. London: Chatto & Windus, 1982.

McCulloch, Margery Palmer. 'Forgotten Founder: The Poetry of Muriel Stuart', *PEN International* 45.1 (1995).

McCullough, Frances, ed. *The Journals of Sylvia Plath*. Consulting ed. Ted Hughes. New York: Dial Press, 1982.

Meynell, Viola. *Alice Meynell: A memoir*. London: Jonathan Cape, 1929.

Michelis, Angelica and Antony Rowland. *The Poetry of Carol Ann Duffy: 'Choosing Tough Words'*. Manchester University Press, 2003.

Minogue, Sally. 'Prescriptions and Proscriptions: Feminist Criticism and Contemporary Poetry'. *Some Problems for Feminist Criticism*. Ed. Sally Minogue. London: Routledge, 1990, pp. 179–236.

Mitchison, Naomi. *All Change Here: Girlhood and Marriage*. London: Bodley Head, 1975.

Mitchison, Naomi. *You May Well Ask: A Memoir 1920–1940*. London: Victor Gollancz, 1979.

Montefiore, Jan. *Feminism and Poetry: Language, Experience, Identity in Women's Writing*. London: Pandora, 1987; revised edition, 1992.

Montefiore, Janet. *Arguments of Heart and Mind: Selected Essays 1977–2000*. Manchester University Press, 2002.

Mulford, Wendy. 'Notes on Writing: A Marxist/Feminist Viewpoint'. *On Gender and Writing*. Ed. Michelene Wandor. London: Pandora, 1983, pp. 31–41.

Mulford, Wendy. *This Narrow Place: Sylvia Townsend Warner and Valentine Ackland – Life, Letters and Politics 1930–1951*. London: Pandora, 1988.

Mulford, Wendy. 'Curved, Odd . . . Irregular. A Vision of Contemporary Poetry by Women'. *Women: a cultural review* 1.3 (Winter 1990), pp. 261–74.

Muske, Carol. *Women and Poetry: Truth, Autobiography, and the shape of the self*. Ann Arbor: University of Michigan Press, 1997.

O'Rourke, Rebecca, 'Mediums, Messages and Noisy Amateurs', *Women: A Cultural Review* 1.3 (Winter 1990), pp. 275–86.

Ostriker, Alicia. *Stealing the Language: The Emergence of Women's Poetry in America*. London: The Women's Press, 1987.

Padel, Ruth. *52 Ways of Looking at a Poem*. London: Chatto & Windus, 2001.

Pearson, John. *Facades: Edith, Osbert and Sacheverell Sitwell*. Basingstoke: Macmillan, 1978.

Plain, Gill. 'Great Expectations: Rehabilitating the Recalcitrant War Poets'. *Feminist Review* 51 (Autumn 1995), pp. 41–65.

Pumphrey, Martin. 'Play, fantasy and strange laughter: Stevie Smith's uncomfortable poetry'. *Critical Quarterly* 28.3 (Autumn 1986), pp. 85–96.

Pykett, Lyn. 'Women Poets and "Women's Poetry": Fleur Adcock, Gillian Clarke and Carol Rumens,' *British Poetry from the 1950s to the 1990s: Politics and Art*. Ed. Gary Day and Brian Docherty. London: Macmillan, 1997, pp. 253 – 67.

Raine, Kathleen. *The Inner Journey of the Poet*. London: Allen and Unwin, 1982.

Raitt, Suzanne. *May Sinclair: A Modern Victorian.* Oxford: Clarendon Press, 2000.

Rees-Jones, Deryn. *Carol Ann Duffy: Writers and their Work.* Plymouth: Northcote House, 1999.

Rees-Jones, Deryn. *Consorting with Angels.* Tarset: Bloodaxe Books, 2004.

Rich, Adrienne. *Blood, Bread and Poetry: Selected Prose 1979–1985.* London: Virago, 1987.

(Riding) Jackson, Laura. *The Word 'Woman' and Other Related Writings.* Eds. Elizabeth Friedman and Alan J. Clark. New York: Persea, 1993.

Riley, Denise. *War In The Nursery: Theories of the Child and Mother.* London: Virago, 1983.

— *Am I That Name? Feminism and the Category of 'Women' in History.* Basingstoke: Macmillan, 1988.

— 'A Short History of Some Preoccupations'. *Feminists Theorize the Political.* Ed. Judith Butler and Joan W. Scott. New York and London: Routledge, 1992, pp. 121–29.

— ed. *Poets on Writing: Britain, 1970–91.* London: Macmillan Academic, 1992.

— 'Denise Riley in conversation with Romana Huk'. *PN Review* 21.5 (1995), pp. 17–22.

— *The Words of Selves: Identification, Solidarity, Irony.* Stanford University Press, 2000.

Rumens, Carol. 'In the Bedroom of the Page'. *Poetry Wales* 30.2 (September 1994), pp. 33–34.

Russell, Arthur, ed. *Ruth Pitter: Homage to a Poet.* London: n.p., 1969.

Salter, Elizabeth and Allanah Harper. *Edith Sitwell: Fire of the Mind.* 1956. London: Michael Joseph, 1976.

Schenck, Celeste M. 'Exiled by genre: Modernism, Canonicity, and the Politics of Exclusion'. Broe and Ingram, pp. 225–50.

Schlack, Beverley Ann. 'The poetess of poets: Alice Meynell rediscovered'. *Women's Studies* 7 (1989), pp. 111–26.

Schweik, Susan. 'Writing War Poetry like a woman'. *Critical Inquiry* 13 (Spring 1987), pp. 532–56.

Sitwell, Edith. 'Some Observations on Women's Poetry'. *Vogue* (London). 65.5 (March 1925), pp. 117–18.

— Review of *The Farmer's Bride* and *The Rambling Sailor,* by Charlotte Mew. *Criterion* 9.34 (October 1929), pp. 130–34.

— *Taken Care Of: an autobiography.* London: Hutchinson, 1965.

Somerville-Arjat, Gillean and Rebecca E. Wilson, eds. *Sleeping with Monsters: Conversations with Scottish and Irish Women Poets.* Edinburgh: Polygon, 1991.

Spalding, Frances. *Stevie Smith: A Critical Biography.* London: Faber, 1988.

Spraggs, Gillian. 'Exiled to Home: The Poetry of Sylvia Townsend Warner and Valentine Ackland'. *Lesbian and Gay Writing: An Anthology of Critical Essays.* Ed. Mark Lilly. Basingstoke: Macmillan, 1990.

Stannard, Julian. *Fleur Adcock in Context: from Movement to Martians.* Lampeter: Edwin Mellen Press, 1977.

Stevenson, Anne. *Between the Iceberg and the Ship: Selected Essays.* Ann Arbor: University of Michigan Press, 1998.

— 'Some Notes on Women and Tradition'. *PN Review* 19.1 (September/October 1992), pp. 29–32.

— 'Writing As A Woman', *Women Writing and Writing About Women.* Ed. Mary Jacobus. Beckenham: Croom Helm, 1979, pp. 168–76.

Taylor, Georgina. *H. D. And The Public Sphere of Modernist Women Writers, 1913–1946: Talking Women.* Oxford University Press, 2001.

Thacker, Andrew. 'Amy Lowell and H.D.: The Other Imagists'. *Women: a cultural review* 4.1. (Spring 1993), pp. 49–59.

Wagner-Martin, Linda, ed. *Critical essays on Denise Levertov.* Boston, Masachusetts: G. K. Hall, 1990.

Wallace, Diana. 'Postwar Women's Poetry'. *Introduction to Women's Writing.* Ed. Marion Shaw. Edinburgh University Press, 1999, pp. 235–63.

Wellesley, Dorothy, ed. *Letters on Poetry from W. B. Yeats to Dorothy Wellesley.* 1940. New edition, ed. Kathleen Raine. Oxford University Press, 1964.

Wellesley, Dorothy. *Far Have I Travelled.* London: James Barrie, 1952.

Wills, Clair. 'Contemporary Women's Poetry: experimentalism and the expressive voice'. *Critical Quarterly* 36.3 (1994), pp. 34–52.

Wilmer, Clive. 'In conversation with Patricia Beer'. *PN Review* 19.5 (May/June 1993), p. 45.

Winters, Yvor. 'A Woman With a Hammer'. Review of *The Contemporary Quarry* and *The Man With a Hammer,* by Anna Wickham. Ed. Murphy Francis. *Uncollected Essays and Reviews of Yvor Winters.* 1973. London: Allen and Lane, 1974., pp. 11–12.

Winters, Yvor. 'Robert Bridges and Elizabeth Daryush.' *American Review* 8.3. (1936–37), pp. 353–67. Repr. in Murphy, pp. 271–83.

Winters, Yvor. *A Woman's Essays.* Harmondsworth: Penguin, 1992.

Yorke, Liz. *Impertinent Voices: Subversive Strategies in Contemporary Women's Poetry.* London: Routledge, 1991.

Special Editions on Women's Poetry

Poetry Wales 23.1 (1987).
Aquarius Women 19/20 (1992).
Poetry Review 84.1 (Spring 1994)
Poetry Review 86.4 (Winter 1996/97).
Feminist Review 62 (Summer 1999).

FURTHER READING

Acheson, James and Huk, Romana, eds. *Contemporary British Poetry: Essays in Theory and Criticism,* State University of New York Press, 1996.

Allnutt, Gillian, Fred D'Aguiar, Ken Edwards and Eric Mottram, eds. *The New British Poetry 1968–1988.* London: Paladin, 1988.

Allott, Kenneth, ed. *The Penguin Book of Contemporary Verse.* 1950.
Harmondsworth: Penguin, 1962.

Alvarez, Al, ed. *The New Poetry.* 1962. Harmondsworth: Penguin, 1966.

Armitage, Simon and Robert Crawford, eds. *The Penguin Book of Poetry from
Britain and Ireland since 1945.* Harmondsworth: Penguin, 1998.

Armstrong, Isobel. *Victorian Poetry: Poetry, Poetics and Politics.* 1993. London:
Routledge, 1996.

Armstrong, Isobel. *The Radical Aesthetic.* Oxford: Blackwell, 2000.

Astley, Neil, ed. *Poetry with an Edge.* Newcastle upon Tyne: Bloodaxe Books, 1993.

— ed. *New Blood.* Newcastle upon Tyne: Bloodaxe Books, 1999.

— ed. *Staying Alive: Real Poems for Unreal Times.* Tarset: Bloodaxe Books, 2002.

Barthes, Roland. *Mythologies.* Selected and trans. Annette Lavers. London:
Paladin, 1973.

Beach, Sylvia. *Shakespeare and Company.* 1956. London: Faber, 1960.

Benstock, Shari. *Women of the Left Bank: Paris 1900–1940.* London: Virago, 1987.

Berger, John. *Ways of Seeing.* Harmondsworth: Penguin, 1972.

Berry, James. *News from Babylon: The Chatto Book of Westindian British Poetry.*
London: Chatto & Windus, 1984.

Blain, Virginia, Patricia Clements and Isobel Grundy, eds. *A Feminist Companion
to English Literature.* London: Batsford, 1990.

Bloom, Clive, ed. *Literature and Culture in Modern Britain, Vol. 1 1900–1929.*
Essex: Longman, 1993.

Bolt, Sidney, ed. *Poetry of the 1920s.* London: Longman, 1967.

Booth, Martin, *British Poetry 1964–84: Driving Through the Barricades.* London:
Routledge and Kegan Paul, 1985.

Brannigan, John. *Orwell to the Present: Literature in England 1945–2000.* London:
Palgrave, 2003.

Broe, Mary Lynn and Angela Ingram, eds. *Women's Writing in Exile.* Chapel Hill:
University of Carolina Press, 1989.

Brown, Andy. *Binary Myths: conversations with contemporary poets.* Exeter: Stride
Publications, 1998.

Brown, Clare and Don Paterson. *Don't Ask Me What I Mean: Poets in their own
words.* London: Picador, 2003.

Bullough, Geoffrey. *The Trend of Modern Poetry.* 1934. London and Edinburgh:
Oliver and Boyd, 1941.

Burnett, Paula, ed. *The Penguin Book of Caribbean Verse in English.*
Harmondsworth: Penguin, 1986.

Butler, Judith and Joan W. Scott, eds. *Feminists Theorize the Political.* London:
Routledge, 1992.

Caddell, Ric and Peter Quartermain, eds. *Other: British and Irish Poetry since 1970.*
Hanover University Press of New England; Wesleyan University Press, 1999.

Chatterjee, Debjani, ed. *The Redbeck Anthology of British South Asian Poetry.*
Bradford: Redbeck Press, 2000.

Chevalier, Tracy, ed. *Contemporary Poets.* 5th edition. New York, Toronto and
London: St James Press, 1991.

Childs, Peter. *The Twentieth Century in Poetry: A critical survey.* London: Routledge, 1999.

Cixous, Hélène and Catherine Clements, *The Newly Born Woman.* Trans. Betsy Wing. *The Theory and History of Literature, vol. 24.* Manchester University Press, 1986.

Clark, Suzanne. *Sentimental Modernism: Women Writers and The Revolution of The Word.* Bloomington and Indianapolis: Indiana University Press, 1991.

Cole, G. D. H. *The Fabian Society, past and present.* London: Fabian Publications, 1942.

Conquest, Robert, ed. *New Lines: An Anthology.* London: Macmillan, 1956.

Conquest, Robert, ed. *New Lines II: An Anthology.* London: Macmillan, 1963.

Coote, Anna and Beatrix Campbell, eds. *Sweet Freedom: The struggle for Women's Liberation.* London: Picador, 1982.

Corcoran, Neil. *English Poetry Since 1940.* London: Longman 1993.

Cosslett, Tess. *Women Writing About Childbirth: Modern discourses of motherhood.* Manchester University Press, 1994.

Crawford, Elizabeth. *The Women's Suffrage Movement: A Reference Guide 1866–1928.* London: Routledge, 2000.

Crawford, Robert. *Identifying Poets: Self and Territory in Twentieth-Century Poetry.* Edinburgh University Press, 1993.

Cunard, Nancy. *These Were the Hours: memories of my Hours Press Réanville and Paris 1928–1931.* London and Amsterdam: Walter Lowenfels, 1969.

Cunningham, Valentine, ed. *The Penguin Book of Spanish Civil War Verse.* Harmondsworth: Penguin, 1980.

Daly, Mary. *Gyn/Ecology: The Metaethics of Radical Feminism.* London: The Women's Press, 1979.

Dawe, Gerald. *The New Younger Irish Poets.* Belfast: Blackstaff, 1991.

Day, Gary, ed. *Literature and Culture in Modern Britain Volume Two: 1930–1955.* Essex: Longman, 1997.

Day, Gary and Brian Docherty, eds. *British Poetry 1900–1950: Aspects of Tradition.* Basingstoke: Macmillan, 1995.

— eds. *British Poetry from the 1950s to the 1990s: Politics and Art.* Basingstoke: Macmillan, 1997.

Day Lewis, C. and L. A. G. Strong, eds. *A New Anthology of Modern Verse 1920–40.* London: Methuen, 1941.

Day Lewis, C. and John Lehmann, eds. *The Chatto Book of Modern Poetry 1915–55.* London: Chatto & Windus, 1959.

Dowson, Jane, ed. *Women's Writing, 1945–1960: After The Deluge.* Basingstoke: Palgrave Macmillan, 2003.

Draper, R. P. *An Introduction to Twentieth-Century Poetry in English.* Basingstoke: Macmillan, 1999.

Easthope, Anthony. *Contemporary Poetry meets Modern Theory.* Hemel Hempstead: Harvester Wheatsheaf, 1991.

Elfyn, Menna and John Rowlands, eds. *The Bloodaxe Book of Modern Welsh Poetry: 20th-Century Welsh-Language Poetry in Translation.* Tarset: Bloodaxe Books, 2003.

Eliot, T. S. ed. *The Little Book of Modern Verse.* 1934. New edition edited by Anne Ridler. London: Faber, 1941.

Eliot, Valerie, ed. *The Letters of T. S. Eliot: Vol. 1. 1898–1922.* London: Faber, 1988.

Enright, D. J. ed, *The Oxford Book of Contemporary Verse 1945–80.* Oxford University Press, 1980.

Forbes, Peter. *Scanning the Century: the Penguin Book of the Twentieth Century in Poetry.* Harmondsworth: Penguin, 1999.

Friedan, Betty. *The Feminine Mystique.* Harmondsworth: Penguin, 1965.

Fyfe, Charlotte, ed. *The Tears of War. The Love Story of a Young Poet and a War Hero.* Upavon: Cavalier, 2000.

Gavron, Hannah. *The Captive Wife: Conflicts of Housebound Mothers.* Harmondsworth: Penguin, 1968.

Gilbert, Sandra and Susan Gubar. *No Man's Land: The Place of the Woman Writer in the Twentieth Century Vol. 1, The War of the Words.* New Haven: Yale University Press, 1988.

— *No Man's Land: The Place of The Woman Writer in the Twentieth Century Vol. 2, Sexchanges.* New Haven: Yale University Press, 1989.

— *No Man's Land: The Place of the Woman Writer in the Twentieth Century Vol. 3, Letters to the Front.* New Haven: Yale University Press, 1994.

Grant, Joy. *Harold Monro and the Poetry Bookshop.* London: Routledge and Kegan Paul, 1967.

Green, Jonathon. *Days In The Life: Voices from the English Underground 1961–1971.* London: Heinemann, 1988.

Gregson, Ian. *Contemporary Poetry and Postmodernism: Dialogue and Estrangement.* Basingstoke: Macmillan, 1996.

Grigson, Geoffrey, ed. *Poetry of the Present: An Anthology of the Thirties and After.* London: Phoenix House, 1949.

Haberkost, Christian. *Verbal Riddim: The Politics and Aesthetics of African-Caribbean Dub Poetry.* Amsterdam: Rodopi, 1993.

Hamilton, Ian, ed. *The Oxford Companion to Twentieth-Century Poetry.* Oxford University Press, 1994.

Hampson, Robert and Peter Barry, eds. *The New British Poetries: The Scope of the Possible.* Manchester University Press, 1993.

Hartley, Jenny, ed. *Hearts Undefeated: Women's Writing of the Second World War.* London: Virago, 1995.

Heaney, Seamus and Ted Hughes, eds. *The School Bag.* London: Faber, 1997.

Heath-Stubbs, John and David Wright, eds. *The Faber Book of Twentieth-Century Verse: An Anthology of Verse in Britain 1900–1950.* London: Faber, 1953.

Herbert, W. N. and Matthew Hollis, eds. *Strong Words: Modern Poets on Modern Poetry.* Tarset: Bloodaxe Books, 2000.

Heron, Liz, ed. *Truth, Dare, Promise: Girls growing up in Fifties Britain.* London: Virago, 1985.

Hewison, Robert. *Under Siege: Literary Life in London 1939–45.* London: Weidenfeld & Nicolson, 1977.

Hidden, Norman, ed. *The State of Poetry Today: A* New Poetry *Survey*. London: The Workshop Press, 1978.

Horovitz, Michael, ed. *Children of Albion: Poetry of the Underground in Britain*. Harmondsworth: Penguin, 1969.

Horovitz, Michael, ed. *Grandchildren of Albion: an illustrated anthology of voices and visions of younger poets in Britain*. London: New Departures, 1992.

Hošek, Chaviva and Patricia Parker. *Lyric Poetry: Beyond New Criticism*. Ithaca, New York and London: Cornell University Press, 1985.

Hulse, Michael, David Kennedy and David Morley, eds. *The New Poetry*. Newcastle upon Tyne: Bloodaxe Books, 1993.

Hyland, Paul. *Getting into Poetry: A Readers' and Writers' Guide to the Poetry Scene*. Newcastle upon Tyne: Bloodaxe Books, 1996.

Ingram, Angela and Daphne Patai, eds. *Rediscovering Forgotten Radicals: British Women Writers 1889–1939*. Chapel Hill: University of North Carolina Press, 1993.

Innes, C. L. *A History of Black and Asian Writing in Britain: 1700–2000*. Cambridge University Press, 2002.

International Who's Who in Poetry and Poets Encyclopaedia. 9th Edition. Cambridge: Melrose Press, 1999.

Jacobus, Mary, ed. *Women Writing and Writing about Women*. Beckenham: Croom Helm, 1979.

Jeffries, Lesley and Peter Sansom, eds. *Contemporary Poems: Some Critical Approaches*. London: The Poetry Business, 2001.

Jennings, Elizabeth, ed. *An Anthology of Modern Verse 1940–1960*. London: Methuen, 1961.

Jennings, Elizabeth. *Every Changing Shape: Mystical experience and the making of poems*. 1961. Manchester: Carcanet, 1996.

Joannou, Maroula. *'Ladies, Please Don't Smash those Windows': Women's Writing, Feminist Consciousness and Social Change 1918–1938*. Oxford: Berg, 1995.

Joannou, Mary, ed. *Women Writers of the 1930s: Gender, Politics and History*. Edinburgh University Press, 1999.

Jones, Peter and Michael Schmidt, eds. *British Poetry Since 1970: a critical survey*. Manchester: Carcanet, 1980.

Jump, Harriet Devine, ed. *Diverse Voices: Essays on Twentieth-Century Women Writers in English*. Sussex: Harvester Wheatsheaf, 1991.

King, Bruce. *Modern Indian Poetry in English*. Oxford University Press, 2001.

Klein, Yvonne. *Beyond the Home Front: Women's Autobiographical Writing of the Two World Wars*. Basingstoke: Macmillan, 1997.

Larissy, Edward. *Reading Twentieth-Century Poetry: The Language of Gender and Objects*. Oxford: Blackwell, 1990.

Larkin, Philip, ed. *The Oxford Book of Twentieth-Century English Verse*. London: Oxford University, 1973.

Leavis, F. R. *New Bearings in English Poetry*. 1932. London: Chatto & Windus, 1979.

Lewis, Jane. *Women in England 1870–1950: Sexual Division and Social Change.* Bloomington: Indiana University Press, 1984.

Lidderdale, Jane and Mary Nicholson. *Dear Miss Weaver: Harriet Shaw Weaver 1876–1961,* London: Faber, 1970.

Light, Alison. *Forever England: Femininity, Literature and Conservatism between the Wars.* London: Routledge, 1991.

Longley, Edna, ed. *The Bloodaxe Book of 20th-Century Poetry from Britain and Ireland.* Tarset: Bloodaxe Books, 2000.

Longley, Edna. *The Living Stream: Literature and Revisionism in Ireland.* Newcastle upon Tyne: Bloodaxe Books, 1994.

Lowell, Amy, ed. *Some Imagist Poets: an anthology Vols. i–iii.* Boston: Houghton Mifflin Company, 1915–17. New York: Kraus Reprint, 1969.

Lucas, John. *The Radical Twenties.* Nottingham: Five Leaves, 1997.

Lucie-Smith, Edward and Philip Hobsbaum eds. *A Group Anthology.* London: Oxford University Press, 1963.

Ludwig Hans-Werner and Lothar Fietz. *Poetry in the British Isles: Non-metropolitan perspectives.* Cardiff: University of Wales Press, 1995.

Maitland, Sara, ed. *Very Heaven: Looking Back at the 1960s.* London, Virago, 1988.

Markham, E. A., ed. *Caribbean Poetry from the West Indies and Britain.* Newcastle upon Tyne: Bloodaxe Books, 1989.

Marsh, Eddie, ed. *Georgian Poetry.* London: The Poetry Bookshop. Annually 1912–1922.

Marsland, Elizabeth A. *The Nation's Cause: French, English and German Poetry of the First World War.* London: Routledge, 1991.

Maslen, Elizabeth. *Political and Social Issues in British Women's Fiction 1928–1968.* Basingstoke: Palgrave Macmillan, 2001.

Mitchell, Juliet. *Women: The Longest Revolution; Essays on feminism, literature and psychoanalysis.* London: Virago, 1984.

Monro, Alida and Harold, eds. *Recent Poetry 1923–1933.* London: Gerald Howe & Co. and The Poetry Bookshop, 1933.

Monro, Harold. *Some Contemporary Poets.* London: Leonard Parsons, 1920; London: Simpkins and Marshall, 1928.

Monro, Harold, ed. *Twentieth-Century Poetry.* London: Chatto & Windus, 1929. Revised and enlarged by Alida Monro, 1933.

Monteith, Moira, ed. *Women's Writing: A Challenge to Theory.* Sussex: Harvester Wheatsheaf, 1986.

Morris, Pam, ed. *The Bakhtin Reader: Selected Writings of Bakhtin, Medvedev, Voloshinov.* London: Edward Arnold, 1994.

Morrison, Blake. *The Movement: English Poetry and Fiction of the 1950s.* Oxford University Press, 1980.

Morrison, Blake and Andrew Motion, eds. *The Penguin Book of Contemporary British Poetry,* Harmondsworth: Penguin, 1982.

Mottram, Eric. 'Editing Poetry Review', *Poetry Information* 20/21 (1979–80), pp. 154–55.

Mulvey, Laura. *Visual and Other Pleasures.* London: Macmillan, 1989.

Murphy, Gwendolen, ed. *The Modern Poet: An Anthology*. London: Sidgwick & Jackson, 1938.

O'Brien, Sean, ed. *Firebox: Poetry in Britain and Ireland after 1945*. London: Picador, 1998.

O'Brien, Sean. *The Deregulated Muse: Essays on Contemporary British and Irish Poetry*. Newcastle upon Tyne: Bloodaxe Books, 1998.

O'Donnell, Margaret J., ed. *An Anthology of Contemporary Verse*. London: Blackie and Son, 1953.

Olsen, Tilly. *Silences*. London: Virago, 1980.

Paige, D. D., ed. *The Selected Letters of Ezra Pound 1907–1941*. New York: New Directions, 1950.

Perkins, David. *A History of Modern Poetry vol. 1, From The 1890s To The High Modernist Mode*. Cambridge, Massachusetts: Harvard University Press, 1976.

Perkins, David. *A History of Modern Poetry Vol. 2, From the 1920s to the Present Day*. Cambridge, Massachusetts: Harvard University Press, 1976.

Persoon, James. *Modern British Poetry 1900–39*. New York: Twayne Publishers, 1999.

Peschmann, Hermann, ed. *The Voice of Poetry 1930–1950*. London: Evans, 1950.

Plain, Gill. *Women's Fiction of the Second World War: Gender, Power, Resistance*. Edinburgh University Press, 1996.

Press, John. *Rule and Energy: Trends in British Poetry since the Second World War*. Oxford University Press, 1963.

Press, John. *A Map Of Modern English Verse*. Oxford University Press, 1969.

Pugh, Martin. *Women and the Women's Movement in Britain 1914–1959* Basingstoke: Macmillan, 1992. Revised Edition, 2000.

Quinn, Sr. Berenetta. *The Metamorphic Tradition in Modern Poetry: Essays on the work of Ezra Pound, Wallace Stevens, William Carlos Williams, T. S. Eliot, Hart Crane, Randall Jarrell and W. B. Yeats*. New York: Gordian Press, 1966.

Raverat, Gwen. *Period Piece: A Cambridge Childhood*. 1952. London: Faber, 1960.

Rety, John, ed. *In the Company of Poets*. London: Hearing Eye Press, 2003.

Rexroth, Kenneth, ed. *New British Poets*. New York: New Directions, 1949.

Rich, Adrienne. *Of Woman Born: Motherhood as experience and institution*. London: Virago, 1977.

(Riding)Laura and Schuyler B. Jackson. *Rational Meaning: A New Foundation for the Definition of Words and Supplementary Essays*. Ed. William Harmon. Introduction by Charles Bernstein. Charlottesville and London: University Press of Virginia, 1997.

Riggs, Thomas, ed. *Contemporary Poets*. New York, Toronto and London: St James Press. 6th Edition. 1996.

Riggs, Thomas, ed. *Contemporary Poets*. New York, Toronto and London: St James Press. 7th Edition. 2001.

Roberts, Michael, ed. *The Faber Book of Modern Verse*. 1936. Revised edition with supplement by Anne Ridler, 1951. London: Faber, 1954.

Robins, Peter, ed. *Doves For The Seventies.* London: Corgi, 1969.

Robinson, Alan. *Instabilities in Contemporary British Poetry.* Basingstoke: Macmillan, 1988.

Russ, Joanna. *How To Suppress Women's Writing,* London: The Women's Press, 1984.

Saguaro, Shelley, ed. *Psychoanalysis and Woman: A Reader.* Basingstoke and London: Macmillan, 2000.

Schmidt, Michael and Grevel Lindop, eds. *British Poetry since 1960: A Critical Survey.* Manchester: Carcanet, 1972.

Schmidt, Michael, ed. *Some Contemporary Poets of Britain & Ireland: An Anthology.* Manchester: Carcanet, 1983.

Scott, Bonnie Kime, ed. *The Gender of Modernism.* Indianapolis: Indiana University Press, 1990.

Sergeant, Howard, ed. *Poets of the 1940s.* London: Longman, 1970.

Seymour-Smith, Martin, ed. *Who's Who in 20th-Century English Literature.* London: Weidenfeld & Nicolson, 1976.

Shapcott, Jo and Matthew Sweeney, eds. *Emergency Kit: Poems for Strange Times.* London: Faber, 1996.

Shattock, Joanne. *The Oxford Guide to British Women Writers.* Oxford University Press, 1994.

Shaw, Marion, ed. *Introduction to Women's Writing.* Edinburgh University Press, 1999.

Shelton, Pamela L. *Contemporary Women Poets.* New York, Toronto, London: St James Press, 1998.

Shils, Edward and Carmen Blacker, eds. *Cambridge Women: Twelve Portraits.* Cambridge University Press, 1996.

Showalter, Elaine. *A Literature of Their Own: British Women Novelists from Bronte to Lessing.* New Jersey: Princeton University Press, 1977.

Sitwell, Edith. *Poetry and Criticism.* London: Hogarth, 1925.

Sitwell, Edith. *Aspects of Modern Poetry.* London: Duckworth, 1934.

Sitwell, Edith. *A Poet's Notebook.* London: Macmillan, 1943.

Skelton, Robin, ed. *Poetry of the Forties.* Harmondsworth: Penguin, 1968.

Smith, Stan. 'The things that words give a name to: The "New Generation" poets and the politics of the hyperreal'. *Critical Survey* 8.3 (1996), pp. 306–22.

Spacks, Patricia M. *The Female Imagination: A Literary and Psychological Investigation of Women's Writing.* London: Allen and Unwin, 1976.

Spender, Dale. *Time and Tide Wait For No Man.* London: Pandora, 1984.

Spender, Stephen. *The Struggle for the Modern.* London: Methuen, 1977.

Thwaite, Anthony. *Poetry Today: A Critical Guide to British Poetry 1960–1984.* Harlow: Longman, 1985.

Todd, Janet. *British Women Writers: A Critical Reference Guide.* New York: Continuum, 1989.

Trodd, Anthea. *Women's Writing in English 1900–1945.* London: Longman, 1998.

Tuma, Keith. *New Anthology of Twentieth-Century British and Irish Poets.* Oxford University Press, 2001.

Tylee, Claire. *The Great War and Women's Consciousness: Images of Militarism and Womanhood in Women's Writings 1914–1964*. Basingstoke: Macmillan, 1990.

Waller, Philip and John Rowett. *Chronology of the 20th Century*. Oxford: Helicon, 1995.

Wandor, Michelene, ed. *The Body Politic: Women's Liberation in Britain*. London: Stage One, 1972.

Wandor, Michelene, ed. *On Gender and Writing*. London: Pandora, 1983.

Warhol, Robyn. R. and Diane Price Herndl, eds. *Feminisms: An anthology of literary theory and criticism*. Basingstoke: Macmillan, 1997. Revised edition.

Warner, Marina. *Fantastic Metamorphoses, Other Worlds: Ways of Telling The Self*. Oxford University Press, 2002.

Waugh, Patricia. *Harvest of the Sixties: English Literature and its Background 1960–1990*. Oxford University Press, 1995.

Wheels. Oxford: Blackwell, 1916–1921. Liechtenstein: Kraus Reprint, 1972.

White, Cynthia. *Women's Magazines 1693–1968*. London: Michael Joseph, 1971.

Williams, John. *Twentieth-Century Poetry: A Critical Introduction*. London: Edward Arnold, 1987.

Wills, Clair. *Improprieties: Politics and Sexuality in Northern Irish Poetry*. Oxford: Clarendon, 1993.

Wilson, Elizabeth. *Only Halfway to Paradise: Women in Post War Britain 1945–1968*. London: Tavistock, 1980.

Woolf, Virginia. *A Room of One's Own*. 1929. London: Grafton, 1977.

Woolf, Virginia. *Three Guineas*. Florida: Harcourt Brace & Co, 1938.

Yeats, W. B., ed. *The Oxford Book of Modern Verse 1892–1935*. Oxford University Press, 1936.

Index